Software Construction Set
for the IBM® PC and PCjr

Software Construction Set for the IBM® PC and PCjr

Eric Anderson

HAYDEN BOOK COMPANY
a division of Hayden Publishing Company, Inc.
Hasbrouck Heights, New Jersey

Acquisitions Editor: M. CHRIS VARLEY
Production Editor: ALBERTA BODDY
Copy Editor: JULIANN COLVIN
Text design: JOHN M-RÖBLIN
Compositor: ENQUIRE PRINTING AND PUBLISHING COMPANY, INC.
Printed and bound by: MAPLE-VAIL BOOK MANUFACTURING GROUP

Library of Congress Cataloging in Publication Data

Anderson, Eric
    Software construction set for the IBM PC and PCjr.
    1. IBM Personal Computer—Programming   2. IBM PCjr (Computer)—
Programming.   3. Basic (Computer program language)   I. Title.
QA76.8.I2594A53   1984   001.64′2   84-12869
ISBN 0-8104-6353-9

	1	2	3	4	5	6	7	8	9 PRINTING
	84	85	86	87	88	89	90	91	92 YEAR

In memory of
John Stafford Anderson
September 3, 1929–August 27, 1982

Contents

Software Construction Set
for the IBM® PC and PCjr

1

Introduction

"I need this data analyzed by tomorrow's group meeting. How soon can the computer people work it over?" asked Tim Fenson, the product manager for the new and improved User-Friendly Bunnies product line.

"Come on, Tim, you and I both know that the computer people can't get anything out on time. It'd be days, probably not until next week's meeting at the earliest."

"You know BASIC. Why don't you program the analysis yourself? It can't be that hard," Lissa Sims, the company's new public relations representative, said.

"Well sure, I know BASIC. But I really don't know how to write an entire program. I've only done little, silly things, like printing my name 50 times," Tim said. "Heck, I wouldn't know where to start."

"But you know how to program, right?"

"Well, sort of. I speak BASIC. But that's not quite the same as actually knowing how to program," said Tim.

"So you mean that learning BASIC is only part of the story. You still haven't really learned how to program?" asked Lissa.

"Well, yes, that's it. In my programming class we were working on the programs but not actually writing BASIC. We were figuring out what programs look like and how they work."

"Like how much money we can make from them?"

"Oh, no, that's what we do in marketing. Besides, we'd have to hold a few committee meetings for that. No, it was the technical details—like drawing blueprints as a plan of action," said Tim.

"I see," Lissa said. "So there is really more to programming than just knowing how to speak BASIC."

"Exactly," Tim said. "And that, unfortunately, is where my college class left off. It's a lot like learning a bunch of French words but not really learning how to string them together to say anything interesting."

"So," quizzed Lissa, "what you need now is a class in building programs, right?"

"Yes, that's it. How do I build a program?"

Does this conversation sound familiar to you? If it does, you need this book, which is a "how to do it" reference guide you can turn to when you are faced with a difficult and challenging program.

This book is full of techniques and ideas for:

- Designing and building programs
- Creating user-friendly software
- Storing and retrieving information
- Searching rapidly through data
- Sorting and arranging information
- Building windows
- Using disk files
- Displaying charts and graphs

Everything is described in clear, concise English. The programming examples are written in IBM PC BASIC. You can put the examples to work now, to make your programs faster, more efficient, more reliable and easier to use.

Programming is like constructing a building. Even though buildings may look quite different from the outside, the internal framework, piping, and wiring are remarkably similar. And so it is with programs. Instead of concrete frames, there are fundamental ways of organizing data. And instead of wiring and pipes, there are specific fast and efficient ways to manipulate data. Knowing the best technique to use in each situation makes programming much easier.

This book gives you the background that you need to design and construct the right solution to your problem. You'll learn about clever programming methods and how to use them to your advantage. This means that you'll spend less time programming and debugging—and more time enjoying your programs and your IBM PC.

But this book is much more than a mere collection of specialized subroutines. It is about fundamental programming techniques that are applicable to all programming problems. These fundamental techniques are the building blocks for assembling your programs, for creating solutions to your application, for getting your job done.

ALGORITHMS AND DATA STRUCTURES

Don't panic!

These buzzwords—*algorithms* and *data structures*—are just about the only jargon that you need to work with.

Computer scientists say that information is organized into data structures. That is just a fancy way of saying that data can be organized into formats suitable for processing by computer. A telephone book, for example, would be awkward to use if all the entries were arranged by telephone number instead of by name. Proper data organization improves the efficiency of information processing.

To look for the name Nolan in the telephone book you begin by turning to roughly the middle of the phone listings. Then you move backward or forward as needed until you find the name. Unless the phone book is very small, it's pointless to begin at the beginning of the phone book and scan forward one name or page at a time.

The sequence of steps that you perform when searching through the telephone book is called an algorithm. Algorithms describe the techniques used to manipulate and process information, such as how to find a name in a telephone book. An algorithm is a detailed set of instructions telling the computer exactly what to do with data.

For example, consider the set of instructions that you might give someone for finding your house:

1. Take 280 southbound from San Francisco.
2. Take the Page Mill Road exit and turn right at the stop sign.
3. At the first road on the right, make a right turn onto Arastradero Road.
4. Drive 1.7 miles.
5. After passing the large hill, pull into the driveway marked with a D.

Each step is a specific instruction in the algorithm "find my house." Each step must be completed before moving on to the next.

In a way, algorithms are similar to road maps because they show you how to get from one point in a problem to the final solution or destination. And often, the most obvious route is not the best. If you study the geography carefully, a better route may become apparent. Similarly, if you study a computing problem intently, a better algorithm or set of step-by-step instructions may be developed.

Software Construction Set for the IBM PC and PCjr is about algorithms and the data structures that the algorithms operate upon.

The correct data structure and the best algorithm greatly improve the efficiency of programs. For example, a simple way to search through a list of names is to start at the beginning of the list and just move from one name to the next until you locate the name. But the example of the telephone book shows that it's better to take advantage of how the data is organized. You know that names beginning with the letter *Z* are near the end of the phone book, while names beginning with *A* are near the beginning. This book explains how to program alternative search methods and how special techniques can be applied to a large class of programming problems.

How to Use This Book

Software Construction Set does not provide "ready-to-run" program listings. Instead, it provides techniques, guidance, and individual routines that can be assembled to produce a program. Building a program from these algorithms is like assembling a component stereo system. When you purchase a receiver, turntable, cassette deck, and speakers, you need only connect the units. You don't have to study electronics to learn how each unit operates. On the other hand, if your computer application is somewhat out of the ordinary, understanding how the system works can be rather useful. So this book also explains what makes these techniques work.

Use this book like a cook book. Do you need a recipe for a faster sorting technique? Just look in the sorting chapter, pull out the algorithm or program code, and plug it into your program. It's as simple as that. Or if you need a special-purpose version, study the descriptions and learn how to adapt the technique for your application.

Like the cook book, each chapter or recipe can be studied individually. Study only the material that you need to accomplish your goal. Occasionally, some of the techniques require knowledge of other methods. When this is the case, you will be directed to the appropriate sections of the book.

Even though you don't have to understand the theory of each algorithm, there are times when you'll want to understand how a method works, so study the examples and the text. Try to work through similar problems with paper and pencil; then try to transfer what you've discovered into a short program to test your ideas. Experiment! The worst that can happen is that your program won't do what you expected. And quite by accident, you may discover a new technique for solving an entirely different problem.

This book does not teach you how to program in BASIC but acts as a guide to getting the most from your BASIC programs for your personal computer applications. To make the best use of this book, you should have some experience with BASIC and know about subroutines (GOSUB and RETURN), FOR-NEXT loops, and IF-THEN-ELSE statements. Expertise is not required! Familiarity with BASIC and an insatiable curiosity are the only requirements.

Some experience in using disk files would be helpful but is not necessary; a fairly detailed introduction is provided in Chapter 7.

A brief introduction to arrays is provided in the next section. Arrays are the basis for nearly all of the programming examples contained in this book— and they are handy devices for solving many problems. If you haven't discovered arrays yet, be sure to read the next section. Otherwise, you can skip ahead to Chapter 2.

For additional reference material, you could use *IBM BASIC from the Ground Up*, by David E. Simon. Additional information is also available in the IBM PC BASIC manual.

All examples in this text assume that you will be using Advanced BASIC, which is available on the IBM PC Disk Operating System (DOS) diskette. To run Advanced BASIC, run the BASICA program when you see the DOS prompt A>:

    A>BASICA

(Running BASIC on the PCjr requires the use of the plug-in BASIC cartridge.) Some of the examples will work with other versions of BASIC: however, most are geared to the disk-based Advanced BASIC language. Don't let the word *advanced* scare you away—after all, it's still BASIC!

BASIC Variables and Arrays

In BASIC, information is stored in variables. Variables are names that you assign to data. For example, an employee's salary might be respresented by

    GROSSPAY = 250.00

This indicates that a variable named GROSSPAY has the value 250.00, probably representing $250.00 dollars.

GROSSPAY is a simple variable; it keeps track of a single value. But when the gross pay of several employees must be processed, you need some way of keeping track of each employee's pay. One way to do this is to create separate variables for each employee.

GROSSPAY1 = 250.00
GROSSPAY2 = 275.00
GROSSPAY3 = 280.00

Separate variables are acceptable only when the number of employees stays the same. If you have to change the program each time you lose or gain an employee, the computer will become very frustrating to use. A better way of storing data is to use an *array*.

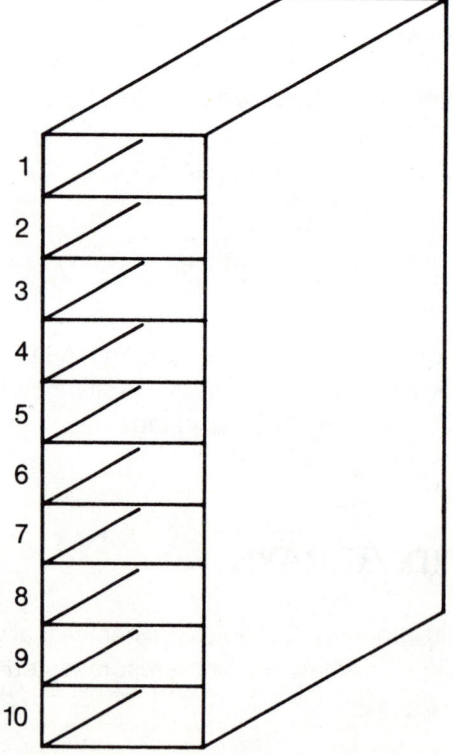

Figure 1-1   GROSS SALARY *storage box with space for 10 salary levels.*

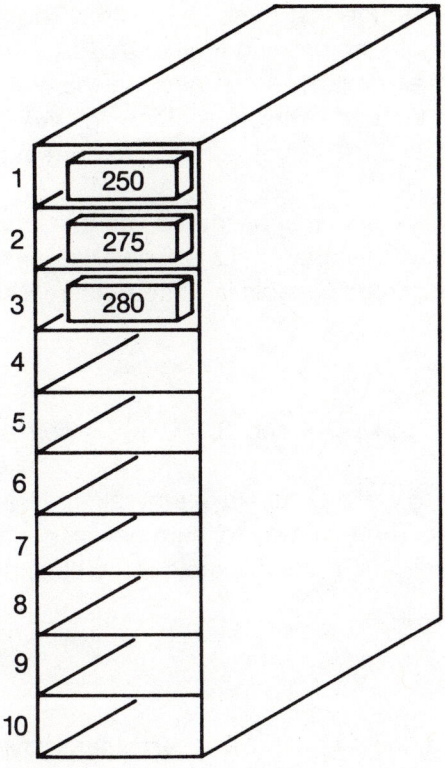

Figure 1-2

An array is a collection of information. To understand how the array stores information, look at some examples. In BASIC, the statement

DIM GROSSSALARY(10)

reserves memory space for an array of 10 variables. (Actually, space is allocated for 11 variables but for now, ignore the technical details.) You can think of an array as a storage box with 10 empty slots where you can put things (see Figure 1-1). Each slot is numbered.

Each of the 10 values in GROSSSALARY is distinguished from the others because it is a specific member of the array.

GROSSSALARY(1) = 250.00
GROSSSALARY(2) = 275.00
GROSSSALARY(3) = 280.00

These statements assign values to the first three elements of the array. (Fig. 1-2 shows the numbers placed into the holes in the GROSSSALARY box.) So 1, 2, and 3 can be thought of as employee numbers. In this way, GROSS-SALARY(1) refers to the storage location of the salary for employee 1. Because the array contains space for 10 different values, it can hold current pay values for up to 10 employees.

Each element of the array is called a subscripted variable. For example, GROSSSALARY(3) is a subscripted variable. That's technical jargon that comes from mathematics, where a subscripted variable is written with real subscripts:

GROSSSALARY$_3$

This variable is read as "GROSSSALARY sub 3," which is sort of a verbal shorthand.

If you've never seen an array before, then take a break from reading and start playing with your computer. The best way to learn new material is to use it! Get BASIC on the screen and type in some simple array statements. Start with

DIM N(100)

(You don't need a line number at the moment.) The computer should respond with

Ok

This allocates space for 100 numbers. They are referenced as N(1), N(2), N(3), and so on, up to N(100). Now, type

N(1) = 15

And then type

N(2) = 33

You have just given "N sub 1" and "N sub 2" the value 15 and 33, respectively. To confirm these assignments, type

PRINT N(1), N(2)

You should see

    15   33

Subscripted variables can be used just like any other variables. Type

    PRINT N(1) + N(2)

The result is

    48

Then type

    INPUT N(3)

When the computer displays ?, enter a number.

    ? 17

Then print N(3).

    PRINT N(3)
    17

You do not need to use the array values in sequential order. For example, type

    N(50) = N(3)
    PRINT N(50)

You'll see

    17

To illustrate how arrays are sometimes used in programs, create a simple program to keep track of names and salaries of up to 100 employees, each referenced by an employee number from 1 to 100. Two arrays are used to keep track of name and salary.

    DIM NAMES$(100)

allocates space for up to 100 names. The "$" is not a typographical error—it's possible to have arrays of strings as well. If string arrays seem unusual, do as before and try them out on your computer.

Next, a second array,

```
DIM PAY(100)
```

allocates space for up to 100 salary levels.

Suppose employee 10 is Herbert Kliegel and he earns $450.00 per week. This information is stored in the arrays as

```
NAMES$(10) = "HERBERT KLIEGEL"
PAY(10) = 450.00
```

As shown, these statements would be directly coded into the program. But if Herbert quits, then the program has to be changed. If there are 100 employees, then there must be at least 200 lines of program just to store the values. Obviously, you need a better approach.

In this example, you don't have to put the actual employee number into the program. Instead, the program can contain the following:

```
1000 REM — Add A New Employee
1010 INPUT "Enter Employee Number to Add ? ",N
1020 INPUT "Employee Name ? ",NAM$
1030 INPUT "Weekly Salary ? ",SALARY
1040 NAMES$(N) = NAM$
1050 PAY(N) = SALARY
1060 RETURN
```

Of course, these statements only add or change data in the arrays. You still need to be able to display the data to see what you have entered. To do that, makes lines 1000 through 1060 a subroutine and then add a command processor.

```
100 INPUT "Enter command: A)dd P)rint D)elete C)hange?
          ",C$
110 IF C$ = "A" THEN GOSUB 1000 : GOTO 100
    ELSE IF C$ = "P" THEN GOSUB 2000 : GOTO 100
    ELSE IF C$ = "D" THEN GOSUB 3000 : GOTO 100
    ELSE IF C$ = "C" THEN GOSUB 4000 : GOTO 100
```

ELSE IF C$ = "Q" THEN GOTO 32000
120 PRINT "Please Enter One of the Commands Shown"
130 GOTO 100

To practice using arrays, you might complete the program by adding subroutines to print, delete, and change information. You may wish to set NAMES$(N) for employee N to the empty string "" when the data is deleted. Then in the print subroutine, you can see if NAMES$() is blank or if it contains a name. That way, you'll need to print only the name records that are actually in use. Listing 1-1 shows one version of the program.

Listing 1-1

```
10        REM - Simple Employee Record Keeper
20        DIM NAMES$(100), PAY(100)
100       INPUT "Enter command:  A)dd P)rint D)elete C)hange? ",C$
110       IF C$ = "A" THEN GOSUB 1000 :
            GOTO 100 ELSE IF C$ = "P" THEN GOSUB 2000 :
            GOTO 100ELSE IF C$ = "D" THEN GOSUB 3000 :
            GOTO 100ELSE IF C$ = "C" THEN GOSUB 4000 :
            GOTO 100 ELSE IF C$ = "Q" THEN GOTO 32000
120       PRINT "Please Enter One of the Commands Shown"
130       GOTO 100
1000      REM - Add A New Employee
1010      INPUT "Enter Employee Number to Add ? ",N
1015      IF N = 0 THEN RETURN
1017      IF NAMES$(N) <> "" THEN PRINT "Choose another employee number." :
            GOTO 1010
1020      INPUT "Employee Name ? ",NAM$
1030      INPUT "Weekly Salary ? ",SALARY
1040      NAMES$(N) = NAM$
1050      PAY(N) = SALARY
1060      RETURN
1070      REM
1080      REM
2000      REM - Print Employee Records
2010      FOR I = 1 TO 100
2020        IF NAMES$(I) <> ""  THEN  PRINT I, NAMES$(I), PAY(I)
2030      NEXT I
2040      RETURN
2050      REM
2060      REM
3000      REM - Delete an Employee Record
3010      INPUT "Enter Employee Number to Delete ? ",N
3015      IF N = 0 THEN RETURN
3020      IF  NAMES$(N) = ""  THEN PRINT "Employee #";N;" does not
            exist - try again":
            GOTO 3010
3030      PRINT NAMES$(N), PAY(N)
3040      INPUT "Delete (Y or N) ? ",C$
3050      IF C$ <> "Y" AND C$ <> "N"  THEN GOTO 3040
3060      IF C$ = "Y" THEN NAMES$(N) = "" :
            PRINT "Deleted" ELSE PRINT "Not Deleted"
3070      RETURN
3080      REM
3090      REM
4000      REM - Change an Employee Record
4010      INPUT "Enter Employee Number to Change ? ",N
4015      IF N = 0 THEN RETURN
```

```
4020    IF NAMES$(N) = "" THEN PRINT "Employee #";N;" does not exist -
        try again" :
        GOTO 3010
4030    PRINT NAMES$(N), PAY(N)
4040    INPUT "Enter new name (or ENTER if no change)? ",T$
4050    IF T$ <> "" THEN NAMES$(N) = T$
4060    INPUT "Enter new pay (or ENTER if no change)? ",T
4070    IF T <> 0 THEN PAY(N) = T
4080    RETURN
4090    REM
4100    REM
32000   END
```

This simple program illustrates how arrays can be used in BASIC to store information. In most applications, however, data is not stored by number. For example, if you wish to find out where George Fenbon lives, you'd probably like to tell the computer: "Look up George Fenbon and tell me where he lives." But if you must first find George Fenbon's employee number, there's not much point to using the computer. To be useful, the computer must solve problems in a friendly way. In this case, the employee pay program would be easier to use if it worked with employee names instead of numbers.

REVIEW

- This book is a how-to-do-it reference guide providing programming techniques, tricks, theory, and much more.
- Algorithms are precise descriptions of the rules that the computer follows to carry out a particular operation or function.
- Data structures are the techniques used to organize the information that the computer works with. Any organized collection of information, such as a telephone book, is a data structure.
- Variables store individual quantities for later processing. The variable

SALARY = 300

keeps track of someone's salary. If the salary changes, you need only change the value assigned to the variable.

Arrays allocate space for many pieces of data. For example, the array defined as DIM NAME$(100) has space for 100 separate names. Each name in the array is referenced with a subscript. The following statement is an example:

NAME$(1) = "John Smith"

Coming Up

The following chapters show how this simple employee-records system can be organized so that you can request information by name rather than by number. Of course, the array NAMES$() could be searched in order. But that method can be much too slow when dealing with large amounts of data or if the search must be performed repeatedly. Instead, there are some clever programming techniques, like the binary table search and hashing, that greatly reduce the number of comparisons needed to find an employee's data record.

Before delving too deeply into actual programming, this book first examines the designing and building of programs. The design phase begins with a concept or idea and progresses through a description of the program to a detailed design or blueprint from which a program is constructed.

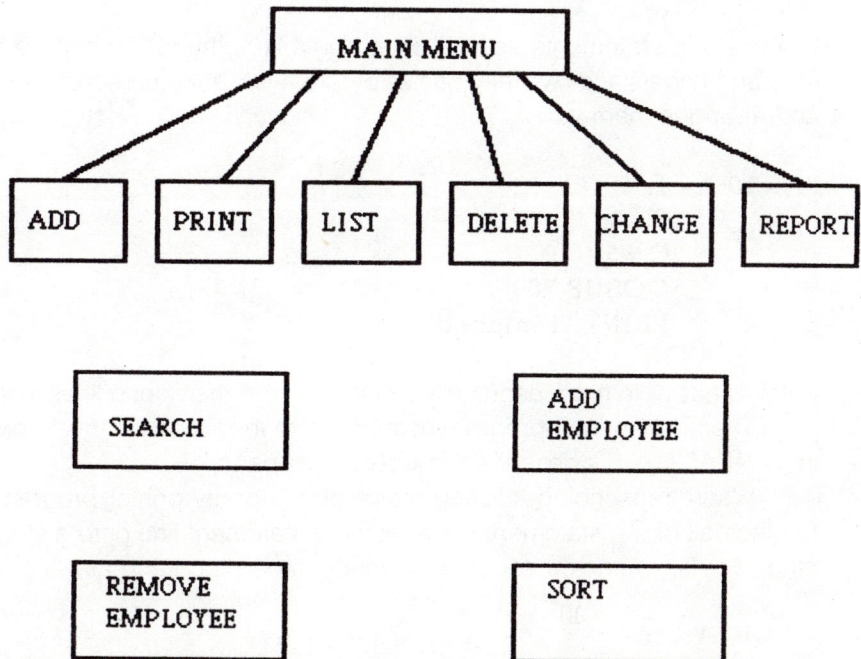

Figure 1-3   *Employee records program structure.*

A Note on the BASIC Listings

Most of the BASIC program listings in this book were not made by typing LIST in BASIC. Instead, a special program called a "pretty printer" was used to display the listings in a more readable format.

A pretty printer program takes an ordinary BASIC listing and arranges the lines and statements into a format that makes the listing easier to read and understand. IBM BASIC lets you place multiple statements on a single line by separating each statement with a colon.

10 A = 1: B = 3: C = 5: GOSUB 700: PRINT "Finished"

is roughly equivalent to these five separate lines:

10 A = 1
20 B = 3
30 C = 5
40 GOSUB 700
50 PRINT "Finished"

When all the statements appear on a single line, the listing can be difficult to read and understand. A pretty printer program takes the collection of statements and arranges them as

10 A = 1:
      B = 3:
      C = 5:
      GOSUB 700:
      PRINT "Finished"

which is easier to read, especially when there are many long lines in the listing.

The pretty printer program used to make the listings in this book is written in IBM BASIC—it is described in detail in Appendix B.

When transcribing a listing made by the pretty printer program, be sure to place all of the statements of a multiple statement line onto a single line. In other words, when you see a statement in the listing such as

10 A = 1:
      B = 3:
      C = 5:
      GOSUB 700:
      PRINT "Finished"

type it at your computer as

10 A = 1: B = 3: C = 5: GOSUB 700: PRINT "Finished"

CHAPTER 2

Building Programs

Before you look at the subroutines that you'll use to build programs, you need to look at the big picture: How is an entire program built? This chapter presents a plan of attack for some big programming projects.

You may be thinking that you'll never write a big program, but small programs often turn into big programs—and big programs often turn into messes. Rather than allow programs to grow uncontrolled, you can plan ahead so that adding new features later is easy.

Structured design and programming techniques help you build programs faster and reduce the likelihood of bugs. Also, the techniques keep future expansion orderly and neat.

The key to program design is the work you do before you write a single line of code. You certainly wouldn't try to build a house without blueprints. Nor would you try to write a book without planning its organization. Programming is no different: Creating a good program requires a certain amount of planning. The steps you should follow are listed here; an overview of each step is given later.

1. Decide what the program will do.
2. Choose the needed features.
3. Describe the operation of the program.
4. Construct a mock-up of the program.
5. Write a detailed design of the program.
6. Code the program.
7. Test the program.
8. Enhance the program.

Steps 1 through 4 define the *user interface,* which is jargon for that portion of the program that interacts with the user, displays menu selections, provides error messages, and accepts input to process commands and selections.

As you can see, approximately half of the steps in program design deal with user interface. In fact, this portion of the program is the most important part. Few people (other than the programmer) care that the program uses the best algorithm in the world to accomplish its task. All that users ever see is the outside of the program. If it's not user friendly, people won't use the program.

Consequently, a carefully designed user interface often takes up to half of the time needed to produce the entire program. The other half of the steps deal with the design of the program code, proper selection of algorithms and data structures, and finally, actual programming. Many professional programmers spend several months on steps 1 through 4, even for a program that may take only a few months to write. It's very important that the initial design steps be undertaken—if they are not, you may find that you have produced a wonderful solution to a problem that does not exist.

DECIDE WHAT THE PROGRAM SHOULD DO

Deciding what the program should do is an obvious way to start. But making this decision is easier said than done.

Sometimes, you start with what seems like a fairly simple idea. But then, as you start to develop the program, you think of other things that you can squeeze in with just a little more work. Soon your simple idea isn't so simple anymore and you start to lose direction. By the time you finish the project, you have forgotten what it was that you were trying to do.

Maybe you'd like to write a program to manage your checking account. This seems simple enough. But maybe what you're really after is a program to organize expenses or a program to track income. The key to your success is to identify exactly what your program is going to do. Try to identify precisely what service your program will perform or what problem it will solve. Narrow your scope so that you're working on just the problems that need to be computerized. In other words, determine the objectives you want your program to meet.

Finish this statement: "My program will . . ." Give a simple description of what the program will do. Don't try to explain how the program works or how someone will run it. Just give a simple statement that says what it will do. Here are some examples:

> My program balances my checkbook.
>
> My program displays azimuth-elevation tracking information for the AMSAT-OSCAR-10 communications satellite.
>
> My program keeps track of expenditures and income.
>
> My program displays plots of antibody concentration versus optical density.
>
> My program chooses the most fuel-efficient route for an airplane flight by examining possible routes, winds aloft, and fuel consumption at various altitudes.

This process helps you determine your objectives. Then you can devise a plan to achieve your objectives. You can probably identify your objectives for a small program without writing anything down. Nevertheless, do not skip this most important step!

CHOOSE THE NEEDED FEATURES

After deciding what the program does, you need to choose the features needed to achieve the program's objectives. If the program plots antibody concentration versus optical density, then you need a way to enter the data and possibly to change the data if you make an error during data entry. After the data is entered, you need a way to display the graph, a way to print the graph on a printer, and perhaps a way to scale and rotate the graph to accommodate different printers.

If you're writing a word processor, then you probably want file commands, editing commands, and cursor-movement commands. You probably also want some sort of "cut and paste" feature. Now is the time to identify the general features in the program.

DESCRIBE THE OPERATION OF THE PROGRAM

Describe what the program looks like from the user's point of view. Describe what appears on the screen, what happens if certain keys are pressed, and so on. A sample description of the plotting program might appear like this:

```
To run the program, type

A>BASICA PLOT

Once plot is loaded into memory and running, it will display

the following screen,


               PLOTTING PROGRAM

                  Version 1

            1   ENTER DATA

            2   CHANGE DATA

            3   DISPLAY PLOT

            4   PRINT PLOT

            5   CHANGE SCALING/ROTATION


               Choose Selection?

Selection 1 - ENTER DATA

      When  the ENTER DATA selection is made,  the screen  is

cleared and the following prompt is displayed,

      Enter Number of Data Elements?

The  user should respond with the number of data points that

are to be entered.    If an invalid entry is made, one of the

following errors will be displayed,

      Invalid Number Entered - Reenter

Or,

      Number of Data Points Must Be Less Than 100 - Reenter

Next, the program will prompt,

      Enter Data Point #1 (X,Y) ?

The  user  should  type the X and Y values  separated  by  a

comma, as for example,

      Enter Data Point #1 (X,Y) ? 10, 20
```

Continue in this manner, describing each feature in the program. Anticipate possible errors and list each of the error messages that the program might issue.

Construct a Mock-up of the Program

The user interface consists of the menus, the displays, and the error messages. Chapter 3 provides guidelines for designing software that are easy to use, ideas for prompting and displaying data, and program examples that show you what you need to do to program the user interface.

At this stage in the design of your program, you're basically describing how the program operates from the user's point of view. Your description should be detailed enough so that someone could use it as the instruction guide to run your program.

A simple way to test the cleanliness and thoroughness of your design is to construct a mock-up of the program. A mock-up isn't a complete version of the program; it is just a program that displays the menu or menus, enables you to make choices, and displays the various screens. For example, the ENTER DATA option of the plotting program should be displayed, although you probably would not allow data entry in your mock-up.

The DISPLAY PLOT option should probably display a sample graph so that you can see just what type of output may be produced by your program. But again, the data you use will probably be fictitious.

The mock-up program is a quick prototype that you'll likely throw away. If you can, try to show it to the people who will use the program. Perhaps you work in a lab with several other people who may use your program. In that case, have a few of them try to run through the mock-up. Take notes on their reactions and comments. You may find that you'll want to make some changes to the user interface.

In addition, it's easy to leave out a feature that is essential to the operation of the program. At this stage, potential users can spot the omission and you can easily put it into the mock-up. After you've made any necessary changes, run the mock-up for them again.

Even though mock-ups are not absolutely essential, and sometimes impossible to create, they are a valuable tool for evaluating a new program design. Software design is an iterative process: Every review helps polish the final product.

Write a Detailed Design of the Program

You're almost ready to write the program! But first, you need to lay the framework by writing a detailed design of data layouts and subroutines.

Start by splitting the program into smaller sections. For example, the plotting program provides some logical ways of segmenting (see Figure 2-1).

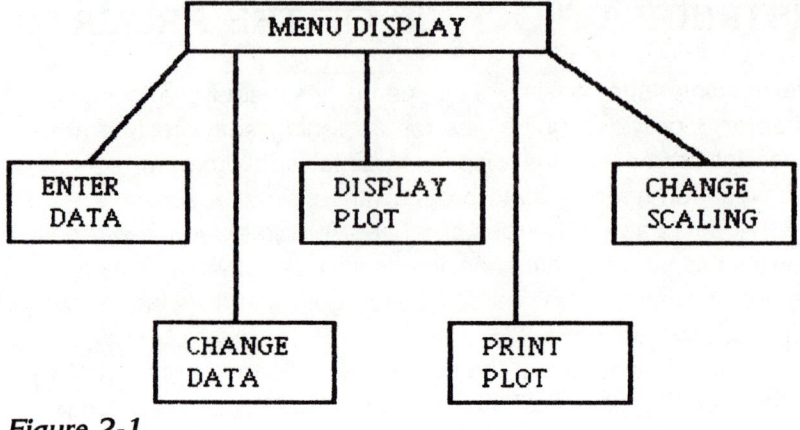

Figure 2-1

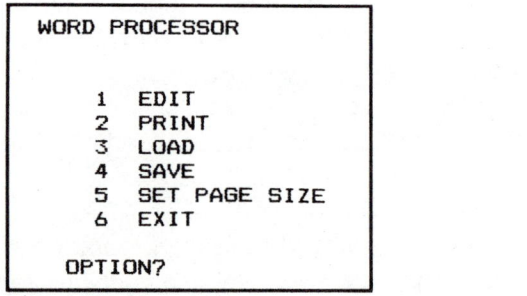

Figure 2-2

Segmenting helps you attack the programming problem. Take a big problem (or program) and split it into several smaller and simpler problems (program subroutines). The design is simplified because you can then concentrate on each of the smaller problems or subroutines individually.

Using a main menu as a guide (Figure 2-2), start a detailed design by sketching the subdivisions of the program. Figure 2-3 shows a sketch of a word-processing program. The sketch shows the flow through the program. When option 1 is selected, the program drops to the EDIT display.

As the design progresses, additional subdivisions can be incorporated into the design. Figure 2-4 shows many more divisions in the editor's layout. Occasionally, as the design becomes more detailed, you will notice that you chose the wrong subdivisions. In that case, rearrange things; Start over if necessary. It's far easier to fix a problem during the design stage than to alter it once the program has been almost completely written. Imagine building a 10-floor building and forgetting to put in the stairway. It'd be far simpler to catch that during design than to blast holes through someone's office space later.

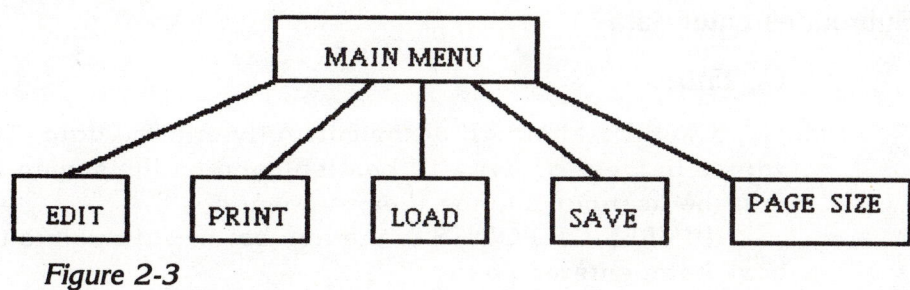

Figure 2-3

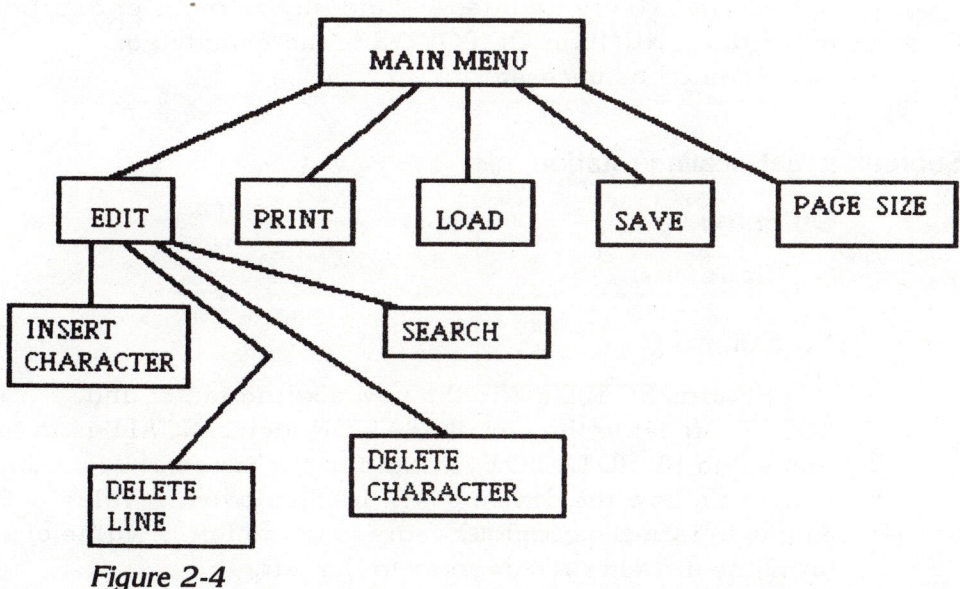

Figure 2-4

Outline the data that you expect your program to operate on. For example, the word-processing program needs an array for storing the entered text. And the plotting program outlined previously needs to store the entered data in an array. It also needs information on the scaling and rotation to be applied to the graph. Note that at this stage it helps to keep the design in a pictorial representation. If a picture is worth a thousand words, then these pictures will make it much easier to understand the overall design.

Next, choose the subroutines you need to implement each of the functions. Specify what values need to be passed to the subroutines and what values will be passed back. Descriptions of two subroutines used in the plotting program follow.

Subroutine enter data

On Entry:

X() and Y() hold all of the currently entered data. The values in these arrays will be displayed on the screen so that the user can change them if needed.

NUMBER.OF.POINTS is the number of data points that have been entered so far.

On Exit:

X() and Y() are updated to hold any changes or additions to the data. NUMBER.OF.POINTS is incremented or decremented as necessary.

Subroutine get scaling/rotation info

On Entry:

No inputs.

On Exit:

Returns SCALE set to the new scaling factor and ROTATION set to the new ROTATION factor. SCALE is in the range 0 to 10. ROTATION is angle in the range of 0 to 359 indicating how the drawing will be displayed. A value of 90 means to turn the graph 90 degrees to the left. A value of 180 turns the drawing 180 degrees to the left.

Each subroutine should perform one function, although each may call other subroutines. For example, if the subroutine computes total expenditures, then it should not also print them. Computing total expenditures may be a fairly involved process that calls other subroutines to compute subtotals. Create a separate subroutine to print out the totals in whatever format might be required.

When you create a subroutine that calls other subroutines, be sure that it makes sense to call the other subroutines. For example, it makes sense to have this subroutine:

Subroutine — Compute and Display Total Expenditures
    GOSUB — Compute Total Expenditures
    GOSUB — Display Total Expenditures

It does not make sense to have a subroutine that makes extraneous calls, like this one:

Subroutine — Compute and Display Total Expenditures
    GOSUB — Compute Total Expenditures
    GOSUB — Display Total Expenditures
    GOSUB — Compute Gas Mileage
    GOSUB — Print Telephone Usage Summary

The last two calls do not belong in the subroutine.

Partitioning a program is not easy. Neither is selecting the appropriate divisions within subroutines. The best way to learn how to partition and design the subroutines is to do it! Designing becomes easier with practice. Be patient: the first attempt at design may be a trying experience.

Describe the Subroutines

A subroutine is basically a short section of BASIC that implements an algorithm. In many cases, you can simply take a published algorithm, such as one from this book, and write your BASIC code directly from it. In other instances, you'll need to describe the algorithm or program flow yourself. In these cases, you may wish to write pseudo code, a shorthand notation for describing an algorithm. Pseudo code is explained a little later in this section. Other techniques for describing a subroutine include flowcharts, outlines, and a newer method called data flow diagrams.

Flowcharting is an older design technique that is not used very often today. Flowcharts are diagrams that use specially labeled symbols to represent the steps of an algorithm. Figure 2-5 shows a flowchart that explains how to search sequentially through a list of names for a specific name. The rectangular boxes describe an operation to be performed, like I = I + 1 or G$ = S$. The diamonds are decision points: they pose questions that can be answered either yes or no. If the answer to the question posed is yes, then a branch is made to some location in the flowchart. A no causes a branch to a different point. A large variety of symbols are provided to indicate input/output, procedures, and decisions. The problem with flowcharts is that they are difficult and time-consuming to draw and are often so detailed that it would be easier just to write the actual code.

An outline is useful for describing simple logic or for capturing a broad view of the program. An outline may look just like the outlines you use when writing a research paper. Or, the outline may be quite detailed.

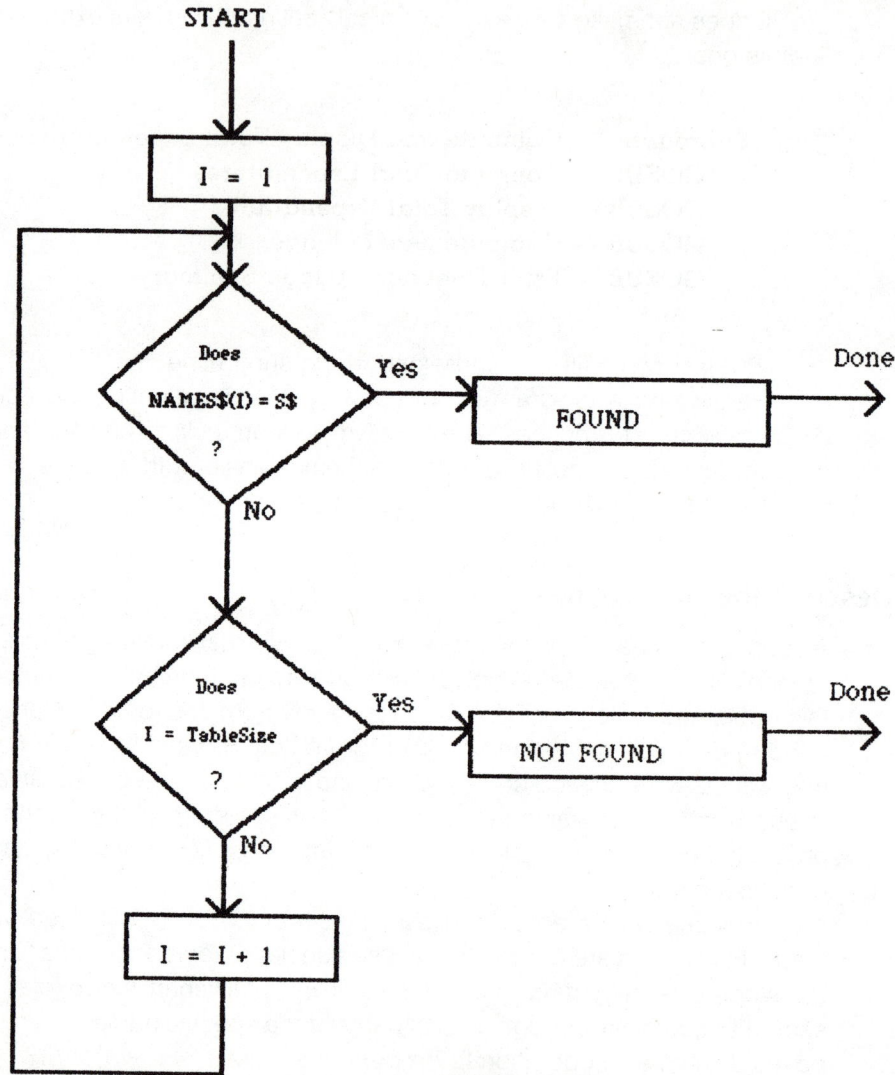

Figure 2-5

Sometimes the techniques are combined. Often a programmer begins with one technique, such as a data flow diagram, and then translates into another specification, such as pseudo code, as the design becomes more detailed. Use whatever technique suits your needs. There really isn't a right or wrong technique. As you gain design experience, you'll no doubt discover what works best for you.

Write the Pseudo Code

Pseudo code is an English-like description of how a subroutine operates. It's called pseudo code because it resembles a cross between English prose and a programming language. Pseudo code describes the steps needed to carry out the operations of a subroutine. Algorithm descriptions in this book are written in pseudo code.

For some people, pseudo code closely resembles the actual program code. For others, the pseudo code may be less specific, giving only a hint as to what should be done in each step. To practice, write a pseudo code for a subroutine that translates all characters in a text file into lower case. Begin with a file containing the following lines.

> THE QUICK BROWN FOX JUMPED OVER THE LAZY DOG
> AND BROKE A LEG. NOW IS THE TIME FOR ALL GOOD MEN
> TO COME TO THE AID OF THE INJURED FOX.
> FORTUNATELY, THE FOX WAS TAKEN TO A LOCAL
> HOSPITAL AND IS REPORTED IN SATISFACTORY
> CONDITION.
> HOWEVER, THERE IS SOME QUESTION AS TO WHETHER
> THE FOX CAN PAY HIS HOSPITAL BILLS.

The subroutine scans through this text and changes each upper-case letter into a lower-case letter. The output looks like this:

> the quick brown fox jumped over the lazy dog and broke
> a leg. now is the time for all good men to come to the aid of
> the injured fox.
> fortunately, the fox was taken to a local hospital and is
> reported in satisfactory condition.
> however, there is some question as to whether the fox can
> pay his hospital bills.

Now that you've specified the goal of the subroutine, write a pseudo-code description of how it operates. A very general description might look like this:

Subroutine to Scan File and Convert to Lower Case

1. Input line
2. If any character in the line is upper case, change it to lower case
3. Output the line

4. If not at end of file, then go to step 1
5. Return

A more detailed description might look like this:

Subroutine to Scan File and Convert to Lower Case

1. Input Line L$
2. For I In 1 to Length L$ Do
   If MID$(L$,I,1) is upper case, change it to lower case.
3. Print L$
4. If Not end of file, then to go to step 1
5. Return

Note that the second description includes variable names and more detail. In fact, translation to BASIC is quite simple. There is no rule as to how detailed a pseudo-code description should be. Many programmers dispense with pseudo code altogether and just write out the program.

Exactly why someone would want a subroutine to convert upper case to lower case is unclear. But it does provide us with a reasonably short example of pseudo code.

CODE THE PROGRAM

After you write the pseudo code, you will find the actual coding of the program in BASIC remarkably easy. In fact, if you've done all the design work described so far, you've probably completed about 80% of the project.

Coding is usually approached in one of two different ways: "top down" or "bottom up." Top-down programming is the process of writing all of the high-level routines, such as the menu displays, first. In a way, coding a program in top-down fashion is like a business that just hires a lot of managers. Each manager then hires employees to do the actual work.

You may be able to use the mock-up created while designing the user interface as the framework for the top-down program. All it contains is the top-level display routines. It's missing the lower-level routines that do the actual work. To turn it into a real program, begin adding the subroutines that perform the requested functions. For example, the plotting program has six main menu selections:

1. ENTER DATA
2. CHANGE DATA
3. DISPLAY PLOT
4. PRINT PLOT
5. CHANGE SCALING/ROTATION

In the mock-up, selecting option 1 probably calls a subroutine that displays a sample screen used for data entry. To build the actual program, add the program statements and subroutines needed to allow data entry and verification.

Bottom-up coding begins with the low-level subroutines. Each subroutine is tested individually and then combined with the others. When the tested subroutines are combined, there is a good chance that the entire group of subroutines will function correctly. As individual subroutines are written, tested, and added to the program, each function becomes operative.

The best approach is often a combination of the two techniques. Begin by writing the low-level routines, but once enough have been written, add the highest-level menu displays and other routines at the top. At this stage, the low-level routines can be tested in the actual program just by making menu selections.

In practice, each program is unique, but these guidelines help you tackle your programming project.

TEST THE PROGRAM

Debugging is the process of removing the errors in a program. Bugs occur in nearly all programs and they are nothing to feel ashamed about. Proper design helps eliminate bugs, but it is very difficult to identify all potential problems until the program is actually running. For this reason, extensive testing must be done to try all functions in a program with all different types of data.

Testing should occur at all stages of development. Sometimes it seems like you should write the entire program and then see if it runs. But, of course, you will almost certainly discover that the program does not run at all. Then you're forced to begin attacking each problem one by one until you've eliminated all the bugs.

A better approach is to test each section as it is produced. Then, as you assemble the program from completed and tested sections, you're much more likely to produce a working program. To test individual subroutines, you need to create special testing code, most of which will eventually be thrown away.

The first step in locating bugs is to play computer. That is, you should walk through the program statements, keeping track of how variables are changed and following the flow through the code. In essence, you pretend that you are the computer and you are running the program.

An easy way to keep track of variables is to write them in a table on a piece of paper. For example, consider the employee-records system.

NUMBER.EMPLOYEES		NAMES$( )	PAY( )
1	#1	GEORGE	350

As you run through the program, variables may change. You indicate the changes by writing the new values in the table.

NUMBER.EMPLOYEES		NAMES$( )	PAY( )
1	#1	GEORGE	350
2	#2	LISA	375

By cycling through the program, you can sometimes locate problems. Often a variable doesn't really have the value that you expect it to, and this, of course, is a bug.

You can add statements to print out the contents of variables. When you start the program, leave gaps in the line numbering sequence so that you have room to add statements such as PRINT. For example, you usually begin numbering a program at line 100 or 1000. This leaves room for adding special code at the beginning of the program. When you add a new subroutine, say a routine to perform a search through a table of names, you add some statements at the beginning of the program to put names into the table. Then you call the subroutine and see if the routine can find each of the names. Once you're convinced that the routine is working correctly, you can delete the testing code.

If the subroutine is normally called by some other routine, you might set up the test to call the next subroutine that calls the search routine in order to make sure everything works out.

When testing is conducted throughout the development process, there will be no major surprises when the program is completed. If testing hasn't been thorough, you really won't know where to look when a bug is encountered. Is the problem in the new routine you just added? Or is the problem in the subroutine called at line 2030? Knowing that each low-level subroutine works correctly helps eliminate potential problem areas.

When debugging, it's often nice to trace the execution of the program. IBM BASIC provides a built-in trace feature that causes BASIC to print the current line number as it executes each line in the program. Tracing is activated by typing TRON, which is a mnemonic for "trace on." TRON may be issued as an immediate-mode statement, or it may be included in the body of your program. For example, you might place TRON at the beginning of a subroutine, and then turn off tracing just before the RETURN statement.

Tracing is turned off by typing TROFF, which, of course, means "trace off." Like TRON, TROFF, may also be used as statement anywhere in your program.

When tracing is in use, BASIC displays each line number within brackets. A sample display might look like this:

[10] [20] [30] Enter your name? ED [40] [50]

The number of each line is displayed when the line is first encountered. Your program's input and output are mixed on the display with the tracing information.

Another way to trace execution is to place PRINT statements throughout your program. These statements may be removed when the program has been completed. Alternately, we might place a statement like

IF DEBUG% THEN PRINT "SEARCH"

at the beginning of each subroutine. If the variable DEBUG% has a nonzero value, then the name of the subroutine is displayed whenever the routine is called. During development, set DEBUG% to a nonzero value. When the program has been completely written and tested, you can change the initial value of DEBUG% to zero.

You could delete all of the debugging code from the program once you've finished writing it. But chances are good that you'll uncover more bugs later. Or you may add new features later. So, if possible, try to keep at least some of the debug code. If you don't want to delete the debug code, you can turn it into program comments by placing REM before each statement or by using the shorthand comment symbol '.

ENHANCE THE PROGRAM

Programs are dynamic organisms, growing and changing throughout their life cycle. New features are added and old ones are changed to accomplish new tasks. These changes are a normal part of all programs. The rest of the world changes, so why shouldn't a program?

Additions or changes are handled just like the original development. You write a description of the new function's operation and possibly create a mock-up so that others can see how the new feature looks. Next, you do detailed design and write the program code.

Adding or changing minor features is easy. But occasionally, large changes are required that may necessitate a major redesign. In these cases, you may need to start from scratch. That means rewriting the program's description, user interface, mock-up, and detailed design. Often, many of the original program statements and subroutines may be incorporated into the new program.

THE EMPLOYEE-RECORDS SYSTEM

As a demonstration of the program-building techniques presented in this chapter, let's now build a slightly bigger and more elaborate version of the employee-records system described in Chapter 1.

Objective

The program will keep track of information related to each employee and summarize that information in printed reports.

Features

- A maximum of 100 employees can be included in the program.
- The information stored for each employee is name, salary, telephone number, and department number.
- New employees can be added.
- Existing employees can be deleted.
- Information concerning an individual employee can be easily changed.
- The information related to an individual employee can be displayed on the screen or printed.
- A report summarizing all employee information can be printed. This report can be sorted by name or by department number.

Description of the Program

The program is called RECORDS. When it is run, the following prompt is displayed on the screen:

Select: A)dd, P)rint, L)ist, D)elete, C)hange, R)eport, Q)uit?

You select the desired operation by entering the letter shown. If a letter other than one in the prompt line is entered, the message

"Incorrect Selection — Try Again"

is displayed and the prompt line reappears.

ADD

When ADD is selected, the prompt

Enter Name of Employee to Add?

is shown. Pressing the ENTER key without entering a name returns you to the main menu. Otherwise, an employee name should be entered. If an employee with that name has already been entered, the following message is displayed:

'name' has already been added.

The "Enter Name of Employee to Add?" prompt then reappears.
Assuming no errors so far, RECORDS next prompts:

Department Number?
Telephone Number?
Salary?

RECORDS is not smart enough to know what is considered a valid department or telephone number, so it will accept just about anything.

PRINT

This prints the information associated with an employee. When selected, PRINT displays

Name of Employee to Print?

Pressing ENTER without entering a name returns you to the main menu.
If the name that is entered is not in the records, then RECORDS displays

'name' is not in the records — Try again

and reprompts for the employee name.

If the name is found in the table of names, then the following is printed:

Name	Department #	Telephone #	Salary
GEORGE	3	444-8888	$ 425

LIST

LIST works exactly like PRINT, except that the information is shown on the screen rather than the printer.

DELETE

Employees can be removed from the records system by selecting DELETE. DELETE prompts

Name of employee to Delete?

Pressing ENTER without entering a name returns you to the main menu.

If the name is not found, this message is displayed following the enter-name prompt:

'name' is not in the records — Try again

Otherwise, DELETE displays something like

GEORGE   Department # 3
Delete (Y or N)?

Answering Y displays

GEORGE removed

Answering N displays

GEORGE not removed

CHANGE

Sometimes the information associated with one of the employees has to change. When selected from the main menu, CHANGE displays

Name of Employee to Change?

Pressing ENTER without entering a name returns you to the main menu.
If the employee is not located, then CHANGE displays

'name' is not in the records — Try again

Once the name is found, CHANGE displays

Department = 3
Enter new department (CR = no change)?

Telephone # = 444-8888
Enter new telephone # (CR = no change)?

Salary = 425
Enter new salary (CR = no change)?

REPORT

REPORT provides printed reports sorted by employee name or by department number. When selected, REPORT prompts

Report by: 1) Employee name, or 2) Department?

Pressing ENTER returns you to the main menu.
Selecting 1 sorts the report into ascending order by employee name, while selecting 2 sorts the report into ascending order by department number.
When the report is sorted by name, the output appears as shown:

Employee	Department	Telephone	Salary
ALAN	9	x 37	275
BETTY	6	x 11	325
CHARLIE	8	x 87	300
DAVID	3	x 33	375
ERIC	8	x 86	425

When the report is organized by department, it appears as

Department	Employee	Telephone	Salary
3	DAVID	x 33	375
6	BETTY	x 11	325
8	CHARLIE	x 87	300
8	ERIC	x 86	425
9	ALAN	x 37	275

Detailed Design

The program is arranged in the structure shown in Figure 1-3 (refer to page 13). Additional routines are needed to search for a specific name, add a name to the table, delete a name, and change the data associated with a name. The report option requires a sorting routine.

The following list displays the names of the variables used in the employee-records system in the form of a variable dictionary.

Variable	*Description*
DEPT(100)	Array containing the department number that employee number i, as in DEPT(i), is within.
NAMES$(100)	Contains each of the employee names.
PHONE$(100)	Contains each employee's telephone number.
SALARY(100)	Contains each employee's weekly salary.
TOTAL.NAMES	Counts the number of names currently stored in the employee-records system.

Pseudo Code

The next step is to write each of the routines. You can write either pseudo code or the actual BASIC routines. Listing 2-1 shows pseudo code for the main menu prompt, as well as the ADD and DELETE routines.

Chapter 4 shows you how to write a program to implement the employee-records system. Chapter 8 tells you how to store the records on a disk file Finally, in Chapter 9, the report function is added.

Listing 2-1   *Sample pseudo code for the employee-records system.*

```
MAIN MENU
     Display Prompt
     If invalid selection then
          display an error and repeat the prompt
     Jump to the appropriate subroutine based on the
          command that was entered.


ADD
     Prompt for the name to add.
     If nothing was entered, then return to MAIN MENU
     Search for the name
     If it was found, then
          display error saying the name already exists
          Redisplay the name prompt
     Otherwise, prompt for each item to be stored,
          DEPT(), SALARY() and PHONE$() and
          place them in the table.
     Return
```

```
DELETE
     Prompt for the name to delete
     If nothing was entered, then return to MAIN MENU
     Search for the name
     If it was not found, then
          display error saying that the name wasn't found
          and prompt for another
     If it was found, then
          verify that we really want to delete it
     If yes, then
          call the delete entry subroutine
          and say Deleted
     If no, then
          say wasn't deleted.
     Return
```

REVIEW

- Proper design of personal computer software requires careful planning and thought. In many instances, the design phase occupies most of the development time. With practice, you'll learn how much time to spend on each application.

- The first four steps in the design process are the following: decide what the program will do; choose the needed features; describe the operation of the program; construct a mock-up of the program. These steps specify the user interface, which describes how the program looks to the end user. This is the "what the program does" description.

- The remaining steps in the design process are the following: write a detailed design of the program; code the program; test the program; enhance the program. These steps describe "how the program will do it." They define the data and the subroutines and programming code.

- During detailed design, specify as many details as you can about the program. These details include the structure of the program's data and an overview of the sections needed within the program.

- Pseudo code is an abbreviated, English-like description of an algorithm or subroutine. Pseudo code is often used to bridge the gap between the general description of the subroutine and the actual program statements.

- Rather than waiting until all programming is complete, you should test throughout the program's development. Seldom, if ever, does a big program fall together and work perfectly on the first run.

CHAPTER
3

Designing Software for People

Just for a moment, imagine an interactive personal computer. What sort of mental image do you have? Do you see your IBM PC with a printer or a disk drive on the desk next to it? A red light might be flashing on the disk drive. Or maybe you see a modem with a row of little red lights. You haven't forgotten anything, have you?

Do you see a person sitting in front of the display?

"Hmmmm," you may be thinking, "what's a person have to do with a computer system?" The answer: everything! You see, computers are tools for people. Yet when you write a program, you generally spend more time on the computing aspects than the people aspects of the applications.

In fact, most of this book is concerned with the details of programming for personal computers. But actually, good software isn't made for computers at all; it's made for people. Program design is a two-step process: design a solution for people and design a program to implement that solution.

A solution created for people is *user friendly*. Software is made user friendly by careful attention to the qualities that make it easy to learn and use. Guidelines for designing user-friendly software are given in this chapter. These guidelines are not wild ideas but are based on human factors research. Creating user-friendly software is similar to designing subroutines—just look in the appropriate section of this book and find a routine that fits your application.

THE IMPORTANCE OF USER-FRIENDLY SOFTWARE

Many cynics say that computer power can help you get your job done faster— or let you snarl things up faster. These snarls are often caused by computer software that is hard to use. Maybe you can't remember a particular command. So what do you do? Many people just guess at the command. But stand back if the command is wrong and it erases the entire disk!

The interface between humans and machines is so important that it was blamed for some of the problems that occurred at the Three Mile Island nuclear power plant. According to an investigation of the Three Mile Island incident, "There is little evidence of modern information technology within the control room . . . it is seriously deficient under accident conditions . . . Information was not presented in a clear and sufficiently understandable form . . . Overall, little attention had been paid to the interaction between human beings and machines under the rapidly changing and confusing circumstances of an accident." (Bowyer, 1980) In essence, the power plant technicians did not understand the information presented to them by their equipment.

Another example is the six digital displays on the flight deck of a Boeing 767 airliner. These displays provide primary control information to the pilots. For obvious reasons, it is crucial that the information be displayed in a clear and meaningful way.

Even though your programs do not control power plants or fly airliners, they still need to be user friendly. Designing a good user interface is an absolute necessity.

A well-designed program has these qualities:

Is easy to learn
Makes sense to its user
Deals with errors logically
Is simple and uncluttered

UNDERSTANDING THE USER

Once you decide to use a computer to solve a problem or to aid you in your work, you should next look at who will use the program. In most cases, the program user is not the programmer who created it. As programmers, you must recognize the needs of that end user and design an appropriate system.

Software is often created for a specific group. For example, a DNA modeling program used by researchers to study methods of gene transfer in cancer cells is very specialized and used only by highly trained scientists. The program must be geared to the needs of the cancer researchers, not the general public.

At the other extreme is a filing system used by both an order entry clerk and corporate vice president. That software needs to satisfy the needs of many users.

Another way to classify computer users is to group them into one of two categories: naive or casual users and experienced users. A naive or casual user is someone who doesn't use the program eight hours a day, five days a week. For example, a businessman might use a business graphics package at the end of each month to display a bar graph of weekly sales. Because he uses the program so infrequently, chances are good that he will have trouble remembering all the details of the program. And he probably doesn't have time to read the instruction manual before he produces a graph each month, so his software needs to be fairly simple and easy to use.

On the other hand, an airline reservations agent is a frequent, well-trained computer user. Because the agent interacts with the computer daily, he is unlikely to forget the little details of system operation.

The goals of the business-graphics package and the airline-reservations system are different. The graphics software is designed to be simple and easy to use. But the reservations system is designed for quick interrogation and flight selection. Therefore, the user interfaces chosen for these two applications are likely to be very different. These examples illustrate the importance of creating software that is appropriate for the end user.

DEVELOPING A CONCEPTUAL MODEL

The first part of designing a new piece of software is to develop a model that explains the operation of the system. When you sit down at your computer, you have a mental image of how things work. You understand that if you give a certain command, then a specific operation will take place. For example, if you type

```
A>DIR
```

you expect PC DOS to list the files on the diskette. It would not make sense if PC DOS did something else. Software has to do what is expected of it. The idea that software has to make sense is the key to designing user-friendly software.

When users sit down at computer terminals, they have an expectation of how the program operates. The goal of software designers is to produce a program that matches the user's expectations. The program should never surprise the user. One way to design software that makes sense is to model software after objects and procedures that you and the program's users are familiar with.

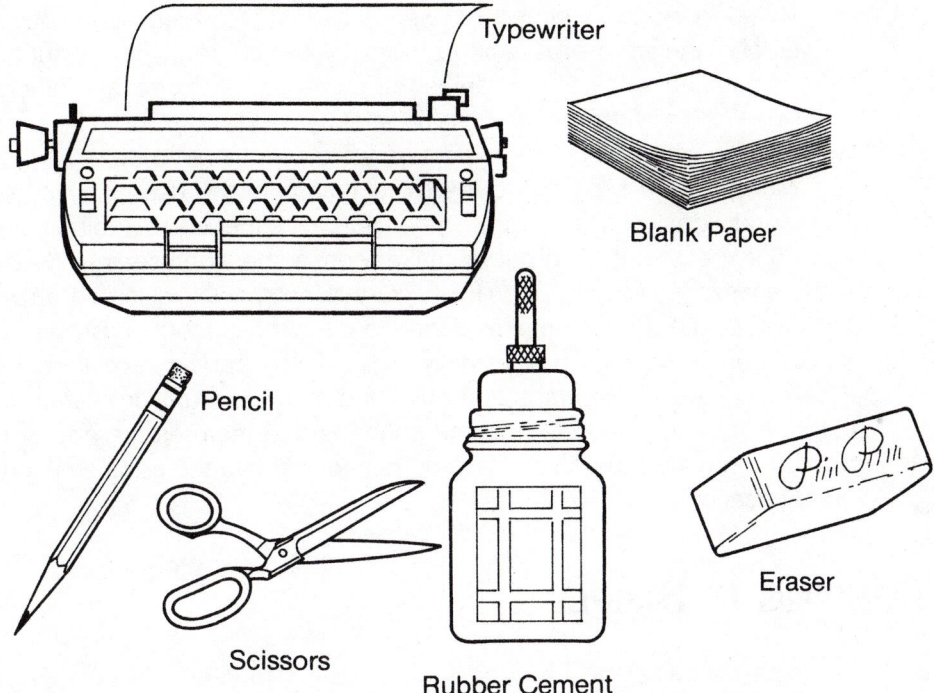

Typewriter

Blank Paper

Pencil

Scissors

Rubber Cement

Eraser

Figure 3-1   *The objects of a word processor.*

For example, consider a word-processing program. The goal of the word processor is to eliminate tedious editing and retyping. The tools of a writer's old-fashioned work station are a typewriter, blank typing paper, erasing liquid, a pencil, and maybe scissors and rubber cement to cut and paste. These pieces suggest features that should be found in the word-processing software. Since these features are familiar to those who do a great deal of writing, a word-processing program based on these ideas will likely make sense to its users.

To see how this works, start a design for a word processor based on these objects. Begin by displaying a blank piece of paper on the computer's video screen. New text is entered by typing it at the appropriate place on the page. Some of the conventional tools used by the writer suggest other features. For example, cutting and pasting is used to rearrange the body of the text. The writer snips out some portion of the text and glues it in place elsewhere in the document. On the computer, this might be handled by marking off the block of text to be cut and then moving the cursor to the spot where the text should be pasted.

By adopting the process that writers use on a conventional typewriter as the model of the word-processing program, you've already layed out much of the design. And since the model is the same as that used by authors, they likely will find the program easy to understand and use. Our word processor does exactly what the author expects a word processor to do.

Matching the program to the expectations of the user is a key point in user-friendly design. The program never surprises the user by doing something that is unexpected. If the program makes sense, then the user intuitively knows how to operate the program. You might call this the principle of least astonishment: Software should do what makes sense to the user, without surprises.

Of course, you don't necessarily want to follow traditional methods exactly. If the designers of the first automobile had followed tradition, cars would be steered with reins. Therefore, some changes and features are appropriate to the medium of the computer that may not have fit into the traditional model for the application.

KEEPING IT SIMPLE

The most difficult part of any designer's task is to keep it simple. Resist the temptation to keep adding one feature after another. In many instances, 90% of a program's users never use more than 10% of the program's features. Adam Osborne, author and creator of the Osborne 1 portable computer, stated this rather succinctly at the 1983 West Coast Computer Faire: "Adequacy is sufficient, he said. "All else is irrelevant." Put into the software only the features that are truly needed.

For example, consider a text-editing program that has a command that deletes a single line of text and another command that deletes multiple lines of text. Surprisingly, to delete five lines of text, most users will choose the command to delete a single line five times rather than choose the command to delete multiple lines once. In fact, in most programs, a small group of commands is used most. This preference for a small group of frequently used commands is probably related to the human short-term memory capacity. Psychological research has established a seven-plus-or-minus-two phenomenon. Researchers have noted that most people can keep track of about seven, plus or minus two, things simultaneously. Increasing the number of events leads to degradation in performance.

Often programmers add just one more feature that, they claim, makes the software easier to use. Weigh such claims very carefully. How many people really notice the lack of a certain feature? In fact, when reviewing commercially produced software, you should keep in mind that feature lists are often a poor way to compare similar software products, since 90% of the features are rarely used anyway. When purchasing software or writing your own, give careful thought to the real usefulness of each feature. The hardest part of design is knowing which features to throw away—not which features to add.

Avoid the technology-for-the-sake-of-technology syndrome. There are a lot of consumer goods, and certainly some famous military weapons systems, that have no useful purpose. Why, then, were these machines created? Basically, because technology is fun. People build super-technical gadgets and gizmos because they are fun to build, not necessarily because they are really useful. Avoid the temptation to add frivolous features that do not enhance the software.

Programming can be very fun and often addicting. People who program computers are notorious for creating wonderfully complex programs that are not particularly good for any purpose. What happens is that the program is developed from the inside out. Programmers start with a great idea for a subroutine and then build a program around the code. When they finish, they look for a problem that fits the solution.

The correct approach is to start by recognizing the problem to be solved. The nature of the problem should dictate the features for the program.

When you get an idea, first think of the applications, because there may not be any. Only after recognizing possible uses for the program can you think about the program in detail.

By allowing the application to drive the design, you can avoid adding, pointless and complicated features. This, in turn, leads to simple and correct design.

Another fact to consider: Each feature that makes the system easier to use must be documented somewhere. That means the instruction manual becomes more complicated. And a complex instruction manual may mask the actual simplicity of your software.

System design boils down to this maxim: Keep it simple. In practice, keeping it simple is seldom easy because the solution that is both simple and complete is rarely obvious. A good practice is that when you think you've reached the ideal design, start over and come up with another. By forcing the design through several interations, you narrow the focus of the product and explore all possible alternatives.

Look at similar features and see if they might be combined into a single concept. For example, many word-processing programs save the document in a special format disk file. But you may want your word processor to create either its own, special format file, or a standard text file, suitable for sending to a printer or using as input to another program. Your first idea might be to make the type of file an option for the SAVE command. That would work, but it also would complicate the SAVE command. Instead, why not take advantage of the PRINT command? PRINT sends standard text to a printer, so why not also allow PRINT to print to a file?

Combining features greatly reduces the complexity of a program. Further, a surprising outcome is that the program may actually be easier to write because what might have required two subroutines may now be a single command implemented by a single subroutine.

CONSISTENCY

The program must be consistent in all aspects of its operation. If you use a key to delete a filing-system record in one area of the program, then you should also use that key elsewhere to delete something. If the DELETE key is used instead to print a file, then the program is inconsistent. Further, it will be hard for the user to remember what command to use—the program may surprise the user by doing something that is totally unexpected.

DESIGNING THE DIALOGUE

There are many methods that you can use to create dialogue between people and machines. A dialogue is the two-way communication between two parties. When you talk with a friend, you expect some sort of response, verbal or otherwise. Similarly, when typing at a keyboard, you expect the computer to respond in a meaningful way.

On the computer, these dialogues can take the form of simple prompts, menus, command languages, pointing devices like mice and light pens, and graphical input and output such as graphics tablets for input and color charts for output.

The type of dialogue to use depends largely on the user and the application. Menus tend to be best for infrequent, naive users, while command languages are sometimes better for skilled, frequent users. For example, an airline re-servations agent needs information from the computer quickly. Passengers do not have the time to wait while the operator runs through a series of menus to reach the needed flight information. Instead, shorthand command language lets the operator interrogate the database quickly, using a minimum number of keystrokes. Consequently, these agents require substantial training to learn the system.

Self-teaching dialogues that contain an explanation of all features may seem like a good idea, but are a poor choice in many real systems. Anyone who uses the system frequently soon tires of the repetitive instructions. A better approach is to make the help messages available through a HELP command or selection.

PROMPTS

Prompts are a frequently used portion of the user interface. But there are correct and incorrect ways to use them. Most prompts should be self-explanatory, such as

ENTER LAST NAME

A prompt like

ENTER NAME?

is ambiguous. The user doesn't know if this means to enter just the last name, or first name, or both. And if the computer does expect both names, in what order should they be entered?

Always try to make your prompts descriptive.

ENTER FILE SIZE (1 TO 100)?

is better than just

ENTER SIZE

The first prompt clearly indicates what size refers to and what is considered an acceptable response. There is no need to make the user guess. Another common input is the date:

ENTER DATE

This prompt is almost useless because you have no idea in what format you are to enter the date. A better prompt is

ENTER DATE (MMDDYY)?

or

ENTER DATE (DD/MM/YY)?

Both prompts indicate the exact format for the date entry. Even though it is easy to make prompts meaningful, many programmers continue to write short or mnemonic messages.

DEFAULT ENTRIES

Many entry methods allow quick entry of commonly entered or assumed values. These assumed values are known as default entries. For example, in a banking system it's reasonable to assume that most transactions occur on the date that they are entered into the computer, so the prompt

ENTER TRANSACTION DATE (CR = 01/25/82)?

indicates that pressing the return key automatically enters the default value of January 25, 1982.

Make sure that the value or values chosen for defaults reflect commonly used values, not just the value that was convenient to program. The computer must also make clear to the user what default value will be used. For example, if users press the ENTER key in response to

ENTER STARTING DATE?

they should see either an error message or the default value:

ENTER STARTING DATE?   [ENTER]
01/25/83 ASSUMED

It is important to always detect incorrect input and issue an appropriate message. Suppose that in response to the prompt

ENTER DATE (DD/MM/YY)?

the user enters

ENTER DATE (DD/MM/YY)? 25/13/83

Your program should tell the user that the date is incorrect (here, the 13th month) and must be reentered. Erroneous input leads to erroneous output.

Avoid defaults that can have catastrophic consequences. For example, do not prompt

Delete FILE.3 (CR = YES)?

Instead, display

Delete FILE.3 (YES or NO)?

In your program or its documentation, you may wish to refrain from calling these values defaults. The word default has legal connotations in the banking and loan industry and it can be suprisingly upsetting to people to learn that a computer has just defaulted on them! A better term might be assumed entry.

```
 _____
|                                |
|  PROGRAM SELECTOR              |
|                                |
|     1   Spreadsheet            |
|                                |
|     2   Filing System          |
|                                |
|     3   Word Processor         |
|                                |
|     4   Electronic Mail        |
|                                |
|     5   Games                  |
|                                |
|  ENTER SELECTION ?             |
|_____|
```

Figure 3-2   *A menu selection display.*

MENUS

Menus present alternatives from which the user chooses a single selection (see Figure 3-2). Computer menus are just like restaurant menus. But instead of choosing entrees, you choose functions or features of a program. Menus are ideal for new users. If kept simple and uncluttered, menus are perfectly fine for advanced users as well.

Try not to display too many options at once. Eight is generally thought to be the maximum number of options that should appear on a single menu. If there are more, it takes too long to scan the menu to find the appropriate choice. (For new users, even eight selections can be overwhelming.)

Menus should not be nested too deeply. For example, if you select an option from one menu, and that option displays another menu, and that option displays yet another menu, you're likely to get lost in the maze of menus. A good practice is to have a single key escape that returns you to the main menu.

Listing 3-1 and 3-2 show two methods of programming a menu-style entry selection. Listing 3-1 displays the menu shown in Figure 3-2, a menu of six options and the prompt ENTER SELECTION?. By entering the number corresponding to the desired option, the user selects the function.

Listing 3-2 displays a mini-menu in which the entire menu is displayed on a single line. Because there are more commands than will fit on a line, the mini-menu is set up so that selecting "+" displays an additional set of options. Figure 3-3 illustrates how this menu display looks and what happens when "+" is selected.

Listing 3-1

```
1000      REM - Example of a 5 Option Menu Display
1010      REM
1020      CLS                       ' Clear the screen
1030      LOCATE 4 , 27
1040      PRINT "PROGRAM SELECTOR"
1050      LOCATE 6 , 29
1060      PRINT "1  Spreadsheet"
1070      LOCATE 8 , 29
1080      PRINT "2  Filing System"
1090      LOCATE 10 , 29
1100      PRINT "3  Word Processor"
1110      LOCATE 12 , 29
1120      PRINT "4  Electronic Mail"
1130      LOCATE 14 , 29
1140      PRINT "5 Games"
1150      LOCATE 17 , 24
1160      INPUT "ENTER SELECTION ? ",SELECTION
```

Listing 3-2

```
1000      REM - Example of a mini-menu
1010      REM
1020      WHICH.MENU = 1
1030      PRINT
1035      IF WHICH.MENU = 1  THEN PRINT "Enter:
          I)nsert A)dd D)elete F)ind R)eplace  + ? ";
1040      IF WHICH.MENU = 2  THEN PRINT "Enter:
          T)ranslate S)ave L)oad S)witch Q)uit  + ? ";
1050      SELECTION$ = INPUT$(1)            ' Input 1 character

1060      PRINT SELECTION$
1070      IF  SELECTION$ = "+"  THEN IF WHICH.MENU
          = 1  THEN WHICH.MENU = 2 ELSE WHICH.MENU = 1
1080      IF SELECTION$ = "+" THEN GOTO 1030
1090      REM - Determine which selection was entered
1100      IF SELECTION$ = "I" THEN GOSUB 2000:
          GOTO 1030
1110      IF SELECTION$ = "A" THEN GOSUB 3000:
          GOTO 1030
1120      IF SELECTION$ = "D" THEN GOSUB 4000:
          GOTO 1030
```

```
Enter:  I)nsert  A)dd  D)elete  F)ind  R)eplace  + ? +

Enter:  T)ranslate  S)ave  L)oad  S)witch  Q)uit  + ? +

Enter:  I)nsert  A)dd  D)elete  F)ind  R)eplace  + ? I

Insert:  Type in your text, finished by pressing ESC
```

Figure 3-3 *The "mini-menu" in operation. The "+" at the end of the line indicates that there are more selections available. Pressing + displays the second set of options.*

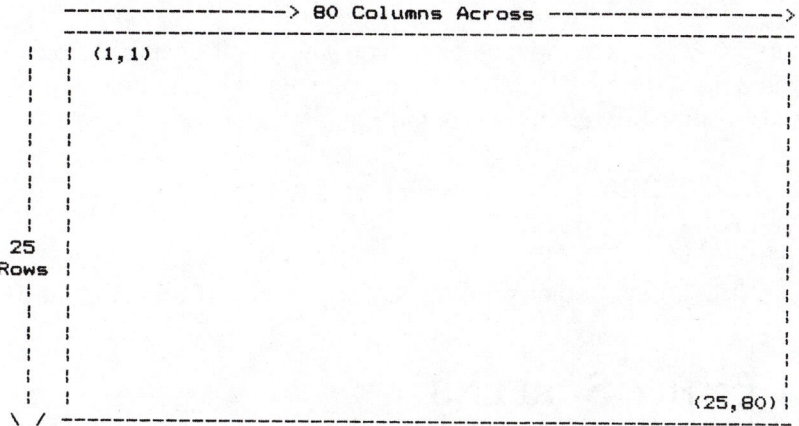

Figure 3-4 *The IBM PC screen is 25 rows high and 80 columns across. Location (1,1) is at the upper left corner of the screen and (25,80) is at the lower right.*

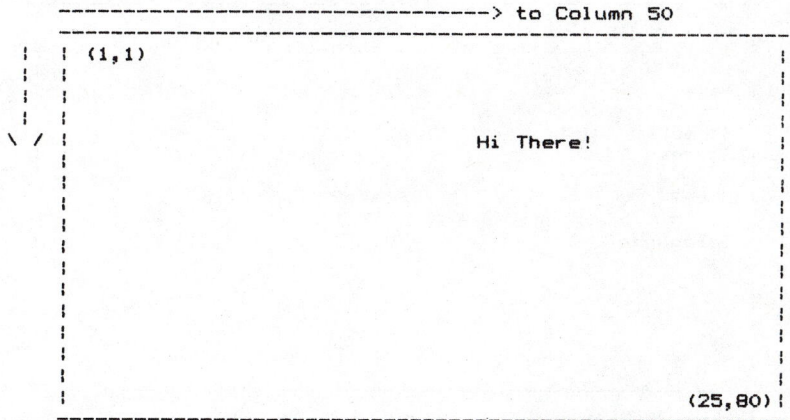

Figure 3-5 *A LOCATE 50,10 statement positions the cursor and subsequent output to the 50th column on row 10.*

In Listing 3-1, the LOCATE statement is used to position the cursor to a specific location on the screen. Text can be written anywhere on the display using LOCATE. On the IBM PC, the screen is arranged into 25 vertical rows and 80 horizontal columns (or 40 columns if the screen is used in 40-column mode). (See Figure 3-4.) LOCATE specifies on which row and at which column the cursor is to be placed. Subsequent PRINT or INPUT statements appear at that location on the screen. LOCATE has the form

LOCATE ROW, COLUMN

where ROW refers to the row, beginning with 1 at the top and 25 at the bottom of the screen, and COLUMN is the horizontal position, beginning with 1 at the left side of the screen and 80 at the right.

LOCATE 10, 50
PRINT "Hi There!"

prints "Hi There!" beginning at column 50 on line 10. See Figure 3-5.

DATA ENTRY SCREENS

Data entry screens present a blank entry form (see Figure 3-6). The user positions the cursor to the desired entry and types in data. If your program requires that the entered data conform to a certain range, such as 1 to 100

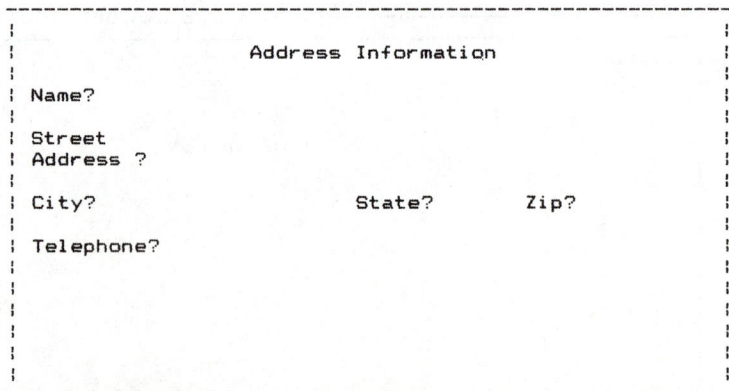

Figure 3-6   *Data entry screens display several items on the screen simultaneously, much like the blank items on a form that need to be filled in. The cursor is moved from item to item on the form. Once all necessary items have been entered, the ENTER key is pressed.*

```
Enter Name (First Last) ? George Smith

Enter Birthdate (MM/DD/YY) ? 2/15/83

Enter Street Address (Up to 30 Chars.) ?        ENTER

Enter Birthdate (MM/DD/YY) ?        ENTER

Enter Name (First Last) ? George Smith

Enter Birthdate (MM/DD/YY) ?

Enter Street Address (Up to 30 Chars.) ?
```

Figure 3-7 *Sometimes questions prompt for information. When the prompts appear one after another, the user should be able to go backward in dialogue in the event of an error.*

for numeric data, then validate the data as soon as practical. If only one of the entered items is in error, then be specific with your error message. Don't display INCORRECT ENTRY and expect the user to locate the problem field. The program should display something like AGE MUST BE LESS THAN 50 and then automatically reposition the cursor to the appropriate field. If only one field contains erroneous input, then only that field should have to be reentered. Never force the user to redo all the input just because one piece of data is incorrect.

Sometimes a series of questions is presented on the display, much like a data entry screen (see Figure 3-7). Keep the number of questions on a single screen low. Too many questions slow down the user's responses and often lead to errors. In one study, a group of users did better at correctly answering

```
Name:
Street:

City:              State:              Zip:

Telephone:

Occupation:

Last Seen (YY/MM/DD):
```

Figure 3-8 *PFS: FILE form.*

a single question on each of three separate screens than at answering three questions on a single screen. Providing too much information on a single screen leads to information overload and should be avoided.

While entering data, the user must be able to move back and forth between the entry fields. If you answer a question and realize that you made a mistake, you should be able to back up and fix the problem, rather than start the series of questions all over again.

The PFS:FILE filing program provides an example of an excellent data entry system. With FILE, a blank form is created on the screen, specifying items that need to be filled in (see Figure 3-8). A form is just like a blank form on a piece of paper, such as a job application or an insurance form. With PFS:FILE, the form is created simply by typing the form design on an empty screen. No programming is involved.

The cursor is moved from one item to the next by pressing the TAB key. Pressing SHIFT/TAB moves the cursor back to the previous item. When some or all of the items have been entered, pressing the F10 key moves you to the next operation.

Listing 3-3 shows one way to program a similar data entry screen in BASIC. In this example, the TAB key moves you from item to item. When you complete the entries, you press the ENTER key. In Listing 3-3, the form is implemented as a subroutine. On return from the subroutine, the array ITEM$() holds the values that were entered for each item. For example, if NAME: and ADDRESS: are JOHN SMITH and 12 SOUTH 15TH STREET, then

ITEM$(1) = "JOHN SMITH"
ITEM$(2) = "12 SOUTH 15TH STREET"

Listing 3-3

```
1000      REM - Data Entry Screen Input/Output
1010      REM
1020      REM - On Entry:
              ITEM$() holds the current values
1030      REM -              These are displayed as
              the default entries
1040      REM - Returns :
              ITEM$() corresponds to the values entered on
              the form
1050      REM
1060      CLS   ' Clear the screen
1070      REM
1080      REM - Display the blank form on the screen
1090      REM
1100      LOCATE 3 , 30
1110      REM
1120      PRINT "Address Information"
1130      LOCATE 6 , 1
1140      PRINT "Name ? "; ITEM$(1)
```

```
1150      LOCATE 8 , 1
1160      PRINT "Street"
1170      LOCATE 9 , 1
1180      PRINT "Address ?"; ITEM$(2)
1190      LOCATE 11 , 1
1200      PRINT "City ? "; ITEM$(3)
1210      LOCATE 11 , 23
1220      PRINT "State ? "; ITEM$(4)
1230      LOCATE 11 , 41
1240      PRINT "Zip ? "; ITEM$(5)
1250      LOCATE 13 , 1
1260      PRINT "Telephone ? ";ITEM$(6)
1270      REM
1280      REM - Let the user fill in the items
1290      ITEM = 1                    ' Initial to first item
1300      REM
1310      REM                         ' Position to
            end of current item
1320      REM
1330      IF ITEM = 1 THEN LOCATE 6, 8 + LEN(ITEM$(ITEM))
1340      IF ITEM = 2 THEN LOCATE 9, 11 + LEN(ITEM$(ITEM))
1350      IF ITEM = 3 THEN LOCATE 11, 8 + LEN(ITEM$(ITEM))
1360      IF ITEM = 4 THEN LOCATE 11, 31 + LEN(ITEM$(ITEM))
1370      IF ITEM = 5 THEN LOCATE 11, 47 + LEN(ITEM$(ITEM))
1380      IF ITEM = 6 THEN LOCATE 13, 13 + LEN(ITEM$(ITEM))
1390      PRINT "_";               ' Display a cursor
            because INPUT$() turns it off
1400      CH$ = INPUT$(1)
1410      LOCATE CSRLIN, POS(0) - 1
1420      PRINT " ";               ' Erase the cursor
1430      LOCATE CSRLIN, POS(0) - 1
1440      IF CH$ = CHR$(9) THEN ITEM = ITEM + 1:
            IF ITEM > 6 THEN ITEM = 1:
            GOTO 1330ELSE GOTO 1330
1450      IF CH$ = CHR$(13) THEN RETURN
1460      IF CH$ = CHR$(8) THEN GOSUB 1530 :
            GOTO 1330
1470      PRINT CH$;
1480      ITEM$(ITEM) = ITEM$(ITEM) + CH$
1490      NUMCH = NUMCH + 1
1500      GOTO 1330
1510      REM
1520      REM
1530      REM - BackSpace key pressed
1540      IF LEN(ITEM$(ITEM)) = 0 THEN RETURN
1550      LOCATE CSRLIN, POS(0) - 1
1560      PRINT " ";
1570      LOCATE CSRLIN, POS(0) - 1
1580      NUMCH = NUMCH - 1
1590      ITEM$(ITEM) = LEFT$(ITEM$(ITEM),
            LEN(ITEM$(ITEM)) - 1)
1600      RETURN
```

Listing 3-4 shows another type of data entry. In this example, questions are displayed as prompts. Normally, when the ENTER key is pressed, the next prompt in the series of questions appears on the screen. In Listing 3-4, however, if you press ENTER in response to a question without having typed any characters, the dialogue returns to the previous prompt. This is a simple way of allowing for corrections to previous entries.

Listing 3-4

```
1000     REM - Prompt for data entry, allowing
             back up in questioning
1010     REM
1020     REM
1030     REM
1040     PRINT
1050     INPUT "Enter Name (First Last ) ? ", NAM$
1060     IF  NAM$ = ""   THEN RETURN
1070     PRINT
1080     INPUT "Enter Birthdate (MM/DD/YY) ? ", BIRTH.DATE$
1090     IF  BIRTH.DATE$ = ""  THEN  1040
1100     PRINT
1110     INPUT "Enter Street Address (Up to 30
             Chars.) ? ", ADDRESS$
1120     IF  ADDRESS$ = ""  THEN 1070
```

USING FUNCTION KEYS FOR INPUT

You should use function keys in your program if the user will benefit. Reaching away from home row on the keyboard to press a function key can slow down skilled typists. It might be best to use control key/character combinations for these people, because they are quick at accessing characters on the keyboard.

On the other hand, special function keys are ideal for naive terminal operators and people who are not touch typists (and 80% of the people in the United States are not touch typists). Properly labeled function keys work well for applications in which the user has little or no training. A key on an automated bank teller labeled DEPOSIT TO CHECKING ACCOUNT is self-explanatory and easy to use. The same key on a human bank teller's typewriter keyboard provides for rapid input of transaction data. When used properly, function keys can also help reduce data entry errors. One hospital used a data entry system that used exactly three keys, labeled YES, NO, and ?. Such a simple input device practically eliminates input errors.

The IBM PC provides 10 function keys, labeled F1 through F10. These keys are found in two vertical columns to the left of the keyboard. In additon, if the CTRL, SHIFT, or ALT keys are depressed in combination with the function keys F1 through F10, an additional 30 key combinations are possible.

IBM BASIC lets you use the F1 through F10 keys in the following ways: as soft keys that make a text substitution; as special interrupt keys; and as direct input keys.

Using Soft Keys

When you first run BASIC, line 25 of the screen displays a compressed listing of the current function key values. If you press F2, for example, the command

RUN is executed. All 10 keys are predefined by BASIC, but you can change their values with the KEY statement. These function key values are called soft keys because they are easy to change, just like software.

For example, your program might have a sequence of commands. Rather than make users type frequently used commands, you can define a function key equivalent to the command name. Then, when the function key is pressed, BASIC automatically substitutes the command name. Suppose your program uses the commands PLOT, PRINT, SAVE, LOAD, and ENTER. You'd like to set up your program so that when it prints the COMMAND prompt the user can press F1, F3, F5, F7, or F9 rather than typing in a command.

To do this, you redefine the function keys using the KEY statement:

```
KEY 1, "PLOT"
KEY 3, "PRINT"
KEY 5, "SAVE"
KEY 7, "LOAD"
KEY 9, "ENTER"
```

Your program does not use the keys F2, F4, F6, F8, and F10, so they are set to empty strings.

```
KEY 2, " "
KEY 4, " "
KEY 6, " "
KEY 8, " "
KEY 10, " "
```

The new function key definitions can be shown on the screen by typing

KEY LIST

If you don't want the keys to display on line 25, type

KEY OFF

And to turn their display back on, type

KEY ON

These are the soft keys. They are easy to redefine and use.

See Listing 3-5 for an example of how the key definitions have been programmed into a simple command prompt subroutine.

Listing 3-5

```
1000      REM - Demonstration of Soft Function Key input
1010      REM
1020      REM
1030      KEY 1, "PLOT "
1040      KEY 3, "PRINT "
1050      KEY 5, "SAVE "
1060      KEY 7, "LOAD "
1070      KEY 9, "ENTER "
1080      KEY 2, ""
1090      KEY 4, ""
1100      KEY 6, ""
1110      KEY 8, ""
1120      KEY 10, ""
1130      REM
1140      REM
1150      INPUT "Enter Command? ",COMMAND$
1160      IF   LEFT$(COMMAND$,4) = "PLOT"   THEN GOSUB 2000
1170      IF   LEFT$(COMMAND$,5) = "PRINT" THEN GOSUB 3000
1180      IF   LEFT$(COMMAND$,4) = "SAVE"  THEN GOSUB 4000
1190      IF   LEFT$(COMMAND$,5) = "ENTER"   THEN GOSUB 5000
1200      GOTO 1150
```

Using Interrupt Function Keys

Sometimes you might like your program to take some action whenever a function key is pressed, even if the program is doing something else at the moment. You want it to stop whatever it is that it's doing and immediately deal with another command. For example, maybe the program is printing a long report, but you'd like to interrupt the print for a moment so that you can save a working copy of the file. Press the F1 key. The print stops and the COMMAND prompt appears on the screen. Type the SAVE command: the file is written out to disk, and the print resumes.

IBM BASIC makes it easy to deal with this type of operation. One approach is to constantly check for input from the function key as each line is sent to the printer. But an easier way is to let BASIC check automatically.

ON KEY(n) GOSUB line

sets the program up so that if function key n is pressed, the program automatically jumps to the subroutine at the indicated line. For example,

ON KEY(1) GOSUB 3000

tells BASIC that whenever function key 1 is pressed, the program should jump to the subroutine at line 3000.

The ON KEY statement just tells BASIC what to do; it doesn't actually activate the special handling of the function key. If you type

ON KEY(1) GOSUB 3000

and then press F1 when your program is running, nothing happens. You need to use this statement:

KEY (n) ON

This activates the detection of the function key. So, to trap the F1 key, you'd do two things: First you'd type:

ON KEY(1) GOSUB 3000

Then when you're ready to begin using the F1 key, you'd type:

KEY (1) ON

You can also disable the key by typing

KEY (1) OFF

All ten keys may be given this special treatment by BASIC. Just vary the value of n from 1 to 10 in the appropriate KEY statement. The cursor-movement keys, UP ARROW, DOWN ARROW, LEFT ARROW, and RIGHT ARROW, may also be detected in this manner. See the description of the ON KEY(n) statement in your IBM PC BASIC manual for all of the possible key codes.

Direct Input from Function Keys

Finally, function keys may also be entered as regular characters. But first, you need to disable the soft-key setting of the function keys. Do this with a KEY n, " " statement:

KEY 1, " "
KEY 2, " "

Next, you want to see if a particular key has been pressed. The function INKEY$ is used to check for an input character. INKEY$ may be called any

time. If no character has been entered, then INKEY$ returns a null string (" ").
Otherwise, INKEY$ returns the character that was typed. Here's an example
that you should try out on your computer.

```
10 T$ = INKEY$
20 IF T$ = " " THEN GOTO 10
30 PRINT " You Typed: "; T$, ASC(T$)
40 GOTO 10
```

This short program echoes back to you any character that you type, plus the
corresponding ASCII code. (The ASCII code is the number that BASIC uses
internally to represent the character.) Since it loops forever, you need to press
CTRL/BREAK (possibly several times) to escape from the program.

Some of the keyboard keys cause T$ to have two characters placed in
it for each key struck. The function keys fall into this category. For these keys,
INKEY$ returns two characters, the first of which is always a null character.
The null character signifies that the entered key is one of the special two-
character codes, and that the second character contains the actual code. IBM
BASIC needs this two-character representation because so many different keys
may be entered that it cannot fit all of them into a single character.

To check for a function key, type the following program.

```
10   FOR I = 1 TO 10
20   KEY I, " "           ' Turn off all function keys
30   NEXT I
40   T$ = INKEY$
50   IF T$ = " " THEN GOTO 40
60   IF ASC(T$) = 0 THEN T$ = RIGHT$(T$,1): E = 1 ELSE E = 0
70   KY = ASC(T$)
80   PRINT E, KY           ' Display code of key pressed
90   GOTO 40
```

Type RUN to start the program. As you press a key, the corresponding internal
numeric code is displayed. For example, if you press the letter A, you will see

```
0      65
```

For the normal keyboard characters, such as the letters and numerals, E has
a value of 0. The extra keys available on the IBM PC cause E to be set to 1,

and the corresponding extra key code is placed in KY. If you press the F1 key, you see

    1   59

Table 3-1 shows the codes returned for many of the IBM function keys. These keys include F1 through F10 plus several other key combinations. If you press the CTRL key together with F1, you get a code that is different from the code you get when you press F1 only. In fact, the function keys used in combination with CTRL, SHIFT, and ALT, provide for 40 separate functions. Additional key codes are available by pressing ALT-0 through ALT-9, CTRL-A through CTRL-Z, and ALT-A through ALT-Z. You may wish to use the example program to experiment with different key combinations and to determine what codes are returned when certain keys are struck.

Table 3-1
Codes returned by INKEY$ to represent function keys

	normal	Shift-F	Ctrl-F	Alt-F
F1	59	84	94	104
F2	60	85	95	105
F3	61	86	96	106
F4	62	87	97	107
F5	63	88	98	108
F6	64	89	99	109
F7	65	90	100	110
F8	66	91	101	111
F9	67	92	102	112
F10	68	93	103	113

RESPONSE TIME

After you tell the computer to do something or after you enter data on a blank entry form, the computer should acknowledge that it received input. The Response time is the time that elapses between a press of the ENTER key and the computer's response. For example, if the program prompts

    COPY FILE A TO FILE B

and you respond with Y, the computer should immediately respond with a message like

WAIT . . . COPYING FILE A TO B

The computer might display a constantly updated message like

15 Records Remaining

or

70% Copied

Never leave users wondering if they forgot to press a key.
Similarly, if you issue a command like

CREATEFILE ACCOUNTS, SIZE = 10

the system must provide confirmation of creating the file by displaying

FILE CREATED

Speed of the response depends on the type of operation. The tracking of a light pen or mouse across the display needs to be done instantly. But a command to copy a file may be obvious once the disk drives begin to whir. In the latter case, once the files are completely copied, the copy command may say

FILE COPIED

There are other instances in which a lengthy delay may be appropriate. For example, after updating several records in a filing system, a logical task completion point is reached. Once a task is completed, a pause may make sense. For example, an order entry system might present a screen of blank fields to be filled in by the order clerk. The clerk can move rapidly between fields on the screen, adding or changing data. Once the editing has been completed, a closure point has been reached, and the user may logically expect a delay while the order entry database is updated.

Command Languages

Command languages are special languages that control or command computer programs. Menus provide a list of all possible inputs. But with command languages, users must remember what command should be entered so that they can command the computer to do something.

Examples of commands include those found in your PC DOS. For example, to obtain a directory listing, you type

A>DIR

Or to copy one file to another, you type

A>COPY FILE1 B:FILE2

Each of these is a command. PC DOS could have been designed so that each of the commands had appeared as a menu choice. A DOS menu prompt might then have appeared as

A>C)opy, D)ir, E)rase, R)ename?

Then, at the press of a key, DOS could have displayed an appropriate prompt, such as

Erase what file?

The major difference between menus and commands is that the user must remember all possible commands. With menus, the computer presents each of the potential choices so that the user is not burdened with remembering exactly how the program works. A novice can learn to use a menu-operated program by guessing and experimenting. Research has shown that what is learned by experimentation is often learned better and retained longer.

A disadvantage of menus is that data entry may be somewhat slower, depending on how large and how fast the menus are displayed. If the menus are displayed so fast that the program keeps up with the user's input, then there is no penalty for using menus. The PFS: Software Series, for example, displays menus in a fraction of a second, far faster than a user can type.

On the other hand, many programs that are operated with commands have convenient abbreviations that can greatly speed operation of the program. But abbreviations only compound the problem of trying to remember the commands.

Interestingly, abbreviated commands do not necessarily mean faster input and control of a program. According to one study, "command languages should employ a structure and notation that is natural and familiar to the user." (Ledgard, 1980.) These researchers found that full English-like command words were used more effectively than shorthand notation.

The researchers, using a group of paid volunteers, compared two text editors and how they were used by both novice and experienced users. The text editors were actually the same; the only difference was that one used English-like commands. The researchers discovered that the editor with the English-like commands proved more usable than the standard editor with its cryptic commands. For example, the standard editor used

RS:/TOOTH/,/TRUTH/

to replace each occurrence of the string TOOTH with the string TRUTH. The English-like editor used

REPLACE "TOOTH" WITH "TRUTH"

You might think that it would be faster to use the editor that used a shorthand notation. But the researchers discovered the opposite. Users of the English-like editor were able to complete their assigned tasks more often than the other group. They used fewer editing commands and made fewer than half the errors the other users did.

Users of the English-like editor probably found the commands easier to remember. Consequently, these users often chose a single, powerful command, rather than use a sequence of less powerful commands.

What all this means is that you should probably design a command language to accept full English-like commands and statements. Users understand a program if it speaks their language. As mentioned earlier, each user creates a mental model of what the program looks like and how it operates. The use of English-like commands means that the user's intuitive notion of how the program works will match the actual operation of the program.

Programming a Command Language

Command languages can be programmed in many different ways; two methods are explained here.

In the examples, commands from a simple line-oriented text editor are used. The commands provided by the editor are summarized in Table 3-2. These commands are recognized by the command processors described in the text.

The first approach to processing the commands is to take a shortcut—only the first character of each command is needed to select the command.

Table 3-2
Summary of commands in a simple text editor

ADD	Type new text at the end of the document.
DELETE n n-m	Delete line n, or the range of lines n to m.
EDIT n	Edit line n.
Find n string	Search for "string" beginning at line n.
INSERT n	Add a new line after line n.
LOAD filename	Load a filename from disk.
PRINT n n-m	List line n or lines n through m on the display.
QUIT	Leave the text-editor program.
REPLACE /s1/s2/n-m	On lines n through m, wherever string s1 is found, replace s1 with string s2.
SAVE filename	Save the document as file "filename"

Of course, simplifying the command language makes the program less user friendly. Single-letter commands are, therefore, not a preferred input method. Full-word and multi-word command processing are discussed later.

Because the computer need only recognize the first character of a command line to act, you could code this as

```
INPUT "Command?", L$
CH$ = LEFT$( L$, 1 )
L$ = MID$( L$, 2 )
IF CH$ = "E" THEN GOSUB 1000 ELSE
IF CH$ = "L" THEN GOSUB 2000 ELSE
IF CH$ = "I" THEN GOSUB 3000 ELSE
    .
    .
    .
```

In this routine, CH$ is given the value of the left-most character in the command line. Then the first character is removed from the line using the MID$() function. If you're not familiar with MID$(), try it out by doing the following:

```
L$ = "ABCDEFGHI"
PRINT MID$(L$,2)
```

Try various values to see just how MID$() functions.

The IF-THEN statements determine which command is selected by testing for each possible command. This is easy to understand, but it is not the best that can be done. In fact, this method uses quite a few IF-THEN statements whenever there are many commands. A better way is to group the first letters of all the commands together into a single string:

"ADEFILPQRS"

If CH$ is the first letter of a command line, you can determine if CH$ holds a valid command character by determining if CH$ is contained in ADEFILPQRS. BASIC's INSTR() or IN STRING function determines if one string is located within another. If CH$ is I, then when you type

PRINT INSTR("ADEFILPQRS", CH$)

you see

5

INSTR() tells you at what location CH$ is found within the first string. In this case, I is the fifth character of the command string. The value that INSTR() returns can be used in an ON-GOSUB statement to quickly determine and jump to the appropriate subroutine.

The format for ON-GOSUB is

On <expression> GOSUB line 1, line 2, line 3, line 4, . . .

Here is an example:

ON I GOSUB 1000, 2000, 3000, 4000

If I is 2, then the program jumps to the subroutine at line 2000. If I is 4, then the subroutine at line 4000 is called.

If you replace I in the ON-GOSUB statement with the INSTR() function, you get a very simple method of jumping to a subroutine based on a single input character:

ON INSTR("ADEFILPQRS", CH$) GOSUB 1000, 2000, 3000, 4000, . . .

If CH$ is A, this jumps to line 1000; if CH$ is D, this jumps to 2000, and so on. One problem, however, is that if CH$ is not a valid command, then INSTR() returns a value of 0. And in that case, the ON-GOSUB fails.

The solution is to always add 1 to the value returned by INSTR() and make the first line number in the list a subroutine that prints an error message. In this form, if an invalid command is entered, INSTR() returns 0, to which 1 is added, resulting in a jump to the first line in the line-number list. Listing 3-6 shows a general purpose, single-character command processor. In Listing 3-6, line 500 catches invalid commands and displays a list of valid entries.

The use of the INSTR() function with ON-GOSUB provides an elegant and simple solution to the problem of recognizing and processing commands entered at the keyboard.

Listing 3-6

```
100     INPUT "COMMAND? ",L$
110     CH$ = LEFT$( L$, 1 )
120     L$ = MID$( L$, 2 )
130     ON INSTR ( "ADEFILPQRS",  CH$ ) + 1 GOSUB 500,   1000,   2000,
        3000, 4000, 5000, 6000, 7000, 8000, 9000, 10000
140     GOTO 100
500     REM - PRINT ERROR MESSAGE
510     PRINT "ENTER A-ADD, D-DELETE, E-EDIT, F-FIND, I-INSERT"
520     PRINT "     L-LOAD, P-PRINT, Q-QUIT, R-REPLACE, S-SAVE"
530     RETURN
1000    REM - ADD
```

Full-Word Commands

Full-word commands are a bit more complicated than single-character commands. One approach is to compare the left-most characters in the command line to each of the possible commands. For example,

```
IF LEFT$(L$,3) = "ADD" THEN GOSUB 1000 ELSE
IF LEFT$(L$,7) = "DELETE" THEN GOSUB 2000 ELSE
IF LEFT$(L$,4) = "EDIT" THEN GOSUB 3000 ELSE
        .
        .
        .
```

This method is entirely satisfactory for a small number of commands, but becomes quite tedious when numerous commands need to be considered. An alternative is to place each of the command names into a DATA statement. Then, using BASIC's READ statement, each command name can be read from the DATA statement and compared to the command entered on the command line. (If the DATA and READ statements are new to you, see Section 5.2 of *IBM BASIC from the Ground Up* by David E. Simon or the IBM PC BASIC manual.)

Here is an example of a command interpreter using DATA and READ statements.

Listing 3-7   *A command interpreter using DATA and READ statements.*

```
50        INPUT "COMMAND? ",L$
60        DATA ADD,DELETE,EDIT,FIND,INSERT,LOAD,PRINT,
              QUIT,SAVE,REPLACE,*
90  REM - PROCESS COMMAND
100       RESTORE
110       I = 1
120       READ C$
130       IF C$ = "*" THEN 170
140       IF LEFT$(L$, LEN(C$)) = C$   THEN 500
150       I = I + 1
160       GOTO 120
170       PRINT "INVALID COMMAND - PLEASE ENTER ONE OF"
180       RESTORE
190       READ C$
200       IF C$ = "*"   THEN GOTO 50
210       PRINT C$;"   ";
210       GOTO 190

490 REM - REMOVE THE COMMAND FROM THE COMMAND LINE
500       L$ = MID$( L$, LEN(C$)+1 )
510       ON I GOSUB 1000, 2000, 3000, 4000, 5000, ...
```

Line 120 reads the first command from the list of commands stored in the DATA statement. This command is ADD. Line 140 compares the first part of line L$ to the command just read. Since C$ is ADD, having a length of 3, this is equivalent to

IF LEFT$(L$,3) = C$ THEN 500

If the routine reads the asterisk, then no matching commands were found, so another routine displays an appropriate error message.

This routine provides a general approach to determining which of many possible commands was entered. New commands can be added by placing the new command name in the DATA statement and adding an appropriate subroutine call in the ON-GOSUB statement in line 500.

Multi-Word Commands

The next approach to deciphering a command line containing one or more full words is based on a subroutine called GET WORD. GET WORD extracts entire words from the command line, one by one. Each call to GET WORD returns the next word on the line in W$. For your purposes, each word of a multi-word command must be separated by a blank. Here are some examples of multi-word commands:

        SAVE FILE1
        GET AXE
        SET PARITY EVEN

Consider the string

        L$ = "SAVE FILE1"

A call to GET WORD returns

        W$ = "SAVE"

and

        L$ = "FILE1"

A second call to GET WORD returns

        W$ = "FILE1"

and

        L$ = " "

This subroutine can be used with several IF-THEN statements to test for various commands. For example,

```
50    INPUT "COMMAND? ",L$
100   GOSUB 800        ' Get Word
110   IF W$ = "ADD" THEN GOSUB 1000 ELSE
      IF W$ = "DELETE" THEN GOSUB 2000 ELSE
      IF 1W$ = "EDIT" THEN GOSUB 3000 ELSE
      .
      .
      .
```

Or you could compare W$ to a set of command names stored in a DATA statement. If the number of command words is quite large, you could do a search through a table of commands to check rapidly for W$. This approach is ideal if the commands are English-like. For example, many adventure-style games accept input in a form like

GET AXE
PICK UP BOTTLE
THROW ROCK
CLIMB STAIRWAY

Such a game may have a very large vocabulary. Hence, a simple comparison of all the words in a series of DATA statements may be unacceptably long. Such words may be stored in a table so they can be retrieved quickly and processed efficiently. The table may also contain other information about the command, such as the subroutine to call to process the input.

Often, a command is followed by several parameters. For example, the single command SET in a communications program can be followed by several options, as in

SET BAUDRATE 300

or

SET PARITY EVEN

The GET WORD subroutine, shown in Listing 3-8(a), makes it easy to process this type of input. A pseudo-code description of a subroutine to process these commands is given in Listing 3-8(b). The routine shown also accepts the following:

SET PARITY ODD
SET PARITY NONE
SET DATABITS 7
SET DATABITS 8
SET DUPLEX HALF
SET DUPLEX FULL

By isolating the routine that extracts words from the command line, you greatly simplify the overall command processing. The routine then is easy to understand and easy to modify. Additional commands can be added by writing new subroutines to process each of them.

Listing 3-8(a)

```
1000      REM - GET WORD
1010      REM - Input:
            L$ holds a command line
1020      REM - Returns:
            W$ is next command in line,
1030      REM           The command in W$ is removed from the start of L$
1040      REM
1050      I = INSTR(L$, " ")          ' Find first blank in L$
1060      IF  I = 0  THEN  I = LEN(L$) + 1
1070      W$ = LEFT$(L$, I - 1)
1080      L$ = MID$(L$, I + 1)
1090      RETURN
```

Listing 3-8(b) *Pseudo code description of the multi-word command processor.*

```
MAIN LOOP
      Repeat
        Prompt for command
        Call GET WORD
        If  W$ = "SET"  Then  Call SET routine
        Check for other commands and
            jump to the appropriate routines
      Until  EXIT command entered


SET ROUTINE
      Call GET WORD
      If  W$ = "BAUDRATE"  Then  Call BAUDRATE Routine
      Else
      If  W$ = "PARITY"  Then  Call PARITY Routine
      Else
      If  W$ = "DATABITS"  Then  Call DATABITS Routine
      Else
      If  W$ = "DUPLEX"  Then  Call DUPLEX Routine
      Else
         Error, invalid entry
      Return


BAUDRATE ROUTINE
      Call GET WORD
      BaudRate = value of W$
      Return


PARITY ROUTINE
      Call GET WORD
      If  W$ = "EVEN"  Then ...
      Else
      If  W$ = "ODD"  Then ...
```

```
        Else
        If  W$ = "NONE"  Then ...
        Else
          Error, invalid parity
        Return


    DATABITS ROUTINE
        Call GET WORD
        If  W$ = "7"  Then ...
        Else
        If  W$ = "8"  Then ...
        Else
          Error, Data bits can only 7 or 8
        Return


    DUPLEX ROUTINE
        Call GET WORD
        If  W$ = "HALF"  Then ...
        Else
        If  W$ = "FULL"  Then ...
        Else
          Error, Can only use HALF or FULL Duplex
        Return
```

DEALING WITH ERRORS

Whenever and wherever an error occurs, some sort of action must be taken. It's never acceptable to assume that "no one will ever make a stupid mistake like that." You must anticipate all errors and inconsistencies that may occur and design your program to handle them.

When a problem is detected, don't ring the computer's bell ten times! Ringing bells attract attention, embarrassing the user. Instead, provide a simple message saying what is wrong and what should be done to correct the problem.

Most programs, unfortunately, concentrate on what is wrong rather than what should be done to fix the problem. Suppose in response to the prompt

ENTER AGE (1 TO 50)?

the user replies

ENTER AGE (1 TO 50)? 75

Don't say

INCORRECT AGE

Instead, say

INCORRECT AGE — MUST BE FROM 1 TO 50

Avoid cryptic error messages. Some programs use a cryptic

ERROR 313

which gives nary a clue to the problem at hand.

Personal computers often lack sufficient memory to store comprehensive error messages. One solution is to store the actual error mesage text in a disk file and to read the message from disk when it is needed. (Disk files are described in Chapter 7.)

Another solution is to at least locate the input problem on the screen or line. For example, if ten item fields are shown on the screen and one of them contains an invalid entry, move the cursor to that field or highlight the entire line. For simple commands, such as

CREATEFILE ACCOUNTS,SIZE = 100

you can use an arrow to point to the problem. For example,

CREATEFILE ACCOUNTS,SIZE = 100
$\wedge$
SIZE MUST BE IN RANGE 1 TO 40

Never use blunt, frightening terminology in an error message. For example,

FATAL ERROR, SCRATCH FILE FULL

is meaningless. This error actually appeared when using a text editor that could only edit a maximum of 1,000 lines. The real problem should have been described as

FILES MUST HAVE FEWER THAN 1000 LINES FOR EDITING

The first of these two errors tells the user what is wrong with the program (file full) rather than what the user did wrong (edited more than 1,000 lines).

Never use words like fatal or illegal when less threatening words can be used instead.

Try to make the error messages specific, but not too wordy. An experienced user often needs only to be informed that something is wrong and does not need a detailed explanation. On the other hand, a novice probably prefers the detailed message. One way to deal with both novice and experienced users is to provide additional error or help messages on demand. For example, when the program cannot recognize a command, simply say

COMMAND NOT RECOGNIZED — PRESS ? FOR A LIST OF COMMANDS

instead of immediately printing out all of the possible commands.

Another possibility is to let the user choose how much help should be given. For example, when the program is first run it may provide comprehensive help and error messages. But a command may be provided for advanced users so that they can disable the help printout.

During program development, have the program tally the errors. Frequent occurrences of the same error may indicate that some part of the program is confusing.

Documentation

Software is not just a program, but a collection of programs, documentation guides, and procedures. All pieces of the software must be designed with people in mind.

Some manufacturers claim that their software is user friendly because the manual explains in a simple manner how to use the program. Yet, the actual software is really quite awful. User-friendly design begins with the program. No amount of documentation can ever make up for the deficiencies of a poor program.

If the documentation appears to be confusing and disorganized, the technical writer may not be the one to blame. Very likely, the software itself is confusing and disorganized. A simple, clean, and logical design leads to easily understood documentation. Therefore, the first step in producing user-friendly reference guides is to produce user-friendly software.

Nearly everyone needs to turn to the manual some time, even if the software is self-teaching. And when you do use the manual, you must be able to find the instructions you need quickly and easily.

If the software that you are describing is designed well, then the manual's organization will be clean and easy to follow. A manual is usually organized as a tutorial, as a reference guide, or as a combination of the two. The tutorial teaches new users by leading them through the program step by step. A new feature is introduced and is followed by examples. An important feature of the tutorial is that numerous examples illustrate suggested applications for the program.

A reference guide details each instruction or command and the possible outcomes of issuing that command. Generally, a reference guide is organized alphabetically by command name. For example, the IBM PC BASIC manual lists all BASIC statements and built-in functions alphabetically. Each command and all possible variations of the command are shown. Examples illustrate how the statement or function is used. The reference guide, however, does not recommend any particular use for the statements or functions.

Many manuals combine the tutorial with the reference format. The manual begins with a tutorial to show you the ropes. But the rest of the guide is primarily reference material. Once you understand the basic operation of the program, you can look up just what you need by turning to the reference section.

Technical writing is a complex task that cannot be covered in a short section in this book. Some of the necessary skills include how to target the writing style and content to a specific audience, choice of wording, use of illustrations, titles, and summaries, sequencing of sentences and paragraphs, and judging the readability and usability of the finished document.

REVIEW

- Software is designed for people. Their needs should be recognized and considered from the very beginning of any programming project.
- The user has an intuitive notion of how the program should operate. Your goal is to match the user's conceptual model so that the program never surprises anyone.
- Avoid the tendency to add additional features. The hardest part of designing a program is deciding what features need to be taken out. Try to combine similar features into a single operation, thereby simplifying the program.
- The operation of the program should be consistent throughout the entire program.
- Display descriptive prompts rather than vague or abbreviated questions.

- Make sure a default is meaningful and indicate what the default is. Avoid defaults that have destructive consequences.

- Menus provide a list of choices from which the user may make a selection. Menus are ideal for new users and are generally easier to use than commands.

- Data entry screens provide a series of questions or items on a single screen, enabling the user to fill in the blanks.

- The IBM PC provides three ways to use function keys: as programmable soft keys; as interrupt keys; and as direct-input keys.

- Always keep the user informed. Never allow the program to run for even several seconds without making it clear that the program is still working.

- Always use English-like commands, although abbreviations also may be accepted.

- Anticipate all possible errors. If an error occurs, try to display not only what the problem is but what should be done to remedy the situation.

- Documentation must be keyed, like the software, to the end user. Provide clear, concise descriptions and always give plenty of examples.

- The user interface is the only part of the system that the user sees. The user judges the entire system by the interface. The software may use the world's greatest algorithm to accomplish its task, but the users won't care about that if they can't communicate with the program.

CHAPTER
4

Searching Techniques

Searching for something always seems easy, unless you're searching for your car keys, contact lenses, or any number of things that never seem to be quite where you put them. How hard can it be to determine whether the name GEORGE FENBON is stored in array NAMES$(100)? After all, you just need to check every name until you find GEORGE FENBON or until you get to the end ·of the list. The search might look something like this:

```
10    FOR I = 1 TO 100
20    IF NAMES$(I) = "GEORGE FENBON" THEN GOTO 100
30    NEXT I
40    PRINT "GEORGE FENBON NOT IN LIST"
50    STOP
100   PRINT "GEORGE FENBON FOUND AT LOCATION "; I
```

But think for a moment. How many comparisons are made if GEORGE FENBON isn't in the list? How many comparisons are made on an average search?

In the first case, in which the searched-for name isn't found, 100 comparisons are needed. And in the average case, 50 comparisons are made. By using a clever technique called a binary search, it's possible to either locate the name or determine that it's not in the list with only seven comparisons. That means that the typical binary search is more than seven times faster than the simple search. Even more surprising is the fact that the binary search isn't the fastest search.

This chapter describes several searching techniques, how they work, and why you'll want to use them. These searches include the sequential search, binary search, and the hashing method.

HOW FAST IS A SEARCH?

Before picking a search technique, you may wish to know which is best for your application. Remember that if the list you need to search is quite short,

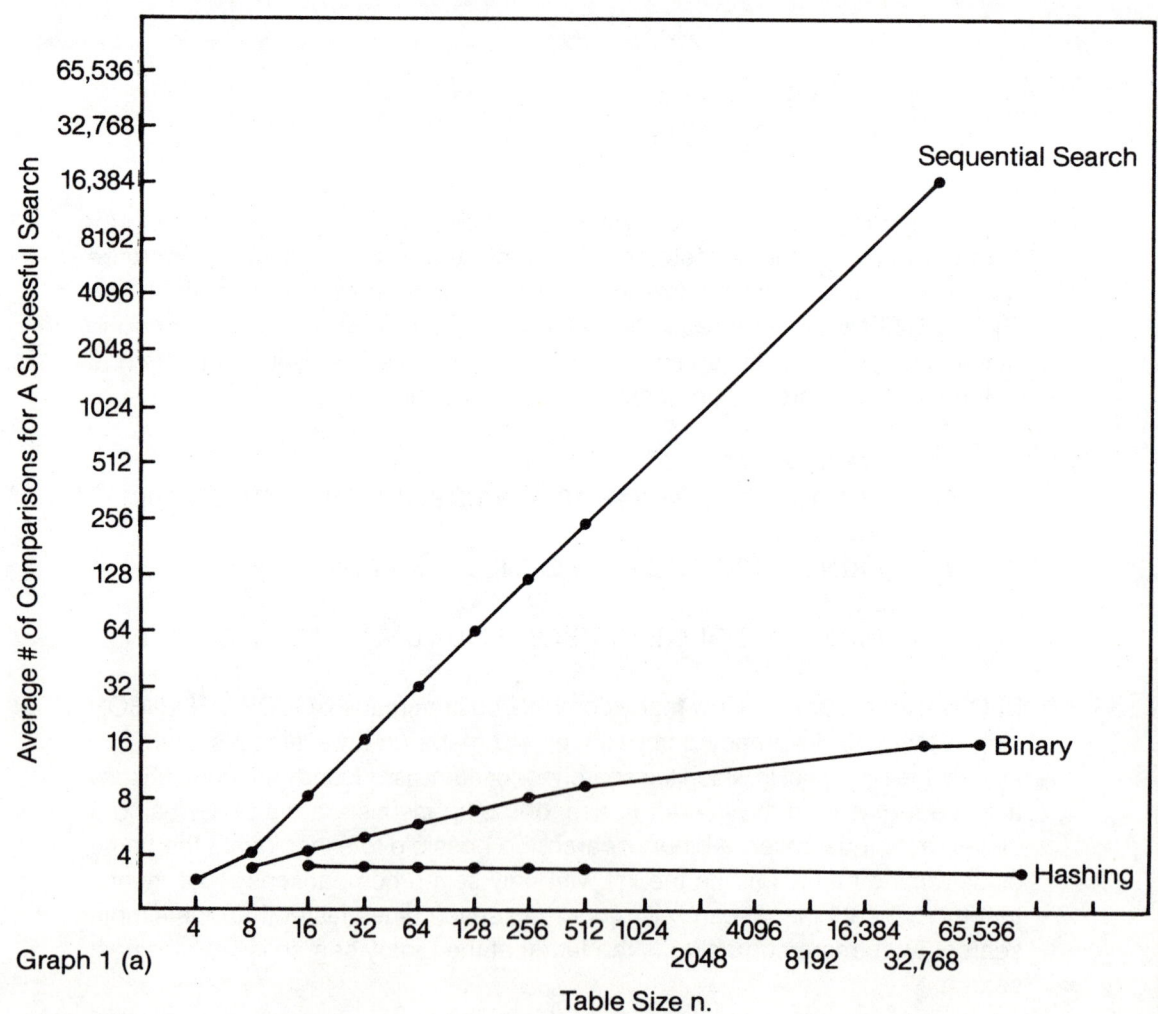

Graph 1 (a)

Figure 4-1

then it may not matter which search method you choose. On the other hand, the fastest method can be hundreds or thousands of times faster on large amounts of data. The storage medium may also influence your algorithm choice. Chapter 7 describes how disk files store information. In addition, Chapter 8 specifically looks at methods of searching through information stored on a diskette.

How can you measure search performance? Some computer scientists like to mathematically model search speed and represent each method by a simple equation. An easier way is simply to time a particular search. In either case, you can approximate how long an average search takes.

For example, if n is the size of the table of names, then on the average, a sequential search takes n/2 comparisons. In other words, a typical search compares against half of the names in the list. The speed of the binary search depends on the base 2 logarithm of n (this is explained later).

Interestingly, the hashing method works at a fairly steady speed, regardless of table size. The hashing method is limited by how full the table becomes. As you'll see later, hashing works best when the space allocated for the table gets no more than about 80% full.

Another way to compare typical search speeds is with a graph. Figure 4-1 compares the relative performance of the three searches.

But there are other considerations. In a binary search, a table of names is automatically sorted into alphabetical order. This is especially useful if some part of your program needs to produce a sorted list of names later. It's already done, so you save memory by avoiding another sort routine.

THE SEQUENTIAL SEARCH

One way to search a list of names is to scan the list until finding a match or until reaching the end of the list. This technique, known as a sequential search, is easy to understand and program. But for a long list, the sequential search can be time-consuming. A list of 100 names requires an average of 50 comparisons for a successful search. If the name being searched for is not even in the list, all 100 names must be examined.

Consider the list of five names in Figure 4-2. To search this list for DAMION, the program begins by checking the name stored at N$(1). Since DAMION does not match N$(1), the search checks N$(2). Detecting a second mismatch, the algorithm moves to N$(3) and finds the name.

In general, a successful sequential search of a list with n entries appearing in random order requires an average of n/2 comparisons. The length of time required to perform the search is directly proportional to the size n. If the size

(a) | N$(1) = "JENNY" | = "DAMION" ?

     N$(2) = "GEORGE"

     N$(3) = "DAMION"

     N$(4) = "LISA"

     N$(5) = "BARBARA"

(b) N$(1) = "JENNY"

     | N$(2) = "GEORGE" | = "DAMION" ?

     N$(3) = "DAMION"

     N$(4) = "LISA"

     N$(5) = "BARBARA"

(c) N$(1) = "JENNY"

     N$(2) = "GEORGE"

     | N$(3) = "DAMION" | = "DAMION" ?

     N$(4) = "LISA"

     N$(5) = "BARBARA"

Figure 4-2

of the list is doubled, the time to do the search also doubles. A list of 1,000 names takes ten times longer to search than a list of 100 names.

Adding a new name to the list is simple. If you let N equal the number of names in the list, you set N = N + 1 and assign the new name to N$(N). Algorithm 4-1 defines the sequential search in a BASIC-like language.

Algorithm 4-1   *Sequential search algorithm.*

Let N$() be an array of character strings containing the list of names to be searched.   Let N be the number of names in N$().   Example: If there are 5 names, then they appear in N$(1) through N$(5), and N is equal to 5.   Let S$ be the name that the algorithm is to search for.   I is used to keep track of the current position in the list.

```
Step  Action
  1)       Set I = 1
  2)       IF I > N THEN terminate search, S$ not found
  3)       IF S$ = N$(I) THEN terminate search, S$ found
                                 at loction I
  4)       Set I = I + 1 and GOTO Step 2
```

Listing 4-1 presents a sample sequential search program including routines to add a new name (line 1000) and to delete an existing name (line 2000). As shown in the listing, names are deleted from the list by locating the name, sliding the remaining names down one place in the list, and setting N to N − 1.

Algorithm 4-1 can be improved by a simple change that reduces the number of steps performed in the search loop.

Add Step 0:
        Set N\$(N + 1) = S\$
Remove Step 2.

All searches now stop when reaching N\$(N + 1). The actual execution time is reduced because only two statements, rather than three, are executed each time through the loop. Step 3 should include a check to determine if I > N, in which case the algorithm should report that S\$ was not found. This simple improvement is shown in Listing 4-2.

Listing 4-1

```
10        MAX = 100
20        DIM N$(MAX)
100       PRINT "Enter:  A)dd  L)ookup  P)rint  D)elete  Q)uit ? ";
110       C$ = INPUT$(1)
120       PRINT C$
130       ON  INSTR ( 1, "ALPDQ", C$) + 1  GOSUB 100, 200, 300, 400, 500, 600
140       GOTO 100
200       REM -------------------------------------------------------------
210       REM - Add Names
220       INPUT "Enter name to add ? ",S$
230       IF S$ = "" THEN RETURN
240       GOSUB 2000
250       IF F = 0 THEN GOSUB 1000 :
              RETURN
260       IF F = 1 THEN PRINT S$; " is already in the table" :
              RETURN
270       IF F = 2 THEN PRINT "Table is full at ";MAX;" entries" :
              RETURN
280       RETURN
300       REM -------------------------------------------------------------
310       REM - Lookup a name
320       INPUT "Enter name to lookup ? ",S$
330       GOSUB 2000
340       IF F = 0  THEN PRINT "Not Found" ELSE PRINT "Found at location ";G
350       RETURN
400       REM -------------------------------------------------------------
410       REM - Print out the entire table
420       GOSUB 3000
430       RETURN
500       REM -------------------------------------------------------------
510       REM - Delete a name
520       INPUT "Enter name to delete ? ",S$
530       GOSUB 2000
540       IF F = 0 THEN PRINT "Not Found" ELSE GOSUB 4000 :
              PRINT "Deleted"
550       RETURN
```

```
600        REM -----------------------------------------------------------------
610        REM - Quit
620        GOSUB 4070
1000       REM -----------------------------------------------------------------
1010       REM - Add a name
1020       IF N = MAX  THEN F = 2 :
              RETURN  ELSE F = 0
1030       N = N + 1
1040       N$(N) = S$
1050       RETURN
2000       REM -----------------------------------------------------------------
2010       REM - Lookup a name
2020       G = 1
2030       IF  G > N  THEN F = 0 :
              RETURN
2040       IF S$ = N$(G)  THEN F = 1 :
              RETURN
2050       G = G + 1
2060       GOTO 2030
3000       REM -----------------------------------------------------------------
3010       REM - Print the entire table
3020       FOR I = 1 TO N
3030         PRINT N$(I),
3040       NEXT I
3050       PRINT
3060       RETURN
4000       REM -----------------------------------------------------------------
4010       REM - Delete a Name
4020       N = N - 1
4030       FOR I = G TO N
4040         N$(I) = N$(I + 1)
4050       NEXT I
4060       RETURN
4070       END
```

Listing 4-2

```
1000       REM -----------------------------------------------------------------
1010       REM - Add a name
1020       IF N = MAX  THEN F = 2 :
              RETURN  ELSE F = 0
1030       N = N + 1
1040       N$(N) = S$
1050       RETURN
2000       REM -----------------------------------------------------------------
2010       REM - Lookup a name using improved sequential search.
2020       G = 1
2030       N$(N+1) = S$
2040       IF S$ = N$(G)   THEN 2080
2050       G = G + 1
2060       GOTO 2040
2070       REM
2080       REM - See if found at end of list
2090       IF G <= N THEN F = 1 ELSE F = 0
2100       RETURN
3000       REM -----------------------------------------------------------------
3010       REM - Print the entire table
3020       FOR I = 1 TO N
3030         PRINT N$(I),
3040       NEXT I
3050       PRINT
3060       RETURN
```

```
4000      REM ----------------------------------------------------------------
4010      REM - Delete a Name
4020      N = N - 1
4030      FOR I = G TO N
4040        N$(I) = N$(I + 1)
4050      NEXT I
4060      RETURN
4070      END
```

Improving the Sequential Search

Put the names that are searched for most often near the beginning of the list. If five names from a list of 100 names are searched for 50% of the time, it makes sense to place those five names at the beginning of the list. Then you can expect 50% of the searches to be satisfied by the fifth comparison. If you assume that the remaining 95 names in the list are distributed randomly, a successful search requires about 27 comparisons, which is better than the 50 comparisons expected when the names appear randomly.

Since you may not know ahead of time which names will be searched for frequently, this technique is best for tables set up in advance to reflect the expected distribution of the search requests. But by using a data structure called a list, it's easy to create a table that automatically orders the entries by frequency of occurrence as names are added or referenced. List structures are described in the next chapter.

THE BINARY SEARCH

A binary search greatly reduces search time. Another benefit is that if the table grows, the search time increases at a much slower rate. A sequential search of a list of 1,000 names takes about ten times longer than a search of a list of 100 names. In the average binary search, a 1,000-name search takes just 1.3 times longer than a 100-name search.

The binary search takes its name from its repeated divisions of the table into two pieces (hence, binary). The algorithm requires the names to appear in some sort of order. In these examples, the names are arranged alphabetically.

Before studying the details of the binary search, run through a search to get a feel for how it works. Instead of starting at the beginning of the list, the binary search begins at the middle. To locate ERIC in the list shown in Figure 4-3, the program compares ERIC to the name appearing in the middle of the list, ERIKA. Since ERIKA is alphabetically greater than ERIC, the entire half of the list with names greater than or equal to ERIKA is ignored.

The binary search makes its next guess by checking the name that appears midway between the middle of the list and the beginning of the list. After comparing CHARLIE to ERIC, you can see that the search has gone too low in the list. All the names less than or equal to CHARLIE are eliminated. Next, examine the name in the middle of the interval running from DAMION to ERIC, which is location 6, or DARLENE. Recognizing that there is only one possible space left to try, the search finds ERIC at location 7. Using the list in Figure 4-3, the binary search finds the name or determines that it does not exist in four or fewer comparisons. The average successful search in a table of 16 names requires about three comparisons. This is fewer than the eight comparisons expected for the sequential search.

The binary search provides a solution with so few comparisons because it repeatedly divides smaller lists in half. After the first comparison, there are only eight possible locations left to check. Following the next comparison, only four locations remain. Each pass through the list divides the number of remaining names in half. Finally, when the list cannot be split again, you know that you

(1) ALAN	(1) ALAN	(1) ALAN	(1) ALAN
(2) ALVIN	(2) ALVIN	(2) ALVIN	(2) ALVIN
(3) BARBARA	(3) BARBARA	(3) BARBARA	(3) BARBARA
(4) CHARLIE	(4) CHARLIE	(4) CHARLIE	(4) CHARLIE
(5) DAMION	(5) DAMION	(5) DAMION	(5) DAMION
(6) DARLENE	(6) DARLENE	(6) DARLENE	(6) DARLENE
(7) ERIC	(7) ERIC	(7) ERIC	(7) ERIC
(8) ERIKA	(8) ERIKA	(8) ERIKA	(8) ERIKA
(9) GEORGE	(9) GEORGE	(9) GEORGE	(9) GEORGE
(10) JOHN	(10) JOHN	(10) JOHN	(10) JOHN
(11) LISA	(11) LISA	(11) LISA	(11) LISA
(12) MIKE	(12) MIKE	(12) MIKE	(12) MIKE
(13) NATHAN	(13) NATHAN	(13) NATHAN	(13) NATHAN
(14) PETER	(14) PETER	(14) PETER	(14) PETER
(15) RICHARD	(15) RICHARD	(15) RICHARD	(15) RICHARD

Figure 4-3

Algorithm 4-2   *The ordered table binary search.*

```
Let  N$() be an array of names appearing in  alphabetical
order.   Let  N be the number of names in the list.  Let  L
mark  the lowest bound of the interval of names to look  at,
and  let  R  mark the upper bound.   Let  G  be  the  "guess"
appearing  midway  between L and R.   S$ is the name  to  be
searched for in table N$().

Step Action
  1)    Set L=1 and R=N
          These are the initial bounds of the interval.
  2)    G = INT ((L + R)/2)
          Make a guess midway between L and R.
  3)    IF R < L THEN terminate search, S$ not found
  4)    IF S$ = N$(G) THEN terminate search, S$ found at G
  5)    IF S$ < N$(G) THEN R = G - 1
          ELSE L = G + 1      Set new boundaries.
  6)    GOTO Step 2
```

have either found the name or that the name isn't in the list. Clearly, a search that eliminates half the list on the first comparison is much faster than the sequential search.

Algorithm 4-2 details the binary-search technique.

Binary Search Performance

For a short list, like the one in Figure 4-3, the time saved by using a binary search is negligible. The computer time needed to search a short list is so little that it makes hardly any difference which method is used. (The computer overhead required for the additional comparisons and for the arithmetic required in the binary search can actually make the binary search take longer than the sequential search when working with small lists.)

But as the size of the list grows, the advantages of the binary search grow. For a list of up to 65,535 names, the binary search guarantees fewer than 16 comparisons before terminating the search. That's 2,000 times better than the average successful sequential search for the same list. The maximum number of comparisons required for any list of size n is equal to the integer base 2 logarithm of n, plus 1. For those not familiar with logarithms, the number of comparisons is roughly equal to the number of times that n can be repeatedly divided by 2 while continuing to have an integer remainder. (For example, log 8 base 2 = 3, because 8/2 = 4, 4/2 = 2, and 2/2 = 1. Hence, 3 divisions is the solution.)

Adding Names to the Ordered Table

Adding names to an ordered table is time-consuming and inefficient. (See Algorithm 4-3.) To add a name, the program first searches the table to see if the name already exists. If it does, then the algorithm reports an error. Otherwise, the binary search has stopped at the point where the name should be added.

Algorithm 4-3   Inserting a new name into an ordered table.

```
N$(), S$, N, and G are the same as for Algorithm 4-2. I is a
dummy variable used as a FOR/NEXT loop control value.

Step Action
  1)   Perform Algorithm 4-2.
  2)   If  S$ was found then terminate with an   error  - the
       name already exists in the table.
  3)   N = N + 1
  4)   FOR I = N TO G + 1 STEP - 1
          N$(I) = N$(I-1)
       NEXT I
       Shift the names over one place in the table.
  5)   N$(G+1) = S$
       Place the name into the table.
```

So all the names that follow are shifted over one entry in the table and the new name is inserted. For example, to insert DAVID into the list in Figure 4-4, first call the binary-search routine (Algorithm 4-2) to see if the name is in the table. Since the name is not in the table, you make a hole where the name will go. Algorithm 4-2 finishes the search. G has the value of the location just before the hole. Figure 4-4 illustrates the insertion. The names that follow DARLENE slide up in the array, and DAVID is inserted at location 7. Algorithm 4-3 may be improved by using pointers to strings and then shifting the pointers rather than the strings. The concept of pointers is introduced in Chapter 5 and discussed further in Chapter 6.

The binary search can also be optimized by ordering the table according to frequency of occurrence. In a binary tree, the most frequently accessed name in the list appears at the center of the table so that it is always examined first. Binary trees are described in Chapter 5.

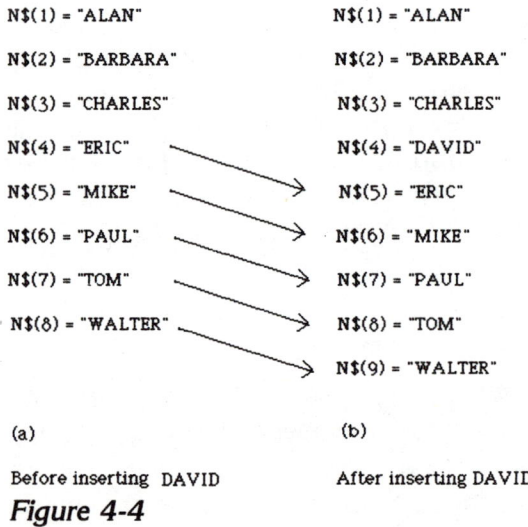

N$(1) = "ALAN"	N$(1) = "ALAN"
N$(2) = "BARBARA"	N$(2) = "BARBARA"
N$(3) = "CHARLES"	N$(3) = "CHARLES"
N$(4) = "ERIC"	N$(4) = "DAVID"
N$(5) = "MIKE"	N$(5) = "ERIC"
N$(6) = "PAUL"	N$(6) = "MIKE"
N$(7) = "TOM"	N$(7) = "PAUL"
N$(8) = "WALTER"	N$(8) = "TOM"
	N$(9) = "WALTER"

(a)   (b)

Before inserting DAVID   After inserting DAVID

Figure 4-4

Listing 4-3 is a set of sample subroutines for implementing a binary search in BASIC. Lines 1 to 999 are omitted because they are the same as the lines in Listing 4-1. Subroutine 1000 adds the name S$ to the table; subroutine 2000 searches the table for the name S$, returning the location in variable G; and subroutine 4000 deletes the name at location G. The program should GOSUB 2000 before jumping to 4000 so that G is set to the proper location.

Listing 4-3   *Binary search routines.*

```
1000      REM  ---------------------------------------------------------
1010      REM - Add a name
1020      IF N = MAX THEN F = 2 :
             RETURN ELSE F = 0
```

```
1030      N = N + 1
1040      FOR I = N TO G + 1 STEP -1
1050        N$(I) = N$(I - 1)
1060      NEXT I
1070      N$(G+1) = S$
1080      RETURN
2000      REM -----------------------------------------------------------------
2010      REM - Lookup a name
2020      L = 1 :
            R = N :
            REM - Set left and right boundaries
2030      G = INT ( (L + R) / 2 ) :
            REM - Make guess between boundaries
2040      IF R < L THEN F = 0 :
            RETURN
2050      IF S$ = N$(G)   THEN F = 1 :
            RETURN
2060      IF S$ < N$(G)   THEN R = G - 1 ELSE L = G + 1
2070      GOTO 2030
3000      REM -----------------------------------------------------------------
3010      REM - Print the table of names
3020      FOR I = 1 TO N
3030        PRINT N$(I),
3040      NEXT I
3050      PRINT
3060      RETURN
4000      REM -----------------------------------------------------------------
4010      REM - Delete a Name
4020      N = N - 1
4030      FOR I = G TO N
4040        N$(I) = N$(I + 1)
4050      NEXT I
4060      RETURN
4070      END
```

HASHING

The best search would be a crystal ball that reveals the location of the name sought. Envision a magic box, like the one in Figure 4-5. When it is given a name, it simply outputs the correct location. Such a strategy is called hashing. Hashing turns the search name into a number that is the actual index into an array of names.

Suppose that there is a function called HASH(STRING), which converts a string to an integer.

```
Location = HASH (S$)
```

S$ is the name that you're looking for. A name is converted to a number by assigning a numeric value to each character in the name and then summing the values. Equate the letter A with the number 65, the letter B with 66, and so on, up through the letter Z, which has the value of 90. This letter-number correspondence is used because these numbers are the ASCII codes that the computer uses to represent characters internally. Most versions of BASIC have a function like

```
C = ASC (S$)
```

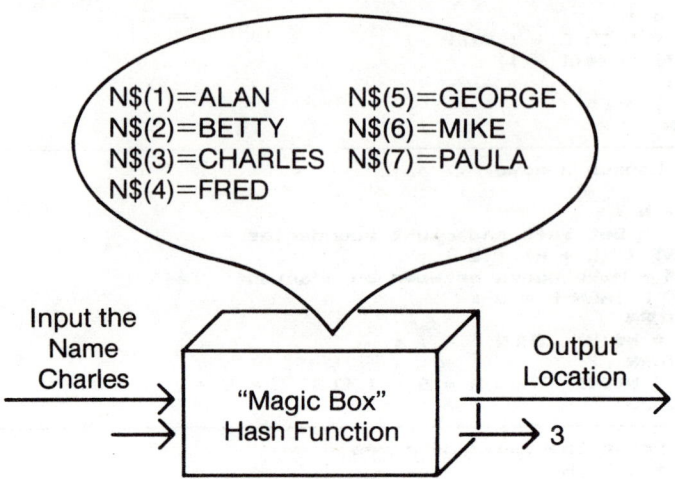

Figure 4-5 *The hash function works like a magic box converting the name Charles into a number that is also the location where Charles is kept on the list. Actually, no magic is involved. The hash function uses simple arithmetic to convert the character string into a number. Of course, more than one name may hash to the same number, producing a collision.*

which returns the ASCII code of the first character in S$. For example, if S$ = D, then ASC(S$) yields 68.

To produce the hash, the hash function sums the codes for each of the characters in the string. For example, to hash DOUG, the values for each of the characters are summed as follows:

D	O	U	G	Sum
68	+ 79	+ 85	+ 71	= 303

DOUG has a hash value of 303. If the names are stored in an array defined as DIM N$(100), then there is a slight problem: How do you use the number 303 as an index to N$() when the index must be less than or equal to 100? To scale the hash value to the range 1 to 100, divide 303 by 100. The remainder of 3 is the actual hash value.

For example, if you define R as the remainder of X/Y, then in IBM BASIC, you write

    R = MOD (X, Y)

To place DOUG in the hash table, N$(3) is set to DOUG. Later, when searching for DOUG, the same hash index of 3 is produced, immediately locating the name at N$(3). Listing 4-4 is a BASIC subroutine that computes the hash value of a character string.

Listing 4-4   *Hashing routines.*

```
1000    REM ------------------------------------------------------------
1010    REM - Add a name
1020    IF N >= MAX - 1 THEN F = 2 :
            RETURN
1030    N = N + 1
1040    F = 0
1050    GOSUB 5000 ' Compute Hash
1060    IF N$(HASH) = ""  OR  N$(HASH) = "*" THEN  N$(HASH) = S$ :
            RETURN
1070    HASH = HASH - 1
1080    IF HASH = 0 THEN HASH = MAX
1090    GOTO 1060
2000    REM ------------------------------------------------------------
2010    REM - Lookup a name
2020    GOSUB 5000
2030    IF N$(HASH) = "" THEN F = 0 :
            RETURN
2040    IF N$(HASH) = S$ THEN F = 1:
            G = HASH :
            RETURN
2050    HASH = HASH - 1
2060    IF HASH = 0 THEN HASH = MAX
2070    GOTO 2030
3000    REM ------------------------------------------------------------
3010    REM - Print the entire table
3020    FOR I = 1 TO MAX
3030      IF LEN(N$(I)) > 0 THEN IF N$(I) <> "*"  THEN PRINT N$(I),
3040    NEXT I
3070    RETURN
4000    REM ------------------------------------------------------------
4010    REM - Delete a Name
4020    N$(HASH) = "*"
4030    N = N - 1
4040    RETURN
5000    REM ------------------------------------------------------------
5010    REM - Compute HASH = Hash(S$)
5020    HASH = 0
5030    FOR I = 1 TO LEN(S$)
5040      HASH = HASH + ASC(MID$(S$, I, 1))
5050    NEXT I
5060    HASH = HASH MOD MAX + 1
5070    RETURN
6000    END
```

Algorithm 4-4   *Searching the hash table.*

```
Let  S$ be the name to search for in the table of names N$().
The function HASH() is as described in the text.   S is equal
to the size of the array N$().

Step   Action
  1)   H = HASH ( S$ )
  2)   IF  N$(H) = ""  THEN exit, S$ was not found
  3)   ELSE  IF  N$(H) = S$  THEN exit, S$ found at location H
  4)   H = H - 1      Decrement and try next position
  5)   IF  H = 0  THEN  H = S
  6)   Goto Step 2
```

Algorithm 4-5   *Adding new names to the hash table.*

```
S is equal to the maximum table size - 1.  For example, if
MAX = 100, then S = MAX - 1, or 99.
```

```
Step  Action
  1)  IF N = S  THEN error, the table is full
  2)  N = N + 1                Increment total entries
  3)  H = HASH (S$)            Compute Hash
  4)  IF  N$(H) = ""  OR  N$(H) = "*"  THEN
                N$(H) = S$;   Exit with the name inserted
  5)  H = H - 1               Collision occurred, so decrement
  6)  IF  H = 0  THEN  H = S
  7)  Goto Step 4
```

Algorithm 4-6   *Deleting names from the hash table.*

```
Step  Action
  1)  Call Algorithm 4
  2)  If  S$ was not found then error
      Else N$(H) = "*", Mark it as deleted.
```

Handling Collisions

A problem arises when you give the hash function a name that also hashes to location 3. For example, DEB hashes to 203.

D	E	B	Sum
68	+ 69	+ 66	= 203

The hash of 203 is scaled to the range of 1 to 100, giving it the value of 3. DOUG is already in the table at that location. The algorithm detects a collision whenever two or more names hash to the same location. There are several ways of dealing with collisions.

When DEB hashes to an index that is already used, the algorithm decrements the hash value and tries the next entry at location 2. If N$(2) is not in use, then the algorithm sets N$(2) to DEB. But if N$(2) is already used, the algorithm decrements the index again. The hash index continues to decrease until a free entry is found. Upon reaching zero, the index wraps around to 100 and continues decrementing until finding a free spot in the table. In the worst case, the hashing algorithm can degenerate into a sequential search of the list, looking for the next-to-the-last free spot.

A problem with this simple scheme for handling collisions is that quite often, names cluster around a single location within the table. If you handle collisions by decrementing the hash value, you make the problem worse because you end up with an entire block of names located in one area. The solution is to change the hash value by a larger amount or to perform some arithmetic on the value. This operation moves the hash index elsewhere in the table, which alleviates clustering.

The present scheme is to set

HASH = HASH − 1

whenever a collision occurs. You can change the −1 to any other constant. Some examples are:

HASH = HASH + 10
HASH = HASH + 100
HASH = HASH − 47

Of course, as a result of this change, you may skip some entries in the table. And this can be a problem when you're looking for a free entry in a crowded table. Making the table size a prime number improves the situation. In any event, the problem occurs only when the table is nearly full.

Another approach is to change the increment each time through the search loop. For example, instead of

HASH = HASH + 1

you might use the following:

HASH = HASH + DIFFERENCE
DIFFERENCE = DIFFERENCE + 2

DIFFERENCE is initially given a value of 1. If the initial HASH value is 0, this formula yields the following:

	DIFFERENCE	New HASH
After 1st Collision	HASH = HASH + 1	1
After 2nd Collision	HASH = HASH + 3	4
After 3rd Collision	HASH = HASH + 5	9
After 4th Collision	HASH = HASH + 7	16

The search routine begins with an initial hash value of zero. (For this example, assume that whatever you are searching for hashed to location 0). Since location 0 in the table is already occupied, the routine computes a new hash index by adding DIFFERENCE to HASH. At this first collision, DIFFERENCE has the value 1, so this gives a new hash location of 1. DIFFERENCE is now increased by 2 to 3.

But location 1 is also occupied, so a second collision occurs. The routine adds DIFFERENCE to the current HASH value once more. Since HASH is now 1 and DIFFERENCE is 3, this gives a new hash location at 4.

The third probe, at location 4, also collides. So once more, HASH is recomputed as HASH + DIFFERENCE or 4 + 5, giving HASH a new value, 9. Since location 9 is also occupied, one more rehash is done, yielding a hash location of 16.

Have you spotted the pattern in the new hash locations? Each new hash index corresponds to the square of the number of collisions that have occurred so far. Collision 1 rehashes to 1, collision 2 rehashes to 4, collision 3 to 9, and collision 4 to 16. A fifth location rehashes to location 25. This particular formula is based on a quadratic equation. The resulting hash sequence tends to avoid clustering. Groups of closely spaced names are skipped fairly rapidly when the table is nearly full. Listing 4-5 shows the hash routines for search, add, and delete, modified to use the new quadratic rehash whenever a collision occurs.

Listing 4-5 *Quadratic hashing routines.*

```
1000      REM  -----------------------------------------------------------
1010      REM - Add a name
1020      IF N >= MAX - 1 THEN F = 2 :
            RETURN
1030      N = N + 1
1040      F = 0
1045      DIFFERENCE = 1
1050      GOSUB 5000 ' Compute Hash
1060      IF N$(HASH) = ""   OR   N$(HASH) = "*" THEN   N$(HASH) = S$ :
            RETURN
1070      HASH = HASH + DIFFERENCE
1075      DIFFERENCE = DIFFERENCE + 2
1080      IF   HASH > MAX   THEN   HASH = HASH MOD MAX + 1
1090      GOTO 1060
2000      REM  -----------------------------------------------------------
2010      REM - Lookup a name
2020      GOSUB 5000
2025      DIFFERENCE = 1
2030      IF N$(HASH) = "" THEN F = 0 :
            RETURN
2040      IF N$(HASH) = S$ THEN F = 1:
            G = HASH :
            RETURN
2050      HASH = HASH + DIFFERENCE
2055      DIFFERENCE = DIFFERENCE + 2
2060      IF   HASH > MAX   THEN   HASH = HASH MOD MAX + 1
2070      GOTO 2030
```

```
3000    REM -----------------------------------------------------------
3010    REM - Print the entire table
3020    FOR I = 1 TO MAX
3030      IF LEN(N$(I)) > 0 THEN IF N$(I) <> "*"  THEN PRINT N$(I),
3040    NEXT I
3070    RETURN
4000    REM -----------------------------------------------------------
4010    REM - Delete a Name
4020    N$(HASH) = "*"
4030    N = N - 1
4040    RETURN
5000    REM -----------------------------------------------------------
5010    REM - Compute HASH = Hash(S$)
5020    HASH = 0
5030    FOR I = 1 TO LEN(S$)
5040      HASH = HASH + ASC(MID$(S$, I, 1))
5050    NEXT I
5060    HASH = HASH MOD MAX + 1
5070    RETURN
6000    END
```

A warning is in order. It's possible that because of the increasing gap in each rehashed location, you may skip some entries when the table is nearly full and you're looking for the last free spot. In fact, it's quite possible that quadratic rehashing may miss about half the entries. Therefore, you need to do two things: avoid letting the table get completely full; and choose a prime number for the size of the table. A prime number is a number that is not evenly divisible by any numbers other than 1 and itself. For example, the numbers 3, 5, 7, 11, 13, 17, 19, 23, 29, and 31 are all prime numbers because they cannot be divided by any others.

Any of the following prime numbers are useful for building tables up to 1,000 entries: 101, 199, 211, 307, 401, 503, 601, 701, 809, 907, 997. Listing 4-6 is a simple program that lists prime numbers; any of the numbers produced are good choices for the size of a hash table. The prime number that you use should be placed in the DIM statement that defines the size of the array that contains the names.

Listing 4-6

```
INPUT "Produce Primes Up to What Number? ",N
PRINT 3, 5,
FOR I = 7 TO  N  STEP  2
  FOR J = 3  TO  SQR(N)  STEP  2
    IF  I MOD J  = 0  THEN  GOTO 80
  NEXT J
PRINT I,
NEXT I
```

Because of collisions, an ideal hash function initially tries to compute a unique hash, which eliminates collisions and alleviates clustering within the table. For maximum efficiency, the table should never be more than 80% full. At about 80% of table capacity, the hashing method averages about three comparisons for a successful search. For an unsuccessful search, even in a large table, only 13 comparisons are expected.

Searching the Hash Table

When searching for DEB, the same process that had been used to add DEB to the table is repeated. DEB is hashed to location 3. Finding a mismatch, the index value is decremented to 2 and the name is found.

The search finishes when the algorithm finds the name or when the index points to an unused slot in the table. If the name doesn't appear in the table and there are no unused slots, then the search loops indefinitely. Therefore, a table of size n can only hold n − 1 names; there must always be at least one empty slot in the table.

Removing Hash Entries

Deleting names from the hash table is not as simple as it first appears. For example, if you remove DOUG from location 3, the first time you search for DEB, you'll hash to location 3, and seeing it empty, conclude that DEB is not in the table. To solve this problem, mark location 3 as deleted, rather than unused, so that the search will correctly continue to location 2.

Lines 4000-4040 of Listing 4-5 show the deletion of a name from a hash table. As with the previous listings, S$ holds the name to add to or search for in the table. To delete a name, call subroutine 2000 and verify that the name exists, and then GOSUB 4000 to actually delete it.

It's not necessary to sum all of the characters in the name. If you know that there are only a few names, you might form the hash from just the first few characters of each name. This technique is very useful in a compiler or interpreter's keyword symbol table or as a command recognizer in a program. As an example, consider a small BASIC interpreter having the keywords, IF, THEN, GOTO, GOSUB, FOR, NEXT, RETURN, PRINT, and INPUT. If you hash all of those keywords by their first letter, the only collision that occurs is between GOTO and GOSUB.

Hashing the Employee Records

In Chapter 2, a complete employee-records system was designed. The program permits the addition, deletion, and changing of information concerning the employees. The program can also display information about individual employees or produce summary reports about all the employees.

The entire employee-records system (except for the report subroutine) is shown in Listing 4-7. The report routine is explained in Chapter 9.

The employee records program's user interface is described in Chapter 2. The implementation is fairly straightforward. The table of names is organized using the hashing-search technique. This allows fast lookups by name and makes it easy to add new names or delete existing entries.

Listing 4-7

```
10        REM - Employee Records System
20        MAX = 100
30        DIM NAMES$(MAX), DEPT(MAX), PHONE$(MAX), SALARY(MAX)
100       REM
110       REM
120       REM - Prompt for Command
130       PRINT
140       INPUT "Select:  A)dd, P)rint, L)ist, D)elete, C)hange,
            R)eport, Q)uit ? ",CH$
150       ON INSTR("APLDCRQ",CH$) + 1 GOSUB 170, 1010, 2010, 3080, 5000,
            6000, 7000, 11080
160       GOTO 130
170       PRINT "Incorrect Selection - Try Again"
180       GOTO 130
190       REM
200       REM
1000      REM --------------------------------------------------------------
1010      REM - Add A New Employee
1020      PRINT
1030      INPUT "Enter Name of Employee to Add? ",S$
1040      IF S$ = "" THEN RETURN
1050      GOSUB 9000 ' Lookup the name
1060      IF F = 1  THEN PRINT "'";S$;"' has already been added":
            GOTO 1020
1070      NAMES$(G) = S$
1080      INPUT "Department Number ? ",DEPT(G)
1090      INPUT "Telephone Number ? ",PHONE$(G)
1100      INPUT "Salary ? ",SALARY(G)
1110      RETURN
1120      REM
1130      REM
2000      REM --------------------------------------------------------------
2010      REM - Print Employee Records
2020      GOSUB 3000 ' Prompt for name to list
2030      IF S$ = "" THEN RETURN
2040      LPRINT "Name"; TAB(20); "Department #"; TAB(35); "Telephone
            #"; TAB(50); "Salary"
2050      LPRINT NAMES$(G); TAB(25); DEPT(G); TAB(35); PHONE$(G);
            TAB(50); SALARY(G)
2060      RETURN
2070      REM
2080      REM
3000      REM --------------------------------------------------------------
3010      REM - Prompt for name of employee to print or list
3020      PRINT
3030      INPUT "Name of Employee to Display? ",S$
3040      IF S$ = "" THEN RETURN
3050      GOSUB 9000 ' lookup S$
3060      IF F = 0  THEN PRINT "'"; S$; "' is not in the records - Try again":
            GOTO 3020
3070      RETURN
```

```
3080        REM
3090        REM
4000        REM -----------------------------------------------------------
4010        REM - List a record to the display
4020        GOSUB 3000
4030        IF S$ = "" THEN RETURN
4040        PRINT "Name"; TAB(20); "Department #"; TAB(35); "Telephone
            #"; TAB(50); "Salary"
4050        PRINT NAMES$(G); TAB(25); DEPT(G); TAB(35); PHONE$(G);
            TAB(50); SALARY(G)
4060        RETURN
4070        REM
4080        REM
4090        REM
5000        REM -----------------------------------------------------------
5010        REM - Delete an employee
5020        PRINT
5030        INPUT "Name of Employee to Delete ? ", S$
5040        IF  S$ = ""  THEN RETURN
5050        GOSUB 9000 ' Lookup the employee
5060        IF F = 0 THEN PRINT "'"; S$; "' is not in the records - Try again":
            GOTO 5020
5070        PRINT NAMES$(G); TAB(20); "Department #"; DEPT(G)
5080        INPUT "Delete (Y or N) ? ",C$
5090        IF C$<> "Y" AND C$<>"N" THEN 5080
5100        IF C$ = "Y" THEN GOSUB 10000 :
            PRINT "Deleted" :
            RETURN
5110        PRINT "Not Deleted"
5120        REM
5130        REM
5140        REM
6000        REM -----------------------------------------------------------
6010        REM - Change Employee Data
6020        PRINT
6030        INPUT "Name of Employee to Change ? ",S$
6040        IF  S$ = ""  THEN RETURN
6050        GOSUB 9000 ' Lookup
6060        IF  F = 0  THEN PRINT "'"; S$; "' is not in the records - Try again" :
            GOTO 6020
6070        PRINT
6080        PRINT "Department ="; DEPT(G)
6090        INPUT "Enter new department (CR=no change) ? ",NEWDEPT
6100        IF  NEWDEPT <> 0  THEN DEPT(G) = NEWDEPT
6110        PRINT
6120        PRINT "Telephone # = ";PHONE$(G)
6130        INPUT "Enter new telephone # (CR=no change) ? ",NEWPHONE$
6140        IF  NEWPHONE$ <> ""  THEN  PHONE$(G) = NEWPHONE$
6150        PRINT
6160        PRINT "Salary = ";SALARY(G)
6170        INPUT "Enter new salary (CR=no change) ? ", NEWSALARY
6180        IF  NEWSALARY <> 0  THEN  SALARY(G) = NEWSALARY
6190        RETURN
6200        REM
6210        REM
7000        REM -----------------------------------------------------------
7010        REM - Print a Report
7020        RETURN
7030        REM
7040        REM
8000        REM -----------------------------------------------------------
8010        REM - Add a name
8020        IF N >= MAX - 1 THEN F = 2 :
            RETURN
8030        N = N + 1
8040        F = 0
```

```
8050      GOSUB 11000 ' Compute Hash
8060      IF NAMES$(HASH) = ""  OR  NAMES$(HASH) = "*" THEN  G = HASH :
            RETURN
8070      HASH = HASH - 1
8080      IF HASH = 0 THEN HASH = MAX
8090      GOTO 8060
8100      REM
8110      REM
9000      REM --------------------------------------------------------
9010      REM - Lookup a name
9020      GOSUB 11000
9030      IF NAMES$(HASH) = "" THEN F = 0 :
            G = HASH :
            RETURN
9040      IF NAMES$(HASH) = S$ THEN F = 1:
            G = HASH :
            RETURN
9050      HASH = HASH - 1
9060      IF HASH = 0 THEN HASH = MAX
9070      GOTO 9030
9080      REM
9090      REM
10000     REM --------------------------------------------------------
10010     REM - Delete a Name
10020     NAMES$(HASH) = "*"
10030     N = N - 1
10040     RETURN
10050     REM
10060     REM
11000     REM --------------------------------------------------------
11010     REM - Compute HASH = Hash(S$)
11020     HASH = 0
11030     FOR I = 1 TO LEN(S$)
11040        HASH = HASH + ASC(MID$(S$, I, 1))
11050     NEXT I
11060     HASH = HASH MOD MAX + 1
11070     RETURN
11080     END
```

REVIEW

- The sequential search is the simplest way to look through a table of names or records for a particular item. It is easy to understand and easy to program. The search is faster if the data is stored in the order it will be searched.

- Binary searches are fast because they split the list in half on the first comparison.

- Hashing converts the name that is being searched for into a number, which is then used to directly locate a data record.

- Sometimes a problem seems impossible to solve. But by looking at it from a different perspective, a solution may almost pop out at you. And when you analyze the problem in detail, still more solutions may appear. Certainly, the sequential, binary, and hashing searches show that there are many ways to do something as "simple" as searching a table.

CHAPTER
5

Data Structures

The term *data structure* refers to the way data is structured or organized. Data that has been organized properly is easier to use and process. A telephone book, organized alphabetically by name, is easy to use. If the phone book were sorted by telephone number, it would be very difficult to use.

The telephone book is only one example of how proper data-structure techniques improve the efficiency of information processing. In this chapter, several data structures are examined—*stacks, queues, lists, trees, and records.* Their use is demonstrated in table searches, arithmetic-expression evaluations, subroutine calls, simulations, process-waiting areas in computer operating systems, and application programs. The proper choice of a problem's data organization can markedly improve both memory and execution time requirements.

DEFINING A DATA STRUCTURE

A data structure is an organized collection of data. In this book, the smallest piece of data used is a single character or integer. An integer consists of bits of storage. The bit, or binary 0 or 1, is the basic unit of a computer's memory. A single memory cell on the IBM PC consists of 8 bits. Each bit holds either a 0 or 1, as shown here:

```
-------------------------------
¦ 0¦ 1¦ 0¦ 0¦ 1¦ 0¦ 1¦ 0¦
-------------------------------
```

In most computers, including the IBM PC, a byte (usually equivalent to a single character like A or B) is 8 bits. A number like 7,234 or 9,283 occupies 16 bits of storage. A bit, a byte, and an integer might be depicted like this:

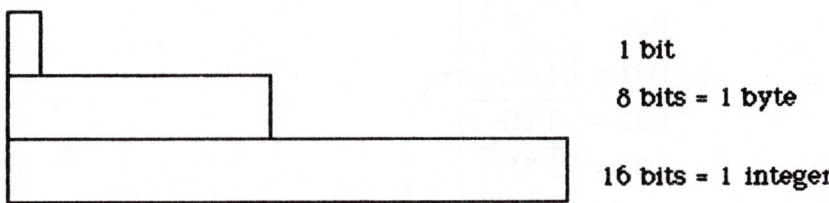

1 bit

8 bits = 1 byte

16 bits = 1 integer

Typically, these are the fundamental storage units that the computer circuitry recognizes. Fortunately, you don't need to understand all the details of how bits are turned into numbers and characters.

The software manipulates these basic building blocks to develop more complex data structures. For example, a character string is little more than a sequence of characters strung together.

Similarly, the array

DIM N%(100)

is just a sequence of integer storage locations.

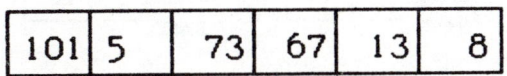

The building blocks of characters and integers can be combined and referenced in numerous ways to form new data types. By treating the value of an integer as the address of another integer, a pointer is created. For example, in the small section of memory shown here, the value of memory cell 101 is interpreted as the location or address of another cell.

Cell Number	Cell Contents
99 =	10
100 =	20
101 =	105
102 =	110
103 =	236
104 =	17
105 =	-1

In this case, cell 101 points to cell 105, hence the name pointer.

By combining groups of characters, integers, and pointers, new and complex data types are created. When collections of data types are brought together, they are called a record. Many languages, including Pascal, PL/1, COBOL, and Ada provide language support for record structures; BASIC does not. But records can be simulated in a number of ways.

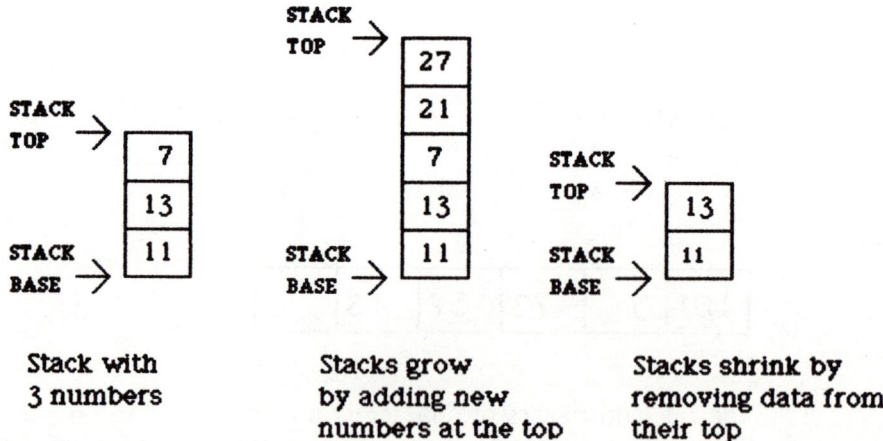

Stack with
3 numbers

Stacks grow
by adding new
numbers at the top

Stacks shrink by
removing data from
their top

Figure 5-1 *The stack in operation. Data is added by pushing it on to the top of the stack. When data is removed, it is popped off the top. Consequently, the last number put on the stack is also the first to be removed.*

STACKS

The stack is a structure that grows and contracts and is often used to store data that is later thrown away. Stacks are used for subroutine calls, recursive subroutine calls (recursive routines call themselves), arithmetic-expression evaluation, sorting and searching algorithms, and many other applications. In some cases, the stack is like an array that grows at one end (see Figure 5-1). Data are always added to and removed from the top of the stack. Consequently, the piece of data placed on the stack most recently is the first to be removed.

Data are added and removed by pushing a new element onto the stack and popping it off the top of the stack.

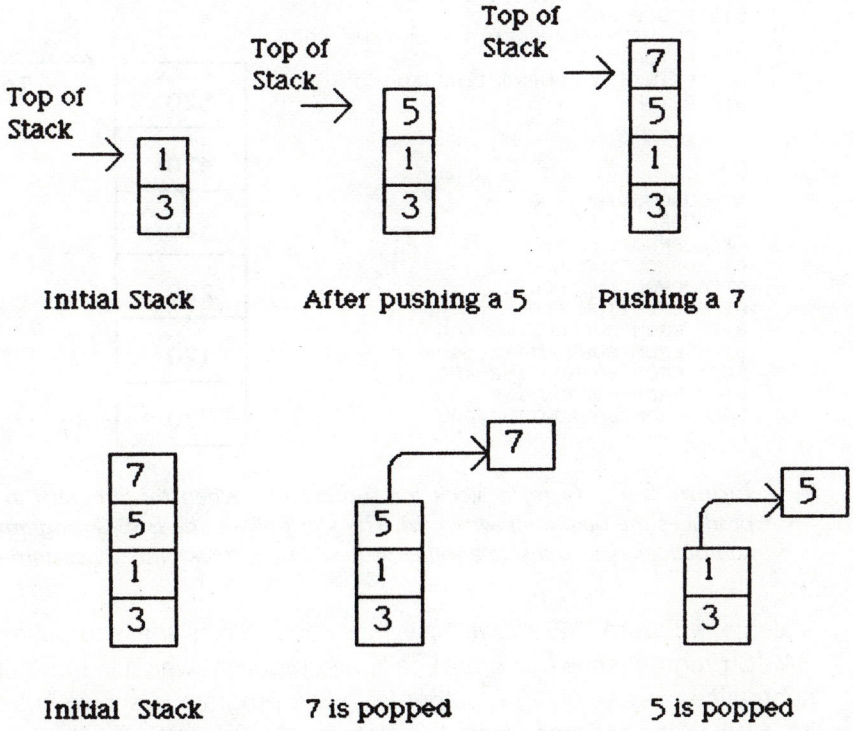

Stacks and Subroutine Calls

Every time your program executes a GOSUB, BASIC uses a stack to keep track of where the program should branch when it encounters the RETURN

(a)

```
10 GOSUB 100
20 PRINT "ALL DONE"
30 STOP
100 PRINT "AT SUBROUTINE 100"
110 GOSUB 200
120 PRINT "BACK FROM SUBROUTINE 200"
130 RETURN
200 PRINT "AT SUBROUTINE 200"
210 GOSUB 300
220 PRINT "BACK FROM SUBROUTINE 300"
230 RETURN
300 PRINT "AT SUBROUTINE 300"
310 GOSUB 400
320 PRINT "BACK FROM SUBROUTINE 400"
330 RETURN
400 PRINT "AT SUBROUTINE 400"
410 GOSUB 500
420 PRINT "BACK FROM SUBROUTINE 500"
430 RETURN
500 PRINT "AT SUBROUTINE 500"
510 GOSUB 600
520 PRINT "BACK FROM SUBROUTINE 600"
530 RETURN
600 PRINT "AT SUBROUTINE 600"
610 RETURN
```

(b)

```
AT SUBROUTINE 100
AT SUBROUTINE 200
AT SUBROUTINE 300
AT SUBROUTINE 400
AT SUBROUTINE 500
AT SUBROUTINE 600
BACK FROM SUBROUTINE 600
BACK FROM SUBROUTINE 500
BACK FROM SUBROUTINE 400
BACK FROM SUBROUTINE 300
BACK FROM SUBROUTINE 200
ALL DONE
```

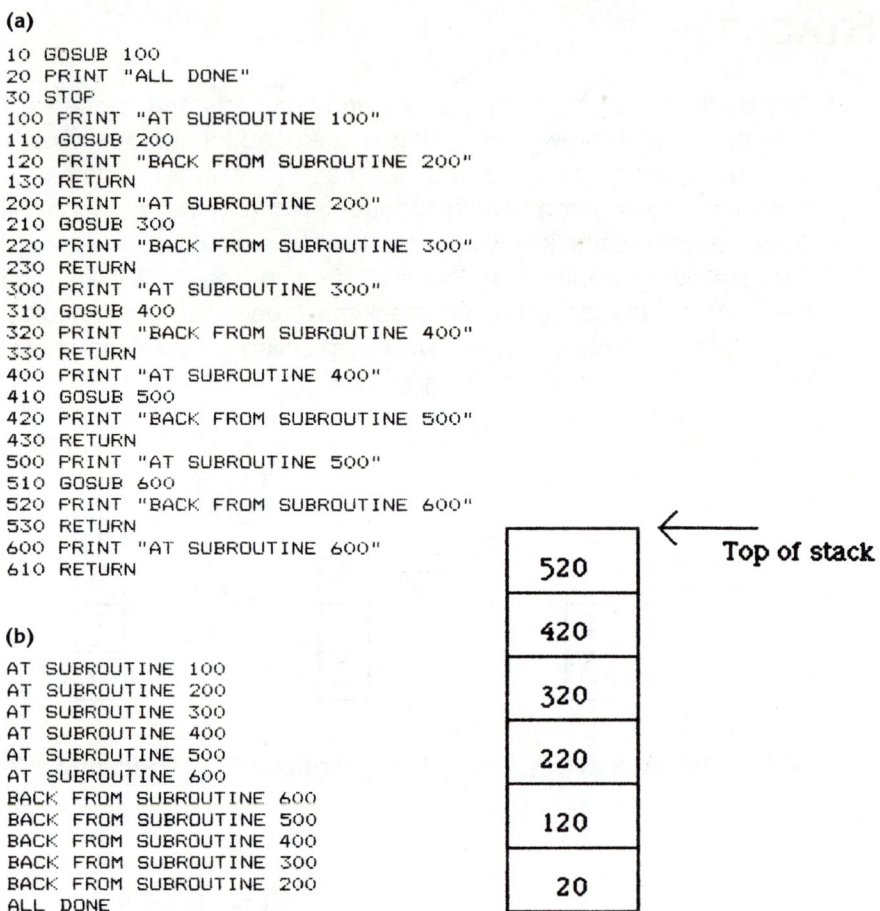

Figure 5-2 Using a stack for subroutines. When the program in (a) runs, it produces the output shown in (b). The stack allows the BASIC program to jump to subroutines nested inside another without losing track of their assignments.

statement. Figure 5-2 shows how the stack makes the subroutine call. The BASIC program shown in 5-2(a) calls a subroutine, which in turn calls another subroutine, and so on. The output from this program is shown in 5-2(b).

When the program runs, the statement at line 10 calls the subroutine at line 100. When the subroutine at line 100 ends, the program returns to line 20. Internally, BASIC uses a stack to remember the return location. When it executes the GOSUB statement at line 10, it places line 20 on the stack.

20

The subroutine at line 100, in turn, calls the subroutine at line 200, placing the return location of 120 onto the stack.

```
| 120 |
|  20 |
```

By the time the program reaches line 600, the stack contains

```
| 520 |
| 420 |
| 320 |
| 220 |
| 120 |
|  20 |
```

At line 610, the RETURN statement causes the subroutine to return to the line where it was called. So BASIC pops the return address from the stack, yielding line 520. At line 520 another RETURN statement is executed, and again, the return address is popped. The program continues popping return addresses until it reaches the STOP at line 30.

Stacks and Expression Evaluation

Stacks are often used to evaluate arithmetic expressions. If you've used a reverse polish notation (RPN) calculator, such as those made by Hewlett-Packard, then you are already familiar with the notion of stacks and their use to evaluate expressions. Pressing the ENTER key is synonymous with a push onto the stack.

Consider the expressison (3 + 5)/(2 + 2). To solve this, you add 3 and 5, giving 8, and then 2 and 2, giving 4. Then you divide 8 by 4, giving 2. During evaluation, two temporary solutions are obtained: 8 and 4. The expression might be expressed as:

```
T1 = (3 + 5)
T2 = (2 + 2)
Answer = T1/T2
```

When the computer evaluates this expression, it uses a stack to store the temporary results.

Evaluating expressions by computer is fairly complicated because some operators, like * and /, have a higher precedence than + and −. This means that the expression 3 + 5 * 3 should give the answer (5 * 3) + 3 or 18, not (3 + 5) * 3 or 24. A program that takes an input like "3 + 5 * 3" requires a "parser" to properly split each part of the expression and to deal with the issue of operator precedence. Chapter 13 describes a method for evaluating expressions using IBM BASIC.

In this chapter the parser is treated as a "black box" that does the evaluation for you. You can then concentrate on stacks and data-structure techniques. Given the expression (3 + 5)/(2 + 2), the parser begins work at the left-most parenthesis. Seeing the number, 3, the parser places 3 on the stack:

Next, the parser sees the + symbol and temporarily saves it as the arithmetic operator. Then the 5 is placed on the stack:

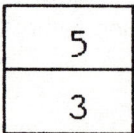

The operator + is applied to the top two elements of the stack to give:

Recognizing that expressions within parentheses must be evaluated first, the parser scans to the next subexpression. Both 2s are placed onto the stack:

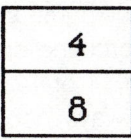

and then added to give:

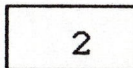

Finally, the second number from the top of stack is divided by the number on the top to produce the answer:

2

Programming Stacks

A simple way to create a stack is to use an array and an index or pointer variable. Let DIM S(100) be space for a stack of up to 100 elements, and let P be a pointer to the top of the stack. Initialize P to 1. To add or push data onto the stack, the program executes these statements:

$S(P) = D$
$P = P + 1$

For example, here is a stack containing five elements:

$P = 6$
    $S(5) = 21$
    $S(4) = 13$
    $S(3) = 8$
    $S(2) = 5$
    $S(1) = 3$

A pop is the reverse of the push:

$P = P - 1$
$D = S(P)$

Appropriate checks should ensure that P does not exceed the dimensions of S(100). If P is greater than 100, BASIC gives an error message.

Using Stacks

Stacks are often used in BASIC to store the values of variables when calling other subroutines. One problem that some people have is that they'll use a variable such as T1 or T2 in one subroutine. Then they'll GOSUB to another subroutine, which GOSUBs to yet another subroutine, which just so happens to also use variables T1 and T2. Presto! The original subroutine crashes and they just can't figure out what happened to the values of T1 or T2. No matter how hard they try to avoid this, the problem almost always occurs as the program grows.

One way to prevent this is to create a stack like this:

```
DIM S(50)
```

and a stack pointer variable P. Inside the first subroutine, save the values of T1 and T2 on the stack, call the other subroutine that also uses T1 and T2, and after returning restore the values of T1 and T2. The code for this looks like this:

```
S(P) = T1
P = P + 1
S(P) = T2
P = P + 1
GOSUB other routine
P = P - 1
T2 = S(P)
P = P - 1
T1 = S(P)
```

Now you won't have to worry about T1 and T2 being changed.

You can even do the same for strings by creating a stack S$() and a separate stack pointer PS. To save T$ on the stack, use these statements:

```
S$(PS) = T$
PS = PS + 1
```

To restore T$, use these statements:

    PS = PS − 1
    T$ = S$(PS)

Stacks are used extensively in computer programs. Some languages, like Pascal, are built on the notion of a stack machine. Pascal programs are translated by a compiler into a set of stack instructions. On these machines, not only is arithmetic evaluated on the stack, but everything is kept there, including memory for variables and return addresses for subroutines.

Stacks are also used within numerous algorithms. Quicksort, a very fast sorting routine presented in Chapter 6, depends on the stack to hold temporary values, in much the same way that we used the stack S() to save the values of T1 and T2. Other algorithms that use stacks include binary-tree searching and special window displays, both described in this book.

QUEUES

The line that bank customers make when they wait for a teller is a queue. New customers (assuming that they are polite and do not cut in) arrive at the tail of the line. When a teller is free, a customer leaves the head of the line and advances to the teller window.

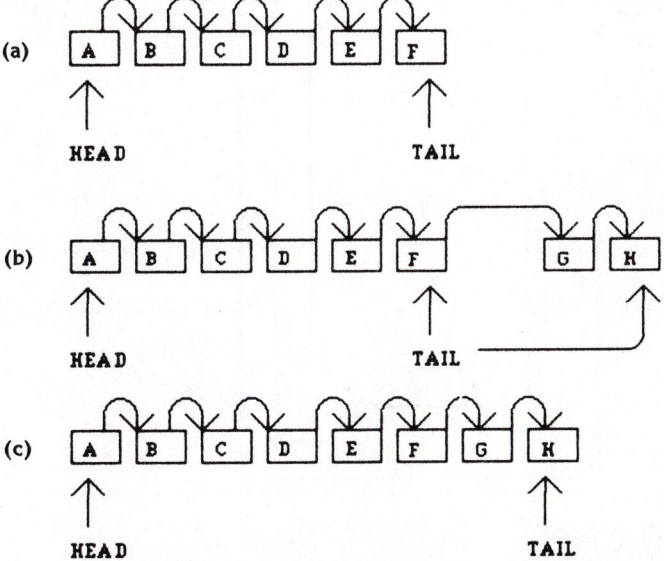

Figure 5-3 As a data structure, a queue is a list for which new items are always added at the tail and removed from the head.

Figure 5-3 shows a typical queue structure as it might appear on the computer. Elements are added to the queue as in Figure 5-3(b) and removed as in Figure 5-3(c).

Queues are often used in simulations to keep track of events. For example, in an airport simulation, aircraft are waiting for clearance to taxi to the runway, to take off, and to land. In a simulation, each of the holding points is represented

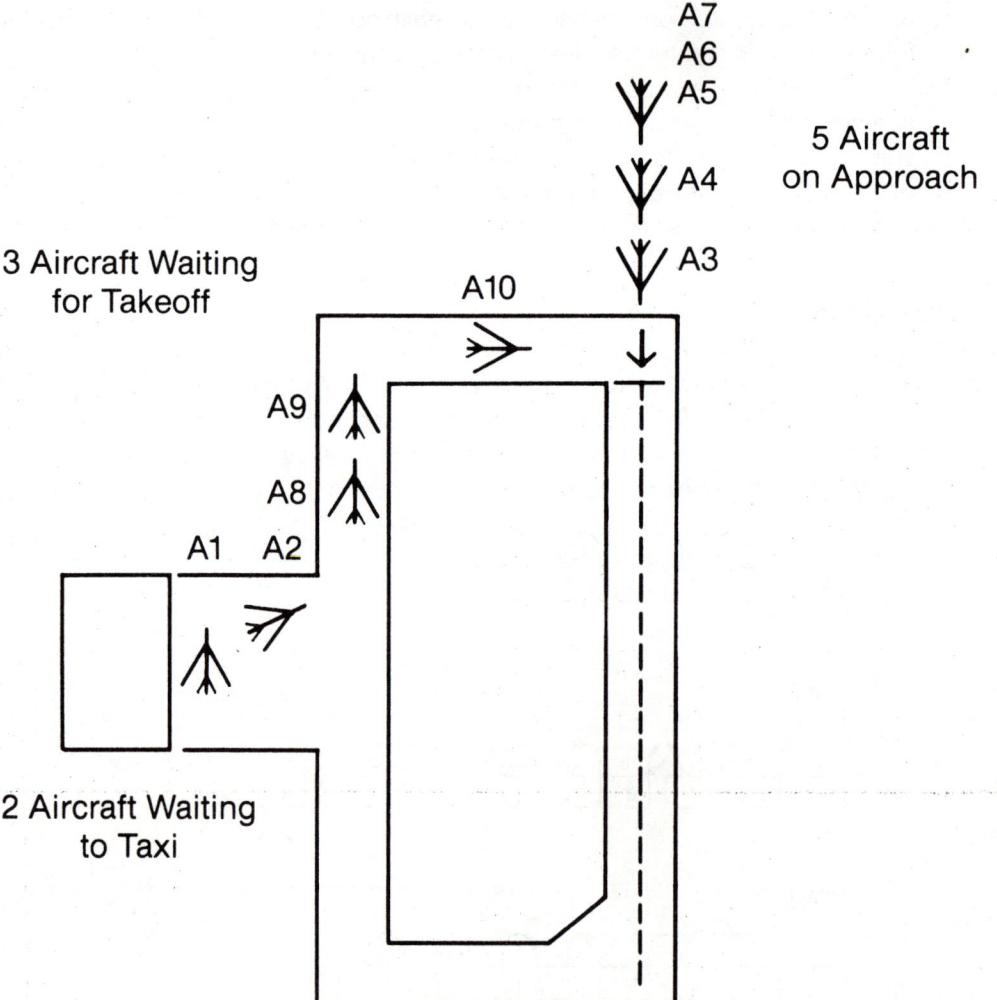

Figure 5-4(a)   *An Airport.*

Approach Queue

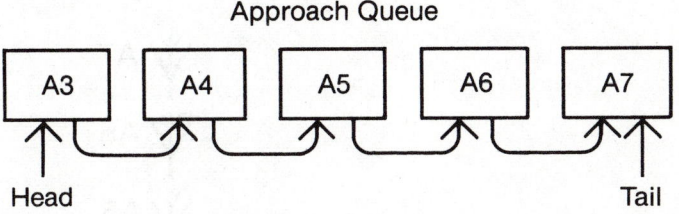

Departure Queue

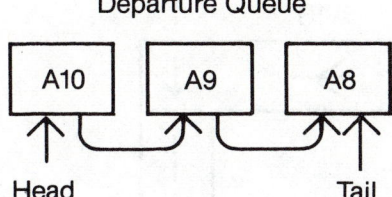

Taxi Queue

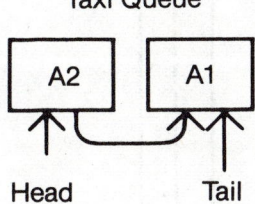

Figure 5-4(b)

by a queue structure. You'd create three queues, one to hold the aircraft waiting to taxi, one to hold the aircraft ready to take off, and one to hold the aircraft approaching for landing. Figure 5-4(a) shows an airport with five aircraft ready to land, three waiting for takeoff, and two requesting clearance to taxi. Translated to a set of queues, the airport simulation looks like that shown in Figure 5-4(b). Once aircraft A3 lands, it taxis off the side of the runway (see Figure 5-5). There it must wait for taxi clearance before continuing to the terminal. In the simulation, you represent this change by moving A3 from the landing queue and attaching it to the taxi-clearance queue. In this manner, you can simulate the operation of an airport.

Another example is a multi-user computer system in which several users want to simultaneously print on the single printer attached to the system. Since

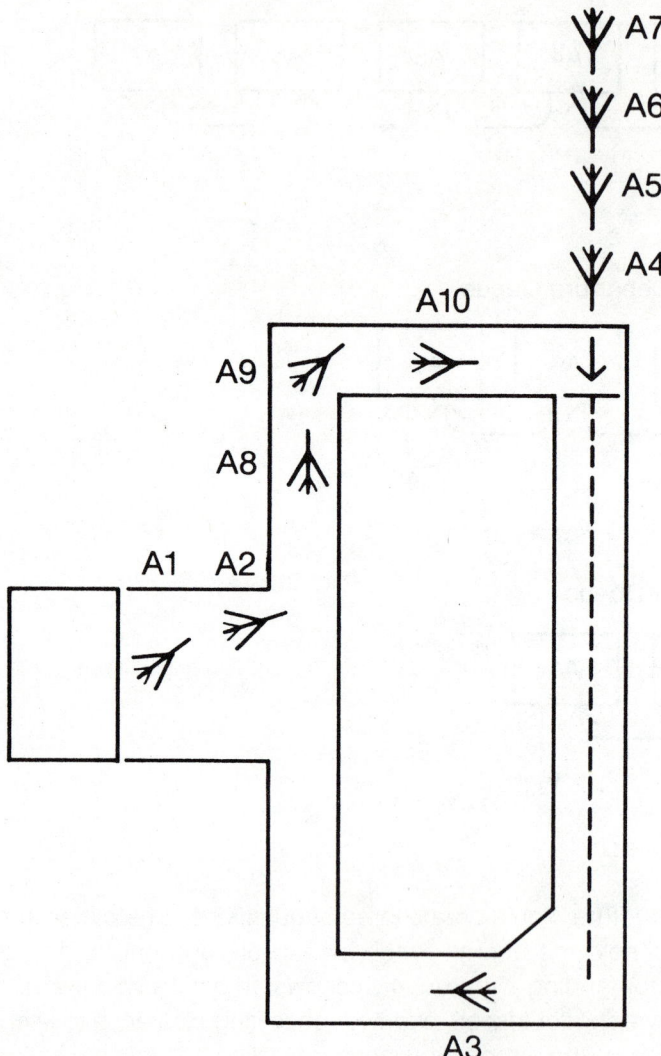

Figure 5-5(a)   *Airport simulation after A3 has landed.*

the printer can print only one file at a time, additional print requests are placed into a queue where they wait for processing by the printer. Figure 5-6 shows this queue. New print requests are added to the end of the queue. The program that does the actual printing checks the front of the queue to get the next file to print. If there are no files, then it just waits for a new print request.

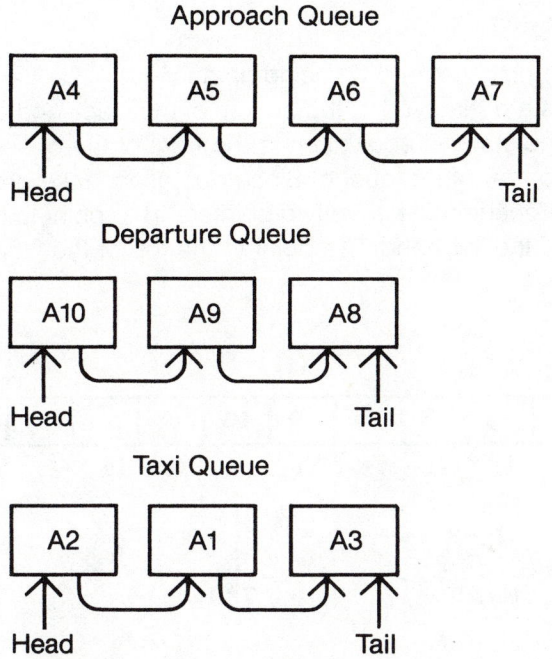

Figure 5-5(b)   *After A3 has landed, it is removed from the approach queue and added to the taxi queue.*

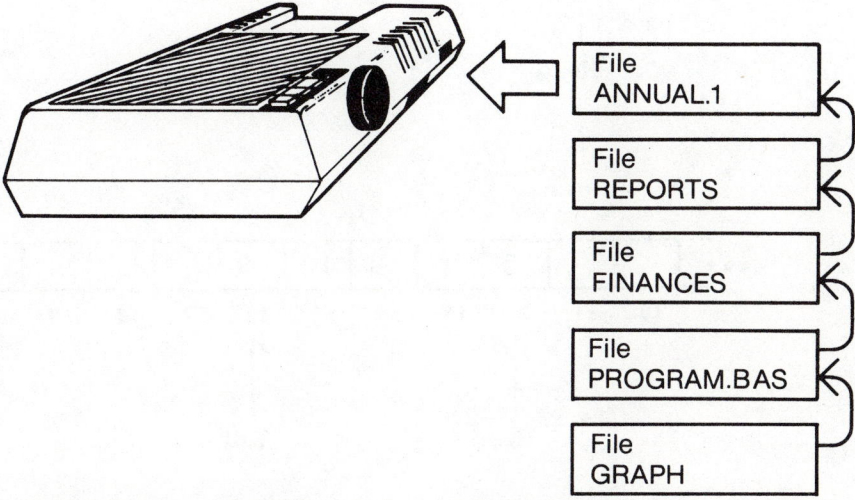

Figure 5-6   *Example of a printer queue showing four files to be printed. When GRAPH is sent to the printer, it is attached to the end of the queue rather than printing immediately.*

Programming Queues

A queue can be programmed by using a variation of the stack. To simulate a queue, elements are removed at the bottom of the stack and added at the top. The bottom of the stack is equivalent to the front of the queue, and the top is equivalent to the rear of the queue. Since operations take place at both ends of the stack, the queue must have two pointers; B to point to the bottom of the stack (or front of the line) and T to point to the top of the stack (or rear of the

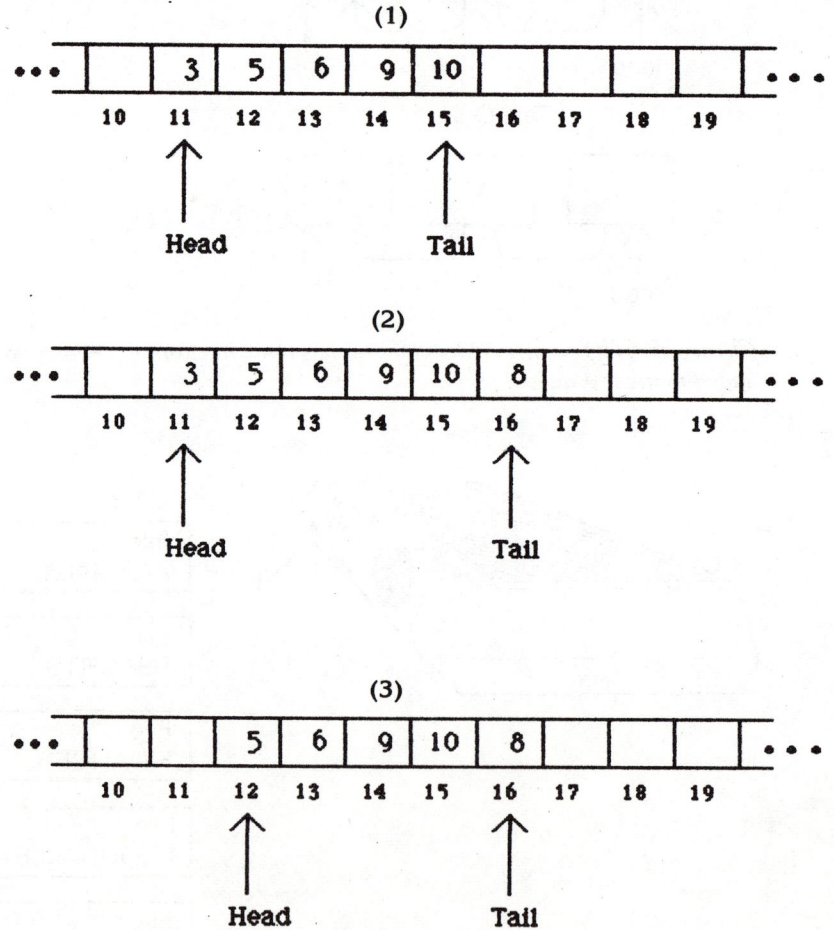

Figure 5-7(a)   *A queue data structure represented in an array. (1) shows a queue with five items. A new element is added to the tail in (2), while another is removed from the head in (3).*

line). Let DIM Q(100) be a queue having 100 elements. At first, the queue is empty, so you have

$$B = 1 \qquad and \qquad T = O$$

T is the location in Q() where you'll add the next entry. To add a value D to the end of the line or top of the queue, set

$$T = T + 1$$
$$Q(T) = D$$

Adding to the queue is the same as a push onto the stack. The major difference occurs when an element is removed from the bottom:

$$D = Q(B)$$
$$B = B + 1$$

Adding and deleting elements to the queue is illustrated by Figure 5-7(a). Initially there are five elements in the queue. At (2) a new element is added to the top and at (3) one element is removed from the bottom.

Two problems must be dealt with in this arrangement. First, what happens when either T or B exceeds 100? The solution is to reset either value to 1 so that the queue wraps around to the first element of Q(). Element 1 then follows element 100 in a circular fashion, as illustrated in Figure 5-7(b).

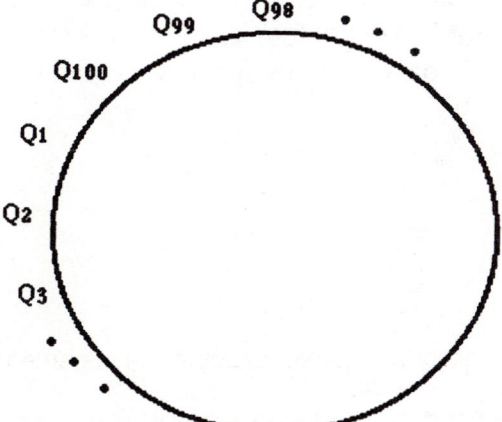

Figure 5-7(b)   *A circular queue is easily implemented in a fixed-size array. If we define DIM Q(100) as an array of 100 numbers, then the queue can be made to grow by having it "wrap around" when reaching Q(100). In effect, Q(100) is followed by Q(1). Listing 5-2 uses this technique to implement a queue structure.*

Second, if the queue has more than 100 entries the bottom overtakes the top as it goes around the circle, and data are destroyed. To detect a full queue, a variable N is used to count the number of elements in the queue. A complete set of subroutines to add and delete queue entries is shown in Listing 5-1. Before adding or deleting elements, the program should GOSUB 1000 to initialize the queue variables. The variable MAX should be set to the maximum size of the queue and a DIM Q(MAX) should be placed near the start of the program.

Listing 5-1

```
1000      REM - Initialize the Queue
1010      H = 1 :
              T = 0 :
              N = 0
1020      RETURN
2000      REM - Add an element to the head of the Queue
2010      IF N = MAX THEN F = 1 :
              RETURN ELSE F = 0
2020      N = N + 1
2030      T = T + 1
2040      IF T > MAX THEN T = 1
2050      Q$(T) = D$
2060      RETURN
3000      REM - Remove an element from Queue tail
3010      IF N = 0 THEN F = 2 :
              RETURN ELSE F = 0
3020      D$ = Q$(H)
3030      N = N - 1
3040      H = H + 1
3050      IF H > MAX THEN H = 1
3060      RETURN
```

A queue can hold more than just numbers if you change the array Q() to some other type. By changing DIM Q(100) to Q$(100) and D to D$, the queue may contain a list of names. Several arrays can hold additional data in parallel. For example, use the statements DIM Q1(100), Q2(100), and Q3(100) and let D1, D2, and D3 be additional data variables. To add the name D$ and the three numeric values, perform

$$T = T + 1$$
$$Q\$(T) = D\$$$
$$Q1(T) = D1$$
$$Q2(T) = D2$$
$$Q3(T) = D3$$

To remove data from the head of the queue, execute the statements

$$D\$ = Q(B)$$
$$D1 = Q1(B)$$
$$D2 = Q2(B)$$
$$D3 = Q3(B)$$
$$B = B + 1$$

Using Queues

To illustrate the use of queues, let's program the airport simulation described previously. For the actual simulation, you need to add an element of time because planes cannot land one after another on the runway. There must usually be at least 30 to 60 seconds between aircraft to prevent a collision. For the simulation, this means that once an aircraft lands or takes off you'll need to wait some time before using the runway again.

Use a variable called MINUTES to keep track of the number of minutes that have elapsed since the simulation began. At the start of the simulation, MINUTES will be set to zero. At each one minute interval, move aircraft and then print the contents of the queues so that you can see what has transpired.

Several assumptions are made to simplify the simulation. First, only one aircraft can be taxiing at a time. Second, assume that it takes exactly one minute to taxi from any spot on the airport to the runway. Third, aircraft that are approaching to land always have priority over all other aircraft. If an aircraft is one minute away from the runway, another aircraft can immediately take off. Otherwise, the departing aircraft must wait until the other plane has landed.

In addition, since aircraft can arrive for landing at unpredictable times, there may be cases in which no planes are on approach. For example, one plane may be just landing but the next airplane on final approach is still five minutes out. To simplify the programming of the simulation, at every one minute interval, if no new plane has entered the approach pattern, a dummy entry is added to the queue. This way, at each one minute interval during the simulation, the program can look at the landing approach queue. If the entry at the front of the queue is a dummy entry, then the program can send one of the departing aircraft on its way. The dummy entry is simply discarded.

To make the simulation interesting, aircraft will randomly request to taxi from their parking place to the runway. Further, aircraft will enter the pattern for landing at random intervals. The probability that an aircraft will appear at one of these locations can be changed. By changing the probabilities you can explore what effect differing traffic has on airport operations.

Listing 5-2(a) is the BASIC implementation of this airport simulation. Sample output is shown in Listing 5-2(b).

Listing 5-2(a)

```
10       REM - Airport Simulation
20       REM
30       REM
40       QSIZE = 20
50       DIM APPROACH.Q(QSIZE), DEPARTURE.Q(QSIZE),
         TAXI.Q(QSIZE), TAXI.DEST(QSIZE)
60       GOSUB 1000 ' Initialize Queues
70       GOSUB 2000 ' Do the simulation
```

```
80      STOP
1000    REM - Initial Queues
1010    APPROACH.P = .5 ' Initial probabities of new aircraft
1020    TAXI.P = .5
1030    REM
1040    MINUTES = 0
1050    REM
1060    APPROACH.H = 1
1070    APPROACH.T = 0
1080    APPROACH.TOTAL = 0
1090    DEPARTURE.H = 1
1100    DEPARTURE.T = 0
1110    DEPARTURE.TOTAL = 0
1120    TAXI.H = 1
1130    TAXI.T = 0
1140    TAXI.TOTAL = 0
1150    REM
1160    REM - Add the initial aircraft to the approach queue
1170    AIRCRAFT = 3 :
           GOSUB 5000
1180    AIRCRAFT = 4 :
           GOSUB 5000
1190    AIRCRAFT = 0 :
           GOSUB 5000
1200    AIRCRAFT = 5 :
           GOSUB 5000
1210    AIRCRAFT = 6 :
           GOSUB 5000
1220    AIRCRAFT = 7 :
           GOSUB 5000
1230    REM
1240    REM - Add initial aircraft to Departure queue
1250    AIRCRAFT = 10 :
           GOSUB 6000
1260    AIRCRAFT = 9 :
           GOSUB 6000
1270    AIRCRAFT = 8 :
           GOSUB 6000
1280    REM
1290    REM - Add initial aircraft to Taxi queue
1300    AIRCRAFT = 2 :
           D = 1 :
           GOSUB 7000
1310    AIRCRAFT = 1 :
           D = 1 :
           GOSUB 7000
1320    REM
1330    COUNTER = 11
1340    LANDING.AIRCRAFT = 0
1350    RETURN
1360    REM
1370    REM
2000    REM - The Simulation
2010    MINUTES = MINUTES + 1
2020    DEPARTURE.AIRCRAFT = 0
2030    REM - Check Taxi Queue
2040    IF TAXI.TOTAL = 0 THEN 2070 ' skip if none taxiing
2045    IF  DEPARTURE.TOTAL = QSIZE  THEN 2070 '
           departures is full
2050    GOSUB 7500 ' Remove from taxi queue
2060    IF D = 1 THEN GOSUB 6000 ' Add to the departure queue
2070    REM - See if an aircraft just taxiied off of the runway
2080    IF LANDING.AIRCRAFT = 0  THEN 2130 ' skip if no landings
2090    AIRCRAFT = LANDING.AIRCRAFT
2100    D = 2 ' Set destination to terminal bldg.
```

```
2110        GOSUB 7000 ' Add to taxi queue
2120        LANDING.AIRCRAFT = 0
2130        REM - Check the Approach queue for landing traffic
2140        IF APPROACH.TOTAL = 0   THEN 2170 ' skip if nobody landing

2150        GOSUB 5500 ' Remove from approach queue
2160        LANDING.AIRCRAFT = AIRCRAFT
2170        REM - Check for pending departures
2180        IF LANDING.AIRCRAFT <> 0 THEN 2200 ' skip if
               runway is in use
2190        IF DEPARTURE.TOTAL <> 0 THEN GOSUB 6500 :
               DEPARTURE.AIRCRAFT = AIRCRAFT
2195        REM
2200        GOSUB 3000 ' Display Simulation status
2210        GOSUB 4000 ' Create more aircraft
2220        GOTO 2010
2230        REM
2240        REM
3000        REM 'Display Simulation Status
3010        PRINT "Time = ";MINUTES
3020        IF LANDING.AIRCRAFT <> 0 THEN PRINT "Aircraft
               #";LANDING.AIRCRAFT;" is landing"
3030        IF DEPARTURE.AIRCRAFT <> 0 THEN PRINT
               "Aircraft #";DEPARTURE.AIRCRAFT;" is departing"
3040        REM - Display contents of queues
3050        PRINT "The Aircraft on Approach are:"
3060        I = APPROACH.H
3070        FOR J = 1 TO APPROACH.TOTAL
3080           IF  APPROACH.Q(I) <> 0  THEN PRINT APPROACH.Q(I);
3090           I = I + 1
3100           IF  I > QSIZE   THEN  I = 1
3110        NEXT J
3120        PRINT
3130        PRINT "The Aircraft Awaiting for Departure are:"
3140        I = DEPARTURE.H
3150        FOR J = 1 TO DEPARTURE.TOTAL
3160           PRINT DEPARTURE.Q(I);
3170           I = I + 1
3180           IF  I > QSIZE   THEN I = 1
3190        NEXT J
3195        PRINT
3200        PRINT "Total Aircraft Awaiting Taxi = ";TAXI.TOTAL
3210        I = TAXI.H
3220        FOR J = 1 TO TAXI.TOTAL
3230           IF TAXI.DEST(I) = 1 THEN PRINT
               "#";TAXI.Q(I);" is taxiing to departure" ELSE PRINT
               "#";TAXI.Q(I);" is taxiing to the terminal bldg"
3240           I = I + 1
3250           IF  I > QSIZE   THEN  I = 1
3260        NEXT J
3270        PRINT
3280        PRINT
3290        RETURN
3300        REM
3310        REM
4000        REM - Create Additional aircraft
4010        IF RND(1) < APPROACH.P  AND  APPROACH.TOTAL <
               QSIZE   THEN AIRCRAFT = COUNTER :
               COUNTER = COUNTER + 1 :
               GOSUB 5000 ELSE AIRCRAFT = 0 :
               GOSUB 5000
4020        IF RND(1) < TAXI.P  AND  TAXI.TOTAL < QSIZE
               THEN AIRCRAFT = COUNTER :
               COUNTER = COUNTER + 1 :
               D = 1 :
               GOSUB 7000
```

```
4030     RETURN
4040     REM
4050     REM
5000     REM - Add to Approach Queue
5010     APPROACH.TOTAL = APPROACH.TOTAL + 1
5020     APPROACH.T = APPROACH.T + 1
5030     IF  APPROACH.T > QSIZE  THEN  APPROACH.T = 1
5040     APPROACH.Q(APPROACH.T) = AIRCRAFT
5050     RETURN
5500     REM - Remove aircraft from approach queue
5510     AIRCRAFT = APPROACH.Q(APPROACH.H)
5520     APPROACH.TOTAL = APPROACH.TOTAL   - 1
5530     APPROACH.H = APPROACH.H + 1
5540     IF  APPROACH.H > QSIZE THEN APPROACH.H = 1
5550     RETURN
6000     REM - Add to Departure Queue
6010     DEPARTURE.TOTAL = DEPARTURE.TOTAL + 1
6020     DEPARTURE.T = DEPARTURE.T + 1
6030     IF  DEPARTURE.T > QSIZE   THEN  DEPARTURE.T = 1
6040     DEPARTURE.Q(DEPARTURE.T) = AIRCRAFT
6050     RETURN
6500     REM - Remove aircraft from departure queue
6510     AIRCRAFT = DEPARTURE.Q(DEPARTURE.H)
6520     DEPARTURE.TOTAL = DEPARTURE.TOTAL   - 1
6530     DEPARTURE.H = DEPARTURE.H + 1
6540     IF  DEPARTURE.H > QSIZE THEN DEPARTURE.H = 1
6550     RETURN
7000     REM - Add to Taxi Queue
7010     TAXI.TOTAL = TAXI.TOTAL + 1
7020     TAXI.T = TAXI.T + 1
7030     IF  TAXI.T > QSIZE  THEN  TAXI.T = 1
7040     TAXI.Q(TAXI.T) = AIRCRAFT
7045     TAXI.DEST(TAXI.T) = D
7050     RETURN
7500     REM - Remove aircraft from taxi queue
7510     AIRCRAFT = TAXI.Q(TAXI.H)
7515     D = TAXI.DEST(TAXI.H)
7520     TAXI.TOTAL = TAXI.TOTAL   - 1
7530     TAXI.H = TAXI.H + 1
7540     IF  TAXI.H > QSIZE THEN TAXI.H = 1
7550     RETURN
```

Listing 5-2(b)

```
Time =  1
Aircraft # 3  is landing
The Aircraft on Approach are:
 4  5  6  7
The Aircraft Awaiting for Departure are:
 10  9  8  2
Total Aircraft Awaiting Taxi =   1
# 1  is taxiing to departure


Time =  2
Aircraft # 4  is landing
The Aircraft on Approach are:
 5  6  7
The Aircraft Awaiting for Departure are:
 10  9  8  2  1
Total Aircraft Awaiting Taxi =   2
# 11  is taxiing to departure
# 3  is taxiing to the terminal bldg
```

```
Time = 3
Aircraft # 10  is departing
The Aircraft on Approach are:
 5  6  7
The Aircraft Awaiting for Departure are:
 9  8  2  1  11
Total Aircraft Awaiting Taxi =  2
# 3  is taxiing to the terminal bldg
# 4  is taxiing to the terminal bldg


Time =  4
Aircraft # 5  is landing
The Aircraft on Approach are:
 6  7  12
The Aircraft Awaiting for Departure are:
 9  8  2  1  11
Total Aircraft Awaiting Taxi =  2
# 4  is taxiing to the terminal bldg
# 13  is taxiing to departure


Time =  5
Aircraft # 6  is landing
The Aircraft on Approach are:
 7  12
The Aircraft Awaiting for Departure are:
 9  8  2  1  11
Total Aircraft Awaiting Taxi =  2
# 13  is taxiing to departure
# 5  is taxiing to the terminal bldg


Time =  6
Aircraft # 7  is landing
The Aircraft on Approach are:
 12
The Aircraft Awaiting for Departure are:
 9  8  2  1  11  13
Total Aircraft Awaiting Taxi =  2
# 5  is taxiing to the terminal bldg
# 6  is taxiing to the terminal bldg
```

At Time = 1, Listing 5-2(b) shows that aircraft 3 is landing. (You may wish to refer to Figure 5-4(a) on page 104, which shows the initial traffic pattern at the airport.) Four aircraft are still on approach and four are waiting for departure. One aircraft is at the terminal awaiting taxi clearance to the runway area.

At Time = 2, you see that aircraft 4 is now landing. This leaves just three aircraft on final approach. The number of aircraft waiting to take off has increased because aircraft 1 has finally taxied from the terminal to the departure line. An since aircraft 3 just landed, it's now waiting to taxi to the terminal. But note that aircraft 11 is just ahead of it. As part of the simulation, the program automatically creates new aircraft arrivals and departures; 11 was created automatically. At Time = 4, you see that aircraft 12 has been added to the arrivals.

At Time = 3, you see that aircraft 5 is still approaching so aircraft 10 is able to depart.

There are seven aircraft awaiting departure at Time = 6. With only one aircraft arriving, it's safe to assume that many of these aircraft will soon be able to depart.

The program operates by internally managing three separate queues, APPROACH.Q(), DEPARTURE.Q(), and TAXI.Q(). These correspond to the aircraft that are shown at the various waiting points in Listing 5-2(b).

The subroutine at line 1000 initializes all the queues, including placing the initial set of aircraft into the various locations. (If you wanted, you could leave these initialization statements out. New arrivals and departures are created automatically; therefore, the program could be self-initializing.)

The variables APPROACH.P and TAXI.P are the probability that a new aircraft will be added to approach and taxi queues, respectively, at each one minute interval. If APPROACH.P is 0.5, on approximately half of the intervals a new arrival will be added to final approach. Setting APPROACH.P to 0.9 means that 90% of the time, a new arrival will appear on approach.

Interestingly, you might think that setting APPROACH.P to 0.9 would create a large number of aircraft on final approach. But the actual results may be somewhat surprising!

Landing aircraft always have priority over all other aircraft. So what happens is that the landing aircraft come down and taxi off the runway as fast as they can. Meanwhile, all of the departures have to wait until a free space appears on final approach. The result of all this is that the queues of departing and taxiing aircraft become quite long. This is exactly what happens at real airports when long delays occur for departing aircraft.

The guts of the simulation appear in lines 2000 through 2220. After incrementing the time, the program checks the queues one by one. If there is an aircraft waiting to taxi to the departure area, then the aircraft is taken off the taxi queue and added to the tail of the departure line. Subroutine 7500 removes the aircraft from the queue, returning in variable AIRCRAFT the aircraft's number and in variable D the destination on the airport. If D is 1, the destination is the runway. If D is 2, the destination is the terminal.

At line 2140, if an aircraft just landed it is added to the taxi queue headed for the terminal. If there are any aircraft on approach, then the next in line is cleared for landing. The variable LANDING.AIRCRAFT is set to the number of the aircraft that is currently landing on the runway.

If no aircraft is currently landing (line 2180), you check to see if there are any departures. If there are, then the first plane waiting in line is sent on its way.

Finally, you display the current status of the airport simulation by calling the subroutine at line 3000. Then you GOSUB 4000 to add additional aircraft to the simulation.

Routines to add and remove elements from the queues appear in lines 5000 through 7500.

Simulations based on queues are studied with queueing theory. Examples of simulations include metropolitan mass transit systems, assembly lines, and software development projects. As mentioned earlier, the results of a simulation based on queues can be surprising.

LISTS

A list is a sequence of memory cells linked by pointers. The first group of cells has a pointer to the second group, which in turn has a pointer to the third, and so on. This is illustrated in Figure 5-8. The first element of the list is called the head and the last element is called the tail. If elements are always added at

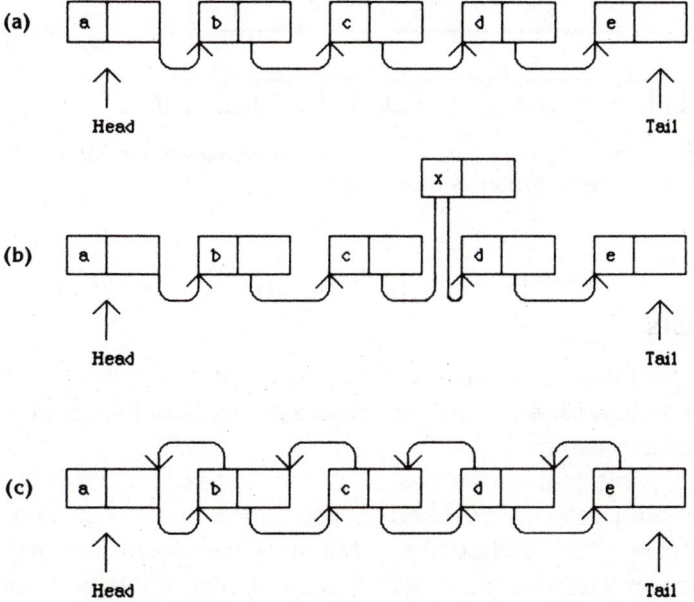

Figure 5-8 *A list is a sequence of memory cells that are linked together. (a) identifies the parts of a list structure; new elements are easily inserted or deleted simply by changing the pointer connections (b); (c) shows the addition of a backpointer so that the list can be traversed in both directions.*

the tail, the list is another way of representing a queue. The list is more powerful because new elements can be inserted anywhere by setting the appropriate pointers.

In Figure 5-8, much of memory is used for pointers and doesn't hold any data. If you increase the size of the data area, memory use improves. For example, a data type made from 16 characters and a pointer appears in Figure 5-9, in which the ratio of useful data memory to pointer memory is much higher.

In Figure 5-8, the only way to get to element D is to start at the head of the list and traverse the pointers. As shown, the list is only traversed in the direction of the pointers. But by adding a backpointer to each list element, the list can be traversed in either direction. Element C can then be reached by starting at the tail and traversing the list in the reverse direction.

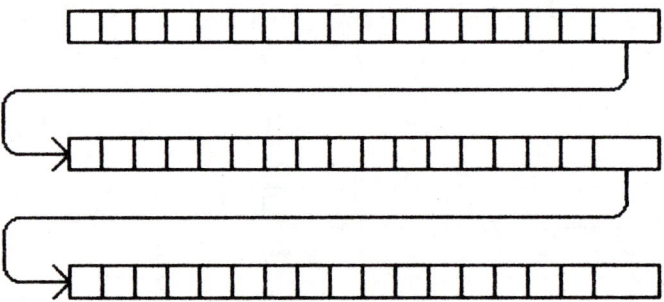

Figure 5-9   *When the data area per element is increased, the ration of useful data memory to pointer memory is much higher.*

Self-Organizing Lists

Lists are useful for tables that are subject to frequent changes because it's easy to add or delete a list entry from anywhere in the table by just changing the pointers between elements.

One type of table that undergoes a lot of changes is a self-organizing list. A self-organizing list can be used to improve a sequential search by reordering the table after each search. Chapter 4 discussed improving the sequential search by organizing the search table so that the most frequently sought names appear first. When the names are stored in a simple array, it's difficult to reorder the names this way. But with a list structure it's easy to reorder the table based on the frequency of occurrence.

The list structure is well-suited to constructing a self-organizing table. As names are added, they are attached at the head of the list. For example, when the name PAUL is added to a list already containing the names GEORGE, LISA, and BERNADETTE, the following list is produced:

To search the list for LISA, the names are examined in the sequence, PAUL, GEORGE, and finally LISA. Once LISA is found, the algorithm puts the name at the head of the list, giving:

Every time a name is found, it is relocated to the head of the list. Names that are accessed frequently stay near the front of the list, while seldom referenced names remain at the rear.

Programming Lists

As mentioned earlier, list elements do not have to appear one after the other, but may instead appear in any order. That means a simple array and a couple of head and tail pointers will not work. If a list element in the middle of the array is deleted, the program must keep track of the freed space. Otherwise, unusable holes develop.

For a list of names, three arrays are created. DIM N$(100) holds the name part of each field. DIM P(100) is the pointer to the previous entry in the list, and DIM N(100) is a pointer to the next entry in the list. Let H point to the head of the list, and let T point to the tail of the list. Like the queue, these two variables point to the first and last elements of the list, respectively. Graphically, a short list of names appears as:

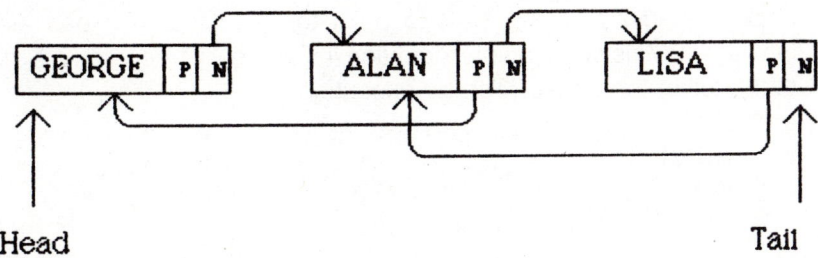

Head   Tail

The previous field for GEORGE (denoted by P) and the next field for LISA (denoted by N) don't point anywhere because they are at the head and tail of the list, respectively.

When represented as arrays, the list might appear as:

$$N\$(7) = \text{"LISA"} \qquad N(7) = 0 \qquad P(7) = 5$$
$$N\$(5) = \text{"ALAN"} \qquad N(5) = 7 \qquad P(5) = 4$$
$$N\$(4) = \text{"GEORGE"} \qquad N(4) = 5 \qquad P(4) = 0$$
$$H = 4 \qquad T = 7$$

Note that the elements are not consecutive, and that they do not have to begin at the first element in the arrays. $P(4)$ and $N(7)$ are both 0 because they don't point anywhere. By tracing the $P()$ and $N()$ pointers, verify for yourself that the three names are correctly linked. In this example, the head of the list begins at 4 with GEORGE and the tail is at 7, where LISA is located.

In the $N\$()$, $P()$, and $N()$ arrays, each of the elements is either used or unused. The used entries are all linked by the $P()$ and $N()$ pointers. To keep track of the free entries, the program may link the unused elements, again using the $P()$ or $N()$ arrays. For example, let U1 be the index of the first unused entry and let U2 be the tail of the unused list. The list consisting of GEORGE, ALAN, and LISA might be represented as follows:

	(1)	(2)	(3)	(4)	(5)	(6)	(7)	(8)
N$	—	—	—	GEORGE	ALAN	—	LISA	
P	—	—	—	0	4	—	5	
N	2	3	6	5	7	8	0	9
	U1=1			H=4			T=7	

In effect, the arrays are holding two lists simultaneously—the list of names and the list of unused entries.

To remove ALAN from the list, the entry at location 5 must be unhooked from the name list and added to the tail of the unused entries list. The deletion is performed by setting $N(4)$ to point to 7, so that it bypasses location 5. Similarly, $P(7)$ is set to point to location 4. The newly freed entry is then attached to the tail of the unused list, by executing

$$N(U2) = 5$$
$$N(5) = 0$$
$$U2 = 5$$

Listing 5-3 presents sample routines to implement a list structure. To insert names, select option A. When the program asks for the location, enter 0 and then the name. Thereafter, to add names, enter the location that the new name should follow. For example, after entering the first name, the head and tail are both set to 1. The second name is then attached after 1 by entering 1. Option D displays the list structure, showing both the list of free space and each of the list elements, including the next and previous pointers.

Listing 5-3

```
10        MAX = 100
20        DIM N$(MAX), N(MAX), P(MAX)
30        GOSUB 1000
100       PRINT "Enter A(dd R(emove D(isplay Q(uit ? ";
110       C$=INPUT$(1):
              PRINT C$
120       ON INSTR(1,"ARDQ",C$)+1 GOSUB 100,200,300,400,4060
130       REM
140       REM
200       INPUT "Enter Location ? ",G
210       INPUT "Enter Name ? ",S$
220       GOSUB 2000
230       IF F>0 THEN PRINT "Error ";F
240       RETURN
250       REM
260       REM
300       INPUT "Remove what location ? ",G
310       GOSUB 3000
320       IF F>0 THEN PRINT "Error ";F
330       RETURN
340       REM
350       REM
400       GOSUB 4000
410       PRINT "Trace of List Control Information"
420       PRINT "Free Space List -"
430       P = U1
440       IF P = 0 THEN GOTO 460
450       PRINT P,:
              P = N(P) :
              GOTO 440
460       PRINT :
              PRINT "Used Space List -"
470       PRINT " Head=";H,"Tail=";T
480       P = H
490       IF P = 0 THEN RETURN
500       PRINT "Element ";P
510       PRINT "Name=";N$(P),"Previous=";P(P),"Next=";N(P)
520       P = N(P)
530       GOTO 490
540       REM
550       REM
1000      REM - Initialize List
1010      REM - Set up list of all unused space
1020      FOR I = 1 TO MAX
1030      N(I) = I + 1
1040      NEXT I
1050      N(MAX) = 0
1060      REM - Initial unused list Head and Tail pointers
1070      U1 = 1 :
              U2 = MAX
```

```
1080     RETURN
1090     REM
1100     REM
1110     REM
2000     REM - Add an element at location G
2010     IF N = MAX THEN F = 1 :
             RETURN ELSE F = 0
2020     REM - Get a free location from the unused space list
2030     L = U1
2040     IF U1 = U2 THEN U1 = 0:
             U2 = 0 ELSE U1 = N(U1)
2050     N$(L) = S$
2060     REM - Adjust the previous pointer of adjacent element
2070     IF G > 0 THEN IF N(G) > 0 THEN P(N(G)) = L
2080     REM - Set up L's Next and Previous pointers
2090     IF G > 0 THEN N(L) = N(G) ELSE N(L) =0
2100     IF G > 0 THEN N(G) = L
2110     REM - Special case:
             Inserting before the head of a list
2120     IF G = 0 AND N>0 THEN P(H) = L :
             N(L) = H
2130     IF G = 0 THEN P(L) = 0 ELSE P(L) = G
2140     N = N + 1
2150     REM - If the insert affects the head or tail,
             then update H or T
2160     IF N = 1 OR G = T THEN T = L
2170     IF G = 0 THEN H = L
2180     RETURN
2190     REM
2200     REM
2210     REM
3000     REM - Remove an element at location G
3010     IF N = 0 THEN F = 2 :
             RETURN ELSE F = 0
3020     REM - Update the head or tail pointers if
             deleting the head or tail
3030     IF H = G THEN H = N(G)
3040     IF T = G THEN T = P(G)
3050     N = N - 1
3060     REM - Update the next and previous pointers of
             adjacent elements
3070     IF N(G) > 0 THEN P(N(G)) = P(G)
3080     IF P(G) > 0 THEN N(P(G)) = N(G)
3090     REM - Place the deleted element on the free space list
3100     IF U2 = 0 THEN U1 = G:
             U2 = G ELSE N(U2) = G
3110     P(G) = 0
3120     U2 = G
3130     N(U2) = 0
3140     RETURN
3150     REM
3160     REM
3170     REM
4000     REM - Display the list
4010     P = H
4020     IF P = 0 THEN PRINT :
             RETURN
4030     PRINT N$(P),
4040     P = N(P)
4050     GOTO 4020
4060     END
```

Using Lists

The routines in Listing 5-3 give you all the power needed to create a self-organizing list. Remember that a self-organizing list is one whose order is changed depending on what names are searched for within the list.

To program the self-organizing list, all you need is a routine that searches the list from head to tail, looking for a given name and a routine that removes the name from its current location and adds it to the head of the list. In this manner, the most frequently searched for names are always found near the head of the list. And this results in faster searches.

Listing 5-4 is the list program modified to include the searching and reordering routines. Line 5000 is the subroutine that searches the list for the name in S$. If the subroutine finds the name, it sets the variable F to 1 (otherwise, F is 0). When F is 1, G contains the location of the name.

Listing 5-4

```
10        MAX = 100
20        DIM N$(MAX), N(MAX), P(MAX)
30        GOSUB 1000
100       PRINT "Enter A)dd L)ookup R)emove D)isplay Q)uit ? ";
110       C$=INPUT$(1):
              PRINT C$
120       ON INSTR(1,"ARDLQ",C$)+1 GOSUB 100,200,300,400,600,4120
130       GOTO 100
140       REM
150       REM
200       INPUT "Enter name ? ",S$
210       REM - If list is empty then insert at 0
220       REM - Otherwise, insert in front of the head P(H)
230       IF N = 0 THEN G = 0  ELSE  G = P(H)
240       GOSUB 2000
250       IF F>0 THEN PRINT "Error ";F
260       RETURN
270       REM
280       REM
300       INPUT "Remove what location ? ",G
310       GOSUB 3000
320       IF F>0 THEN PRINT "Error ";F
330       RETURN
340       REM
350       REM
400       GOSUB 4000
410       PRINT "Trace of List Control Information"
420       PRINT "Free Space List -"
430       P = U1
440       IF P = 0 THEN GOTO 460
450       PRINT P,:
              P = N(P) :
              GOTO 440
460       PRINT :
              PRINT "Used Space List -"
470       PRINT " Head=";H,"Tail=";T
480       P = H
```

```
490      IF P = O THEN RETURN
500      PRINT "Element ";P
510      PRINT "Name=";N$(P),"Previous=";P(P),"Next=";N(P)
520      P = N(P)
530      GOTO 490
540      REM
550      REM
600      REM - Lookup a name
610      INPUT "Enter name ? ",S$
620      GOSUB 4060 ' Search
630      IF F = O THEN PRINT "Not found":
             RETURN
640      PRINT "Found at ";G
650      GOSUB 3000 ' Remove
660      G = P(H) ' Insert in front of the head
670      GOSUB 2000 ' Add at head of list
680      RETURN
690      REM
700      REM
1000     REM - Initialize List
1010     REM - Set up list of all unused space
1020     FOR I = 1 TO MAX
1030     N(I) = I + 1
1040     NEXT I
1050     N(MAX) = O
1060     REM - Initial unused list Head and Tail pointers
1070     U1 = 1 :
             U2 = MAX
1080     RETURN
1090     REM
1100     REM
2000     REM - Add an element to the list at Position G
2010     PRINT G
2020     IF N = MAX THEN F = 1 :
             RETURN ELSE F = O
2030     REM - Get a free location from the unused space list
2040     L = U1
2050     IF U1 = U2 THEN U1 = O:
             U2 = O ELSE U1 = N(U1)
2060     N$(L) = S$
2070     REM - Adjust the previous pointer of adjacent element
2080     IF G > O THEN IF N(G) > O THEN P(N(G)) = L
2090     REM - Set up L's Next and Previous pointers
2100     IF G > O THEN N(L) = N(G) ELSE N(L) =O
2110     IF G > O THEN N(G) = L
2120     REM - Special case:
             Inserting before the head of a list
2130     IF G = O AND N>O THEN P(H) = L :
             N(L) = H
2140     IF G = O THEN P(L) = O ELSE P(L) = G
2150     N = N + 1
2160     REM - If the insert affects the head or tail,
             then update H or T
2170     IF N = 1 OR G = T THEN T = L
2180     IF G=O THEN H=L
2190     RETURN
2200     REM
2210     REM
2220     REM
3000     REM - Remove an element at location G
3010     IF N = O THEN F = 2 :
             RETURN ELSE F = O
3020     REM - Update the head or tail pointers if
             deleting the head or tail
3030     IF H = G THEN H = N(G)
```

```
3040    IF T = G THEN T = P(G)
3050    N = N - 1
3060    REM - Update the next and previous pointers of
          adjacent elements
3070    IF N(G) > 0 THEN P(N(G)) = P(G)
3080    IF P(G) > 0 THEN N(P(G)) = N(G)
3090    REM - Place the deleted element on the free space list
3100    IF U2 = 0 THEN U1 = G:
          U2 = G ELSE N(U2) = G
3110    P(G) = 0
3120    U2 = G
3130    N(U2) = 0
3140    RETURN
3150    REM
3160    REM
3170    REM
4000    REM - Display the list
4010    P = H
4020    IF P = 0 THEN PRINT :
          RETURN
4030    PRINT N$(P),
4040    P = N(P)
4050    GOTO 4020
4060    ' Search for S$ in the list
4070    P = H
4080    IF  P = 0  THEN  F = 0 :
          RETURN
4090    IF  S$ = N$(P)  THEN F = 1:
          G = P :
          RETURN
4100    P = N(P)
4110    GOTO 4080
4120    END
```

To remove the name, call the subroutine at line 3000, which deletes a list entry. Then set G to H, the head pointer, and add the name at the head of the list. That's all there is to it.

To run the program, select option A to add a new name to the table. The add routine always adds new names to the list at the tail. When you wish to search, select option S, and enter the name to look for. If the name is found, it will be removed from its current location in the list and moved to the head. You can verify that all this takes place by using Option D to display the list before and after searching for a name.

TREES

Trees are used to organize data for searching, to represent the syntactic structure of compilers, and in database management systems. A family tree, illustrated in Figure 5-10(a) is a tree structure showing relationships among family members. Each of the parts of the tree has a name, as shown in 5-10(b). Since the tree is upside down, the top point is called the root, and the lines emerging downward from the root are branches. Each of the branching points is called a node.

A Family Tree

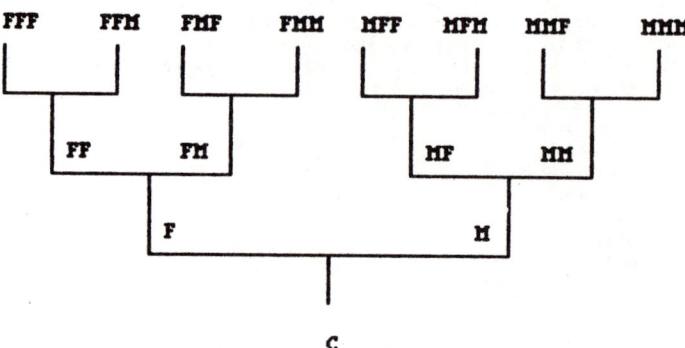

Figure 5-10(a)   The family tree *shows the relationship among family members.*

Leaves are at the extreme ends of the branches. A tree with two or fewer branches at each node is called a binary tree. Trees containing more than two branches at each node do exist, but they aren't explored in this chapter.

An ordered table could be represented as the following tree:

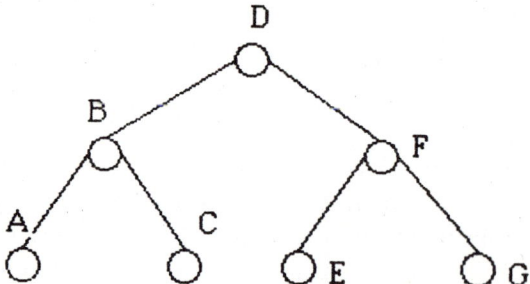

The arrows trace the table entries in alphabetical order. The D at the root position is at the alphabetic center of the table. According to Algorithm 4-1, the ordered table binary search begins at the name in the middle of the table. Similarly, the root of the tree corresponds to the middle of the table and is used as the starting position for the binary tree search.

Placing the names from Figure 4-3 into a tree gives the structure shown in Figure 5-11. Chapter 4 gave a detailed example of how to search for the name ERIC within the ordered table. That search began with the name ERIKA, which appeared at the midpoint of the ordered table. Since ERIC is alphabetically less than ERIKA, all names greater than or equal to ERIKA were removed from further consideration.

A Data Structure Tree

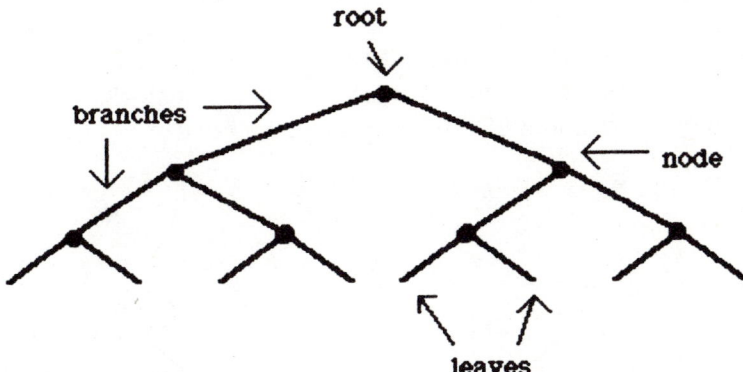

Figure 5-10(b) *In data structures, a tree is usually represented upside down, so that C would be on the top, with father and mother just beneath.*

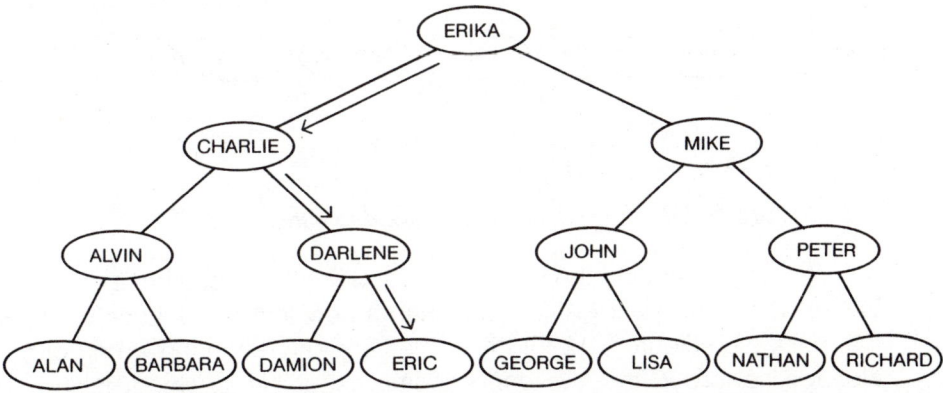

Figure 5-11 *Searching a binary tree for the name Eric. Starting at the root, Eric is less than Erika, so the name must be situated along the left branch. But since Erika is greater than Charlie, it must be to the right of Charlie. Eventually, the search finds Eric to the right of Darlene in just four tries.*

When the table is a tree structure, the binary search begins at the tree's root, where ERIKA appears. Since the names appearing on the branch to the right of ERIKA are all alphabetically greater than ERIC, that entire branch may be removed from further consideration. The search then descends the left branch to CHARLIE. Comparing CHARLIE to ERIC, the algorithm chooses the right subbranch as the only possibility, so it descends to DARLENE. But ERIC is greater than DARLENE, so the search descends to the right, where ERIC is found. The branches within the tree lead directly to the next guess, just as arithmetic is used to select the next guess when using the binary ordered table search.

Here's what happens when you search for EDWARD, a name not in the tree. The search starts like the search for ERIC, descending the left branch from ERIKA to CHARLIE, from CHARLIE to DARLENE, and from DARLENE to ERIC. At ERIC the search tries the left. The left branch doesn't exist, so the algorithm concludes that EDWARD is not in the table.

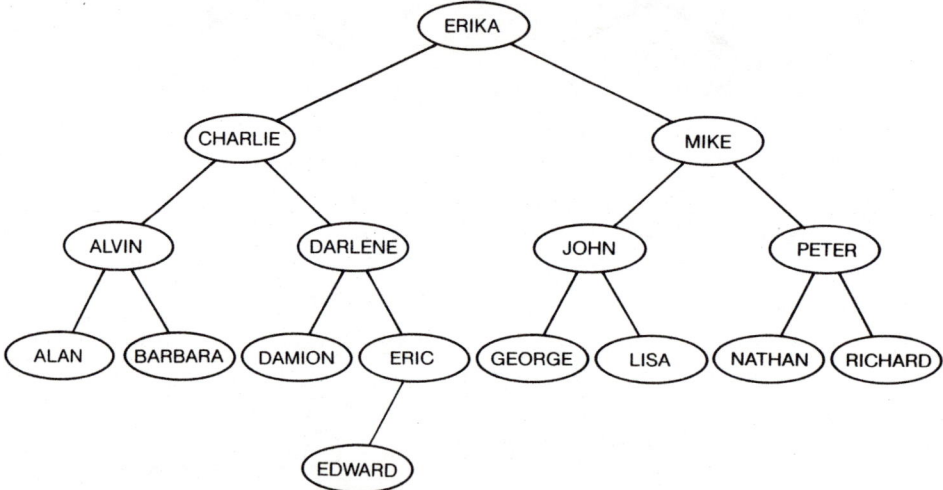

Figure 5-12   *Adding the name Edward to a tree.*

Adding a name to the tree is simple. Since the algorithm expects to find EDWARD to the left of ERIC, it attaches a new leaf and places EDWARD at that point (see Figure 5-12). If the names are entered in the wrong order, like alphabetical order, the tree can become extremely lopsided, taking on the appearance of a list:

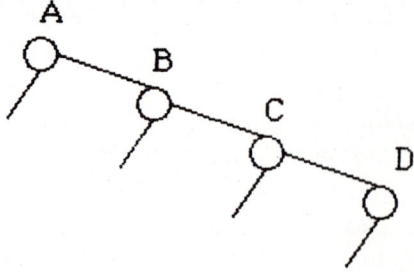

Fortunately, if you assume that the names will be entered in random order, then the tree will probably organize into a structure that is not lopsided.

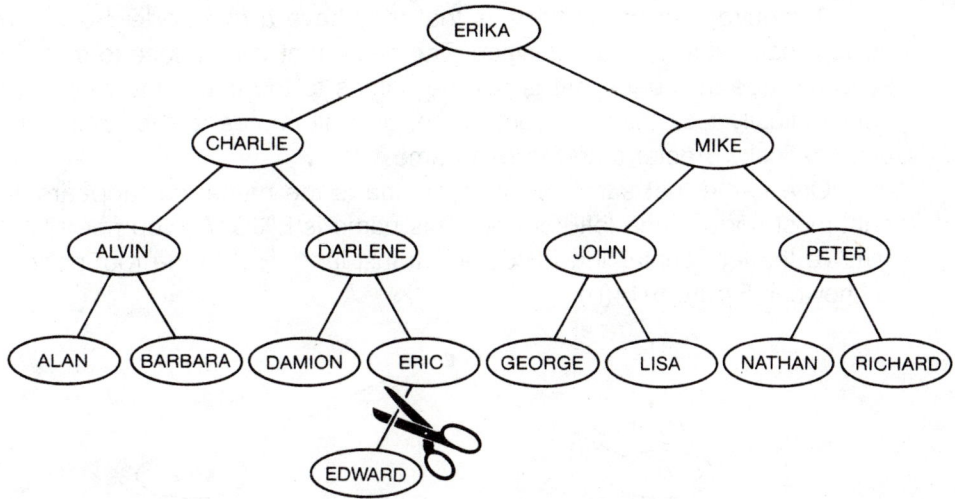

Figure 5-13   *To delete the name Edward, simply cut the branch.*

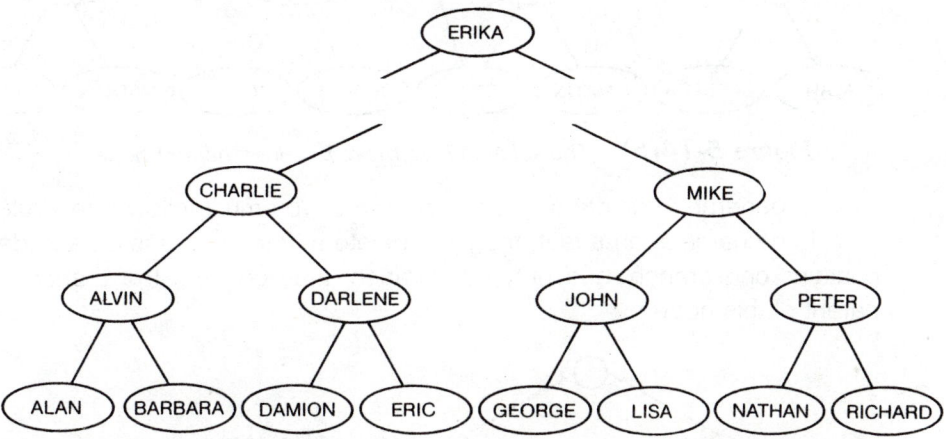

Figure 5-14(a)   *When the name Erika is deleted, the tree is split in two.*

Deleting from a Tree

You will sometimes need to delete information from a tree. Deleting a leaf from a tree is easy—just cut it off, as shown in Figure 5-13.

But if you remove the name ERIKA (see Figure 5-14a), you encounter some problems because you split the tree. There are now two branches with no root. You can't connect the two dangling branches because the tree would no longer be a binary tree. Instead, you need to do some minor tree surgery.

A requirement for all trees is that they have a root node. So you must move a name into the root position. The name that you choose to move must keep the tree in order. That is, all the names to the left of the root must be alphabetically less than the root name, and all names to the right must be alphabetically greater than the root name.

One name that satisfies these criteria is the name that appears in the right-most node of the left subtree. This name is ERIC. All you need to do is remove the leaf containing ERIC, and transplant ERIC to the root node. This is shown in Figure 5-14(b).

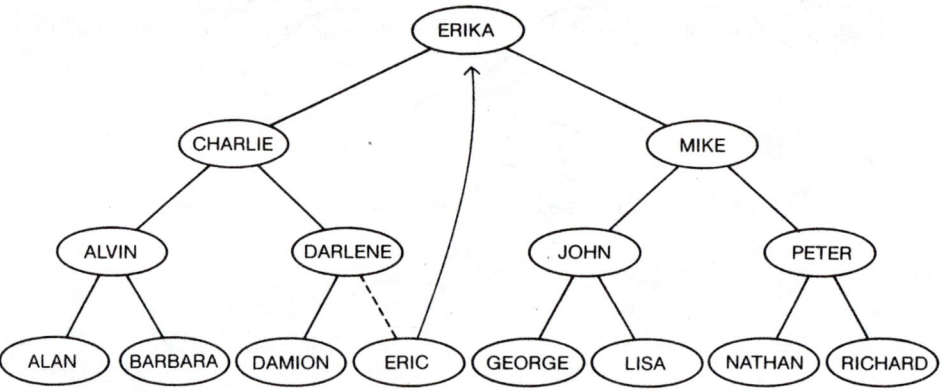

Figure 5-14(b)   *The solution is to move Eric into the root node.*

In general, to delete a name from a tree, you must follow a few rules.

If the name is on a leaf, then just delete it. If the name is on a node that contains one branch, and only one branch, then connect the branch to the parent of this node.

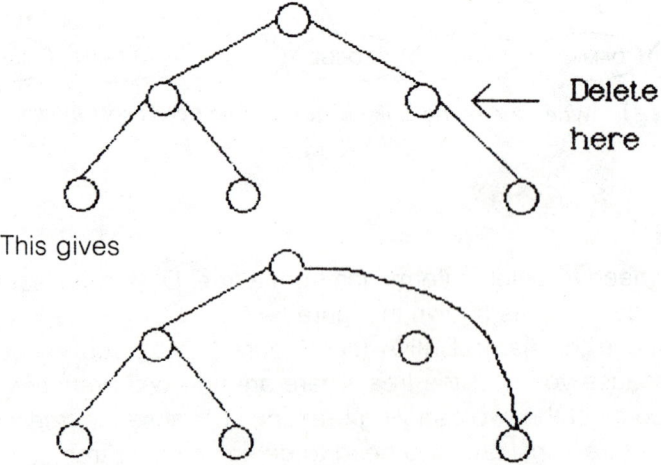

If the node contains two branches, then find the name at the right-most branch of the left subtree.

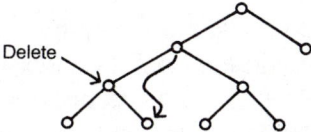

Remove this leaf node, and place its name in the node that you are trying to delete.

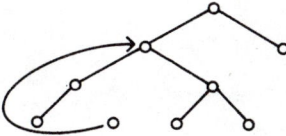

These are the rules to follow when removing a section of the tree.

Programming Trees

Trees are programmed like lists—pointers to the left and right subtrees of each node are kept in arrays. Like the list, the names are stored in array N$(). Pointers to the left and right subtrees beneath any node are kept in L() and R(), respectively.

This small tree

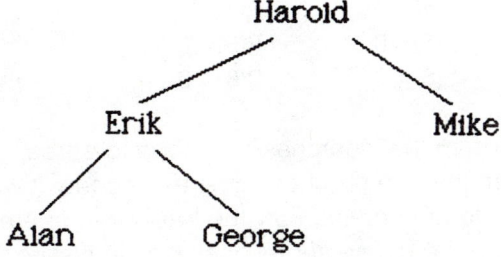

might be represented in the arrays N$(), L(), and R() as

N$(1) = "HAROLD"	L(1) = 2	R(1) = 5
N$(2) = "ERIC"	L(2) = 0	R(2) = 4
N$(3) = "ALAN"	L(3) = 0	R(3) = 0
N$(4) = "GEORGE"	L(4) = 0	R(4) = 0
N$(5) = "MIKE"	L(5) = 0	R(5) = 0

The 0 in the L() and R() values shows that there is no subtree beneath those nodes. You should verify that the values shown do indeed represent the tree structure.

New names are added to the tree by linking in a new branch and leaf at the appropriate node. First, a binary search is used to see if the name to be added already exists. If the name is already in the tree, it cannot be added. When the search ends without finding the name, it has stopped at the point where the name should appear. For example, to add RICHARD to the previous tree, the algorithm first searches the tree. RICHARD is not found to the right of MIKE, so the search terminates. Therefore, the name should be placed along a new branch descending to the right of MIKE, giving the following tree:

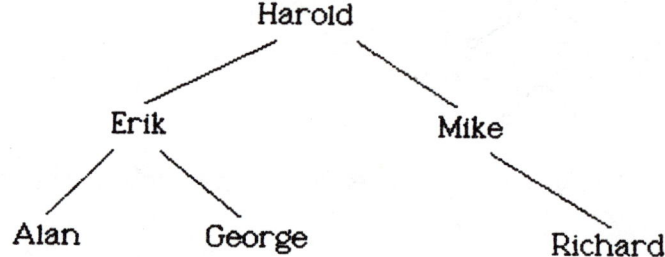

The arrays are updated to show the addition of the new name.

N$(1) = "HAROLD"	L(1) = 2	R(1) = 5
N$(2) = "ERIK"	L(2) = 0	R(2) = 4
N$(3) = "ALAN"	L(3) = 0	R(3) = 0
N$(4) = "GEORGE"	L(4) = 0	R(4) = 0
N$(5) = "MIKE"	L(5) = 0	R(5) = 6
N$(6) = "RICHARD"	L(6) = 0	R(6) = 0

Listing 5-5 is a BASIC program that searches and adds to a tree.

Because deleting from the tree requires some extra code, it will be done separately. Use Listing 5-5 to understand how the basic tree operations work before you try to understand the delete subroutine code in Listing 5-6.

Listing 5-5

```
10      MAX = 100
20      DIM N$(MAX), L(MAX), R(MAX), S(20)
21      REM - S() is a stack needed when displaying the tree
30      GOSUB 1000
40      PRINT "Enter A(dd S(earch D(isplay L(ist Q(uit ? ";
50      C$ = INPUT$(1):
        PRINT C$
```

```
60        ON INSTR(1,"ASDLQ",C$)+1 GOSUB 40, 80, 130,
             120, 170, 32767
70        GOTO 40
71        REM
72        REM
73        REM
80        INPUT "Enter Name ? ",S$
90        GOSUB 3000
100       IF F>0 THEN PRINT "Error ";F
110       RETURN
111       REM
112       REM
113       REM
120       GOSUB 4000
125       RETURN
126       REM
127       REM
128       REM
130       INPUT "Search for what name ? ",S$
140       GOSUB 2000
150       IF F = 0 THEN PRINT S$;" Is in the list at ";G
             ELSE PRINT "Error ";F
160       RETURN
170       PRINT "Root = ";R
180       FOR I = 1 TO N
190       PRINT I;N$(I),"Left=";L(I),"Right=";R(I)
200       NEXT I
210       RETURN
220       REM
230       REM
240       REM
1000      REM - Initialize Tree
1010      R = 0 :
             REM - Set Root of tree to nil
1020      RETURN
1030      REM
1040      REM
1050      REM
2000      REM - Search the tree for name s$
2010      G = R :
             G1 = R
2020      IF G = 0 THEN F = 1 :
             G = G1 :
             RETURN
2030      IF S$ = N$(G) THEN F = 0 :
             RETURN
2040      G1 = G
2050      IF S$ < N$(G) THEN G = L(G) ELSE G = R(G)
2060      GOTO 2020
2070      REM
2080      REM
2090      REM
3000      REM - Add a name S$ to the tree
3010      IF N = MAX THEN F = 4 :
             RETURN
3020      GOSUB 2000 :
             REM - See if the name is already in the tree
3030      IF F = 0 THEN F = 2 :
             RETURN ELSE F = 0
3040      N = N + 1
3050      IF G = 0 THEN R = N ELSE IF S$ > N$(G) THEN
             R(G) = N ELSE L(G) = N
3060      N$(N) = S$
3070      RETURN
4000      REM - Display the entries in the tree
```

```
4010      G = R :
          P = 0 :
          REM - P is the stack pointer
4020      IF L(G) <> 0 THEN S(P) = G :
          P = P + 1:
          G = L(G) :
          GOSUB 4020 :
          P = P - 1 :
          G = S(P)
4030      PRINT N$(G)
4040      IF R(G) <> 0 THEN S(P) = G :
          P = P + 1 :
          G = R(G) :
          GOSUB 4020 :
          P = P - 1 :
          G = S(P)
4050      RETURN
32767     END
```

Listing 5-6

```
10        MAX = 100
20        DIM N$(MAX), L(MAX), R(MAX), S(20)
30        REM - S() is a stack needed when displaying the tree
40        GOSUB 1000
100       PRINT "Enter A(dd S(earch D(isplay L(ist R)emove Q(uit ? ";
110       C$ = INPUT$(1):
          PRINT C$
120       ON INSTR(1,"ASDLRQ",C$)+1 GOSUB 100, 210, 410, 310, 450, 610, 8060
130       GOTO 100
140       REM
150       REM
200       REM - Add a name
210       INPUT "Enter Name ? ",S$
220       GOSUB 3000
230       IF F>0 THEN PRINT "Error ";F
240       RETURN
250       REM
260       REM
300       REM - Print tree
310       GOSUB 4000
320       RETURN
330       REM
340       REM
400       REM - Lookup a name
410       INPUT "Search for what name ? ",S$
420       GOSUB 2000
430       IF F = 0 THEN PRINT S$;" Is in the list at ";G ELSE PRINT "Error ";
440       RETURN
450       PRINT "Root = ";R
460       FOR I= 1 TO U1-1
470       PRINT I;N$(I),"Left=";L(I),"Right=";R(I)'
480       NEXT I
490       RETURN
500       REM
510       REM
600       REM - Remove a name
610       INPUT "Name to remove ? ",S$
620       GOSUB 2000
630       IF F <> 0 THEN PRINT "Error ";F:
          RETURN
640       GOSUB 5000
650       RETURN
660       REM
670       REM
```

```
680       REM
1000      REM - Initialize Tree
1010      R = 0 :
              REM - Set Root of tree to nil
1020      REM - Initialize free space list
1030      U1 = 1 :
              U2 = MAX
1040      FOR I = 1 TO MAX
1050      R(I) = I + 1
1060      NEXT I
1070      R(MAX) = 0
1080      RETURN
1090      REM
1100      REM
1110      REM
2000      REM - Search the tree for name s$
2010      G = R :
              G1 = R
2020      IF G = 0 THEN F = 1 :
              G = G1 :
              RETURN
2030      IF S$ = N$(G) THEN F = 0 :
              RETURN
2040      G1 = G
2050      IF S$ < N$(G) THEN G = L(G):
              D=-1 ELSE G = R(G):
              D=1
2060      GOTO 2020
2070      REM
2080      REM
2090      REM
3000      REM - Add a name S$ to the tree
3010      IF N = MAX THEN F = 4 :
              RETURN
3020      GOSUB 2000 :
              REM - See if the name is already in the tree
3030      IF F = 0 THEN F = 2 :
              RETURN ELSE F = 0
3040      N=U1:
              IF U1=U2 THEN U1=0:
              U2=0 ELSE U1=R(U1)
3050      IF G = 0 THEN R = N ELSE IF D = 1 THEN R(G) = N ELSE L(G) = N
3060      N$(N) = S$
3070      L(N)=0:
              R(N) = 0
3080      RETURN
3090      REM
3100      REM
4000      REM - Display the entries in the tree
4010      IF R = 0 THEN RETURN ' Nothing to display
4020      G = R :
              P = 0 :
              REM - P is the stack pointer
4030      IF L(G) <> 0 THEN S(P) = G :
              P = P + 1:
              G = L(G) :
              GOSUB 4030 :
              P = P - 1 :
              G = S(P)
4040      PRINT N$(G)
4050      IF R(G) <> 0 THEN S(P) = G :
              P = P + 1 :
              G = R(G) :
              GOSUB 4030 :
              P = P - 1 :
              G = S(P)
```

```
4060    RETURN
4070    REM
4080    REM
5000    REM - Remove node at G
5010    T = G
5020    IF R(G) = 0 THEN GOSUB 6000 ELSE IF L(G) = 0 THEN GOSUB 7000
            ELSE T=L(G) :
            GOSUB 8000
5030    REM - Add T to free space list
5040    IF U2 = 0 THEN U1 = T:
            U2=T ELSE R(U2) = T
5050    R(T) = 0
5060    U2 = T
5070    RETURN
5080    REM
5090    REM
6000    REM - Set parent to point to left branch of G
6010    IF R = G THEN IF R(G) = 0 THEN R = L(G) :
            RETURN
6020    IF D = - 1 THEN L(G1) = L(G) ELSE R(G1) = L(G)
6030    RETURN
6040    REM
6050    REM
7000    REM - Set parent to point to right branch of G
7010    IF R = G THEN IF L(G) = 0 THEN R = R(G) :
            RETURN
7020    IF D = -1 THEN L(G1) = R(G) ELSE R(G1) = R(G)
7030    RETURN
7040    REM
7050    REM
8000    REM - Descend along right most branch of T
8010    WHILE R(T) <> 0 :
            T1 = T :
            T = R(T) :
            WEND
8020    N$(G) = N$(T)
8030    R(T1)= L(T) ' T s parent no longer points to T
8040    IF L(G) = T THEN L(G) = L(T)
8050    RETURN
8060    END
```

The delete subroutine is at line 5000. It begins by checking to see if the node has one branch or if it has no branches. If there is no right branch (R(G)=0), it calls the subroutine at 5100. At 5100, you test to see if you are deleting the root (IF R=G). If you are, then you update R to point to the left subtree in L(G). Bear in mind that if L(G) is 0, then R is 0, and the tree is now empty.

If it is not deleting the root, the subroutine sets the parent's left or right subbranch pointers, as appropriate, to point to the left or right subbranch of the node that is being deleted. G1 is the location of the parent. If you reached the node that you are deleting by following the parent's left branch, then you update the parent's left branch pointer. If you reached this node by following the parent's right branch, then you update the parent's right branch.

A similar operation is performed at subroutine 5150, which is reached if the node you are deleting has no left branch.

If the node has both right and left branches, neither of the IF tests in line 5020 test true. You call the subroutine at 5200 to handle this case.

As described previously, you begin by finding the right-most node in the left subtree. On entry to 5200, T is the location of the top of the left subtree. If the subtree has a right branch, then line 5210 descends the right branch as far as it can.

Next, at line 5220, you copy the name at the right-most node into the node that you are deleting, hence N$(G) = N$(T). Next, the leaf whose name you just copied into node G needs to be deleted. But it's quite possible that the right-most node is not on a leaf. It might contain a left branch, as shown here:

So you set the deleted node's parent's right-branch pointer to point to the left branch of the deleted node.

Now you are almost done. You've taken care of the delete problem, but you must figure out what to do with the node that was deleted.

On the computer, a deleted node becomes an unused location in an array. You need to keep track of the unused locations so you can use them when memory starts to run short. To do all this, create a list of unused entries. Initially, all the nodes in the tree are unused. Organize an unused entry list by creating two pointers. U1 points to the head of the unused list. U2 points to the tail. Link all of the array entries into a list structure using the R() array. Initially, set R(1) to point to 2, R(2) to point to 3, R(3) to point to 4, all the way to up R(100), which doesn't point to anything because it's at the end of the list. Figure 5-15 shows how the entries are linked.

When you add a new name to the tree, you remove the entry at the head of the unused entry list. Initially, this is location 1, so the first entry goes in location 1, N$(1), L(1) and R(1). U1 is updated; the head now points to R(2).

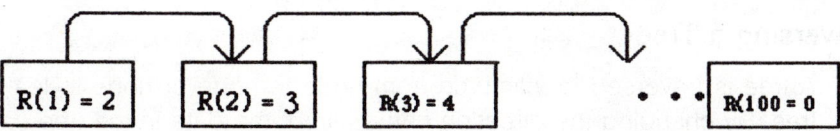

Figure 5-15   *Initially, all of the elements are linked together using the R( ) array.*

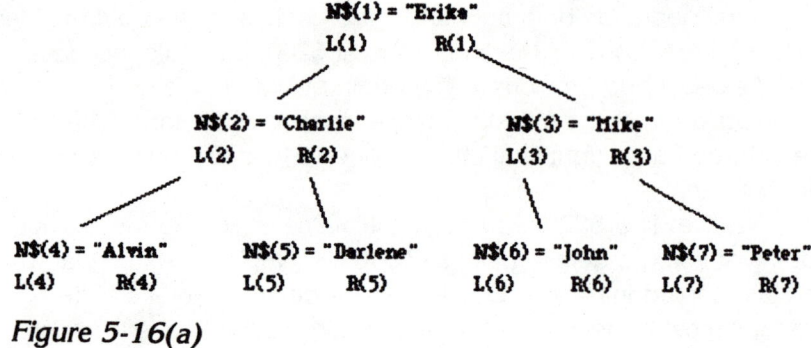

Figure 5-16(a)

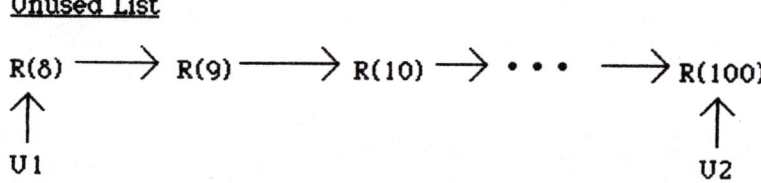

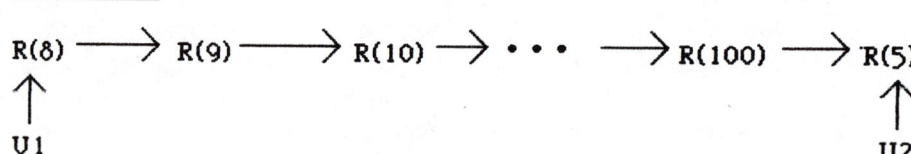

Figure 5-16(b) *After deleting the name Darlene at location 5, location 5 is added to the unused list.*

After a while, much of the array has become filled with names. See Figure 5-16(a). When you delete a name in the middle of the tree, for example, location 5, this location must be added to the free-space list. This is done by setting the entry at R(U2), which is currently the last entry in the list, to 5, and setting R(5) to 0. U2, in turn, now points to 5 because 5 is at the tail of the list. Figure 5-16(b) shows the resulting unused entry list.

Traversing a Tree

A tree is traversed by climbing from node to node or node to leaf within the tree. By changing the direction of the climb, the data in the tree can be read in either ascending or descending order.

To produce an ascending traversal (sometimes called inorder or symmetric), the traversal algorithm descends as far as it can on the left side of tree. After visiting the leaf on the far left, it moves up to the node immediately above and visits nodes along the right branch. An ascending traversal algorithm is shown in Algorithm 5-1. Algorithm 5-1 is a recursive procedure because it calls itself.

Algorithm 5-1   *In order tree traversal.*

```
Step Action
____ _____
1)   Set S = Root
2)   Traverse Tree (S) (see Algorithm 5-2)
3)   Stop
```

When programmed in BASIC, a stack is used to keep track of the return positions within the tree. To traverse the tree in Figure 5-17, S is set to 1. Since (1) has a left branch, you place 1 on a stack and descend to (2) by setting S to 2.

(a)

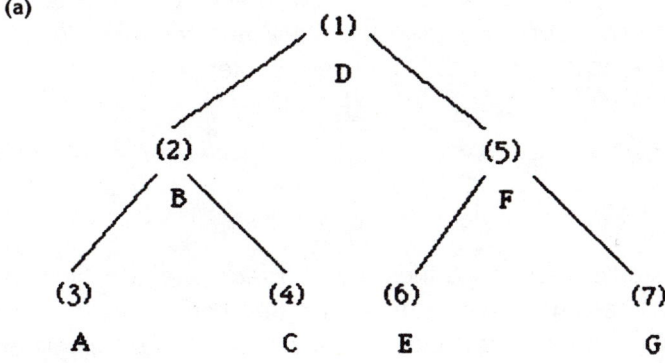

(b)

Stack

Figure 5-17(a) and (b)   *Transversing a tree. A stack-based algorithm (see Algorithms 5-1 and 5-2) reads the tree from left to right. It descends the tree as far as it can along left branches. At each node it places a return point on the stack. At (b) the algorithm has reached node (3) where it prints "A." It then pops the return node (2) from the stack and climbs back up the tree to (3) to print "B." It then descends to the right and prints "C." Finally, it returns to (1) and descends node (1)'s right branch.*

Algorithm 5-2   *Traverse tree.*

```
S is the tree to traverse

Step Action
---- ------
1)    If Left Branch (S) exists then
            PUSH S              Save S on stack
            S = Left Branch (S)
            Traverse Tree (S)
            S = POP          Get old value of S back
2)    Display the name at node S
3)    If Right Branch (S) exists then
            PUSH S
            S = Right Branch (S)
            Traverse Tree (S)
            S = POP
4)    Return
```

Since (2) has a left branch, 2 is placed on the stack and the algorithm descends to (3), which has no left branch. The algorithm goes to step 3 and prints "A". Since there is no right branch, it simply moves back up to the previous node by popping 2 from the stack and returning to step 3 of the original call in Algorithm 5-1. "B" is printed. At step 4, the algorithm descends the right branch.

RECORDS

This chapter earlier mentioned the idea of a *record* as a collection of related data, such as a person's name, address, and telephone number. This information logically belongs together. It is convenient to think of it as a single entity called a *data record*. Each piece of the record, such as name or address, is a *field* within the record. Figure 5-18 shows a name and address record.

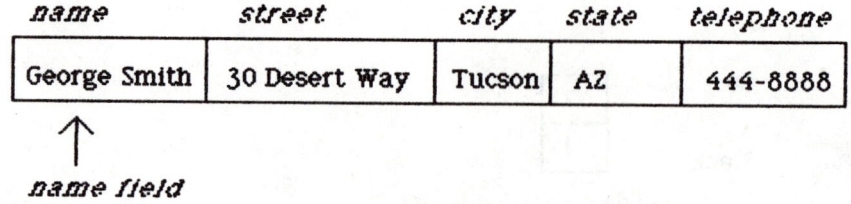

Figure 5-18   *A record is a collection of related data, such as this name and address record.*

Even though BASIC does not provide a direct representation for records, since it only has simple variables, there are a number of tricks that can be used to simulate records. You often must use logical records because the record structure provides a natural representation of the problem to be solved.

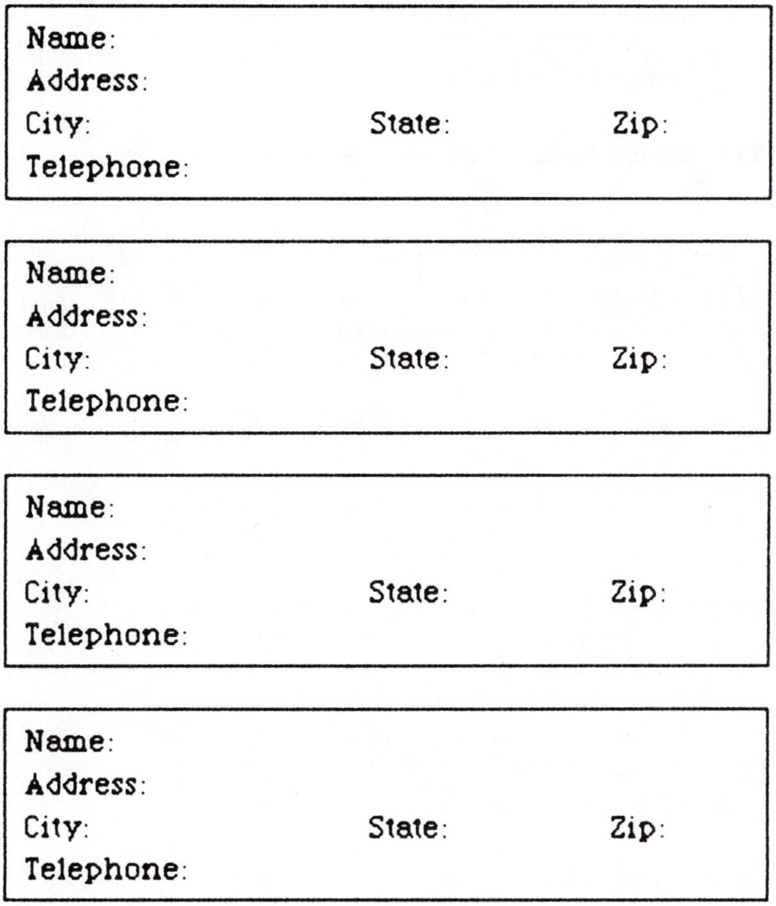

Name:
Address:
City: State: Zip:
Telephone:

Name:
Address:
City: State: Zip:
Telephone:

Name:
Address:
City: State: Zip:
Telephone:

Name:
Address:
City: State: Zip:
Telephone:

Figure 5-19   *Each entry in an address book is a record.*

For example, consider an address book like the one shown in Figure 5-19. Each entry in the book is a separate entity, yet each contains several pieces of information: name, address, and telephone number. When you remove an entry from the address book, you remove all of it—name, address, and telephone number—not just a small portion of the entry.

The first approach to creating a record is to store all of the information into a single string. For example, if you define a record with a layout like that shown in Figure 5-18, you can store each of the fields within a larger string. This means that the first 25 characters store the name, the next 40 store the address, and the next 13 store the telephone number. Call this string R$. Figure 5-20 shows how the record is mapped onto the characters in R$.

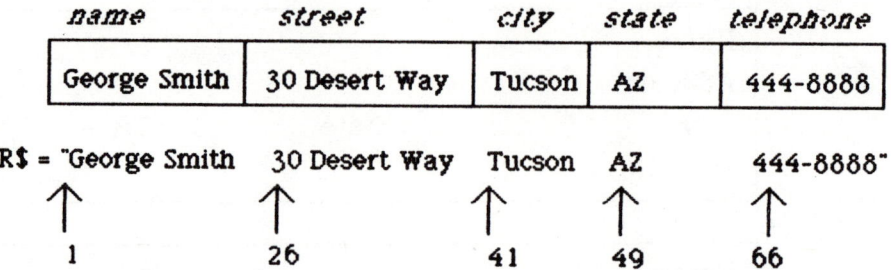

Figure 5-20 *A typical record can be stored as a single BASIC string by combining all of the fields together. To reference a particular field, use the MID$() function. For example, to extract the city field, use MID$(R$, 41, 8).*

To look at the name field within R$, you need to use the MID$() function,

    PRINT MID$(R$, 1, 25)

which displays the leftmost characters within R$. Similarly, the address is extracted with

    PRINT MID$(R$, 26, 40)

and the telephone number field is extracted with

    PRINT MID$(R$, 66, 13)

To assign values to R$, you use the LEFT$() and MID$() functions. For example, to change the name field in R$ to GEORGE SMITH, type

    N$ = "GEORGE SMITH"
    R$ = N$ + SPACE$(25 − LEN(N$)) + MID$(R$, 26)

The first part of this statement adds blanks to N$ so that there are 25 characters in the name field. In this example, N$ has a length of 12, so the SPACE$() function creates the number of blanks equal to SPACE$(25-12) or SPACE$(13).

If you're not familiar with SPACE$(), try the following examples. SPACE$() returns a string containing the number of blanks that you have requested. For example,

    PRINT "/";SPACE$(10);"/"

prints 10 blanks between the slashes. Similarly,

PRINT "/";SPACE$(50);"/"

displays 50 blanks between the slashes.

The MID$() function used in the statement

R$ = N$ + SPACE$(25 − LEN(N$)) + MID$(R$, 26)

appends the remaining portion of R$ to the first 25 characters. MID$() normally has a third parameter specifying the number of characters to extract. For example, MID$(R$,1,3) begins at postion 1 and returns the next three characters in R$. When the third parameter is omitted, MID$() returns the remainder of the string. In this case, MID$(R$,26) means all the characters in R$ beginning at position 26 and continuing to the end of the string.

To set the address field, you need to use

R$ = LEFT$(R$,25) + ADDRESS$ + SPACE$(40 −
    LEN(ADDRESS$)) + MID$(R$, 66)

Records like this can be combined into arrays, as in

DIM R$(100)
    "
    "
    "

R$(I) = N$ + SPACE$(25 − LEN(N$)) + MID $(R$(I), 26)

When you store data on a disk, using this form means you need only output the single record R$ to the disk.

Another way to store this type of information is to use separate arrays— one for the name, one for the address, and one for the telephone number:

DIM NAMES$(100), ADDRESS$(100), TELEPHONE$(100)

This form makes it easy to store, search, and retrieve information:

NAMES$(I) = "GEORGE SMITH"
ADDRESS$(I) = "11 MAIN STREET, SOUTH"
TELEPONE$(I) = "444-8888"

A disadvantage of this method is that if you add a new record to the middle of these arrays, then you must make a hole in all of the arrays to make room for the next entry. Figure 5-21 illustrates what must be done to shift the arrays upward to make room for the new entry.

```
NAMES$(1)        = "ALAN"              NAMES$(1)        = "ALAN"
ADDRESS$(1)      = "27 FLUID WAY"      ADDRESS$(1)      = "27 FLUID WAY
TELEPHONE$(1)    = "786-9876"          TELEPHONE$(1)    = "786-9876"

NAMES$(2)        = "JULIE"             NAMES$(2)        =
ADDRESS$(2)      = "19 MAGNETICS DR"   ADDRESS$(2)      =
TELEPHONE$(2)    = "345-8465"          TELEPHONE$(2)    =

NAMES$(3)        = "LANCE"             NAMES$(3)        = "JULIE"
ADDRESS$(3)      = "789 COM LANE"      ADDRESS$(3)      = "19 MAGNETICS
TELEPHONE$(3)    = "234-1234"          TELEPHONE$(3)    = "345-8465"

NAMES$(4)        = "TESSIE"            NAMES$(4)        = "LANCE"
ADDRESS$(4)      = "234 STOCKS RD"     ADDRESS$(4)      = "789 COM LANE
TELEPHONE$(4)    = "234-2348"          TELEPHONE$(4)    = "234-1234"

                                      NAMES$(5)        = "TESSIE"
                                      ADDRESS$(5)      = "234 STOCKS R
                                      TELEPHONE$(5)    = "234-2348"
```

Figure 5-21   *When the name "CHARLIE" is added to the record array, the items locations 2, 3, and 4 must be moved into the next higher locations.*

TABLES

Numbers are often arranged into tables for readability. Spreadsheet programs arrange all work into cells on the screens, which are really just entries within a table. Figure 5-22 shows a table of income information for the hypothetical Scented Drug Company, makers of the famous Lemony-Fresh Polio Vaccine, New Improved Strawberry Flavored Penicillin, and Insulin-On-Tap.

On the left side of the chart are names of the months. Across the top are the years 1975, 1976, 1977, 1978, 1979, and 1980. Within the table, each entry holds the revenue for the indicated month of the year.

In IBM BASIC, you can store this information in a table as a *two-dimensional* array. You have already seen that you can define an array as

DIM NAMES$(100)

You can also add a second subscript to an array by including the second dimension in the DIM statement. To create an array to store the table shown in Figure 5-22, define array TABLE() as

DIM TABLE(12,6)

	1975	1976	1977	1978	1979	1980
JAN	100	110	115	130	140	155
FEB	100	109	112	132	139	150
MAR	101	110	114	129	137	157
APR	104	112	116	131	136	149
MAY	102	111	117	125	131	143
JUN	99	116	103	120	143	143
JUL	104	118	109	123	147	149
AUG	106	105	104	108	150	153
SEP	109	111	108	119	135	155
OCT	110	112	111	123	135	156
NOV	111	113	113	125	138	159
DEC	112	114	115	127	139	160

Figure 5-22   *Table of income figures for the Scented Drug Company.*

This allocates space for 12 rows and 6 columns. This is represented as

TABLE(1,1) TABLE(1,2) TABLE(1,3) TABLE(1,4) TABLE(1,5) TABLE(1,6)
TABLE(2,1) TABLE(2,2) TABLE(2,3) TABLE(2,4) TABLE(2,5) TABLE(2,6)
TABLE(3,1) TABLE(3,2) TABLE(3,3) TABLE(3,4) TABLE(3,5) TABLE(3,6)

and so on.

In this form, the entry corresponding to July 1975 is stored in TABLE(7,1) because 7 corresponds to July and 1 to 1975. Similarly, the entry for June 1977 is in TABLE(6,3).

REVIEW

- Data structures organize information. The proper organization makes processing data easier and more efficient.
- A stack is like a stack of plates in a cafeteria. New items are added to the stack by pushing them onto the top. Existing items are removed by popping them from the top. Stacks are essential in implementing many

algorithms. They are also useful for storing temporary results and for evaluating arithmetic expressions.

- Queues are like waiting lines. New items are added at the end of the line, while items that have been waiting are removed from the front of the line. Queues are useful for keeping track of multiple events and for storing information.
- Lists are memory cells linked by pointers. A structure like the self-organizing list produces a sequence of names that can be searched fairly quickly, especially when only a few names are searched for most of the time.
- Trees are data structures that resemble an upside down tree, with a root at the top and leaves at the bottom. Trees are used for keeping track of information in filing systems, command processors, and in applications like geneology. They combine the flexibility of lists with the speed of the binary search.
- Records store related pieces of information as a single entity. The information in each record is subdivided into fields.
- Tables can be used to store any type of data that is arranged into rows and columns. In IBM BASIC, you use two-dimensional arrays to store the table.

C H A P T E R
6
Sorting

Sorting may at first seem like a simple problem for solving with a computer. There a number of fairly simple sorting methods that you may have discovered on your own. But there are also several fast sorting techniques that are not very obvious. This chapter presents several sort algorithms, from the simple to the extremely clever.

You may want to scan through an entire array of numbers and select the lowest number. Here's a simple way to find the lowest number:

```
10   M = 9999
20   FOR I = 1 TO N
30      IF X (I)<M THEN M = X(I):J = I
40   NEXT I
```

This routine operates by setting M to some arbitrarily large number. Each time through the loop, if X(I) is less than the current value, M is given that value. In this way, M is assigned a new low value each time a lower value is found. At the end of the loop, M is equal to the lowest value in array X(). The variable J remembers the location of the lowest number. To see how the routine works, you might run through it by hand.

A sort based on selecting the lowest number from an array is known as a selection sort. Unfortunately, this is quite slow, especially when the array is large. There are sorts that work faster than simple selection sorts.

147

CHOOSING A SORT PROCEDURE

Some techniques are obviously better than others. But how much better? How do you choose a sort?

By analyzing parameters associated with each algorithm, such as the total number of comparisons and exchanges expected for a list, a simple formula may be derived to indicate the speed of a sort. For example, a sort called the bubble sort requires about n^2 time units to sort a list of n numbers. This means that the time is roughly equal to the size of the list squared. Doubling the size of n quadruples the time needed to perform the sort.

Another way to evaluate sort performance is to time the sorts with different arrays. The resulting times can be plotted. Figure 6-1 is a graph that shows the sorting time required by four sorting methods.

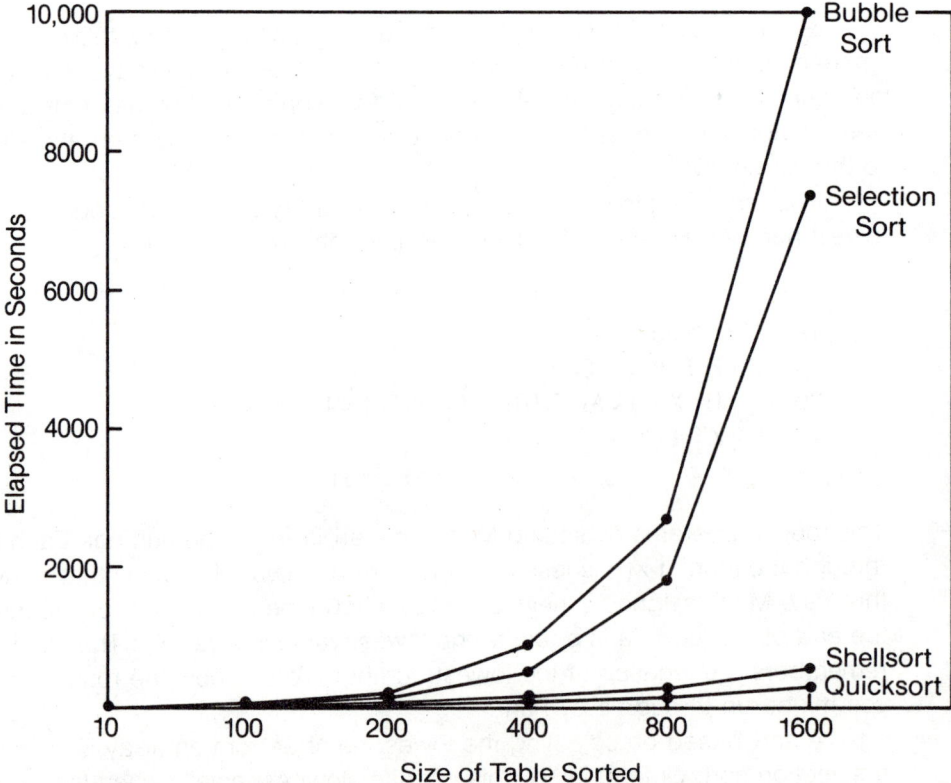

Figure 6-1 *A comparison of running time versus table size for four sorting algorithms. Bubble sort takes more than 10,000 seconds to sort 1,600 numbers, while Quick sort takes about 350 seconds.*

Keep in mind that when the data records are almost ordered, the sort algorithms may behave much differently than expected.

Of course, the speed of the sort may be irrelevant, simply because the computer functions so quickly. Sometimes you may not care whether the sort runs in one hour or eight hours. Keep in mind that the difference in sorting performance becomes a factor only when the amount of data increases, and then only when the time in human terms becomes significant.

SELECTION SORT

Selection sort is the first sort to be discussed in detail. To sort the following array into ascending order

$S1(1)$	$S1(2)$	$S1(3)$	$S1(4)$	$S1(5)$	$S1(6)$
7	11	12	3	31	9

the selection sort starts at the left and scans the list for the lowest number. It finds the lowest value at position $S1(4)$. The contents of the cell is printed and $S1(4)$ is set to 99999, giving

$S1(1)$	$S1(2)$	$S1(3)$	$S1(4)$	$S1(5)$	$S1(6)$
7	11	12	99999	31	9

By setting $S1(4)$ to 99999, the algorithm eliminates the number at $S1(4)$ from further consideration. It then repeats the scan, this time choosing 7. The number is printed and $S1(1)$ is set to a large number.

$S1(1)$	$S1(2)$	$S1(3)$	$S1(4)$	$S1(5)$	$S1(6)$
99999	11	12	99999	31	9

The algorithm loops through the list until all the values in S1() are set to the same large value. Listing 6-1 is a simple selection sort.

Listing 6-1

```
1        REM - Simple Selection Sort
10       DIM S1(100)
20       N = 1
100      INPUT "Enter number (-999 when done)? ",S1(N)
110      IF S1(N) = -999 THEN GOTO 200
120      N = N + 1
130      GOTO 100
200      N = N - 1
210      GOSUB 1000    ' Sort the array S1()
400      STOP
```

```
999        REM - Simple Selection Sort Subroutine
1000       FOR I = 1 TO N
1010       S = 999999!
1020       FOR J = 1 TO N
1030          IF S1 (J) < S THEN S = S1 (J):
              L = J
1040       NEXT J
1050       PRINT S1(L),
1060       IF POS(0) > 60 THEN PRINT
1070       S1 (L) = 999999!
1080       NEXT I
1090       RETURN
```

LINEAR SELECTION WITH REPLACEMENT SORT

The linear selection with replacement sort scans the list until finding any number that is lower than the first, but not necessarily the lowest overall. Once a number is found, the two values are exchanged, and the algorithm continues searching. For example, using

(1)	(2)	(3)	(4)	(5)	(6)
9	11	12	7	31	3

the scan begins at (1) and compares 9 to the other numbers. As soon as 7 is found, the two numbers are exchanged.

(1)	(2)	(3)	(4)	(5)	(6)
7	11	12	9	31	3

Resuming at (5), the algorithm finds 3 at (6). Three is less than 7; the two numbers are exchanged, giving

(1)	(2)	(3)	(4)	(5)	(6)
3	11	12	9	31	7

At this point, the first number in the list is the lowest number. The algorithm begins a second pass at (2). It scans until (4), and an exchange produces

(1)	(2)	(3)	(4)	(5)	(6)
3	9	12	11	31	7

Finally, (2) is compared to (6) and the two values are exchanged.

(1)	(2)	(3)	(4)	(5)	(6)
3	7	12	11	31	9

Now the first two numbers of the list are in order. Beginning at (3), the sort continues to scan the list. It scans until all of the numbers are in ascending order.

The linear selection sort with replacement is shown in Listing 6-2.

Listing 6-2

```
1         REM - Linear Selection Sort
10        DIM S1(100)
20        N = 1
100       INPUT "Enter number (-999 when done)? ",S1(N)
110       IF S1(N) = -999 THEN GOTO 200
120       N = N + 1
130       GOTO 100
200       N = N - 1
210       GOSUB 1000   ' Sort the array S1()
300       FOR I = 1 TO N
310       PRINT S1(I),
320       IF POS(0) > 60 THEN PRINT
330       NEXT I
400       STOP
999       REM - Linear Selection Sort Subroutine
1000      FOR I = 1 TO N - 1
1010        FOR J = I TO N
1020          IF S1 (J) < S1 (I) THEN T = S1 (J):
              S1(J) = S1(I):
              S1(I) = T
1030        NEXT J
1040      NEXT I
1050      RETURN
```

INSERTION SORT

The ordered table binary search described in Chapter 4 is an insertion sort. The ordered table keeps the names in alphabetical order. In effect, the searching method both searches and sorts. A new piece of data is added by inserting it into the correct position in the list. To add 13 and 8 to the list

    3   7   9   11   31

you just insert each number at the appropriate position. This gives

    3   7   9   11   31
                    ∧   ∧
                    8   13

An insertion sort removes one number from the input and inserts it into the sorted output list. For example, to sort the list

    9   3   12   7   5

the insertion sort begins by creating an empty table. It then reads the first number from the input, 9, and adds it to the table. This gives two tables. The one on the left is the sorted table and the one on the right is the remaining input.

9   3   12   7   5

Next, 3 is removed from the input and added to the ordered table, giving

3   9   12   7   5

Then 12 is added to the ordered table, giving

3   9   12   7   5

Then 7 is added, giving

3   7   9   12   5

Finally, the last number is read from the input, giving

3   5   7   9   12

Notice how adding the numbers to an ordered table produces a sorted table.

See algorithms 6-1(a) and 6-1(b) and Listing 6-3 for examples of programming the binary search insertion sort routine. As each number is entered (lines 210 through 240), a call is made to the search routine at 2000. The search routine returns G as the location preceding the insertion point. The subroutine at line 1000 then adds the number to the table. When you use the search routine for sorting, you do not care whether the number already exists in the table. You need uniqueness only when you search for a specific item, such as a name.

Algorithm 6-1(a)   *The ordered table binary search insertion sort.*

```
Inserts  names or numbers into an ordered table,  using a  binary
search to locate the proper point for the insertion.

S$  is  the  name  to add to the table.   N$()  is  an  array  of
alphabetically  arranged  names.   N  is  the  number  of  names
currently in the array.

Step        Action
----        ------
 1          Do Algorithm 6.1(b) to find the proper insertion point.
 2          Add the name into the table at G + 1
 3          Return
```

Algorithm 6-1(b)   *Perform binary search on a table.*

Searches for S$ in the table, returning G equal to the position
where the name was found, or equal to the position just before
where the name should be added.

Step	Action
1	Set L = 1 and R = N, as the initial bounds of the interval over which to search.
2	Let G = INT ((L + R)/2) Make a guess midway between L and R
3	If R < L Then S$ was not found. Return with G being one less than where we should add the name.
4	If S$ = N$(G) Then return with G being the location where S$ was found in the table.
5	IF S$ < N$(G) Then we do not need to check any more entries to the right. Set R = G − 1 Else We do not need to check any entries to the left, Set L = G + 1
6	Goto Step 2

Listing 6-3

```
10        MAX = 100
20        DIM N (MAX)
100       INPUT "A)dd numbers, D)isplay Sorted List? ",C$
110       IF C$ = "A"  THEN GOSUB 200
120       IF C$ = "D"  THEN GOSUB 300
130       GOTO 100
200       ' Add numbers and sort them
210       INPUT "Number (-999 when done)? ",S
215       IF  S = -999  THEN RETURN
220       GOSUB 2000                          ' Find where to put the number
230       GOSUB 1000                          ' And put it into the list
240       GOTO 210
300       ' Display the sorted list
310       GOSUB 3000
320       PRINT
330       RETURN
1000      REM ------------------------------------------------------------
1010      REM - Add a number
1020      IF N = MAX THEN F = 2 :
              RETURN ELSE F = 0
1030      N = N + 1
1040      FOR I = N TO G + 1 STEP -1
1050        N(I) = N(I - 1)
1060      NEXT I
1070      N(G+1) = S
1080      RETURN
2000      REM ------------------------------------------------------------
2010      REM - Find the location for the next number
2020      L = 1 :
              R = N :
              REM - Set left and right boundaries
2030      G = INT ( (L + R) / 2 )              ' Make guess between boundaries
2040      IF R < L THEN F = 0 :
              RETURN
2050      IF S = N(G)  THEN F = 1 :
              RETURN
2060      IF S < N(G)  THEN R = G - 1 ELSE L = G + 1
2070      GOTO 2030
```

```
3000      REM ------------------------------------------------------
3010      REM - Print the table of sorted numbers
3020      FOR I = 1 TO N
3030         PRINT N(I),
3040      NEXT I
3050      PRINT
3060      RETURN
```

Algorithms 4-2 and 4-3 and Listing 4-3 in Chapter 4 illustrate the insertion sort technique on an array of character strings. The same algorithms may be applied to numeric arrays by changing the string variables to numeric variables.

The insertion sort does not require that any particular data structure or search technique be used. Depending on the requirements of the data, an array, binary tree, or linked list may be used to represent the data, and a sequential, binary, or binary tree search may find the position at which to insert the new name.

One problem with insertion sorts is that the actual insertion can be fairly time-consuming because so many numbers or strings have to be moved around in memory. There is a trick that can speed up typical insertion sorts, especially when you're sorting strings or data kept in disk files. The trick is described later in this chapter.

SHELLSORT

The Shellsort, named for its creator, Donald Shell, divides a list into many small partitions. The numbers within each partition are then sorted. For example, if you start with the list

(1)	(2)	(3)	(4)	(5)	(6)	(7)	(8)
7	11	12	3	31	9	6	13

and partition it into pairs of elements, you get the list

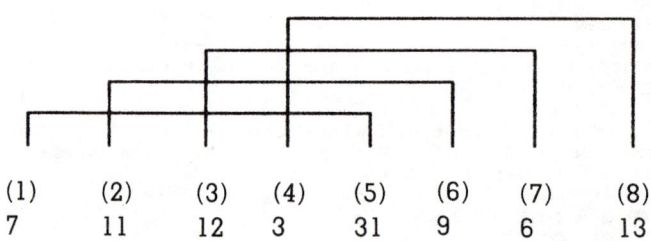

(1)	(2)	(3)	(4)	(5)	(6)	(7)	(8)
7	11	12	3	31	9	6	13

in which (1) is paired with (5), (2) with (6), (3) with (7), and (4) with (8). Each pair is then sorted. Exchanging (2) and (6) and (3) and (7) produces the list

(1)	(2)	(3)	(4)	(5)	(6)	(7)	(8)
7	9	6	3	31	11	12	13

Next, the partitions are doubled so that each contains four elements, giving

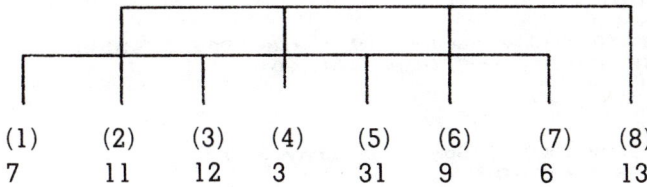

(1)	(2)	(3)	(4)	(5)	(6)	(7)	(8)
7	11	12	3	31	9	6	13

The four elements within each of these partitions are sorted to give

(1)	(2)	(3)	(4)	(5)	(6)	(7)	(8)
6	3	7	9	12	11	31	13

Finally, the partitions are doubled again, this time to encompass the entire list. Note that the list is almost sorted. The first four elements are in the wrong relative positions, but they are indeed the first four elements of the sorted list. The final list is produced by interchanging three adjacent pairs of numbers at locations (1) and (2), (5) and (6), and (7) and (8).

The reason that the Shellsort is fast is because it makes relatively few passes through the list. In the previous example, four iterations sorted eight numbers. In the selection sort, the number of iterations equaled the size of the list.

There are relatively few comparisons because the partition is doubled with each iteration, so it very soon equals the size of the list to be sorted. This is similar to a binary search, in which the list is halved at each comparison. In effect, the Shellsort is like a binary sort because it does a similar doubling operation.

Because of this, the number of iterations is approximately equal to the base 2 logarithm of the list size. (Remember, that's the number of times that the list size can be divided by 2. Sixteen can be divided by 2 exactly 4 times, so the base 2 logarithm of 16 is 4.) You can see that Shellsort can sort a large list much faster than a selection sort.

Shellsort Listing

The Shellsort is shown in BASIC in Listing 6-4. The variable D is the distance between elements within a single partition. Statement 1050 selects the partition to sort. Statements 1060 through 1110 sort the elements of the partition.

Listing 6-4

```
1          REM - Shellsort
10         DIM S1(100)
20         N = 1
100        INPUT "Enter number (-999 when done)? ",S1(N)
110        IF S1(N) = -999 THEN GOTO 200
120        N = N + 1
130        GOTO 100
200        N = N - 1
210        GOSUB 1000    ' Sort the array S1()
300        FOR I = 1 TO N
310        PRINT S1(I),
320        IF POS(0) > 60 THEN PRINT
330        NEXT I
400        STOP
999        REM - Shellsort Subroutine
1000       D = 4
1010       IF D < N THEN D = D + D :
             GOTO 1010
1020       D = D - 1                          ' Let D = largest power of 2 <
1030       D = INT (D/2)
1040       IF D < 1 THEN RETURN
1050       FOR J = 1 TO N - D
1060         FOR I = J TO 1 STEP -D
1070           IF S1(I + D) > S1(I) THEN GOTO 1120
1080           T = S1(I)
1090           S1(I) = S1(I + D)
1100           S1(I + D) = T
1110         NEXT I
1120       NEXT J
1130       GOTO 1030
```

QUICKSORT

The linear selection sort algorithm requires n^2 time units to sort a list of n entries. If the list is split in two, the problem becomes one of sorting two smaller lists, each taking $(n/2)^2$ time units. If n = 10, then the sort takes $n^2 = 100$ time units to sort the list. Dividing the list into two smaller lists of n = 5 gives a sorting time of $5^2 + 5^2 = 50$, which is less than the original time needed. (This does not include the time needed to merge the sorted lists after the sort.)

The Quicksort algorithm, invented by C. A. R. Hoare, uses a divide and conquer approach. It divides the list into subproblems. A number called the pivot value is chosen, and all numbers less than the pivot are placed to the left of the pivot and all numbers greater than the pivot are placed to the right of the pivot. To sort the list containing 9, 31, 11, 7, 12, and 3, you choose the first number in the list, 9, as the pivot value. All numbers less than 9 are arranged to the left of the pivot value and all the numbers that are greater are arranged to the right. This gives two partitions. The partitioning looks like the following tree:

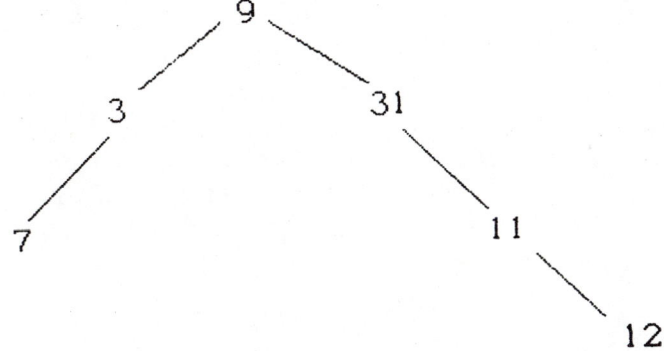

Each partition will be subdivided. There are just two numbers in the left subbranch: they are easily sorted to give

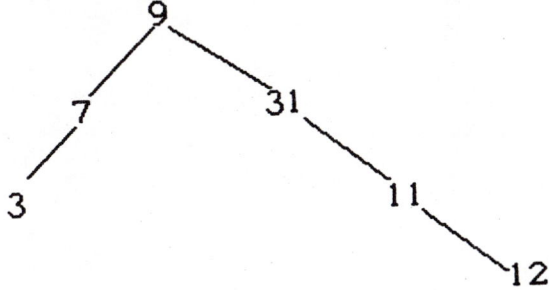

The next step is to select a pivot value for the right subbranch and to partition it. Choosing 12 as the pivot value yields

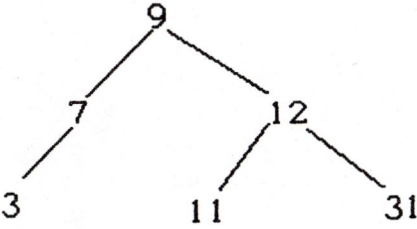

After only three partitions, the list is sorted into the tree shown above. Traversing the tree from left to right yields the sorted list.

Selecting the Pivot Value

There are number of variations of Quicksort, and they vary particularly with respect to choosing the pivot value. Ideally, the pivot should be the median of the list, so that it yields two nearly equal partitions. You can simply choose the first value in the list as the pivot point. If the list is nearly sorted, which is often the case, that is a poor choice because it likely will be the lowest number in the list.

The last value in the list is also a very poor choice when the list is almost sorted. If you think the list is almost sorted, then the middle entry is a good choice. Other choices include averaging the first, last, and middle elements of a partition or averaging a random sample from the list.

Programming Quicksort

Rather than using a tree structure for Quicksort, it is much faster and easier to use an array structure, especially in BASIC. Let the numbers

9	31	11	7	12	3

be contiguous numbers in an array. To partition the array, select 9 as the pivot value and reorder the array as

9	3	7		11	12	31
		<9		>9		

The first three numbers are less than or equal to the pivot, and the last three numbers are all greater than the pivot.

To partition the array, you create two pointers I and J, and set them as follows:

9	31	11	7	12	3
I					J

Let X equal the pivot value of 9. Advance I to the right until finding a number greater than X. This yields

9	31	11	7	12	3
	I				J

Next, decrement J to the left until finding a number less than the pivot. In this case, 3 is less than 9, so J does not need to move. Exchange the two numbers pointed to by I and J, giving

```
    9       3      11      7      12      31
            I                      J
```

Repeat the procedure, advancing I to the right. Then decrement J to the left until reaching a number less than 9.

```
    9       3      11      7      12      31
                    I      J
```

The two numbers are exchanged and the first partition is completed, giving two new partitions.

```
    9       3       7              11      12      31
                    I              J
```

All numbers at or to the left of I are less than or equal to 9, and those to the right are greater. It is now up to the algorithm to sort the two smaller sections. The easiest way to do that is to have Quicksort call itself to partition and sort each of the smaller sections.

Quicksort Algorithm

Quicksort is shown in Algorithm 6-2. After the first partitioning, Quicksort calls itself to sort the two smaller sections. Unfortunately, recursive subroutines cannot be programmed directly in BASIC because each call to the subroutine needs its own copy of the variables. For example, the Quicksort subroutine sorts the numbers between L and R, but as soon as Quicksort is called again, the old values of L, R, I, and J will be lost when the variables are set to the edges of the new partition. Obviously, the values need to be saved. An initial solution might be to write something like

```
R1 = R
J1 = J
```

to save the values of R and J. But what happens if the call to Quicksort, in turn, causes another call to Quicksort? Ultimately, R1 and J1 will be set to some other values.

The solution is to store R and J on a stack. Each time that Quicksort is called, R and J are pushed. For example, to sort the original list, L and R are 1 and 6, respectively. After calling the partitioning routines, two new partitions are created: 1 to 3 and 4 to 6. Quicksort is called recursively to sort each of the two subproblems. The necessary values are placed on the stack, and Quicksort is called. On return, the original values are restored from the stack.

Algorithm 6-2   *Quicksort (L,R).*

On entry, L is the lower bound of a partition and R is an upper bound. This algorithm sorts the numbers in the array S1() between L and R. The partitioning routine is described in the text and is shown in Listing 6.5.

```
Step        Action
----        ------
1           Partition ( L, I, J, R )
2           If  R - L = 1  Then
              If  S1(R) > S1(L)  Then  Exchange S1(R), S1(L)
            Otherwise,
              Quicksort ( L, I )    - Sort the left partition
              Quicksort ( J, R )    - Sort the right partition
```

Quicksort Listing

Listing 6-5 shows Quicksort in BASIC. Even this algorithm can be improved. The stack S() is quite large. The space needed for the stack can be reduced by calling Quicksort to sort the smaller of the two intervals first. This trick is shown in Listing 6-6. The comparison at line 1060 determines which interval is smaller and sets up the values for L and R as appropriate. By sorting the smaller interval, you don't have to stack as much return information. In fact, the maximum size of the stack is equal to n log n, where n is the size of the list to be sorted.

Listing 6-5

```
1          REM - Quicksort
10         DIM S1(100), S(200)                ' S() is a stack for quicksort
20         N = 1
30         P = 1                              ' Initial stack pointer
100        INPUT "Enter number (-999 when done)? ",S1(N)
110        IF S1(N) = -999 THEN GOTO 200
120        N = N + 1
130        GOTO 100
200        N = N - 1
210        L = 1
220        R = N
230        GOSUB 1000                         ' Sort the array S1()
300        FOR I = 1 TO N
310        PRINT S1(I),
320        IF POS(0) > 60 THEN PRINT
330        NEXT I
400        STOP
1000       REM - Quicksort Subroutine
```

```
1010      IF L >= R - 1 THEN GOTO 1160
1020                                              ' Subrtn. 2000 Partitions the segment

1030      GOSUB 2000              \              ' segment between L and R
1040      IF J > R THEN GOTO 1170
1050      P = P + 2                               ' Push J and R on to stack
1060      S (P) = J :
             S (P-1) = R
1070      R = I                                   ' Call Quicksort to sort the
1080                                              ' segment between L and R
1090      GOSUB 1000
1100      L = S (P)                               ' Restore L = J and R from
1110      R = S (P - 1)                           ' the save values on the stack
1120      GOSUB 1000                              ' Sort the second partition
1130                                              ' Pop the saved data from the stack
1140      P = P - 2:
             RETURN                     ' and return
1150                                              ' If only 2 elements
1155                                              ' then do a quick comparison and
1156                                              ' exchange if necessary
1160      IF R - L = 1 THEN IF S1(R) < S1(L) THEN T = S1(L):
             S1(L) = S1(R):
             S1(R) = T
1170      RETURN
2000      REM
2010      REM
2020      REM
2030      REM
2040      REM - Partition the segment between L and R, returning I and J
2050      I = L :
             J = R
2060      X = (S1(I) + S1(J) + S1((I + J)/2))/3 ' Compute pivot value
2070                                              ' Increment I until Finding an
2075                                              ' S1(I) > then X
2080      IF I > R THEN GOTO 2170
2090      IF S1(I) < X THEN I = I + 1:
             GOTO 2080
2100      REM
2110      ' Decrement J Until finding an S1(J) < than X
2120      IF J < L THEN GOTO 2170
2130      IF S1(J) > X THEN J = J - 1:
             GOTO 2120
2140                                              ' If needed, exchange the values at




2150                                              ' S1(I) and S1(J)
2160      IF I < J THEN T = S1(I):
             S1(I) = S1(J):
             S1(J) = T:
             I = I + 1:
             J = J - 1:
             GOTO 2080
2170      I = J :
             J = J + 1                   'Return I and J at edges of partition
2180      RETURN
```

Listing 6-6

```
1         REM - Quicksort Using Trick to Reduce Stack Size
10        DIM S1(100), S(20)                    ' S() is a stack for quicksort
20        N = 1
30        P = 1                                 ' Initial stack pointer
100       INPUT "Enter number (-999 when done)? ",S1(N)
```

```
110     IF S1(N) = -999 THEN GOTO 200
120     N = N + 1
130     GOTO 100
200     N = N - 1
210     L = 1
220     R =•N
230     GOSUB 1000                              ' Sort the array S1()
300     FOR I = 1 TO N
310     PRINT S1(I),
320     IF POS(0) > 60 THEN PRINT
330     NEXT I
400     STOP
1000    REM - Quicksort Subroutine
1010    IF L >= R - 1 THEN GOTO 1160
1020                                            ' Subrtn. 2000 Partitions the segment
1030    GOSUB 2000                              ' segment between L and R
1040    IF J > R THEN GOTO 1170
1050    P = P + 2                               ' Push J and R on to stack
1055                                            ' Sort the smallest partition first
1060    IF  (I - L) > (R - J)  THEN  S(P) = L :
        S(P - 1) = I :
        L = J ELSE S(P) = J :
        S(P - 1) = R :
        R = I
1070    R = I                                   ' Call Quicksort to sort the
1080                                            ' segment between L and R
1090    GOSUB 1000
1100    L = S (P)                               ' Restore L = J and R from
1110    R = S (P - 1)                           ' the save values on the stack
1120    GOSUB 1000                              ' Sort the second partition
1130                                            ' Pop the saved data from the stack
1140    P = P - 2:
        RETURN                      ' and return
1150                                            ' If only 2 elements
1155                                            ' then do a quick comparison and
1156                                            ' exchange if necessary
1160    IF R - L = 1 THEN IF S1(R) < S1(L) THEN T = S1(L):
        S1(L) = S1(R):
        S1(R) = T
1170    RETURN
2000    REM
2010    REM
2020    REM
2030    REM
2040    REM - Partition the segment between L and R, returning I and J
2050    I = L :
        J = R
2060    X = (S1(I) + S1(J) + S1((I + J)/2))/3 ' Compute pivot value
2070                                            ' Increment I until Finding an
2075                                            ' S1(I) > then X
2080    IF I > R THEN GOTO 2170
2090    IF S1(I) < X THEN I = I + 1:
        GOTO 2080
2100    REM
2110    ' Decrement J Until finding an S1(J) < than X
2120    IF J < L THEN GOTO 2170
2130    IF S1(J) > X THEN J = J - 1:
        GOTO 2120
2140                                            ' If needed, exchange the values at
2150                                            ' S1(I) and S1(J)
2160    IF I < J THEN T = S1(I):
        S1(I) = S1(J):
        S1(J) = T:
        I = I + 1:
        J = J - 1:
```

```
            GOTO 2080
2170    I = J :
            J = J + 1
2180    RETURN
```
                                                      'Return I and J at edges of partition

SORTING STRINGS

All of the examples shown so far sort arrays of numbers, but the examples can also be used with arrays of character strings and with records in disk files. The linear selection sort shown in Listing 6-2 is altered to sort character strings by changing the appropriate variables. (See Listing 6-7.)

Listing 6-7

```
1       REM - Linear Selection Sort Using Strings
10      DIM S$(100)
20      N = 1
100     INPUT "Enter string (CR when done)? ",S$(N)
110     IF S$(N) = "" THEN GOTO 200
120     N = N + 1
130     GOTO 100
200     N = N - 1
210     GOSUB 1000   ' Sort the array S$()
300     FOR I = 1 TO N
310     PRINT S$(I),
320     IF POS(0) > 60 THEN PRINT
330     NEXT I
400     STOP
999     REM - Linear Selection Sort Subroutine
1000    FOR I = 1 TO N - 1
1010      FOR J = I TO N
1020        IF S$ (J) < S$ (I) THEN T$ = S$ (J):
          S$(J) = S$(I):
          S$(I) = T$
1030      NEXT J
1040    NEXT I
1050    RETURN
```

Unfortunately, sorting character strings is very inefficient because entire strings need to be shifted around in memory. Microcomputers (and most large computers), do not perform that operation very well. But you don't have to move the strings around. Instead, an array of pointers is used to point to each name in the array to be sorted. Then the pointers, rather than the strings, are exchanged. An example makes this clear. Let D$() be this array of names:

D$(1)	D$(2)	D$(3)	D$(4)	D$(5)
LISA	ALAN	GEORGE	TED	ALICE

Let P() be an array of pointers, initially set as

P(1)	P(2)	P(3)	P(4)	P(5)
1	2	3	4	5

Now, to sort the list of names, exchange the pointer locations as follows:

P(1)	P(2)	P(3)	P(4)	P(5)
2	5	3	1	4

After the sort, D$() is unchanged. Only the P() values have been exchanged. Note that D$(P(1)) = ALAN, which is the first name in the sorted list and D$(P(2)) = ALICE, which is the second name. Verify for yourself that D$(P(I)), for I equals 1 to 5, does indeed yield the sorted list of names. A linear selection sort using pointers is shown in Listing 6-8. Each P(I) value is initialized to I, so that P(1) equals 1, P(2) equals 2, P(3) equals 3, and so on. This initialization occurs at line 115. At line 1020, which compares the strings, only the pointers are exchanged.

Listing 6-8

```
1          REM - Linear Selection Sort Using Strings and Pointers
5          DEFINT A-Z
10         DIM S$(100), P(100)
20         N = 1
100        INPUT "Enter string (CR when done)? ",S$(N)
110        IF C$(N) = "" THEN GOTO 200
115        P(N) = N
120        N = N + 1
130        GOTO 100
200        N = N - 1
210        GOSUB 1000          ' Sort the array S$()
300        FOR I = 1 TO N
310        PRINT S$(P(I)),
320        IF POS(0) > 60 THEN PRINT
330        NEXT I
400        STOP
999        REM - Linear Selection Sort Subroutine
1000       FOR I = 1 TO N - 1
1010         FOR J = I TO N
1020           IF S$ (P(J)) < S$ (P(I)) THEN T = P (J):
                 P(J) = P(I):
                 P(I) = T
1030         NEXT J
1040       NEXT I
1050       RETURN
```

This technique can be used with all the sorting algorithms. For greatest efficiency, the P() array should be declared as an integer array. In IBM BASIC you can do this in two ways:

1. Append % to each integer variable name, as in

```
FOR I% = 1 TO N%
   P%(I%) = I%
NEXT I%
```

2. Define all integer variables with the DEFINT, statement, as in

DEFINT I, P

and then code the statements normally. BASIC automatically uses integers whenever it sees variables I and P. See your IBM PC BASIC manual for details.

Integer variables make most FOR-NEXT loops execute about 30 times faster.

Pointers should also be used when sorting records in a data file. Rather than reading a record from the file and exchanging it with another record elsewhere in the file, simply rearrange the pointers. This and other techniques for sorting disk files are described in Chapter 9.

Quicksort with Strings

Quicksort is excellent for sorting strings. However, special care must be given to selecting the pivot.

You can make the pivot, P$, the first, middle, or last string in the list to be sorted. But as noted earlier, a better approach is to compute the average of several items in the list.

How do you compute the average of a group of strings? Certainly you cannot add them like numbers. But you can convert the strings to numbers by using the string's ASCII codes. The easiest operation is to average the ASCII codes that are used for just the first characters of the first, middle, and last strings in the partition interval. If N$(1), N$(50), and N$(100) are three names to be averaged, you can compute

P$ = CHR$(ASC(N$(1)) + ASC(N$(50)) + ASC(N$(100))) / 3)

This assigns to P$ a single character that is approximately equivalent to the average of the three names. For example, if N$(1) is JACK, N$(50) is LAURA, and N$(100) is ROBERT, the average is computed as

P$ = CHR$((74 + 76 + 82) / 3);
    = CHR$(77)
    = "M"

The ASCII codes corresponding to the first letter of each of the names are 74, 76, and 82. (See the IBM PC BASIC manual for a list of the ASCII codes on the IBM PC.) The result is the letter M, which is roughly the average of the three names. This value can now be used as the pivot to rearrange the numbers. All that needs to be done to convert Quicksort to strings is to use string variables instead of numbers. Listing 6-9 shows the resulting conversion. The statement in line 2060 determines the actual pivot, which is stored in variable X$.

Listing 6-9

```
1          REM - Quicksort to sort strings
10         DIM S$(100), S(200)                    ' S() is a stack for quicksort
20         N = 1
30         P = 1                                  ' Initial stack pointer
100        INPUT "Enter name (CR when done)? ",S$(N)
110        IF S$(N) = "" THEN GOTO 200
120        N = N + 1
130        GOTO 100
200        N = N - 1
210        L = 1
220        R = N
230        GOSUB 1000                             ' Sort the array S$()
300        FOR I = 1 TO N
310        PRINT S$(I),
320        IF POS(0) > 60 THEN PRINT
330        NEXT I
400        STOP
1000       REM - Quicksort Subroutine
1010       IF L >= R - 1 THEN GOTO 1160
1020                                              ' Subrtn. 2000 Partitions the segment
1030       GOSUB 2000                             ' segment between L and R
1040       IF J > R THEN GOTO 1170
1050       P = P + 2                              ' Push J and R on to stack
1060       S (P) = J :
             S (P-1) = R
1070       R = I                                  ' Call Quicksort to sort the
1080                                              ' segment between L and R
1090       GOSUB 1000
1100       L = S (P)                              ' Restore L = J and R from
1110       R = S (P - 1)                          ' the save values on the stack
1120       GOSUB 1000                             ' Sort the second partition
1130                                              ' Pop the saved data from the stack
1140       P = P - 2:
             RETURN                     ' and return
1150                                                ' If only 2 elements
1155                                                ' then do a quick comparison and
1156                                                ' exchange if necessary
1160       IF R - L = 1 THEN IF S$(R) < S$(L) THEN T$ = S$(L):
             S$(L) = S$(R):
             S$(R) = T$
1170       RETURN
2000       REM
2010       REM
2020       REM
2030       REM
2040       REM - Partition the segment between L and R, returning I and J
2050       I = L :
             J = R                             ' Compute X$=pivot character
2060       X$ = CHR$((ASC(S$(I)) + ASC(S$(J)) + ASC(S$((I + J)/2)))/3)
2070                                              ' Increment I until Finding an
2075                                              ' S$(I) > then X$
2080       IF I > R THEN GOTO 2170
2090       IF S$(I) < X$ THEN I = I + 1:
             GOTO 2080
2100       REM
2110       ' Decrement J Until finding an S$(J) < than X$
2120       IF J < L THEN GOTO 2170
```

```
2130      IF S$(J) > X$ THEN J = J - 1:
            GOTO 2120
2140                                        ' If needed, exchange the values at
2150                                        ' S$(I) and S$(J)
2160      IF I < J THEN T$ = S$(I):
            S$(I) = S$(J):
            S$(J) = T$ :
            I = I + 1:
            J = J - 1:
            GOTO 2080
2170      I = J :
            J = J + 1              'Return I and J at edges of partition
2180      RETURN
```

IMPROVING THE BINARY INSERTION SORT

The binary insertion sort (binary table search) is slower than it could be. This is because every time a new name or number is added to the table, strings are rearranged in memory. Instead of moving the strings, you can use pointers to each of the strings and then rearrange the pointers.

Algorithm 4-3 shows how to shift the entries within a table to make room for a new entry. The statements that do this are

$$N = N + 1$$
$$FOR\ I = N\ TO\ G + 1\ STEP\ -1$$
$$\quad N\$(I) = N\$(I-1)$$
$$NEXT\ I$$

G is the location in the array N$() where the new name is to be added. You can open up this bottleneck by using an array P(), consisting of pointers to N$(). Let N$() consist of the names

N$(1)	N$(2)	N$(3)	N$(4)	N$(5)
ALAN	ALICE	GEORGE	LISA	TED

Let P() be an array of pointers, initially set as

P(1)	P(2)	P(3)	P(4)	P(5)
1	2	3	4	5

If you add CHARLIE to this ordered table, you'll need to make room between N$(2) and N$(3). Using the original algorithm, you would just slide N$(5) into N$(6), N$(4) into N$(5), and so on. But it's quicker to just move the pointers in P().

To start, you need to change the code in the FOR-NEXT loop to exchange P() values instead of N$(). This new code looks like

```
N = N + 1
FOR I = N TO G + 1 STEP −1
    P(I) = P(I − 1)
NEXT I
```

Next, you set N$(N) equal to CHARLIE and set P(3) to 6. The two arrays now have the values

N$(1)	N$(2)	N$(3)	N$(4)	N$(5)	N$(6)
ALAN	ALICE	GEORGE	LISA	TED	CHARLIE

P(1)	P(2)	P(3)	P(4)	P(5)	P(6)
1	2	6	3	4	5

You can see that N$(P(I)) for I running from 1 to 6 gives the list of names in alphabetical order.

Listing 6-10 illustrates the use of pointer variables in an improved version of the binary table search. Listing 6-11 shows similar changes to the binary search insertion sort routines.

Listing 6-10

```
1        REM - Improved Binary Table Search Using Pointers
10       MAX = 100
20       DIM N$(MAX), P(MAX)
100      PRINT "Enter:  A)dd  L)ookup  P)rint  D)elete  Q)uit ? ";
110      C$ = INPUT$(1)
120      PRINT C$
130      ON  INSTR ( 1, "ALPDQ", C$) + 1  GOSUB 100, 200, 300, 400, 500, 600
140      GOTO 100
200      REM ---------------------------------------------------------------
210      REM - Add Names
220      INPUT "Enter name to add ? ",S$
230      IF S$ = "" THEN RETURN
240      GOSUB 2000
250      IF F = 0 THEN GOSUB 1000 :
             RETURN
260      IF F = 1 THEN PRINT S$; " is already in the table" :
             RETURN
270      IF F = 2 THEN PRINT "Table is full at ";MAX;" entries" :
             RETURN
280      RETURN
300      REM ---------------------------------------------------------------
310      REM - Lookup a name
320      INPUT "Enter name to lookup ? ",S$
330      GOSUB 2000
340      IF F = 0  THEN PRINT "Not Found" ELSE PRINT "Found at location ";G
350      RETURN
400      REM ---------------------------------------------------------------
```

```
410       REM - Print out the entire table
420       GOSUB 3000
430       RETURN
500       REM -----------------------------------------------------------------
510       REM - Delete a name
520       INPUT "Enter name to delete ? ",S$
530       GOSUB 2000
540       IF F = 0 THEN PRINT "Not Found" ELSE GOSUB 4000 :
            PRINT "Deleted"
550       RETURN
600       REM -----------------------------------------------------------------
610       REM - Quit
620       GOSUB 4070
1000      REM -----------------------------------------------------------------
1010      REM - Add a name
1020      IF N = MAX THEN F = 2 :
            RETURN ELSE F = 0
1030      N = N + 1
1040      FOR I = N TO G + 1 STEP -1
1050        P(I) = P(I - 1)
1060      NEXT I
1070      N$(N) = S$
1075      P(G+1) = N
1080      RETURN
2000      REM -----------------------------------------------------------------
2010      REM - Lookup a name
2020      L = 1 :
            R = N :
            REM - Set left and right boundaries
2030      G = INT ( (L + R) / 2 ) :
            REM - Make guess between boundaries
2040      IF R < L THEN F = 0 :
            RETURN
2050      IF S$ = N$(P(G)) THEN F = 1 :
            RETURN
2060      IF S$ < N$(P(G))  THEN R = G - 1 ELSE L = G + 1
2070      GOTO 2030
3000      REM -----------------------------------------------------------------
3010      REM - Print the table of names
3020      FOR I = 1 TO N
3030        PRINT N$(P(I)),
3040      NEXT I
3050      PRINT
3060      RETURN
4000      REM -----------------------------------------------------------------
4010      REM - Delete a Name
4020      N = N - 1
4030      FOR I = G TO N
4040        P(I) = P(I + 1)
4050      NEXT I
4060      RETURN
4070      END
```

Listing 6-11

```
1         REM - Improved Binary Table Insertion Sort Using Pointers
10        MAX = 100
20        DIM N (MAX), P(MAX)
100       INPUT "A)dd numbers, D)isplay Sorted List? ",C$
110       IF C$ = "A"   THEN GOSUB 200
120       IF C$ = "D"   THEN GOSUB 300
130       GOTO 100
200       ' Add numbers and sort them
210       INPUT "Number (-999 when done)? ",S
215       IF  S = -999  THEN RETURN
```

```
 220        GOSUB 2000                     ' Find where to put the number
 230        GOSUB 1000                     ' And put it into the list
 240        GOTO 210
 300        ' Display the sorted list
 310        GOSUB 3000
 320        PRINT
 330        RETURN
1000        REM -------------------------------------------------------------
1010        REM - Add a number
1020        IF N = MAX THEN F = 2 :
               RETURN ELSE F = 0
1030        N = N + 1
1040        FOR I = N TO G + 1 STEP -1
1050          P(I) = P(I - 1)
1060        NEXT I
1070        N(N) = S
1075        P(G+1) = N
1080        RETURN
2000        REM -------------------------------------------------------------
2010        REM - Find the location for the next number
2020        L = 1 :
               R = N :
               REM - Set left and right boundaries
2030        G = INT ( (L + R) / 2 )              ' Make guess between boundaries
2040        IF R < L THEN F = 0 :
               RETURN
2050        IF S = N(P(G))    THEN F = 1 :
               RETURN
2060        IF S < N(P(G))    THEN R = G - 1 ELSE L = G + 1
2070        GOTO 2030
3000        REM -------------------------------------------------------------
3010        REM - Print the table of sorted numbers
3020        FOR I = 1 TO N
3030          PRINT N(P(I)),
3040        NEXT I
3050        PRINT
3060        RETURN
```

Sorting On Fields

Normally, sorting is not performed on simple data objects like single names or arrays of numbers, but on records. A typical record might have a layout like that shown in Figure 6-2. If a data file with records like R$ is sorted using the string sorts described so far, an alphabetic ordering based on the last name and then the first name is produced. Suppose that the file should be sorted by zip code. All comparisons are then made using just the zip code field. A more complicated sort might be based on several fields. For example, suppose a business needed to sort its customer records by city, and then by zip code within each city, and then by customer name within each of the zip codes.

A fairly easy way to do a multi-field sort is to combine each of the fields into one string. After combining the fields for each record, the strings can be compared and the records rearranged accordingly.

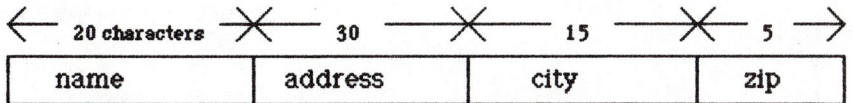

Figure 6-2 *A typical record contains many subfields. Shown here is an address record containing name, address, city, and zip subfields.*

For example, if R$() is an array of variables, each containing a name, address, and zip code, as in

R$(1) = "George Smith   1 Main St   Fremont 96033"

you can sort these records first by zip code, and then by name within each zip code. You do this by extracting the zip code and then the name and combining them into a single string. For example,

K1$ = MID$(R$(1),51,5) + LEFT$(R$(1),16)

This new string is compared to the string that was built for each of the other records. Listing 6-12 shows this multi-field sorting subroutine set up to sort six records containing names and addresses. The output from this program is shown in Listing 6-13. Note that the names are grouped first by zip code and then alphabetically within each zip code.

Listing 6-12

```
1          REM - Demonstration of sorting records
10         DIM S1(100)
20         N = 6                          ' Set up 6 records to sort
100        S$(1) = "George Smith        " + "1 Main Street         "
105        S$(1) = S$(1) + "Sunnyvale      " + "94038"
110        S$(2) = "Pamela Brown         " + "27 El Camino Real     "
115        S$(2) = S$(2) + "Mountain View  " + "94043"
120        S$(3) = "Lester Fenson        " + "1111 Silliness Drive  "
125        S$(3) = S$(3) + "Santa Clara    " + "94038"
130        S$(4) = "Alan Leek            " + "1278 Harper Court     "
135        S$(4) = S$(4) + "Palo Alto      " + "94043"
140        S$(5) = "Tom Molarie          " + "786 Boston Lane       "
145        S$(5) = S$(5) + "Mountain View  " + "94043"
150        S$(6) = "Betty Lancet         " + "76358 Route 85        "
155        S$(6) = S$(6) + "Sunnyvalue     " + "94038"
210        GOSUB 1000  ' Sort the array S1()
300        FOR I = 1 TO N
310        PRINT S$(I),
320        IF POS(0) > 60 THEN PRINT
330        NEXT I
400        STOP
999        REM - Shellsort Subroutine for Strings
1000       D = 4
1010       IF D < N THEN D = D + D :
               GOTO 1010
```

```
1020     D = D - 1                                    ' Let D = largest power of 2 < N
1030     D = INT (D/2)
1040     IF D < 1 THEN RETURN
1050     FOR J = 1 TO N - D
1060       FOR I = J TO 1 STEP -D                     ' Sort by zip code and name
1065         K1$ = MID$(S$(I+D),65,5) + LEFT$(S$(I+D),20)
1067         K2$ = MID$(S$(I),65,5) + LEFT$(S$(I),20)
1070         IF  K1$ > K2$   THEN GOTO 1120
1080         T$ = S$(I)
1090         S$(I) = S$(I + D)
1100         S$(I + D) = T$
1110       NEXT I
1120     NEXT J
1130     GOTO 1030
```

Listing 6-13

```
Betty Lancet           76358 Route 85              Sunnyvalue      94038
George Smith           1 Main Street               Sunnyvale       94038
Lester Fenson          1111 Silliness Drive        Santa Clara     94038
Alan Leek              1278 Harper Court           Palo Alto       94043
Pamela Brown           27 El Camino Real           Mountain View   94043
Tom Molarie            786 Boston Lane             Mountain View   94043
```

REVIEW

- Quicksort and its variations are the fastest sorts. Unfortunately, Quicksort is somewhat harder to program than other sorts.

- Shellsort is almost as fast as Quicksort and is quite easy to program in BASIC.

- Selection sorts are suitable if the list to be sorted is fairly small. If the list is large, Shellsort and Quicksort work better.

- The sorting algorithms can be used for multi-field sorts and disk sorts. The best way to speed up a disk sort is to keep the search keys in memory. Repeated disk accesses slow down all of the sorting algorithms. Disk sorts are described in Chapter 9.

CHAPTER
7
Using Disk Files

Computers use disk files for permanent or semipermanent storage. Using disk files is a little tougher than other programming, but it's not so tough that you need to avoid it. You can use disk files to store data for later processing, for building filing systems, and even for expanding the memory of your computer.

Think of a file as a file folder—the folder contains related information, like your medical bills or insurance records. These files might be collected together in a filing cabinet.

In the computer world, a file is also a collection of related data. Instead of being placed in a file folder, the data is stored in an area on a floppy diskette. Each diskette may contain several files, just as the filing cabinet may contain several filing folders (see Figure 7-1). A document prepared with a word processor is a file. So is a spreadsheet.

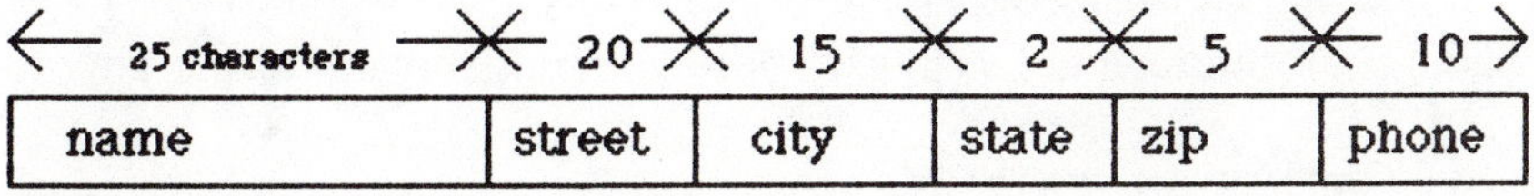

Figure 7-1 *Graphic representation of a record showing the amount of space allocated to each field.*

Programs use files to "permanently" record data. For example, a statistician may enter a set of data. But rather than run all of the needed statistical tests at once, the data may be used over a period of several days. The data need to be entered only once and then stored onto a diskette file. Thereafter, the analysis programs can get input from the stored data files. And the statistician does not have to re-enter any of the data.

Data files are usually classified according to the way data is stored within them. The two most commonly used file types are sequential and random access.

The data in a sequential file must be read in the order that it appears. The random access file permits the data records to be read or written in any order.

PROGRAMMING DISK FILES

BASIC has statements that are used specifically to create and manipulate disk files. For a start, you need to know about OPEN and CLOSE, which tell the computer to open and close an access channel to the disk, and special versions of PRINT and INPUT.

Each file on the diskette has a unique name. MYPROG.BAS, DATAFILE, ACCOUNTS, CUSTOMER.REC are all possible filenames. The OPEN statement uses the filename as a link between the BASIC program and the disk file. For example,

OPEN "DATAFILE" AS 1

establishes DATAFILE as file number 1. Thereafter, PRINT and INPUT statements are used to write data to the file, and read it from the disk, respectively. The file number used with OPEN is also used with PRINT and INPUT. For example, to put data into the file DATAFILE, previously opened as file number 1, you would write

PRINT #1, "ABCDEFGHIJKLMNOPQRSTUVWXYZ"

This statement writes the alphabet into the data file. The next PRINT #1 statement in the program writes to the file space immediately after the first data. So

PRINT #1, "0123456789"

will appear in the file as

ABCDEFGHIJKLMNOPQRSTUVWXYZ
0123456789

Note that this display looks exactly as it would if you had just printed these two strings on the computer's screen. PRINT behaves in exactly the same way whether it is used to print to a disk file or to the display.

Of course, the whole purpose of writing to a disk file is so that you can read the data back later. To do this, you need to use the INPUT statement. Assume that the data file has these two lines:

ABCDEFGHIJKLMNOPQRSTUVWXYZ
0123456789

If you type

OPEN "DATAFILE" AS 1
INPUT #1, S$
PRINT S$

you would see this on your display:

ABCDEFGHIJKLMNOPQRSTUVWXYZ

To see how PRINT and INPUT to a file work, you can type in the following statements exactly as shown (without line numbers).

OPEN "DATAFILE" AS 1
PRINT #1, "ABCDEFGHIJKLMNOPQRSTUVWXYZ"
PRINT #1, "0123456789"
CLOSE 1
OPEN "DATAFILE" AS 1
INPUT #1, S$
PRINT S$
INPUT #1, S$
PRINT S$
CLOSE 1

These statements create a file called DATAFILE and put two lines of data into it. Between the PRINTs and the INPUTs, you have to close and reopen the file. This is necessary because after a PRINT executes, BASIC remembers only the last place it was in the file. After

PRINT #1, "ABCDEFGHIJKLMNOPQRSTUVWXYZ"

is executed, BASIC marks its location just after the letter Z.

ABCDEFGHIJKLMNOPQRSTUVWXYZ∧

When the next PRINT is encountered, BASIC writes the output immediately following the Z.

Unfortunately, this means that you cannot PRINT and then read back what you just wrote. You must close and then reopen the file. In a way, this is like recording on a cassette tape. After you've recorded a piece of music, you must rewind the tape before playing back that music.

This type of file is called sequential because it must be read and written in the same order. You can't write some data here, read some there, and then write again some place else. That type of operation is performed with random access files.

Numeric data may also be written to sequential files. If X is a variable with the value of 2345.88, then the statement

```
PRINT #1, X
```

writes

```
2345.88
```

to the file. The number can be read back later with an INPUT statement, as in

```
INPUT #1, X
```

Of course, you can also print several numbers with a single PRINT statement, as in

```
PRINT #1, X, Y, Z
```

But remember that when INPUT is used to read several numbers typed at the keyboard, as in

```
INPUT X, Y, Z
? 56.7, 34.3, 1223.3
```

You need to separate each number with a comma. You must do the same for numeric data that is kept in a data file. One way to insert the commas is to place them in the original PRINT statement:

```
PRINT #1, X, ",", Y, ",", X
```

This is a bother, and fortunately BASIC provides a way around this. The WRITE statement works just like PRINT—and it adds a comma between each of the items. For example,

    WRITE #1, X, Y, X

will output

    56.7,34.3,1223.3

WRITE works the same whether it outputs to a disk file or to the screen. Try WRITE by typing the following:

    X = 56.7
    Y = 34.3
    Z = 1223.3
    WRITE X, Y, Z

You should see

    56.7,34.3,1223.3

WRITE can also print string variables. If A$ = "THIS IS IT", and you write

    WRITE X, A$, X

you'll see

    56.7,"THIS IS IT",56.7

Note that WRITE automatically puts quotes around all strings that it prints.

BASIC also has another type of input statement called LINE INPUT. Type

    INPUT S$

When the question mark appears, enter

    ? Hi, my name is Hal

Then type

PRINT S$

What will you get?

It may not be what you expect. Since BASIC uses commas to separate items for input, it saw the comma after "Hi" and threw the rest of the input away. Because commas are handled specially for the INPUT statement, there is a LINE INPUT statement. LINE INPUT doesn't care about commas. So now type

LINE INPUT S$
? Hi, my name is Hal

and then

PRINT S$

You'll get

Hi, my name is Hal

LINE INPUT is like the INPUT statement, and it may be used to read through disk files. In fact, you will probably want to use LINE INPUT to read files containing textual material. For example, chances are good that a file produced by your word-processing program contains commas in the middle of lines of text. So be sure to use LINE INPUT whenever commas are likely to be found in the input strings.

PROGRAMMING MULTIPLE FILES

IBM BASIC lets you use several files at the same time. For example, if you type

10 OPEN "DATA1" AS #1
20 OPEN "DATA2" AS #2

you now have two files open. To copy file 1 to file 2, you'd write

```
--->      30 INPUT #1, L$
  |       40 PRINT #2, L$
  |
  |___    50 GOTO 30
```

When you finish, you close both files with

    60 CLOSE 1
    70 CLOSE 2

(The next section explains how to determine when you've reached the end of the first file. Without an end-of-file check, the previous lines would eventually cause an error.)

Normally, BASIC allows only three files to be open at the same time. When more are needed, you can tell BASIC exactly how many when you first start BASICA. At the DOS prompt, type

    A>BASICA /F:5

In this example, you are telling BASIC that you need five files. You can specify more or less by changing the five to the number of files needed. For example,

    A>BASICA /F:10

provides up to 10 files. The maximum number of files permitted is 15.

Each file that is allocated requires 188 bytes of memory. In addition, buffer space must be allocated for random access files. Therefore, if memory is tight, don't casually allocate additional files! In fact, if memory is a problem and your program does not use any files, then you may wish to set the number of files to 0:

    A>BASICA /F:0

To see what files are on your disk, type

    FILES

If you prefer, you may use the DIR (directory) command at the DOS prompt:

    A>DIR

Opening Files for Input and Output

A file, once it is open, is either print-only or input-only. That means that once you have printed some data, then you must either continue to print data or close the file. Similarly, you can't input some data and then try to print to the same file. Remember that BASIC is marking its location in the file as data is written. If you tried to do an INPUT, you'd get the data immediately following what was written, which is usually the end of the file.

Because you can do only PRINTs or only INPUTs, BASIC lets you state your intentions when you open the file. The statement

OPEN "DATAFILE" FOR OUTPUT AS 1

says that you intend to PRINT to the file.

OPEN "DATAFILE" FOR INPUT AS 1

says that you're going to INPUT data. There's another mode, called APPEND, as in

OPEN "DATAFILE" FOR APPEND AS 1

This tells the computer to open the file and position the marker at the end of the file. The first PRINT then appends data to the file.

Be careful! When you open a file for output, all you can do is write to it. Therefore, if you open a file and a file of the same name already exists, the computer sets the length of the existing file to zero. Subsequent prints are to the beginning of the file. Because of this, OPEN FOR OUTPUT is equivalent to deleting the file and then opening it.

An Example

Say you've written a word-processing program. When you give the command

SAVE MYFILE

the word processor saves the edited text into a disk file called MYFILE.

Internally, all of the edited text might be kept in an array of strings L$(). Variable N keeps track of how many lines are in the document. When the SAVE command is given, MYFILE will be opened for OUTPUT, effectively erasing any previous data in MYFILE. The text will be written out and the file will be closed. Listing 7-1 shows the SAVE subroutine.

Listing 7-1

```
1000      REM - SAVE text array to file
1010      '
1020      ' Inputs:
1030      '   F$      is the filename to store the text in
1040      '   L$()    is an array of text
1050      '   N       is the number of lines in the array
1060      '
1070      OPEN F$ FOR OUTPUT AS 1
1080      FOR I = 1  TO  N
1090        PRINT #1, L$(I)
1100      NEXT I
1110      CLOSE 1
1120      RETURN
```

The word processor also has a command to read files from the disk.

LOAD MYFILE

tells the word processor to read all the text from MYFILE into array L$().

One problem is knowing when to stop reading. BASIC has a function called EOF(), which tells you when the end of a file has been reached. EOF() is normally used in an IF statement to check for more input. For example,

IF EOF(1) THEN GOTO 500

says that if file 1 is exhausted, then jump to line 500. Listing 7-2 shows the LOAD subroutine. Note that the subroutine uses the LINE INPUT statement to properly read lines containing commas.

How to Use Sequential Files

Sequential files are often used to initialize variables. For example, a word processor probably contains an array of the valid command names. One way to initialize the array is to read all of the commands from a DATA statement, as shown in Listing 7-3. Another way is to store the command names in a file and INPUT the command names. This method is better if there are many commands. By eliminating the DATA statement, you condense the program and use less memory. Listing 7-4(a) shows a routine that reads an array of commands from a data file. The data file, shown in Listing 7-4(b), was typed using a text editor.

Sequential files can also store data as it is entered. For example, a statistician may need to store statistical data for later processing. Or it may be that not all of the data will fit into memory, so the statistician might write each value to disk as it is entered. When analysis begins, the file is opened for input, and

Listing 7-2

```
2000      REM - LOAD text array from a file
2010      '
2020      ' Inputs:
2030      '   F$      is the filename to read the text from
2040      '   L$()    is an array to read the text into
2050      '   N       is the number of lines that were loaded
2060      '
2070      OPEN F$ FOR INPUT AS 1
2080      N = 0
2090      WHILE  EOF(1) = 0
2100        N = N + 1
2110        LINE INPUT #1, L$(N)
2120      WEND
2130      RETURN
```

Listing 7-3

```
1000      REM - Initialize table of command names
1010      FOR I = 1 TO 10
1020        READ COMMANDS$(I)
1030      NEXT I
1040      RETURN
1050      DATA ADD,CHANGE,DELETE,FIND,INSERT,LIST,LOAD,MOVE,PRINT,SAVE
```

Listing 7-4(a)

```
1000      REM - Initialize array of commands
1010      '                        \
1020      OPEN   "COMMANDS.DAT"   FOR INPUT AS 1
1030      N = 0
1040      WHILE  EOF(1) = 0
1050        N = N + 1
1060        LINE INPUT #1, COMMANDS$(N)
1070      WEND
1080      RETURN
```

Listing 7-4(b)

```
ADD
CHANGE
DELETE
FIND
INSERT
LIST
LOAD
MOVE
PRINT
SAVE
```

the data is read and processed. In this way, only a very small amount of data is kept in memory.

Review of Sequential File Statements

OPEN and CLOSE establish a connection between the file on the disk and the BASIC program. PRINT and WRITE output data to the disk file. WRITE is practically the same as PRINT except that it separates each item with commas.

INPUT and LINE INPUT read data from a disk file. Remember that INPUT needs to have each item separated by a comma or by the end of the input line. LINE INPUT reads lines containing commas, accepting input all the way up to the end of the input line. You can determine if the end of the file is reached by checking the EOF() function.

OPEN, CLOSE, PRINT, INPUT, and EOF allow you to store data produced by your program on a diskette.

RANDOM ACCESS FILES

Random access files are more flexible than sequential files. The same file can be both read from and written to without a reopening of the file.

To understand how random access files work, you need to explore the concept of a record. A record holds a set of related data. For example, a file of customer records would probably contain the customer's name, address, telephone number, item last ordered, and the purchase price of the item.

Each part of the record—name, telephone number, and so on—is a field. Each field is allocated a certain amount of space. The customer name might be 25 characters long. The address might be subdivided into 4 fields: 20 characters for the street, 15 for the city, 2 for the state, and 5 for the zip code. Figure 7-2 illustrates the layout for a typical record. BASIC uses the FIELD statement to map a record definition into a random access file record.

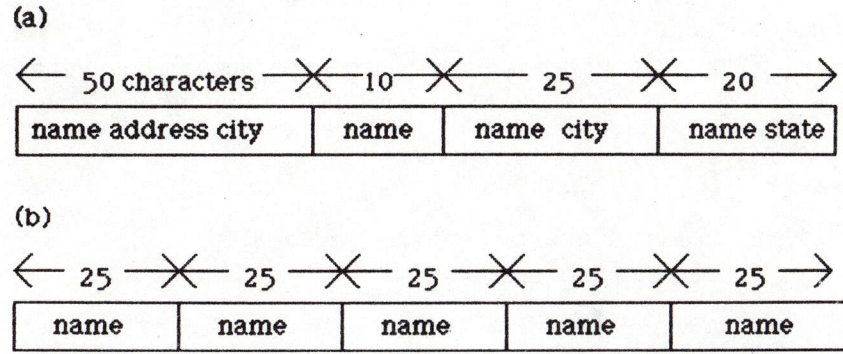

Figure 7-2 *In a sequential file, the record length varies (a). A special character (an ASCII 13) marks the end of each record. On the other hand, each record in a random access file is the same length (b).*

Because the records in the random file are fixed length, it's easy for BASIC to pick out any record in any order. It's not necessary to start at the beginning of the file and read each record until reaching the desired location, as is necessary with sequential files. This flexibility is what makes random access files so useful. In many applications, such as inventory control, one number may point to the desired record.

FIELD, GET, PUT, LSET, and RSET are the statements you need for programming random access.

FIELD describes the layout of a single record. Figure 7-2 shows how a customer record is mapped onto a BASIC record by the FIELD statement.

FIELD indicates which file contains the record and how many characters are allocated to each string variable. It does not put any data into the record nor does it output any data to the disk. It simply describes the record format.

To assign values to the field variables, you use either the LSET or RSET commands. These commands are similar to LET. The command

LSET CUSTOMER$ = "RICHARD SMITH"

assigns the value RICHARD SMITH to the name field. The name field is 20 characters long, so something needs to be placed in the extra character positions. LSET left adjusts RICHARD SMITH and fills the trailing area with blanks. RSET right adjusts RICHARD SMITH and fills the leading area with blanks.

Use caution. If you forget to use LSET or RSET when assigning to a FIELDed variable, BASIC will remove the variable from the FIELD definition and store the data elsewhere in memory. This creates a hole in the record that can no longer be accessed. (BASIC does, however, allow you to redefine the fields at any time, even while the file is open. Therefore, it is possible to just re-execute the FIELD statement to allocate the variables back to fields within the file record.)

Once a record has been assigned some values, you need to tell BASIC to actually write the record to disk. You do this with the PUT statement.

PUT #1, 5

says to write the current record to record 5 in file 1.

To read a record, use

GET #1, 3

This reads record 3 and puts it into the FIELD variables. These variables can then be used normally. They can be compared, copied to other string variables, or printed. Always remember, however, to use either LSET or RSET to assign a new value to any of the FIELD variables.

Opening a Random Access File

Because you can change the field assignments even after the file has been opened, BASIC doesn't know exactly how much room each record in your file requires. In fact, the computer won't know you're using a random file until you tell it so.

You must tell the computer the maximum size of the record. Do this by adding a record length to the OPEN statement. Suppose you're using a file described by the following FIELD statement:

```
FIELD #1, 50 AS T$, 25 AS S$
```

You need only 75 bytes. In the OPEN statement, add the LEN specification shown here:

```
OPEN "DATAFILE" AS 1 LEN = 75
```

Be sure to specify only the number of bytes that you need. If you specify too many, you will waste space.

Storing Numbers in Random Access Files

Technically, only strings may be placed in the FIELD statement. But there are ways around this restriction.

The obvious solution is to use BASIC's STR$() and VAL() functions. STR$(X) converts the number X into a string containing the number. For example, if X is 2.7765, then

```
A$ = STR$(X)
```

gives A$ the value 2.7765.

Even though A$ contains a number, you can't type

```
PRINT A$ * A$
```

instead, you must use VAL() to convert the string representation back into numeric format. You need to write

```
PRINT VAL(A$) * VAL(A$)
```

which is equivalent to

    PRINT 2.7765 * 2.7765

There are some problems associated with using STR$() and VAL(). First, you never really know just how big a string you'll need in the FIELD statement to store some number. For example, if X equals 5, then the length of STR$(X) is 2, but if X is 119, then the length of STR$(X) is 4. You could just allocate a large string within the record, but that wastes space.

The second problem is the time consumed in converting BASIC's internal numeric format into a string and vice versa. You don't notice the time delay when you convert one or two numbers. But if you convert hundreds of numbers, the delay is quite noticeable.

To alleviate these problems, BASIC provides a set of conversion functions to use with random files. These functions are

    CVI(X$)   CVS(X$)   CVD(X$)
    MKI$(X)   MKS$(X)   MKD$(X)

There are two functions for each of the three number formats of BASIC. These three formats are integers, single precision reals, and double precision reals. Integers are numbers that do not contain a decimal part. Single precision numbers are computed to about seven decimal places. Double precision numbers are calculated to about 16 decimal places. You just need to know that there are three different types of numbers in BASIC and that a number in each of the different formats uses a different amount of memory.

Integers take two bytes of memory, single precision reals take four bytes, and double precision reals require eight bytes.

You allocate strings equal to the size of the type of number that will be placed in the record with the FIELD statement. To store three separate real numbers, you write

    FIELD #1, 4 AS R1$, 4 AS R2$, 4 AS R3$

To convert real numbers into strings and vice versa, use the functions CVS(X$) and MKS$(X). MKS$(X) converts X into a four-byte string. Note that MKS$() converts X into a non-printable format. MKS$() is intended to store numbers only. The statement

    LSET R1$ = MKS$(X)

assigns R1$ the four-byte string equivalent to X.

CVS() is the inverse of MKS$(), so CVS(R1$) would convert the four-byte R1$ string back into a single precision real number.

MKI$() is used to convert integers into two-byte strings; CVI() converts the two-byte string back into an integer. MKD$() and CVD() work on double precision numbers, translating between an eight-byte string and the internal double precision format.

The MAKE and CONVERT functions are useful because they produce compact representations of the numbers. And they are from two to 10 times faster than STR$() and VAL(). Generally, you'll want to use the MKS and CVS functions instead of STR$() and VAL().

THE EMPLOYEE-RECORDS SYSTEM REVISITED

We now have enough background to put together a useful program using random access files. The employee records system described in Chapter 1 will be converted to store data on disk. The employee records weren't very useful in the introductory example because there was no way to save them for future use.

To preserve the names and salaries in a disk file, you need to make several minor modifications to the program. First, you no longer need the NAMES$() and PAY() arrays. Instead, you define these values in a FIELD statement for the file that holds the employee records. This FIELD statement looks like this:

FIELD #1, 30 AS NAMES$, 4 AS PAY$

This defines a single record as a name of up to 30 characters in length and a real-number variable stored as the string PAY$.

The subroutine at line 5000 (see Listing 7-5) opens the RECORDS.DAT file, which is the file used to hold the employee records.

Listing 7-5

```
10       REM - Simple Employee Record Keeper
20       GOSUB 5000                         ' Open RECORDS.DAT file
100      INPUT "Enter command:  A)dd P)rint D)elete C)hange Q)uit? ",C$
110      IF C$ = "A" THEN GOSUB 1000 :
             GOTO 100 ELSE IF C$ = "P" THEN GOSUB 2000 :
             GOTO 100ELSE IF C$ = "D" THEN GOSUB 3000 :
             GOTO 100ELSE IF C$ = "C" THEN GOSUB 4000 :
             GOTO 100 ELSE IF C$ = "Q" THEN GOTO 6030
120      PRINT "Please Enter One of the Commands Shown"
130      GOTO 100
```

```
1000      REM - Add A New Employee
1010      INPUT "Enter Employee Number to Add ? ",N
1020      IF N = 0 THEN RETURN
1030      INPUT "Employee Name ? ",NAM$
1040      INPUT "Weekly Salary ? ",SALARY
1050      LSET NAMES$ = NAM$
1060      LSET PAY$ = MKS$(SALARY)
1070      PUT #1, N                               ' Output to record #N in file
1080      RETURN
1090      REM
1100      REM
2000      REM - Print Employee Records
2010      FOR I = 1 TO 100
2020      GET #1, I                               ' Read employee #i's data record
2030        IF LEFT$(NAMES$,1) <> " "  THEN  PRINT I, NAMES$, CVS(PAY$)
2040      NEXT I
2050      RETURN
2060      REM
2070      REM
3000      REM - Delete an Employee Record
3010      INPUT "Enter Employee Number to Delete ? ",N
3020      IF N = 0 THEN RETURN
3030      GET #1, N                               ' Get Employee #n's data record
3040      IF  LEFT$(NAMES$,1) = " "  THEN PRINT "Employee #";N;" does
          not exist - try again":
              GOTO 3010
3050      PRINT NAMES$, CVS(PAY$)
3060      INPUT "Delete (Y or N) ? ",C$
3070      IF C$ <> "Y" AND C$ <> "N"  THEN GOTO 3060
3080      IF C$ = "Y" THEN LSET NAMES$ = " " :
              PUT #1, N :
              PRINT "Deleted" ELSE PRINT "Not Deleted"
3090      RETURN
3100      REM
3110      REM
4000      REM - Change an Employee Record
4010      INPUT "Enter Employee Number to Change ? ",N
4020      IF N = 0 THEN RETURN
4030      GET #1, N                               ' Get Employee #n's data record
4040      IF  LEFT$(NAMES$,1) = " " THEN PRINT "Employee #";N;" does
          not exist - try again" :
              GOTO 4010
4050      PRINT NAMES$, CVS(PAY$)
4060      INPUT "Enter new name (or ENTER if no change)? ",T$
4070      IF T$ <> "" THEN  LSET NAMES$ = T$
4080      INPUT "Enter new pay (or ENTER if no change)? ",T
4090      IF T <> 0 THEN  LSET PAY$ = MKS$(T)
4100      IF T$ <> ""  OR  T <> 0  THEN  PUT #1, N
4110      RETURN
4120      REM
4130      REM
5000      REM - Open the RECORDS.DAT data file
5010      ON ERROR GOTO 5070
5020      OPEN "RECORDS.DAT" FOR INPUT AS 1
5030      CLOSE 1
5040      OPEN "RECORDS.DAT" AS 1 LEN=34
5050      FIELD #1, 30 AS NAMES$, 4 AS PAY$
5060      RETURN
5070      REM - We come here if RECORDS.DAT does not exist
5080      RESUME 5090
5090      INPUT "Initialize Employee Records File (CR=Yes) ? ",C$
5100      IF C$ = ""  OR  C$ = "Y" THEN GOTO 5130
5110      PRINT "Stopped"
5120      STOP
5130      REM - Initialize RECORDS.DAT to all empty records
```

```
5140      OPEN "RECORDS.DAT" AS 1 LEN = 34
5150      FIELD #1, 30 AS NAMES$, 4 AS PAY$
5160      LSET NAMES$ = " "
5170      LSET PAY$ = MKS$(0)
5180      FOR I = 1 TO 100
5190        PUT #1, I
5200      NEXT I
5210      ON ERROR GOTO 0
5220      RETURN
6000      REM
6010      REM
6020      REM - QUIT
6030      CLOSE 1
6040      END
```

Line 5020 attempts to open the data file for input. As we learned earlier in this chapter, a file that is opened for input must exist prior to the OPEN statement. If the file does not exist, then an error occurs. You can take advantage of this procedure to determine if RECORDS.DAT already exists. If it does, then everything is fine. Otherwise, you need to create a new RECORDS.DAT file. This is where the ON ERROR GOTO statement comes into play.

ON ERROR GOTO tells BASIC that as soon as an error occurs, GOTO line 4070. This is contrary to how BASIC normally works. In most instances, if an error occurs, BASIC stops the program and prints an appropriate error message. But with ON ERROR GOTO you can handle all errors within the program itself, thereby avoiding halts and error messages. In the subroutine at line 5020, if RECORDS.DAT does not exist, the open for input fails. The ON ERROR GOTO statement causes a jump to line 5070. Once the program detects an error, it executes a RESUME statement. RESUME is similar to GOTO, but it should be used only after an error. The RESUME directs the computer to pick up normal processing at the indicated line.

In the example in Listing 7-5, the program responds to the error by prompting to find out if you wish the RECORDS.DAT file to be created and initialized. If you do, the program jumps to line 5140, opens the file as a random access file, and proceeds to fill the file with empty name and pay entries. It then executes

ON ERROR GOTO 0

which directs the computer to suspend internal error processing. From this point on, if an error is encountered, BASIC will print the error instead of branching.

(BASIC has two built-in variables, ERR and ERL. Whenever an error occurs, ERR is set to an error code that indicates what type of error occurred. A complete list of errors and error numbers appears in the IBM PC BASIC manual. ERL returns the line number at which the error occurred. Together, these two variables can be used to pinpoint exactly where and why an error occurred.

In many instances, you are expecting the possibility of an error. ON ERROR GOTO, ERR, and ERL are often used to catch these expected errors.)

At line 1050, you can see how new names are added. Instead of assigning to array elements, as was done before, you simply place the entered values into the FIELD variables NAMES$ and PAY$. Then you update the information by writing it with the PUT statement to the data file at record number N.

The CHANGE function is similar. It begins by reading the appropriate employee record from the data file, using the GET statement in line 4030. After accepting changes, the new values are replaced in the FIELD statement and written back to the disk with the PUT in line 4100.

As you can see, disk files provide great power and information-processing ability for your programs.

REVIEW

- A disk file is like a file folder that contains related information, such as insurance forms or monthly bills.
- Disk files permanently record information for future reference.
- Sequential files typically contain text, such as a word-processing document. They are called sequential because each item in the file is accessed in sequence, beginning from the first item in the file. Random access files, on the other hand, let you access items in any order.
- BASIC provides several statements for sequential access to files. These are OPEN, CLOSE, and special versions of PRINT, INPUT, and WRITE.
- For random access disk files, you create record layouts using the FIELD statement. PUT outputs a single record to the file. GET reads a record or item anywhere in the file.
- BASIC provides six special functions for storing and retrieving numeric information in random access files. These functions are: CVI(X$), CVS(X$), CVD(X$) MKI$(X), MKS$(X), and MKD$(X).

CHAPTER

8

File Searching

Chapter 4 describes several ways to search through arrays of data. In this chapter, you will find methods for searching through disk files. These methods include disk-based hashing and binary tree searches.

THE DISK BASED SEQUENTIAL SEARCH

The simplest file search is the sequential search. You just begin at the first record in the file and scan until finding the desired record. Listing 8-1 is a short program that opens a random access file and searches sequentially for the string S$. If S$ is found, the variable F is set to 1. 1 is the number of the record holding S$. If S$ is not found, F is set to 0.

Listing 8-1

```
1000    REM - Open File to Search
1010    OPEN "DATAFILE" AS 1 LEN = 40
1020    FIELD #1, 40 AS NAMES$
1030    RETURN
1040    '
1050    '
1060    '
2000    REM - Sequential Search of a File for the name in S$
2010    S$ = S$ + SPACE$(40 - LEN(S$))      ' Pad with blanks
2020    I = 1
2030    GET #1, I
2040    IF  S$ = NAMES$  THEN  F = 1 :
            RETURN
2050    I = I + 1
2060    IF I <= 50   THEN GOTO 2030
2070    F = 0 ' Not found
2080    RETURN
```

As you saw in Chapter 4, the sequential search needs, on the average, to check half of the records in the disk file. If the records are read from the disk one by one, the search will be very slow for all but the smallest files.

The IBM PC takes about 30 seconds to read 500 records. The machine takes about a half hour to search 30,000 records. If you can reduce the number of times that the disk must be read, you can speed up the search. Techniques like hashing and tree searches reduce the number of disk references.

The Disk Based Hashing Search

Hashing converts a name into a number. The number is then used as an index into a table. In Chapter 4, the hashing algorithm stored the table in an array. The table may be stored just as easily in a disk file.

Hashing works well for disk tables because it normally makes only a few comparisons before finding the name. This keeps the number of disk reads low. The only disadvantage of hashing is that the table is kept in random order. If you wish to have your data sorted in a particular sequence, such as alphabetically, then the binary tree may be a better choice for your application.

Hashing converts the name being searched for, or the search key, into a hash index. The index is then scaled to the size of the file, ensuring that the index will be no greater than the highest record in the file. This guarantees that the hash number will be no larger than the highest record in the file. Chapter 4 shows that the hash search often yields the correct record on the first comparison. This means that very few records, on the average, need to be read from the disk.

All you have to do to implement this method is to use a hash algorithm like Algorithm 4-3, 4-4, 4-5, or 4-6. Instead of indexing an array, read and write records using the hash index as the record number. This requires that the file containing the search keys be a random access file. The index computed by hashing a search name becomes the record number that you should read from the disk file.

Listing 8-2 is a program that keeps track of names, addresses, and telephone numbers. The name is the search key; to look up a particular address, a name is entered, hashed to a record in the file, and the address and telephone number are fetched. The subroutine at lines 930 through 1090 is the heart of the hashed file structure. After the HASH index is computed (line 1000), the corresponding record is read from the disk. If that record is currently unused, then HASH is returned as the number of the record where the new information should be placed. Otherwise, the HASH value is decremented, and the next index location is checked.

Listing 8-2

```
100      REM - Hashed Disk File Searching
110      '
120      '
130      PRINT "Address Keeper Featuring"
140      PRINT "    o   Quick Searches by Name"
150      PRINT
160      '
170      '
180      MAX = 100                              ' Maximum number of names
190      '
200      ' The number of records may be changed by
         setting MAX to a new value
210      '
220      '
230      GOSUB 1300                             ' Open data file
240      '
250      '
260      ' Display Main Menu
270      PRINT
280      PRINT "1  Add"
290      PRINT "2  Search Using Name"
300      PRINT "3  Exit"
310      PRINT
320      INPUT "Selection? ",N
330      PRINT                    '
340      ON N GOSUB 390,530,660
350      GOTO 270
360      '
370      '
380      ' ---------------------------
390      ' Add A new data record
400      PRINT "ADD A NAME"
410      PRINT
420      INPUT "Name ? ",NAM$
430      INPUT "Telephone ? ",PHONENUM$
440      INPUT "Street Address ? ",ADDRESS$
450      INPUT "City ? ",CITY$
460      INPUT "State ? ",STATE$
470      INPUT "Zip Code ? ", ZIP$
480      GOSUB 720
490      RETURN
500      '
510      '
520      ' ---------------------------
530      ' Search for a name
540      INPUT "Name to search for? ",NAM$
550      GOSUB 1150
560      IF F = 0  THEN PRINT NAM$;" is not in the table":
            RETURN
570      GET #1, HASH
580      PRINT NAMES$
590      PRINT PHONE$
600      PRINT STREET$
610      PRINT CITY.NAME$; "  "; STATE.NAME$; "   "; ZIP.CODE$
620      RETURN
630      '
640      '
650      ' ---------------------------
660      REM - Exit Program
670      CLOSE 1
680      END
690      '
700      '
710      ' ---------------------------
```

```
720     REM - Add a Data Record containing the variables:
730     '   NAM$,   PHONENUM$, ADDRESS$, CITY$, STATE$, ZIP$
740     '
750     GOSUB 1150                      ' Check if name is
          already in the table
760     IF F = 1  THEN PRINT S$; " has already been entered" :
          RETURN
770     '
780     GOSUB 930                       ' Find the location
          for the name
790     ' On return, HASH = the record # to contain the data
800     '
810     ' Now place the data into the fields of the
          record and write to disk
820     LSET NAMES$ = NAM$
830     LSET PHONE$ = PHONENUM$
840     LSET STREET$ = ADDRESS$
850     LSET CITY.NAME$ = CITY$
860     LSET STATE.NAME$ = STATE$
870     LSET ZIP.CODE$ = ZIP$
880     PUT #1, HASH
890     RETURN
900     '
910     '
920     ' ------------------------
930     REM - Add a name to the table
940     '
950     ' Check if the table is full
960     IF NUM.NAMES >= MAX - 1  THEN F = 2 :
          RETURN
970     NUM.NAMES = NUM.NAMES + 1
980     S$ = NAM$                       ' Make a copy of the name
990     F = 0
1000    GOSUB 1500                      ' Compute Hash
1010    GET #1, HASH
1020    IF  LEFT$(NAMES$,1) = " "   THEN  RETURN
1030    ' If this space in the table is free, then
          place the name here
1040    ' Return HASH
1050    '
1060    ' Otherwise, try the next entry in the table
1070    HASH = HASH - 1
1080    IF  HASH = 0  THEN  HASH = MAX
1090    GOTO 1010
1100    '
1110    '
1120    '
1130    '
1140    ' ------------------------
1150    REM - Search the table for NAM$
1160    '      Returns:
          HASH = record # containing the data
1170    '
1180    S$ = NAM$
1190    GOSUB 1500
1200    S$ = S$ + SPACE$(20 - LEN(S$))
1210    GET #1, HASH
1220    IF  LEFT$(NAMES$,1) = " "   THEN F = 0 :
          RETURN
1230    IF  NAMES$ = S$  THEN  F = 1 :
          RETURN
1240    HASH = HASH - 1
1250    IF  HASH = 0  THEN  HASH = MAX
1260    GOTO 1210
1270    '
```

```
1280     '
1290     ' ------------------------
1300     REM - Open data file
1310     ON ERROR GOTO 1370
1320     OPEN "datafile" FOR INPUT AS 1
1330     CLOSE 1
1340     OPEN "datafile" AS 1 LEN=62
1350     FIELD #1, 20 AS NAMES$, 10 AS PHONE$, 15 AS
            STREET$, 10 AS CITY.NAME$, 2 AS STATE.NAME$, 5 AS
            ZIP.CODE$
1360     RETURN
1370     OPEN "datafile" AS 1 LEN = 62
1380     PRINT "Initializing Data File ..."
1390     FIELD #1, 20 AS NAMES$, 10 AS PHONE$, 15 AS
            STREET$, 10 AS CITY.NAME$, 2 AS STATE.NAME$, 5 AS
            ZIP.CODE$
1400     LSET NAMES$ = " "
1410     FOR I = 1 TO MAX
1420     PUT #1, I
1430     NEXT I
1440     PRINT "Initialization Completed"
1450     PRINT
1460     RETURN
1470     '
1480     '
1490     ' ------------------------
1500     REM - Compute HASH = Hash (S$)
1510     HASH = 0
1520     FOR I = 1 TO LEN(S$)
1530       HASH = HASH + ASC(MID$(S$,I,1))
1540     NEXT I
1550     HASH = HASH MOD MAX + 1
1560     RETURN
```

The OPEN DATA FILE subroutine (line 1300) determines if the data file already exists. If it does, then the file is opened in random access mode and the FIELD variables are allocated. If this is the first run of the program, the file must be created. The entire file is initialized to blanks so that the search and addition routines can recognize unused entries in the hash table.

You can easily modify the routines to keep track of other information by changing the FIELD statement in line 1390. Be sure to change the LEN parameter of the OPEN statement in lines 1330 and 1370 if your changes decrease or increase the number of bytes in the FIELD statement.

Multiple Hash Tables

Suppose that a certain file must be organized for quick reference by both name and by telephone number. This implies the need for two hash tables: one to store the names and the other to store the telephone numbers. In this form, it's convenient to isolate the search keys from the corresponding data record. The file then becomes split into three separate sections: the names area, the telephone number area, and the data records area.

Associated with each name is the number of the record where the corresponding data record is to be found. Figure 8-1 illustrates this concept. The first part of the file reserves space for 100 names. The next section reserves space for 100 telephone numbers. The actual data records follow the two tables. When you hash a name, you compute an index to one of the name records. If the name record contains the correct name, you use the number of the associated data record to fetch the data from the data records area of the file. Because the names and the telephone numbers are organized as hash tables, you can quickly locate any record in the file by specifying either a name or a telephone number.

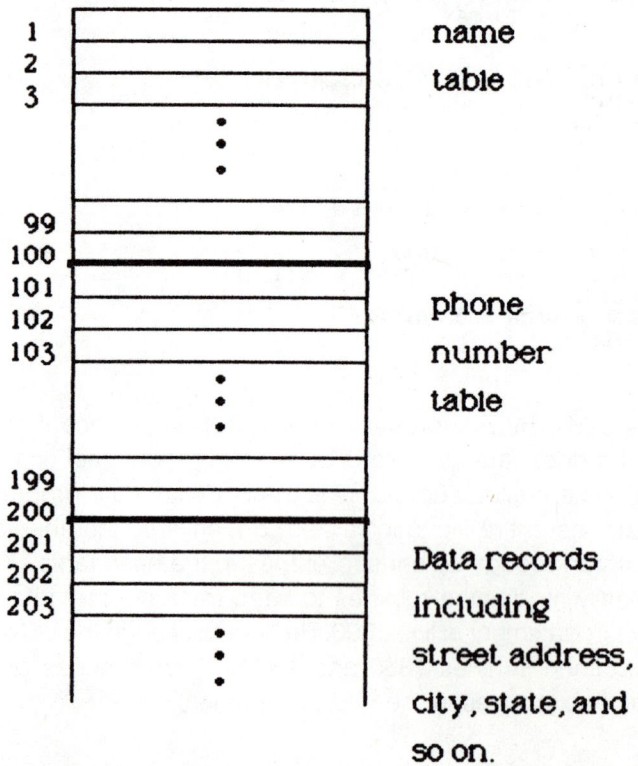

Figure 8-1 *Layout of a file containing two hash tables: one for names and one for phone numbers. The corresponding data records are kept in a third area.*

Listing 8-3 contains the multiple hash table search routines. The maximum number of names and telephone numbers may be changed by altering the value assigned to MAX in line 190. New records are added by the subroutine at line 980. Here, a quick check is made to see if the record has already been added. The routines at 1250 and 1470 add the name and telephone number to their respective tables.

Listing 8-3

```
100     REM - MultiKey File Searching Using Two Hash Tables
110     '
120     '
130     PRINT "Address Keeper Featuring"
140     PRINT "    o   Quick Searches by Name"
150     PRINT "    o   And Telephone Number"
160     PRINT
170     '
180     '
190     MAX = 100                          ' Maximum number
        of names/telephone numbers
200     NUM.DATARECORD = MAX * 2 + 2  ' Location of
        first data record in file
210     ' The data file is layed out in 3 sections, as follows:
220     ' Records 2..101 = are the name table
230     ' Records 102..201 = are the telephone number table
240     ' Records 202 + = the data records
250     ' Record #1 holds total number of data records
260     '
270     ' The number of records may be changed by
        setting MAX to a new value
280     '
290     '
300     GOSUB 1940                              ' Open data file
310     '
320     '
330     ' Display Main Menu
340     PRINT
350     PRINT "1  Add"
360     PRINT "2  Search Using Name"
370     PRINT "3  Search Using Telephone Number"
380     PRINT "4  Exit"
390     PRINT
400     INPUT "Selection? ",N
410     PRINT
420     ON N GOSUB 470,610,750,890
430     GOTO 340
440     '
450     '
460     ' ------------------------
470     ' Add A new data record
480     PRINT "ADD A NAME"
490     PRINT
500     INPUT "Name ? ",NAM$
510     INPUT "Telephone ? ",PHONENUM$
520     INPUT "Street Address ? ",ADDRESS$
530     INPUT "City ? ",CITY$
540     INPUT "State ? ",STATE$
550     INPUT "Zip Code ? ", ZIP$
560     GOSUB 980
570     RETURN
580     '
590     '
600     ' ------------------------
610     ' Search for a name
620     INPUT "Name to search for? ",NAM$
630     GOSUB 1640
640     IF F = 0  THEN PRINT NAM$;" is not in the table":
        RETURN
650     GET #1, DATA.RECORD.NUM
660     FIELD #1, 20 AS NAMES$, 10 AS PHONE$, 15 AS
        STREET$, 10 AS CITY.NAME$, 2 AS STATE.NAME$, 5 AS
        ZIP.CODE$
670     PRINT NAMES$
```

```
680     PRINT PHONE$
690     PRINT STREET$
700     PRINT CITY.NAME$; "  "; STATE.NAME$; "   "; ZIP.CODE$
710     RETURN
720     '
730     '
740     ' ----------------------
750     ' Search by Telephone number
760     INPUT "Telephone Number to search for? ",PHONENUM$
770     GOSUB 1800
780     IF F = 0 THEN PRINT PHONENUM$; " is not in the table" :
        RETURN
790     GET #1, DATA.RECORD.NUM
800     FIELD #1, 20 AS NAMES$, 10 AS PHONE$, 15 AS
        STREET$, 10 AS CITY.NAME$, 2 AS STATE.NAME$, 5 AS
        ZIP.CODE$
810     PRINT NAMES$
820     PRINT PHONE$
830     PRINT STREET$
840     PRINT CITY.NAME$; "  "; STATE.NAME$; "   "; ZIP.CODE$
850     RETURN
860     '
870     '
880     ' ----------------------
890     REM - Exit Program
900     FIELD #1, 2 AS DATA.RECORDS$
910     LSET DATA.RECORDS$ = MKI$(NUM.DATARECORD)
920     PUT #1, 1
930     CLOSE 1
940     END
950     '
960     '
970     ' ----------------------
980     REM - Add a Data Record containing the variables:
990     '   NAM$,  PHONENUM$, ADDRESS$, CITY$, STATE$, ZIP$
1000    '
1010    '
1020    GOSUB 1640                    ' Check if name is
        already in the table
1030    IF F = 1  THEN PRINT S$; " has already been entered" :
        RETURN
1040    '
1050    GOSUB 1800                    ' Check if phone
        number is in the table
1060    IF F = 1  THEN PRINT S$; " has already been entered" :
        RETURN
1070    '
1080    GOSUB 1250                    ' Add the name to
        the names table
1090    ' On return, NUM.DATARECORD = the record # to
        contain the data
1100    GOSUB 1470                    ' Add to telephone
        number table
1110    '
1120    ' Now place the data into the fields of the
        record and write to disk
1130    FIELD #1, 20 AS NAMES$, 10 AS PHONE$, 15 AS
        STREET$, 10 AS CITY.NAME$, 2 AS STATE.NAME$, 5 AS
        ZIP.CODE$
1140    LSET NAMES$ = NAM$
1150    LSET PHONE$ = PHONENUM$
1160    LSET STREET$ = ADDRESS$
1170    LSET CITY.NAME$ = CITY$
1180    LSET STATE.NAME$ = STATE$
1190    LSET ZIP.CODE$ = ZIP$
```

```
1200      PUT #1, NUM.DATARECORD
1210      RETURN
1220      '
1230      '
1240      ' ------------------------
1250      REM - Add a name to the name table
1260      '
1270      ' Check if the table is full
1280      IF NUM.NAMES >= MAX - 1  THEN F = 2 :
              RETURN
1290      NUM.NAMES = NUM.NAMES + 1
1300      S$ = NAM$                     ' Make a copy of the name
1310      F = 0
1320      FIELD #1, 40 AS NAMES$, 2 AS DATA.RECORD.LOCATION$
1330      GOSUB 2160                    ' Compute Hash
1340      GET #1, HASH + 1
1350      IF  LEFT$(NAMES$,1) = " "  THEN  LSET NAMES$ = S$ :
              NUM.DATARECORD = NUM.DATARECORD + 1 :
              LSET DATA.RECORD.LOCATION$ = MKI$(NUM.DATARECORD) :
              PUT #1, HASH + 1:
              RETURN
1360      ' If this space in the table is free, then
              place the name here
1370      ' Return NUM.DATARECORDS = the record
1380      ' number where the corresponding data is kept
1390      '
1400      ' Otherwise, try the next entry in the table
1410      HASH = HASH - 1
1420      IF  HASH = 0  THEN  HASH = MAX
1430      GOTO 1340
1440      '
1450      '
1460      ' ------------------------
1470      REM - Add a telephone number into the phone number table
1480      '
1490      S$ = PHONENUM$                ' make a copy of
              the phone number
1500      F = 0
1510      FIELD #1, 40 AS PHONE$, 2 AS DATA.RECORD.LOCATION$
1520      GOSUB 2160                    ' Compute Hash
1530      GET #1, HASH + MAX + 1
1540      IF  LEFT$(PHONE$,1) = "*" OR LEFT$(PHONE$,1) =
              " "  THEN  LSET PHONE$ = S$ :
              LSET DATA.RECORD.LOCATION$ = MKI$(NUM.DATARECORD) :
              PUT #1, HASH + MAX + 1 :
              RETURN
1550      ' If this space in the table is free, then
              place the phone number here
1560      '
1570      ' Otherwise, try the next entry in the table
1580      HASH = HASH - 1
1590      IF  HASH = 0  THEN  HASH = MAX
1600      GOTO 1530
1610      '
1620      '
1630      ' ------------------------
1640      REM - Search the table for NAM$
1650      '     Returns:
              DATA.RECORD.NUM = record # containing the data
1660      '
1670      S$ = NAM$
1680      FIELD #1, 40 AS NAMES$, 2 AS DATA.RECORD.LOCATION$
1690      GOSUB 2160
1700      S$ = S$ + SPACE$(20 - LEN(S$))
1710      GET #1, HASH + 1
```

```
1720    IF  LEFT$(NAMES$,1) = " "   THEN F = 0 :
           RETURN
1730    IF  NAMES$ = S$   THEN  F = 1 :
           DATA.RECORD.NUM = CVI(DATA.RECORD.LOCATION$) :
           RETURN
1740    HASH = HASH - 1
1750    IF  HASH = 0  THEN  HASH = MAX
1760    GOTO 1710
1770    '
1780    '
1790    ' ----------------------
1800    REM - Search the table for PHONENUM$
1810    '       Returns:
           DATA.RECORD.NUM = record # containing the data
1820    S$ = PHONENUM$
1830    FIELD #1, 40 AS PHONE$, 2 AS DATA.RECORD.LOCATION$
1840    GOSUB 2160
1850    GET #1, HASH + MAX + 1
1860    IF  LEFT$(PHONE$,1) = " "   THEN F = 0 :
           RETURN
1870    IF  LEFT$(PHONE$,LEN(S$)) = S$   THEN  F = 1 :
           DATA.RECORD.NUM = CVI(DATA.RECORD.LOCATION$) :
           RETURN
1880    HASH = HASH - 1
1890    IF  HASH = 0  THEN  HASH = MAX
1900    GOTO 1850
1910    '
1920    '
1930    ' ----------------------
1940    REM - Open data file
1950    ON ERROR GOTO 2030
1960    OPEN "datafile" FOR INPUT AS 1
1970    CLOSE 1
1980    OPEN "datafile" AS 1 LEN=62
1990    GET #1, 1
2000    FIELD #1, 2 AS DATA.RECORD$
2010    NUM.DATARECORD = CVI(DATA.RECORD$)
2020    RETURN
2030    OPEN "datafile" AS 1 LEN = 62
2040    PRINT "Initializing Data File ..."
2050    FIELD #1, 40 AS NAMES$, 2 AS DATA.RECORD$
2060    LSET NAMES$ = " "
2070    FOR I = 2 TO 2 * MAX + 1
2080    PUT #1, I
2090    NEXT I
2100    PRINT "Initialization Completed"
2110    PRINT
2120    RETURN
2130    '
2140    '
2150    ' ----------------------
2160    REM - Compute HASH = Hash (S$)
2170    HASH = 0
2180    FOR I = 1 TO LEN(S$)
2190       HASH = HASH + ASC(MID$(S$,I,1))
2200    NEXT I
2210    HASH = HASH MOD MAX + 1
2220    RETURN
```

The ADD NAME routine at line 1250 does a conventional hash table insertion. It returns a variable NUM.DATARECORD, which is the number of the record where the rest of the data should be stored. These values are stored by the statements in lines 1140 through 1200. Note that duplicate copies of the name and telephone number are also placed into the data record.

Searches are made by name or by telephone number. When a search by name is requested, the subroutine at line 1640 is called. When searching by phone number, the routine at line 1800 is called. If searches must be made on other fields in the data record, a simple sequential search can be done on the data records only.

THE BINARY TREE FILE SEARCH

The binary tree structure (see Chapter 5) provides an ideal method for storing information in disk files. Using the tree structure, you minimize disk use and maintain the data in sorted order.

In Chapter 5, the tree structure routine used three arrays: N$() to hold the names, L() to point to the left subtree, and R() to point to the right subtree. For the disk-based tree, each of these values is stored in a FIELD variable. Each node in the tree contains a name, left tree pointer, and right tree pointer. Therefore, each record in the file is defined as

> FIELD #1, 40 AS N$, 2 AS LEFT.TREE$, 2 AS RIGHT.TREE$

The file is constructed from a sequence of these records. For example, a small tree containing three names might have the form

Translated to a tree structured file, you have three records. The root of the tree is at record 1.

    Record 1
        George   LEFT.TREE = 2   RIGHT.TREE = 3

    Record 2
        Alan   LEFT.TREE = 0   RIGHT.TREE = 0

    Record 3
        Kim   LEFT.TREE = 0   RIGHT.TREE = 0

In addition to the data records, you also need to store some information about the file, including the location of the root record, the number of records in the file, and which records are free. This way, when you leave the file on the diskette, you won't lose track of the file structure. When you reopen the file, the information is read into memory and processing resumes.

A convenient location for this information is in record 1. This means that the actual data records have to begin at record 2 instead of record 1.

Programming the Disk-Based Tree

Programming the tree structured file is similar to programming the array version. But there is one important difference. In the array version, you initialized the R() array as a linked list to keep track of all the unused entries in the arrays. Before any data was added, all the entries were considered unused. They were placed on the unused entries list: U1 pointed to R(1), R(1) to R(2), R(2) to R(3), and so on.

To add a new name, you removed the unused location pointed to by U1 and then set U1 to the next entry in the list. The scheme worked well for the array tree structure, but it must be modified for the disk. Initializing the R() array into a single linked list is time-consuming for a disk file because it requires writing to every record in the file. That would take at least a minute for 1,000 records. Further, that method uses up a great deal of disk space before you have added a single name to the tree.

For the disk tree, you set both U1 and U2 to 0, signifying that the unused list is currently empty. Variable N will count the total number of records used in the file and is initially set to 1 (the first record contains the file information). When you add a new name to the file, you first look at the unused list. If it contains a free location, then you add the new name at that record.

If the free list is empty, you just increment N and use the new value of N as the next record to be added to the tree.

Let's run through some examples to see how this works. Initially, the file is empty and N = 1. Let's add the name GEORGE.

Since U1 = 0, you know that the free list is empty, so you increment N and place GEORGE in record 2.

Next, add ALAN. Again, since U1 = 0, add one to N. Then add KIM, BETTY, and MIKE, giving the tree,

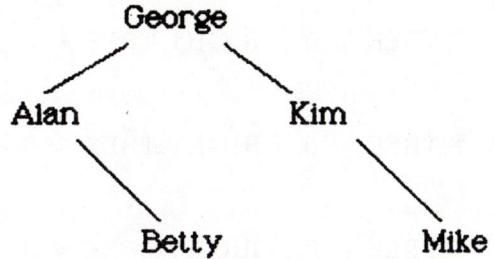

This tree is represented in the data file as

        Root = 2   U1 = 0   U2 = 0

        Record 2
            GEORGE   LEFT.TREE = 3   RIGHT.TREE = 4

        Record 3
            ALAN   LEFT.TREE = 0   RIGHT.TREE = 5

        Record 4
            KIM   LEFT.TREE = 0   RIGHT.TREE = 6

        Record 5
            BETTY   LEFT.TREE = 0   RIGHT.TREE = 0

        Record 6
            MIKE   LEFT.TREE = 0   RIGHT.TREE = 0

Now, let's delete BETTY. This creates a free entry, so you attach record 5 to the free list. This gives U1 = 5 and U2 = 5. Next, delete MIKE. Attaching record 6 to the free list gives U1 = 5 and U2 = 6. Note that RIGHT.TREE for record 5 points to record 6, as shown here.

        Root = 2   U1 = 5   U2 = 6

        Record 2
            GEORGE   LEFT.TREE = 3   RIGHT.TREE = 4

        Record 3
            ALAN   LEFT.TREE = 0   RIGHT.TREE = 0

Record 4
   KIM   LEFT.TREE = 0   RIGHT.TREE = 0

Record 5
   BETTY   LEFT.TREE = 0   RIGHT.TREE = 6

Record 6
   MIKE   LEFT.TREE = 0   RIGHT.TREE = 0

The last two records are now free and will be reused as you add new names. For example, if you add TOM, you remove the entry at the head of the free list. Since U1 = 5, you use this record and set U1 to 6. This gives

Root = 2   U1 = 6   U2 = 6

Record 2
   GEORGE   LEFT.TREE = 3   RIGHT.TREE = 4

Record 3
   ALAN   LEFT.TREE = 0   RIGHT.TREE = 0

Record 4
   KIM   LEFT.TREE = 0   RIGHT.TREE = 5

Record 5
   TOM   LEFT.TREE = 0   RIGHT.TREE = 0

Record 6
   MIKE   LEFT.TREE = 0   RIGHT.TREE = 0

The next name will be placed at record 6. Thereafter, there will be no free spaces, so new names will be added at the end of the file, beginning with record 7.

In this way, deleted records are always reused and the file grows only when all of the current records are in use.

Explanation of the Program

Listing 8-4 is a tree structured filing program. Let's step through it.

The first major operation is opening the data file. Line 130 calls the subroutine at line 1250, which opens the file.

Listing 8-4

```
100       MAX = 100
110       DIM S(20)
120       REM - S() is a stack needed when displaying the tree
130       GOSUB 1250
140       PRINT "Enter A(dd S(earch D(isplay L(ist
            R)emove Q(uit ? ";
150       C$ = INPUT$(1):
            PRINT C$
160       ON INSTR(1,"ASDLRQ",C$)+1 GOSUB 140, 210, 330,
            280, 370, 460, 1500
170       GOTO 140
180       REM
190       REM
200       REM - Add a name
210       INPUT "Enter Name ? ",S$
220       GOSUB 680
230       IF F>0 THEN PRINT "Error ";F
240       RETURN
250       REM
260       REM
270       REM - Print tree
280       GOSUB 810
290       RETURN
300       REM
310       REM
320       REM - Lookup a name
330       INPUT "Search for what name ? ",S$
340       GOSUB 570
350       IF F = 0 THEN PRINT S$;" Is in the list at ";G
            ELSE PRINT "Error ";F
360       RETURN
370       PRINT "Root = ";R
380       FOR I= 2 TO N
390       GET #1, I
400       PRINT I;N$,"Left=";CVI(LEFT.TREE$),
            "Right=";CVI(RIGHT.TREE$)
410       NEXT I
420       RETURN
430       REM
440       REM
450       REM - Remove a name
460       INPUT "Name to remove ? ",S$
470       GOSUB 570
480       IF F <> 0 THEN PRINT "Error ";F:
            RETURN
490       GOSUB 910
500       RETURN
510       REM
520       REM
530       REM
540       REM
550       REM
560       REM
570       REM - Search the tree for name s$
580       G = R :
            G1 = R
590       IF G = 0 THEN F = 1 :
            G = G1 :
            RETURN
600       GET #1, G
610       IF LEFT$(N$,LEN(S$)) = S$   THEN F = 0 :
            RETURN
620       G1 = G
630       IF S$ < N$   THEN G = CVI(LEFT.TREE$):
```

```
                        D=-1 ELSE G = CVI(RIGHT.TREE$):
                        D=1
  640        GOTO 590
  650        REM
  660        REM
  670        REM
  680        REM - Add a name S$ to the tree
  690        IF N = MAX THEN F = 4 :
                 RETURN
  700        GOSUB 570 :
                 REM - See if the name is already in the tree
  710        IF F = 0 THEN F = 2 :
                 RETURN ELSE F = 0
  720        IF U1 = 0 THEN N = N + 1 :
                 RECNUM = N :
                 U1 = 0:
               U2 = 0  ELSE  GET #1, U1 :
                 RECNUM = U1 :
                 U1 = CVI(RIGHT.TREE$) :
                 IF U1 = 0 THEN U2 = 0
  730        IF G = 0 THEN R = RECNUM  ELSE  IF D = 1 THEN GET #1, G :
                 LSET RIGHT.TREE$ = MKI$(RECNUM) :
                 PUT #1, G  ELSE  GET #1, G :
                 LSET LEFT.TREE$ = MKI$(RECNUM) :
                 PUT #1, G
  740        GET #1, RECNUM
  750        LSET N$ = S$
  760        LSET LEFT.TREE$ = MKI$(0) :
                 LSET RIGHT.TREE$ = MKI$(0)
  770        PUT #1, RECNUM
  780        RETURN
  790        REM
  800        REM
  810        REM - Display the entries in the tree
  820        IF R = 0 THEN RETURN ' Nothing to display
  830        G = R :
                 P = 0 :
                 REM - P is the stack pointer
  840        GET #1, G
  850        IF CVI(LEFT.TREE$) <> 0 THEN S(P) = G :
                 P = P + 1:
                 G = CVI(LEFT.TREE$) :
                 GOSUB 840 :
                 P = P - 1 :
                 G = S(P) :
                 GET #1, G
  860        PRINT N$
  870        IF CVI(RIGHT.TREE$) <> 0 THEN S(P) = G :
                 P = P + 1 :
                 G = CVI(RIGHT.TREE$) :
                 GOSUB 840 :
                 P = P - 1 :
                 G = S(P)
  880        RETURN
  890        REM
  900        REM
  910        REM - Remove node at G
  920        T = G
  930        GET #1, G :
                 IF CVI(RIGHT.TREE$) = 0 THEN GOSUB 1010 ELSE IF
                 CVI(LEFT.TREE$) = 0 THEN GOSUB 1070 ELSE T =
                 CVI(LEFT.TREE$) :
                 GOSUB 1140
  940        REM - Add T to free space list
  950        IF U2 = 0 THEN U1 = T:
```

```
                  U2=T ELSE   GET #1, U2 :
                  LSET RIGHT.TREE$ = MKI$(T) :
                  PUT #1, U2
    960       GET #1, T :
                  LSET RIGHT.TREE$ = MKI$(0) :
                  PUT #1, T
    970       U2 = T
    980       RETURN
    990       REM
   1000       REM
   1010       REM - Set parent to point to left branch of G
   1020       IF R = G THEN GET #1, G :
                  IF CVI(RIGHT.TREE$) = 0 THEN   R = CVI(LEFT.TREE$) :
                  RETURN
   1030       IF D = - 1 THEN 'GET #1, G :
                  TEMP$ = LEFT.TREE$ :
                  GET #1, G1 :
                  LSET LEFT.TREE$ = TEMP$ :
                  PUT #1, G1  ELSE   GET #1, G :
                  TEMP$ = LEFT.TREE$ :
                  GET #1, G1 :
                  LSET RIGHT.TREE$ = TEMP$ :
                  PUT #1, G1
   1040       RETURN
   1050       REM
   1060       REM
   1070       REM - Set parent to point to right branch of G
   1080       IF R = G THEN GET #1, G :
                  IF CVI(LEFT.TREE$) = 0 THEN R = CVI(RIGHT.TREE$) :
                  RETURN
   1090       GET #1, G :
                  TEMP$ = RIGHT.TREE$ :
                  GET #1, G1 :
                  IF D = -1 THEN LSET LEFT.TREE$ = TEMP$   ELSE   LSET
                  RIGHT.TREE$ = TEMP$
   1100       PUT #1, G1
   1110       RETURN
   1120       REM
   1130       REM
   1140       REM - Descend along right most branch of T
   1150       GET #1, T
   1160       WHILE  CVI(RIGHT.TREE$) <> 0 :
                  T1 = T :
                  T = CVI(RIGHT.TREE$) :
                  GET #1, T :
                  WEND
   1170       GET #1, T :
                  TEMP$ = N$
   1180       GET #1, G :
                  LSET N$ = TEMP$ :
                  PUT #1, G
   1190       IF  T1 <> 0   THEN GET #1, T :
                  TEMP$ = LEFT.TREE$ :
                  GET #1, T1 :
                  LSET RIGHT.TREE$ = TEMP$ :
                  PUT #1, T1
   1200       GET #1, G :
                  IF  CVI(LEFT.TREE$) = T THEN   GET #1, T :
                  TEMP$ = LEFT.TREE$ :
                  GET #1, G :
                  LSET LEFT.TREE$ = TEMP$ :
                  PUT #1, G
   1210       RETURN
   1220       REM
   1230       REM
```

```
1240        REM
1250        REM - Open Data File
1260        PRINT "Accessing Data File ..." :
               PRINT :
               PRINT
1270        ON ERROR GOTO 1390
1280        OPEN "datafile" FOR INPUT AS 1
1290        CLOSE 1
1300        OPEN "datafile" AS 1 LEN = 44
1310        GET #1, 1
1320        FIELD #1, 2 AS ROOT$, 2 AS N$, 2 AS UNUSED1$,
               2 AS UNUSED2$
1330        R = CVI(ROOT$)
1340        N = CVI(N$)
1350        U1 = CVI(UNUSED1$)
1360        U2 = CVI(UNUSED2$)
1370        FIELD #1, 40 AS N$, 2 AS LEFT.TREE$, 2 AS RIGHT.TREE$
1380        RETURN
1390        RESUME 1400
1400        ON ERROR GOTO 0
1410        OPEN "datafile" AS 1 LEN = 44
1420        FIELD #1, 40 AS N$, 2 AS LEFT.TREE$, 2 AS RIGHT.TREE$
1430        U1 = 0
1440        U2 = 0
1450        N = 1
1460        R = 0
1470        RETURN
1480        REM
1490        REM
1500        REM - CLOSE DATAFILE AND EXIT
1510        FIELD #1, 2 AS ROOT$, 2 AS N$, 2 AS UNUSED1$,
               2 AS UNUSED2$
1520        LSET ROOT$ = MKI$(R)
1530        LSET N$ = MKI$(N)
1540        LSET UNUSED1$ = MKI$(U1)
1550        LSET UNUSED2$ = MKI$(U2)
1560        PUT #1, 1
1570        CLOSE 1
1580        END
```

If the data file does not exist, the OPEN FOR INPUT in line 1280 will fail and cause an error. The ON ERROR GOTO statement in line 1270 catches the error and sends control to line 1390, where the file is opened as a random access file and the variables U1, U2, N, and R are initialized.

If the file already exists, then line 1280 executes successfully. But this opens the file as a sequential file. Lines 1290 and 1300 close the file and reopen it as a random access file. Record 1 is fetched and the original values for the root, number of records, and the unused list head pointers and tail pointers are restored.

Line 140, in the main body of the program, is a prompt. This program provides for adding new names, searching for existing names, displaying the names in sorted order, listing the internal structure of the file, removing a name, and quitting, which also updates record 1 and closes the file.

The add name routine, at line 200, prompts for a name to add and places it in the variable S$. Then it calls the subroutine at line 680. This routine, in turn, calls the SEARCH subroutine at line 590. This subroutine, in turn, calls the SEARCH subroutine at line 480. If the name is already in the tree, an error occurs.

If the name is not already present, the ADD routine places the new name into the tree. If U1 = 0 (line 720), then the free list is empty, so the new name is added at record N + 1. If the unused list contains at least one location, then the new name will be placed at record U1, and U1 is set to point to the next free location (see last part of line 720).

G contains the location of the parent record for the new name. Line 730 determines which subtree in the parent record points to the new record. If D is 1, then the direction taken through the tree was to the right, so the right tree must point to the new record.

Lines 740 through 770 add the new name and record to the file.

Except for the changes to the unused list, the disk tree search is practically identical to Listing 5-6. In the disk version, new code was added to GET a record before modifying the data and PUT the updated record back on the disk.

To store additional information along with the name, just modify the FIELD statements in lines 1370 and 1420 to specify the additional data fields. Also be sure to update the LEN parameter of the OPEN statements in lines 1300 and 1410, as appropriate.

THE EMPLOYEE RECORDS MOVE TO DISK

At last, you have covered enough ground to nearly complete the employee-records system. Listing 4-7 provided an almost complete system. But that program omitted the report function. It also omitted the ability to store records on disk, which is what makes the system truly useful. In this section, you can make the conversion from an array system to a disk system. The necessary changes are shown in Listing 8-5. (Chapter 9 adds the reporting function.)

Listing 8-5

```
10        REM - Employee Records System
20        MAX = 100
30        GOSUB 12000              ' Open/Initialize Data File
100       REM
110       REM
120       REM - Prompt for Command
130       PRINT
140       INPUT "Select:  A)dd, P)rint, L)ist, D)elete, C)hange,
             R)eport, Q)uit ? ",CH$
150       ON INSTR("APLDCRQ",CH$) + 1 GOSUB 170, 1010, 2010, 3080, 5000,
             6000, 7000, 13000
160       GOTO 130
170       PRINT "Incorrect Selection - Try Again"
```

```
180      GOTO 130
190      REM
200      REM
1000     REM -----------------------------------------------------
1010     REM - Add A New Employee
1020     PRINT
1030     INPUT "Enter Name of Employee to Add? ",S$
1040     IF S$ = "" THEN RETURN
1050     GOSUB 9000 ' Lookup the name
1060     IF F = 1  THEN PRINT "'";S$;"' has already been added":
             GOTO 1020
1070     LSET NAMES$ = S$
1080     INPUT "Department Number ? ",DEPT :
             LSET DEPT$ = MKI$(DEPT)
1090     INPUT "Telephone Number ? ",PHONE.NUM$ :
             LSET PHONE$ = PHONE.NUM$
1100     INPUT "Salary ? ",SALARY :
             LSET SALARY$ = MKI$(SALARY)
1105     PUT #1, G
1110     RETURN
1120     REM
1130     REM
2000     REM -----------------------------------------------------
2010     REM - Print Employee Records
2020     GOSUB 3000 ' Prompt for name to list
2030     IF S$ = "" THEN RETURN
2035     GET #1, G
2040     LPRINT "Name"; TAB(20); "Department #"; TAB(35); "Telephone
         #"; TAB(50); "Salary"
2050     PRINT NAMES$; TAB(25); CVI(DEPT$); TAB(35); PHONE$; TAB(50);
         CVI(SALARY$)
2060     RETURN
2070     REM
2080     REM
3000     REM -----------------------------------------------------
3010     REM - Prompt for name of employee to print or list
3020     PRINT
3030     INPUT "Name of Employee to Display? ",S$
3040     IF S$ = "" THEN RETURN
3050     GOSUB 9000 ' lookup S$
3060     IF F = 0  THEN PRINT "'"; S$; "' is not in the records - Try again":
             GOTO 3020
3070     RETURN
3080     REM
3090     REM
4000     REM -----------------------------------------------------
4010     REM - List a record to the display
4020     GOSUB 3000
4030     IF S$ = "" THEN RETURN
4035     GET #1, G
4040     PRINT "Name"; TAB(20); "Department #"; TAB(35); "Telephone
         #"; TAB(50); "Salary"
4050     PRINT NAMES$; TAB(25); CVI(DEPT$); TAB(35); PHONE$; TAB(50);
         CVI(SALARY$)
4060     RETURN
4070     REM
4080     REM
4090     REM
5000     REM -----------------------------------------------------
5010     REM - Delete an employee
5020     PRINT
5030     INPUT "Name of Employee to Delete ? ", S$
5040     IF  S$ = ""   THEN RETURN
5050     GOSUB 9000 ' Lookup the employee
5060     IF F = 0 THEN PRINT "'"; S$; "' is not in the records - Try again":
             GOTO 5020
```

```
5070      PRINT NAMES$; TAB(20); "Department #"; CVI(DEPT$)
5080      INPUT "Delete (Y or N) ? ",C$
5090      IF C$<> "Y" AND C$<>"N" THEN 5080
5100      IF C$ = "Y" THEN GOSUB 10000 :
          PRINT "Deleted" :
          RETURN
5110      PRINT "Not Deleted"
5120      REM
5130      REM
5140      REM
6000      REM ------------------------------------------------------------
6010      REM - Change Employee Data
6020      PRINT
6030      INPUT "Name of Employee to Change ? ",S$
6040      IF  S$ = ""   THEN RETURN
6050      GOSUB 9000 ' Lookup
6060      IF  F = 0   THEN PRINT "'"; S$; "' is not in the records - Try again" :
          GOTO 6020
6065      GET #1, G
6070      PRINT
6080      PRINT "Department ="; CVI(DEPT$)
6090      INPUT "Enter new department (CR=no change) ? ",NEWDEPT
6100      IF  NEWDEPT <> 0   THEN LSET DEPT$ = MKI$(NEWDEPT)
6110      PRINT
6120      PRINT "Telephone # = ";PHONE$
6130      INPUT "Enter new telephone # (CR=no change) ? ",NEWPHONE$
6140      IF  NEWPHONE$ <> ""   THEN  LSET PHONE$ = NEWPHONE$
6150      PRINT
6160      PRINT "Salary = ";CVI(SALARY$)
6170      INPUT "Enter new salary (CR=no change) ? ", NEWSALARY
6180      IF NEWSALARY <> 0   THEN  LSET SALARY$ = MKI$(NEWSALARY)
6185      PUT #1, G
6190      RETURN
6200      REM
6210      REM
7000      REM ------------------------------------------------------------
7010      REM - Print a Report
7020      RETURN
7030      REM
7040      REM
8000      REM ------------------------------------------------------------
8010      REM - Add a name
8020      IF N >= MAX - 1 THEN F = 2 :
          RETURN
8030      N = N + 1
8040      F = 0
8050      GOSUB 11000 ' Compute Hash
8055      GET #1, HASH + 1
8060      IF LEFT$(NAMES$,1) = ""   OR   LEFT$(NAMES$,1) = "*" THEN   G = HASH + 1:
          RETURN
8070      HASH = HASH - 1
8080      IF HASH = 0 THEN HASH = MAX
8090      GOTO 8060
8100      REM
8110      REM
9000      REM ------------------------------------------------------------
9010      REM - Lookup a name
9020      GOSUB 11000
9025      S$ = S$ + SPACE$(18-LEN(S$))
9027      GET #1, HASH + 1
9030      IF LEFT$(NAMES$,1) = " " THEN F = 0 :
          G = HASH + 1:
          RETURN
9040      IF NAMES$ = S$ THEN F = 1:
          G = HASH + 1:
          RETURN
```

```
9050      HASH = HASH - 1
9060      IF HASH = 0 THEN HASH = MAX
9070      GOTO 9027
9080      REM
9090      REM
10000     REM ------------------------------------------------------------
10010     REM - Delete a Name
10015     GET #1, HASH + 1
10020     LSET NAMES$ = "*"
10025     PUT #1, HASH + 1
10030     N = N - 1
10040     RETURN
10050     REM
10060     REM
11000     REM ------------------------------------------------------------
11010     REM - Compute HASH = Hash(S$)
11020     HASH = 0
11030     FOR I = 1 TO LEN(S$)
11040        HASH = HASH + ASC(MID$(S$, I, 1))
11050     NEXT I
11060     HASH = HASH MOD MAX + 1
11070     RETURN
11080     REM
11090     REM
12000     REM ------------------------------------------------------------
12010     REM - Open/Initialize Data File
12020     ON ERROR GOTO 12080
12030     OPEN "records" FOR INPUT AS 1
12040     CLOSE 1
12050     OPEN "records" AS 1 LEN = 32
12060     FIELD #1, 18 AS NAMES$, 2 AS DEPT$, 10 AS PHONE$, 2 AS SALARY$
12065     ON ERROR GOTO 0
12070     RETURN
12080     RESUME 12090
12090     ON ERROR GOTO 0
12100     OPEN "records" AS 1 LEN = 32
12110     PRINT "Initializing Employee Records Data File"
12120     FIELD #1, 18 AS NAMES$, 2 AS DEPT$, 10 AS PHONE$, 2 AS SALARY$
12130     LSET NAMES$ = " "
12140     FOR I = 1 TO MAX
12150        PUT #1, I
12160     NEXT I
12170     RETURN
13000     REM - END
13010     CLOSE 1
13020     END
```

Since the records are now stored on disk, you no longer need the array declarations at the beginning of the program. The DIM statement, originally at line 30, has been removed and replaced with a jump to the subroutine at line 12000. This subroutine either opens or creates the data file. The FIELD statement allocates 18 bytes for a name, 2 bytes for the department number, 10 bytes for a telephone number, and 2 bytes for the salary. You might wish to change these. The SALARY value is limited to integers. By increasing the salary field to 4 bytes and using CVS() and MKS$() instead of CVI() and MKI() throughout the program, you can adapt the system to store fractional values, such as $335.50.

The routines in the program have been modified to read directly from the disk. In the LOOKUP routine (line 9000), you now GET the hashed record (line 9027). Other routines, such as CHANGE, (lines 6000 through 6190) must not only GET the record but must also PUT the altered record back into the file.

REVIEW

- Searching a disk is as easy as searching an array.
- Hash tables provide fast access, but they lack the sorted structure of trees. Nevertheless, hash tables are excellent to quickly search large files.
- To use more than one search key, add hash tables to each file.
- Binary trees are excellent disk storage structures. Trees provide quick searches, updates, and deletions. Trees do not require that the entire file be preallocated, which saves disk space and provides flexibility.

CHAPTER
9
Sorting Files

Chapter 6 describes several sorting algorithms, including the selection sort, Shellsort, and Quicksort. All of these algorithms are suitable for sorting files. The faster methods are preferable, of course. A major problem in sorting a disk file is that many slow and inefficient disk reads and writes must be made.

Listing 9-1 shows a selection sort subroutine that sorts a disk file containing MAX records. This routine is quite slow, partly because the selection sort is inefficient, but especially because it reads, exchanges, and writes many disk records. Each reference to the disk is time-consuming. In addition, the selection sort algorithm destroys the data in the disk file. After it prints a record, the algorithm writes "zzzzzz" back in the file.

Listing 9-1

```
900      REM - Disk based selection sort
1000     FOR I = 1 TO MAX
1010     S$ = "zzzzzz"
1020     FOR J = 1 TO MAX
1030     GET #1, J
1040       IF NAMES$ < S$ THEN S$ = NAMES$:
             L = J
1050     NEXT J
1060     GET #1, L
1070     PRINT NAMES$,
1080     IF POS(0) > 60 THEN PRINT
1090     LSET NAMES$ = "zzzzzz"
1100     PUT #1, L
1110     NEXT I
1120     RETURN
```

IMPROVING THE SORT

You can improve the disk selection sort by reading the entire file into an array, sorting the array, and then writing the file back out to disk. Listing 9-2 is a version of the selection sort that has been modified to read the records into an array. After reading the entire file, Listing 9-2 sorts the array and writes the ordered records back to disk. In this form, the disk file sort routine arranges 50 records in 22 seconds. Listing 9-1 takes 50 seconds to do this.

Listing 9-2

```
1000    REM - Disk based selection sort, reads all into memory
1010    FOR I = 1 TO MAX
1020    S$ = "zzzzzz"
1030    FOR J = 1 TO MAX
1040      IF S$(J) < S$ THEN S$ = S$(J):
            L = J
1050    NEXT J
1060    PRINT S$(L),
1070    IF POS(0) > 60 THEN PRINT
1080    LSET NAMES$ = S$(L)
1090    PUT #1, I
1100    S$(L) = "zzzzzz"
1110    NEXT I
1120    RETURN
1130    '
1140    '
1150    REM - Read the file into memory
1160    FOR I = 1 TO MAX
1170      GET #1, I
1180      S$(I) = NAMES$
1190    NEXT I
1200    RETURN
```

Sorting time depends on the size of each record in the file. Large records take more time, while short records take less time. Unfortunately, if the file is larger than the available memory, this technique will not work. This chapter discusses techniques for solving this and other disk sorting problems.

The first technique reads only the fields of the records that are used in the sort, rearranges a group of pointers P(), and then copies the old file to a new file based on the record order in the P() array. This technique uses much less memory because it reads only the field on which the sort is based. Larger files can thus be sorted.

The second method splits the file to be sorted into one or more smaller files, sorts the smaller files, and then merges the results to produce the final sorted file.

These two methods are not the only disk file sorts, but they likely will be sufficient for your applications.

If you haven't read Chapter 6, do so now. Many basic sorting algorithms are described there and are not repeated here. Additional information on disk files and how they are programmed in BASIC is provided in Chapter 7. If you're not familiar with random access files, you'd best start with Chapter 7.

The Shellsort routine is used in all the program examples in the following sections. Feel free to substitute if other routines would be better for your application.

SORTING WITH POINTERS

In the first technique for improving sorts, the sort program is split into several subroutines. The first subroutine reads the file, extracting and storing the keys in an array K$(). Only the keys are kept in memory. Next, a Shellsort is performed on K$() using a set of pointers P(). Then the records from the file are read and written to a new file in the order determined by the sort of K$(). This routine can handle fairly large files because it only keeps a part of each record in memory. For example, if you need to sort a list of names and addresses, and you're going to sort by zip code, then you need to read only the five characters of the zip code into K$().

Listing 9-3 shows the complete sorting program. It uses a Shellsort with pointers. The routines extract a portion of each record to use as the sort item and then arrange pointers to sort the records. Lines 1000 to 1080 read the sort keys into array K$(). K$() is then sorted using the Shellsort routine at line 2000 through 2140. Finally, the sorted file is constructed based on the new ordering of K$().

Listing 9-3

```
1000      REM - Read file, extracting keys K$()
1010      OPEN "datafile" AS 1 LEN = 40
1020      FIELD #1, 20 AS NAMES$, 20 AS PHONE.NUM$
1030      FOR I = 1 TO MAX
1040        GET #1, I
1050        K$(I) = NAMES$
1060        P(I) = I
1070      NEXT I
1080      RETURN
1090      '
1100      '
2000      ' Do Shellsort of array K$()
2010      D = 4
2020      IF D < MAX THEN D = D + D :
            GOTO 2020
2030      D = D - 1                          ' Let D =
            largest power of 2 < N
```

```
2040      D = INT (D/2)
2050      IF D < 1 THEN RETURN
2060      FOR J = 1 TO MAX - D
2070        FOR I = J TO 1 STEP -D
2080          IF K$(P(I,+ D)) > K$(P(I)) THEN GOTO 2130
2090          T = P(I)
2100          P(I) = P(I + D)
2110          P(I + D) = T
2120        NEXT I
2130      NEXT J
2140      GOTO 2040
2150      '
2160      '
3000      ' Create new, sorted file
3010      OPEN "sorted" AS 2 LEN = 40
3020      FIELD #2, 40 AS BUFFER2$
3030      FIELD #1, 40 AS BUFFER1$
3040      FOR I = 1 TO MAX
3050        GET #1, P(I)
3060        LSET BUFFER2$ = BUFFER1$
3070        PUT #2, I
3080      NEXT I
3090      CLOSE 1
3100      CLOSE 2
3110      KILL "datafile"
3120      NAME "sorted" AS "datafile"
3130      RETURN
```

The Shellsort and the file input routines are self-explanatory. But the final creation of the sorted file needs some explanation. When the file is first read and the sort items extracted, the pointer array P() is initialized to count from 1 to N, as in

P(1)	P(2)	P(3)	. . .	P(N)
1	2	3	. . .	N

These correspond to the sort items in array K$(). For example,

K$(1)	K$(2)	K$(3)	. . .	K$(N)
LISA	BETH	STEVE	. . .	ALAN

After the sort, the values in P() have been rearranged so that K$(P(I)) for I equals 1 to N gives K$() in alphabetical order. This means that the P(I) values look like

P(1)	P(2)	P(3)	. . .	P(N)
N	2	1	. . .	3

If you print the values, K$(P(I)), by varying the value of I from 1 to N, you'll print the names in sorted order.

K$(P(1))	K$(P(2))	K$(P(3))	. . .	K$(P(N))
ALAN	BETH	LISA	. .	STEVE

Each key K$(I) corresponds to the original record I in the file. But P(I) points to the location of the record in the sorted file. So to produce a sorted version of the file, you need to read record I from the original file and then write it out to record P(I) in the new file. See lines 3000 through 3140 of Listing 9-3.

SORTING BY SPLITTING THE FILE

The second disk file sorting method is somewhat simpler. It works by splitting the big file into several smaller files, each of which is small enough to be sorted in memory. The small, sorted files are then merged.

Merging two sorted files is easy. read one record from each file. Compare the two records. If record 1 is less than record 2, output record 1, and read a new record from the first file. Otherwise, output record 2 and then record 1. To see how this works, consider these two sorted lists of names:

List 1	List 2
ALAN	ALICE
CHARLIE	DAVID
FRED	DON
MIKE	LORI
NANCY	PAULA
OLIVER	TOM
SAMANTHA	WANDA

Let's read through these two lists and produce a third list containing the merged result.

Look at the names ALAN and ALICE. Since ALAN is alphabetically less than ALICE, put ALAN in list 3 and read the next name from list 1. Since ALICE is less than CHARLIE, put ALICE in list 3 and read the next name from list 2, DAVID. Compare CHARLIE and DAVID; put CHARLIE in list 3. The next name from list 1 is FRED; put DAVID in list 3 and read DON. DON is still less than FRED, so put DON in list 3 and read the next name, LORI.

So far list 3 looks like

List 3

ALAN
ALICE
CHARLIE
DAVID
DON
FRED

The merge continues until all the names are in list 3.

Special handling is needed when one file is emptied before the other. The merge routine must handle this detail. Listing 9-4 is a subroutine that does so. Before this subroutine is called, files 1 and 2 must be open for input and file 3 must be open for output. Previously sorted files 1 and 2 are read and merged to produce the larger file 3.

Listing 9-4

```
1000      ' Merge Files #1 and #2, producing file #3
1010      GOSUB 1240 ' Get line L1$
1020      GOSUB 1290 ' Get line L2$
1030      '
1040      IF  L1$ < L2$  THEN  PRINT #3, L1$ :
            IF EOF(1) THEN 1080 ELSE GOSUB 1240:
            GOTO 1040
1050      PRINT #3, L2$ :
            IF EOF(2) THEN 1150 ELSE GOSUB 1290 :
            GOTO 1050
1060      '
1070      '
1080      ' End of file on #1
1090      PRINT #3, L2$
1100      WHILE EOF(2) = 0
1110        GOSUB 1290
1120        PRINT #3, L2$
1130      WEND
1140      RETURN
1150      ' End of file on #2
1160      PRINT #3, L1$
1170      WHILE EOF(1) = 0
1180        GOSUB 1240
1190        PRINT #3, L1$
1200      WEND
1210      RETURN
1220      '
1230      '
1240      ' Read a line from #1
1250      LINE INPUT #1, L1$
1260      RETURN
1270      '
1280      '
1290      ' Read a line from #2
1300      LINE INPUT #2, L2$
1310      RETURN
```

Splitting the Files

One way to split a file into two pieces is to use an editor program, read the file, and write the first half to file 1 and the second half to file 2. Another method reads the entire file and counts the records. The routine determines the maximum number of records that can fit in memory and divides the file into the needed number of subfiles.

For example, if the file contains 1,211 records and only 250 records can fit in memory at once, then you need to split the file into 1,211/250 plus 1 subfiles, which gives 5 separate files. The first 4 subfiles contain 250 records each. The fifth file contains only 211 records.

A record from the master file is read and put on file 1. This is repeated until 250 records have been printed. Then, file 1 is closed and file 2 is read. This operation is repeated until all 5 files have been created.

Any sorting method can be used to sort the small files. After the individual files have been sorted, the files are merged. Listing 9-5 is a complete program that performs this operation. The routine at line 1000 scans through the entire file, counting the number of records. The variable N is set to the number of records. (You can preset N if you already know how many records are on the file.)

Listing 9-5

```
100     MAX.FILE.SIZE = 250
110     DIM S$(MAX.FILE.SIZE), P(MAX.FILE.SIZE)
120     OPEN "bigfile" FOR INPUT AS 1
130     GOSUB 1000
140     CLOSE 1
150     OPEN "bigfile" FOR INPUT AS 1
160     GOSUB 2000
170     CLOSE 1
180     GOSUB 3000
190     GOSUB 5000
200     STOP
1000    REM - Read through entire file, counting the
            number of records
1010    '   Return:
             N is the number of records in the file
1020    N = 0
1030    WHILE EOF(1) = 0
1040      LINE INPUT #1, L$
1050      N = N + 1
1060    WEND
1070    PRINT N;" records read."
1080    RETURN
1090    '
1100    ' '
2000    REM - Split the large file into several small files
2010    '   We have room for MAX.FILE.SIZE records in each file
2020    '   Return:
             NUMBER.OF.FILES created by splitting the large file
2030    '
2040    NUMBER.OF.FILES = INT(N/MAX.FILE.SIZE) + 1
2050    FOR I = 1 TO NUMBER.OF.FILES
```

```
2060        PRINT "Creating temporary SORT file # ";I
2070          OPEN "SORT." + CHR$(I+48) FOR OUTPUT AS 3
2080          J = 1
2090          WHILE EOF(1) = 0   AND   J <= MAX.FILE.SIZE
2100            LINE INPUT #1, L$
2110            PRINT #3, L$
2120            J = J + 1
2130          WEND
2140          CLOSE 3
2150        NEXT I
2160        RETURN
2170        '
2180        '
3000        REM - Shell sort each of the temporary files
3010        '  Input:
             NUMBER.OF.FILES is the number of temporary files
3020        '
3030        FOR Q = 1 TO NUMBER.OF.FILES
3040          PRINT "Sorting temporary SORT file # ";Q
3050          OPEN "SORT." + CHR$(Q+48) FOR INPUT AS 2
3060          NUM.LINES = 0
3070          WHILE   EOF(2) = 0
3080            NUM.LINES = NUM.LINES + 1
3090            LINE INPUT #2, S$(NUM.LINES)
3100            P(NUM.LINES) = NUM.LINES
3110          WEND
3120          CLOSE 2
3130          GOSUB 4010
3140          OPEN "sort." + CHR$(Q + 48) FOR OUTPUT AS 2
3150          FOR  I = 1 TO NUM.LINES
3160            PRINT #2, S$(P(I))
3170          NEXT I
3180          CLOSE 2
3190        NEXT Q
3200        RETURN
3210        '
3220        '
4000        ' Shellsort array S$(), using pointer array P()
4010        D = 4
4020        IF D < NUM.LINES THEN D = D + D :
             GOTO 4020
4030        D = D - 1                              ' Let D =
             largest power of 2 < N
4040        D = INT (D/2)
4050        IF D < 1 THEN RETURN
4060        FOR J = 1 TO NUM.LINES - D
4070          FOR I = J TO 1 STEP -D
4080            IF S$(P(I + D)) > S$(P(I)) THEN GOTO 4130
4090            T = P(I)
4100            P(I) = P(I + D)
4110            P(I + D)\ = T
4120          NEXT I
4130        NEXT J
4140        GOTO 4040
4150        '
4160        '
5000        ' Merge the sorted SORT.i files together into
             one big file
5010        '  Input:
             NUMBER.OF.FILES is the number of sort files
5020        '
5030        PRINT "Merging all sorted files"
5040        ON ERROR GOTO 5070
5050        KILL "sorted.big"
5060        GOTO 5080
```

```
5070        RESUME 5080
5080        ON ERROR GOTO 0
5090        GOSUB 5120
5100        NAME "scratch." + CHR$(48 + I - 2)   AS   "sorted.big"
5110        RETURN
5120        '
5130        IF NUMBER.OF.FILES > 1 THEN 5180
5140        NAME "sort.1" AS "scratch.1"
5150        I = 3
5160        RETURN
5170        '
5180        OPEN "sort.1" FOR INPUT AS 1
5190        OPEN "sort.2" FOR INPUT AS 2
5200        OPEN "scratch.1" FOR OUTPUT AS 3
5210        GOSUB 5420
5220        CLOSE 1
5230        CLOSE 2
5240        CLOSE 3
5250        KILL "sort.1"
5260        KILL "sort.2"
5270        I = 3 ' In case there are only 2 files
5280        FOR I = 3 TO NUMBER.OF.FILES
5290          OPEN "scratch." + CHR$(48 + I - 2) FOR INPUT AS 1
5300          OPEN "sort." + CHR$(48 + I) FOR INPUT AS 2
5310          OPEN "scratch." + CHR$(48 + I - 1) FOR OUTPUT AS 3
5320          GOSUB 5420
5330          CLOSE 1
5340          CLOSE 2
5350          CLOSE 3
5360          KILL "scratch." + CHR$(48 + I - 2)
5370          KILL "sort." + CHR$(48 + I)
5380        NEXT I
5390        RETURN
5400        '
5410        '
5420        ' Merge Files #1 and #2, producing file #3
5430        GOSUB 5660 ' Get line L1$
5440        GOSUB 5710 ' Get line L2$
5450        '
5460        IF  L1$ < L2$   THEN  PRINT #3, L1$ :
                IF EOF(1) THEN 5500 ELSE GOSUB 5660:
                GOTO 5460
5470        PRINT #3, L2$ :
                IF EOF(2) THEN 5570 ELSE GOSUB 5710 :
                GOTO 5470
5480        '
5490        '
5500        ' End of file on #1
5510        PRINT #3, L2$
5520        WHILE EOF(2) = 0
5530          GOSUB 5710
5540          PRINT #3, L2$
5550        WEND
5560        RETURN
5570        ' End of file on #2
5580        PRINT #3, L1$
5590        WHILE EOF(1) = 0
5600          GOSUB 5660
5610          PRINT #3, L1$
5620        WEND
5630        RETURN
5640        '
5650        '
5660        ' Read a line from #1
5670        LINE INPUT #1, L1$
5680        RETURN
```

```
5690        '
5700        '
5710        ' Read a line from #2
5720        LINE INPUT #2, L2$
5730        RETURN
```

Line 2000 reads through the large file and creates a series of temporary files—SORT.1, SORT.2, SORT.3, and so on.

The routine at line 3000 reads each subfile, performs a Shellsort, and writes the sorted file back out to the disk.

Finally, the subroutine at line 4000 opens two of the files for input and a third for output. Then the subroutine at line 5000 merges the two opened files into the third file. Subroutine 4000 steps through each of the temporary files until all of the records have been combined into a single file. Each temporary file is deleted after it is no longer needed.

POLISHING THE EMPLOYEE-RECORDS SYSTEM

Finally, you can complete the employee-records system by adding the REPORT function. The REPORT function, when selected, displays

Report by: 1) Employee name, or 2) Department?

By selecting 1, you receive a display of employee data sorted by name. Selection 2 displays the employee records sorted by department number.

The entire report subroutine is shown in Listing 9-6; the routine begins at line 7000. (Look back at Listing 4-7 and Listing 8-5, and you will see room at line 7000 for this routine.) Lines 7100 through 7410 produce the report sorted by name. Lines 7110 through 7140 read the name fields into the array K$(). Note that only records that actually contain a name are read. The test in line 7130 ensures that you place only actual names into array K$(). The number of the record that holds the name is stored in the array RECORD.NUM().

Listing 9-6

```
7000     REM ----------------------------------------------------------------
7010     REM - Print a Report
7020     PRINT
7030     INPUT "Report by:  1) Employee name, or 2) Department? ", COMMAND
7040     IF COMMAND = 0  THEN  RETURN
7050     IF  COMMAND = 1  THEN  7080 ELSE IF  COMMAND = 2  THEN  7420
7060     PRINT "Incorrect Selection"
7070     GOTO 7030
7080     REM - Produce Report sorted by employee name
7090     PRINT :
         PRINT "Please Wait ... Producing Report"
7100     KEYS = 0
```

```
7110    FOR I = 1 TO MAX
7120      GET #1, I
7130      IF  LEFT$(NAMES$,1) <> " "    AND  LEFT$(NAMES$,1) <> "*"
          THEN  KEYS = KEYS + 1 :
          K$(KEYS) = NAMES$ :
          RECORD.NUM(KEYS) = I
7140    NEXT I
7150    REM
7160    REM - Do Shellsort based on K$()
7170    D = 4
7180    IF D < KEYS THEN D = D + D :
          GOTO 7180
7190    D = D - 1                              ' Let D = largest power of 2 < N
7200    D = INT (D/2)
7210    IF D < 1 THEN 7330
7220    FOR J = 1 TO KEYS - D
7230      FOR I = J TO 1 STEP -D
7240        IF K$(I + D) > K$(I) THEN GOTO 7290
7250        T$ = K$(I) :
          T = RECORD.NUM (I)
7260        K$(I) = K$(I + D) :
          RECORD.NUM(I) = RECORD.NUM(I + D)
7270        K$(I + D) = T$ :
          RECORD.NUM(I + D) = T
7280      NEXT I
7290    NEXT J
7300    GOTO 7200
7310    REM - Now display sorted output
7320    PRINT
7330    PRINT "Name"; TAB(20); "Department #"; TAB(35); "Telephone
          #"; TAB(50); "Salary"
7340    PRINT "----"; TAB(20); "------------"; TAB(35); "-----------
          "; TAB(50); "------"
7350    PRINT
7360    FOR I = 1 TO KEYS
7370      GET #1, RECORD.NUM(I)
7380    PRINT NAMES$; TAB(25); CVI(DEPT$); TAB(35); PHONE$; TAB(50);
          CVI(SALARY$)
7390    NEXT I
7400    PRINT
7410    RETURN
7420    REM - Produce report, sorted by department number
7430    PRINT :
          PRINT "Please Wait ... Producing Report"
7440    KEYS = 0
7450    FOR I = 1 TO MAX
7460      GET #1, I
7470      IF  LEFT$(NAMES$,1) <> " "    AND  LEFT$(NAMES$,1)<> "*"
          THEN  KEYS = KEYS + 1 :
          K(KEYS) = CVI(DEPT$) :
          RECORD.NUM(KEYS) = I
7480    NEXT I
7490    REM
7500    REM - Do Shellsort based on K$()
7510    D = 4
7520    IF D < KEYS THEN D = D + D :
          GOTO 7520
7530    D = D - 1                              ' Let D = largest power of 2 < N
7540    D = INT (D/2)
7550    IF D < 1 THEN 7650
7560    FOR J = 1 TO KEYS - D
7570      FOR I = J TO 1 STEP -D
7580        IF K(I + D) > K(I) THEN GOTO 7630
7590        K = K(I) :
          T = RECORD.NUM (I)
```

```
7600         K(I) = K(I + D) :
             RECORD.NUM(I) = RECORD.NUM(I + D)
7610         K(I + D) = K :
             RECORD.NUM(I + D) = T
7620       NEXT I
7630     NEXT J
7640     GOTO 7540
7650     REM - Now display sorted output
7660     PRINT
7670     PRINT "Department #"; "Name"; TAB(35); "Telephone #"; TAB(50); "Salary"
7680     PRINT "------------"; "----"; TAB(35); "------------"; TAB(50); "------"
7690     PRINT
7700     FOR I = 1 TO KEYS
7710       GET #1, RECORD.NUM(I)
7720     PRINT CVI(DEPT$); TAB(15); NAMES$; TAB(35); PHONE$; TAB(50);
           CVI(SALARY$)
7730     NEXT I
7740     PRINT
7750     RETURN
```

At line 7160 you begin a Shellsort of the names in K$(). Each time that
you exchange a name, you also exchange the corresponding RECORD.NUM()
value. (See lines 7250 and 7260.)

Lines 7360 through 7390 read the records from the disk file, in sorted
order, and display them on the screen. You can easily modify these routines
for hard copy by using LPRINT statements.

The employee-records system is not intended to be comprehensive or
even fool-proof. It is intended only as an example of a simple filing system and
reporting utility. Feel free to base your programs around its internal structure
or to modify any of the subroutines.

REVIEW

- File sorting is slow unless disk references are reduced.
- The simplest way to sort is to read all the records from the file and put
  them in an array. Then sort the records in memory and write the sorted
  array back to the disk.
- If memory is limited, read only the part of the record that the sort is based
  on. If you are sorting a name, street address, city, and zip code record
  into alphabetical order by name, then you must read only the name into
  the array. When the sort is finished, rearrange the disk file based on the
  array in memory.
- Again, if memory is limited, you can split a file into several small files.
  Sort each of the small files and merge the result into a single file.

C H A P T E R
10

Condensing Programs

Sometimes your programs keep growing and growing and it seems like you will never have enough memory. But no matter how much memory you have, it will never be enough. In fact, an often stated rule is that most programs require about 10% more memory than the computer currently has.

So what can you do? Your choices are:

1. Make the program shorter
2. Throw out some features
3. Split the program into separate programs and call them with the CHAIN statement
4. Reduce the amount of data kept in memory

Making the program shorter, is of course, an obvious solution. This chapter outlines some general techniques and simple changes that lead to shorter programs.

Another possibility is to take out some features. Most people use only a small subset of the features in a program. So many people won't notice the absence of some features. Chapter 3 gives tips on how to choose features for a program.

The CHAIN statement lets one BASIC program run another BASIC program. This means that a long program might be split into several short programs. Each of the short programs can call each other with the CHAIN statement.

Many programs are not large programs; they just process tremendous amounts of data. And there just isn't room to keep all the data in memory. The solution is placing the data in a disk file and reading only the data that needs to be processed.

Of course, some programs need to have all or at least most of the data in memory at one time. A special *virtual memory* technique lets you trick the program into thinking that it has more memory than it really does. Virtual memory techniques simulate an array of data by storing the data on disk but accessing it in a way that minimizes the slowness of the disk drive. Many applications can use virtual memory techniques with little degradation in performance.

PROGRAM SHRINKERS

Sometimes you get an OUT OF MEMORY error when the program is really quite short. Try this little program to see how this happens.

        10 GOSUB 10

Type RUN. What do you get? Each time BASIC executes a Type GOSUB statement, it uses a little bit of memory. When it encounters a RETURN, it frees the memory. But if the program contains an error, it may end up repeatedly calling GOSUB and never seeing a RETURN statement.

If you're suspicious of the OUT OF MEMORY message, check to see whether you have any unexpected GOSUB calls or other errors in your program.

REM statements take up memory. They can be eliminated, but you risk making the program hard to understand. If possible, use the special ' symbol to put a remark at the end of a line. For example, instead of

        100 REM − X Gets the starting temperature
        100 X = 57

use

        100 X = 57 ' X Gets the starting temperatrure

Comments made this way require slightly less memory than REM statements.

Use integer variables instead of real number variables. IBM BASIC has three different kinds of numbers—integers, single precision real numbers, and double precision real numbers. Integers are numbers that contain no fractional part. On the IBM computer, they fall in the range of −32,768 to +32,767. A number like 3.14159 is not an integer because it contains a fractional part. To store this type of number, BASIC needs to use single or double precision real numbers. Real numbers take up considerably more memory than integers: Two times more for single precision and four times more for double precision numbers. The memory needed for an array of 1,000 integer variables is 2,000 bytes, compared to 8,000 bytes for an array of 1,000 double precision variables.

Single and double precision arthmetic is much slower than integer arithmetic. In fact, a FOR-NEXT loop that uses an integer for the loop control variable runs about 30 times faster than one that uses a single precision number.

You have two ways to tell your computer which type of variable you will use. You can either use the DEF statement or you can add a special character to the end of a variable name.

For example, all variables that end in a % symbol are treated as integers. The variables I%, J%, and MONTH% can hold only values from $-32,768$ to $+32,767$ that have no fractional part. The DEF statement looks like this:

10 DEFINT I, J, MONTH

Whenever I, J, or MONTH is referenced, BASIC knows that these are integer values.

DEFINT can also be used to specify an entire group of integer variables, as in

DEFINT A-Z

This says that all variables beginning with the letters A through Z are integers.

When it is possible, combine statements into a single line. For example, this sequence of lines

```
100 A = 45
110 B = 37.7
120 C = B*2 + A
```

can be combined by separating each of the statements with a colon. For example, the previous lines become

```
100 A = 45 : B = 37.7 : C = B*2 + A
```

Each line number takes memory. In long programs, eliminating lines can provide significant savings.

The same statement is often repeated in a program. For example, your program may do the same calculation in several places. In the following statements, B + 1 is repeated.

    A = (B + 1) * C
    PRINT (B + 1), SQR(A/(B + 1))

Instead of calculating B + 1 in each expression, assign B + 1 to a variable.

    T = B + 1
    A = T/C
    PRINT T, SQR(A/T)

This substitution also will make the program run slightly faster, especially if the calculation is executed within a loop.

You should also look for common strings. These strings might appear in PRINT statements in several places in the program. For example, a common message might be INVALID ENTRY - REENTER. If this appears in, say, seven locations, initialize a variable, such as E$, to the message.

    E$ = "Invalid Entry - Reenter"

Then, whenever that message must be printed, replace the message with the variable.

    PRINT "Invalid Entry - Reenter"

becomes

    PRINT E$

Always dimension array variables with the DIM statement. If you forget to dimension an array, BASIC does it automatically. When it does, it creates an array defined with 10 subscripts. If the array needs fewer than 10 elements, memory will be wasted. Always define the array precisely.

Sometimes the wrong algorithm is used to accomplish a task. Try to find a better way, perhaps one that uses less memory. Generally, there is a trade-off between the amount of memory needed and the speed of an algorithm. The faster the algorithm, the more memory required; the slower the algorithm the less memory required.

Chapter 6 describes two fast sorts: Shellsort and Quicksort. Quicksort uses an array called a stack, which keeps track of Quicksort's internal state. Shellsort doesn't need a stack at all, yet it executes almost as fast as Quicksort. So by giving up some speed, Shellsort releases memory.

THE CHAIN AND COMMON STATEMENTS

CHAIN provides a way for one BASIC program to pass control to another. This exercise illustrates how the command works. Type these statements:

```
10 PRINT "This is program #1"
20 CHAIN "PROGR2"
99 END
```

Save them as PROGR1, by typing

```
SAVE "PROGR1"
```

Next create this program:

```
10 PRINT "This is program #2"
20 STOP
```

Save it as PROGR2, by typing

```
SAVE "PROGR2"
```

Load PROG1 back into memory, type LIST and then run the program.

```
LOAD "PROGR1"
Ok
LIST
10 PRINT "This is program #1"
20 CHAIN "PROGR2"
99 END

RUN
```

You'll see the following output:

> This is program #1
> This is program #2
> Break

Type LIST, and you will see

> 10 PRINT "This is program #2"
> 20 STOP

What happened? The listing is different!
   The CHAIN statement in PROGR1 is equivalent to typing

> RUN "PROGR2"

That is why PROGR2 began running. When it stopped, it was still in memory, and so you could view it by typing LIST.
   Unfortunately, in normal use, CHAINing between programs causes the values of all variables to be lost. Add the following line to PROGR1:

> 15 J = −1:PRINT J

and in PROGR2, add

> 15 PRINT J

The output will be

> This is program #1
> −1
> This is program #2
> 0
> Break

As you can see, the value of J was lost once PROGR2 was loaded and executed by the CHAIN statement. To preserve variables, you need to use the COMMON statement, which makes variables common between programs. Make J common in PROGR1 by adding the line

> 12 COMMON J

This statement passes the value of J through to the called program, PROGR2. When it is run, you'll see

```
This is program #1
 −1
This is program #2
 −1
Break
```

CHAIN and COMMON enable BASIC programs to run other programs and to pass information between the programs. CHAIN can also pass control to a specific line within the called program. For example,

```
CHAIN "PROG2", 3000
```

begins execution of PROG2 at its line 3000.

An alternate for CHAIN and COMMON is the RUN statement. RUN, when used as program statement, has the form

```
RUN "PROG3"
```

and is nearly equivalent to CHAIN. A program that uses the RUN statement does not have access to COMMON variables, though. An easy way around this is to write needed variables to a temporary file. When the called program begins running, it opens the file and reads the variables. Alternately, data can be poked into memory areas outside of BASIC (see Chapter 13), and retrieved with PEEK statements in the called program.

VIRTUAL MEMORY

Virtual memory is a term used to describe a memory system that simulates a large or virtual memory. The concept is easy to apply to programs that normally store their data in an array. In fact, even though virtual memory is a common term, a more descriptive phrase might be virtual array.

To understand the method and its implementation, let's look at a sample text editor that lets you edit up to 1,000 lines of text. Each line can be up to 80 bytes long. That's as much as 80,000 bytes of text. You have no choice but to store the text on disk, each line stored in its own 80-byte record.

```
FIELD #1, 80 AS L$
```

To read line 23, you execute

```
GET #1, 23
```

Displaying 24 lines of text on the screen involves reading 24 separate records.

```
FOR I = 1 to 24
    GET #1, I
    PRINT L$;
NEXT I
```

Needless to say, 24 disk reads are very slow.

A simple improvement is to rearrange the file. Rather than thinking of each 80-byte line as an individual record, you can place a group of lines into a single record. For example,

```
FIELD #1, 80 AS L$(1), 80 AS L$(2), 80 AS L$(3), 80 AS L$(4)
```

In this form, each read gets four lines at a time. Displaying the 24 lines on the screen now takes only eight disk reads. This method is roughly three times faster than the other method. Note that 320 bytes exceeds BASIC's default random file buffer size of 128, so you must specify the buffer size when first starting BASICA:

```
A>BASICA /S:320
```

But using a larger buffer means you can no longer say

```
GET #1, LINE.NUMBER
```

when you wish to read the text corresponding to LINE.NUMBER. You need to translate LINE.NUMBER into a record number, and then determine which line within the record is the one you want.

If you set the variable LINES.PER.RECORD to 4, you can compute which record you need by evaluating

```
RECORD.NUMBER = INT ( (LINE.NUMBER − 1)/
    LINES.PER.RECORD ) + 1
```

For example, if you wish to read line 5, this statement computes

$$\text{RECORD.NUMBER} = \text{INT} ((5-1) / 4) + 1$$
$$= 1 + 1$$
$$= 2$$

This indicates that record 2 contains the text of line 5. The next step is to select which line within the record contains line 5. To do this, you create a variable INDEX, which indexes the appropriate L$() variable in the FIELD statement. INDEX is computed as

$$\text{INDEX} = ((\text{LINE.NUMBER} - 1) \text{ MOD LINES.PER.RECORD}) + 1$$

The MOD or modules math function computes the remainder in a division problem. For example, in the problem $7 \div 3$, the remainder is 1.

So the expression evaluates as

$$\text{INDEX} = ((5 - 1) \text{ MOD } 4) + 1$$
$$= (4 \text{ MOD } 4) + 1$$
$$= 0 + 1$$
$$= 1$$

This tells you that L$(1) is the array element that you need to fetch line 5.

To simplify the routines, place the disk record and index computation in a separate subroutine, as shown in Listing 10-1. This routine also reads the needed record from the disk. To see how the subroutine is used, look again at the routine that writes 24 lines of test to the screen.

```
FOR I = 1 to 24
   LINE.NUMBER = I
   GOSUB 3000
   PRINT L$(INDEX);
NEXT I
```

Rather than reading the record directly, you call the FETCH routine at line 3000. The subroutine reads the required record, and the lines above simply display the corresponding line on the screen. Note that there is a special test in the read record routine. If the RECORD.NUMBER that is computed is equal to the CURRENT.RECORD, then you already have the record in memory and do not have to read the disk again. If the two values are different, then you must read the new record and update CURRENT.RECORD.

Listing 10-1

```
3000 REM - FETCH RECORD FROM DISK
3010 REM Input:
3020 REM    LINE.NUMBER is the line to fetch
3030 REM Returns:
3040 REM    RECORD.NUMBER
3050 REM    INDEX
3060 REM    Reads the record into memory
3070 REM
3080 RECORD.NUMBER = INT( (LINE.NUMBER -1) / LINES.PER.RECORD ) + 1
3090 INDEX = ((LINE.NUMBER - 1) MOD LINES.PER.RECORD) + 1
3100 IF  CURRENT.RECORD = RECORD.NUMBER  THEN  RETURN
3110 GET #1, RECORD.NUMBER
3120 CURRENT.RECORD = RECORD.NUMBER
3130 RETURN
```

So far, so good. But you also need to write lines of text out to disk. To do that, you can LSET the data into the FIELDed variables and put the entire record on disk. But it can be wasteful to output a record containing four lines when you've only changed one line. And it is especially wasteful if the line you need to modify next is in the same record.

You can change the routine in Listing 10-1 to handle this situation. You need to keep track of when you have executed an LSET statement so that you are sure to output any modified lines to disk before reading a new record. Listing 10-2, lines 1180 to 1220 show a subroutine to handle writing to disk. In this subroutine, the variable MODIFIED is set to 1 whenever one of the FIELD variables is changed. The MODIFIED variable is checked before a new record is read. If the current record has been modified, then it is written to the disk.

Listing 10-2

```
100      LINES.PER.RECORD = 10
110      LINE.SIZE = 80
120      GOSUB 1250
130      ,
140      ,
150      INPUT "Enter:  A)dd a line, R)ead a line, Q)uit ? ", C$
160      IF C$ = "A"  THEN GOSUB 200 ELSE IF C$ = "R"
            THEN GOSUB 270 ELSE IF C$ = "Q" THEN STOP
170      GOTO 150
180      ,
190      ,
200      REM - Add a new line
210      INPUT "At What line number? ",LINE.NUMBER
220      INPUT "Text? ",TEXT$
230      GOSUB 1180
240      RETURN
250      ,
260      ,
270      REM - Read a line from virtual memory
280      INPUT "Line number to read? ", LINE.NUMBER
290      GOSUB 1000
300      PRINT L$(INDEX)
310      RETURN
320      ,
330      ,
```

```
1000      REM - Fetch/Read Record From Disk
1010      REM Input:
1020      REM    LINE.NUMBER is the line to fetch
1030      REM Returns:
1040      REM    RECORD.NUMBER
1050      REM    INDEX
1060      REM    Reads the record into memory
1070      REM
1080      RECORD.NUMBER = INT( (LINE.NUMBER - 1) /
            LINES.PER.RECORD ) + 1
1090      INDEX = ((LINE.NUMBER - 1) MOD LINES.PER.RECORD) + 1
1095      PRINT RECORD.NUMBER, INDEX
1100      IF CURRENT.RECORD = RECORD.NUMBER THEN RETURN
1110      IF MODIFIED   THEN PUT #1, CURRENT.RECORD
1120      GET #1, RECORD.NUMBER
1130      CURRENT.RECORD = RECORD.NUMBER
1140      MODIFIED = 0
1150      RETURN
1160      '
1170      '
1180      REM - Write TEXT$ to the disk at LINE.NUMBER
1190      GOSUB 1000
1200      LSET L$(INDEX) = TEXT$
1210      MODIFIED = 1
1220      RETURN
1230      '
1240      '
1250      REM - Initialize/Open data file containing virtual array
1260      REM Input:
1270      REM    LINE.SIZE is size, in bytes, of each line
1280      REM    LINES.PER.RECORD is number of lines per disk block
1290      REM
1300      OPEN "virtual.mem" AS 1 LEN = LINES.PER.RECORD
            * LINE.SIZE
1310      DIM L$(LINES.PER.RECORD)
1320      FIELD #1, LINE.SIZE AS L$(1), LINE.SIZE AS
            L$(2), LINE.SIZE AS L$(3), LINE.SIZE AS L$(4),
            LINE.SIZE AS L$(5), LINE.SIZE AS L$(6), LINE.SIZE AS
            L$(7), LINE.SIZE AS L$(8), LINE.SIZE AS L$(9),
            LINE.SIZE AS L$(10)
1330      GET #1, 1
1340      MODIFIED = 0
1350      CURRENT.RECORD = 1
1360      RETURN
```

On entry to WRITE RECORD, LINE.NUMBER contains the number of the line that is to be updated, and variable TEXT$ is the text to be written to the file. The first step is to get the record containing LINE.NUMBER into memory (this is done by calling FETCH RECORD). Then you LSET the variable into the FIELD buffer. But you don't output the modified record right away. Instead, you set a flag variable called MODIFIED to remind us that the lines in the CURRENT.RECORD have been altered. This way, if the next line that you write to the file is already in the buffer, you avoid a duplicate ouput operation.

Suppose that you have placed a line into the record. Also suppose that the next line you need to fetch is not in the buffer. You can't just read it in directly because one of the lines in the record has been changed and you still need to write it out to disk. This is where you check the MODIFIED flag. If it's set, then you output the current buffer.

Listing 10-2 is a set of sample routines for reading and writing lines into a virtual array file structure. Experiment by changing the number of lines in each record. You can even change the data from text lines to real numbers. Real numbers take only four bytes each, so a 128-byte record has room for 32 variables.

This virtual memory system is one of the most valuable techniques that you can use in your programs. When your data doesn't quite fit into memory, just put it on disk. You can use this technique for binary and hash searches, and sorting techniques. The virtual array works just like a memory array. It is just as easy to program. Furthermore, if you leave a temporary file on disk and then run your program again, the array is already filled with the original data. There is no need to rebuild or reread new data into the array.

REVIEW

Many programs require more memory than is available. Sometimes this is because the program itself grows; in other cases, there is simply too much data. Here are some tips for condensing programs:

- Remove features from the program
- Delete REM statements
- Put data in disk files
- Use virtual memory techniques
- Split programs into sections and link the sections with CHAIN statements

CHAPTER
11

Windows

Windows are an exciting new development in personal computing.* They are used to split a computer screen into several viewing areas. Each window shows a separate program or task. Figure 11-1 shows a screen with two windows. The left window displays a directory listing; the right window shows a word processing program in operation.

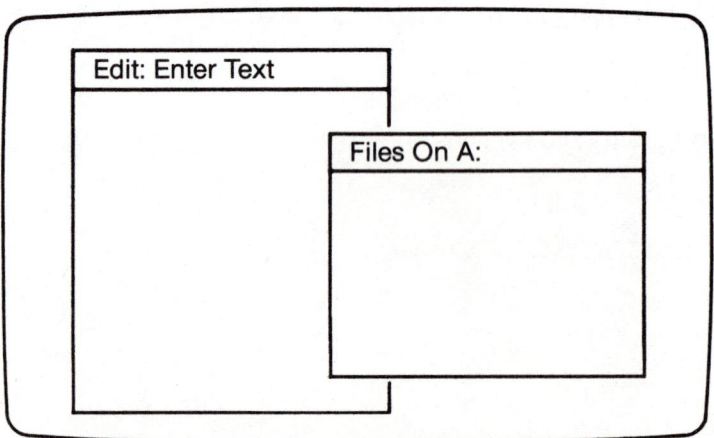

Figure 11-1 *A screen showing two windows.*

*The "windows" described in this chapter are substantially different from BASIC 2.00's WINDOW statement. BASIC 2.00 provides two new graphics statements, VIEW and WINDOW. These statements provide a way to use graphics coordinates that exceed the coordinates of the IBM PC screen. They should not be confused with the windowing technique described in this chapter.

238

You don't have to be a programming wizard to implement windows on the IBM PC. In fact, you can create windows with a remarkably short BASIC program, which you'll do in this chapter.

WHY WINDOWS?

Imagine that your desk is covered with paperwork. When you stop working on one project to begin another, you don't take everything off the desk. Instead, you just plop the new papers on top of the old. Yet most software requires that

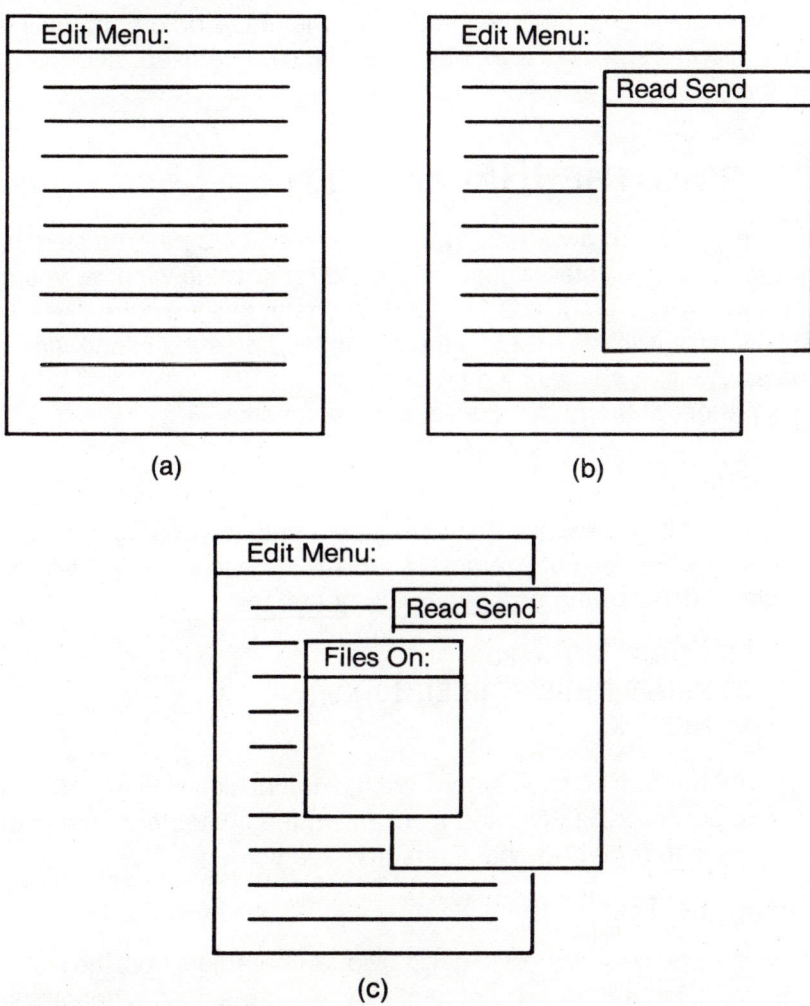

Figure 11-2   *Operations of a typical computer.*

you take everything off the desk to start a new program. You must stop one program, insert a new diskette, and then run the new program.

Windows are like pieces of paper on the desk. Instead of clearing the desk between tasks, the software simply draws windows on top of whatever else is on the screen. The new task is completed within the boundaries of the window. After you finish the new task, the window disappears and the original task is restored. The screen becomes just like stacked pieces of paper on a desk.

Figure 11-2 shows operations of a typical computer. Figure 11-2(a) shows a word processor; at (b) an electronic mailbox is checked, so a window is created. Windows can even be placed on top of windows, as shown in (c), where a quick check of the file directory is made before the mail is handled. When you finish using a window, the window is erased, and the original text on the display is restored.

ACCESSING THE IBM SCREEN

Before you can draw a window on the screen, you need to save the text that is already there. Later, when you wish to remove the window, you can restore the saved text. How do you find out what characters are currently on the screen? This is easy with the IBM PC; the computer stores the image that appears on the screen in a special memory area.

To get at the memory area, use the function

SCREEN (Y, X)

which returns the ASCII code corresponding to the character on the screen at column X of row Y. For example, suppose there is some text on row 10 of the display. The following program will print that text:

```
10 FOR X = 1 to 80
20 PRINT CHR$(SCREEN(10,X));
30 NEXT X
```

Lines 10 through 30 scan across each of the positions in row 10, reading each character with SCREEN() and then writing the character to the display. That's all there is to retrieving characters from the screen.

Preserving the Text

Now that you've seen how to get individual characters from the screen memory, you can look at the next problem: How do you save the characters within an area that will be overwritten by a window?

A window is defined by the coordinate pair that marks its upper-left corner. The window's width and height complete the definition. Figure 11-3 shows a window at (10,5) on the screen. It is 10 lines high and 20 columns wide. This window is completely described by the location of its upper-left corner (10,5), its height (10), and its width (20).

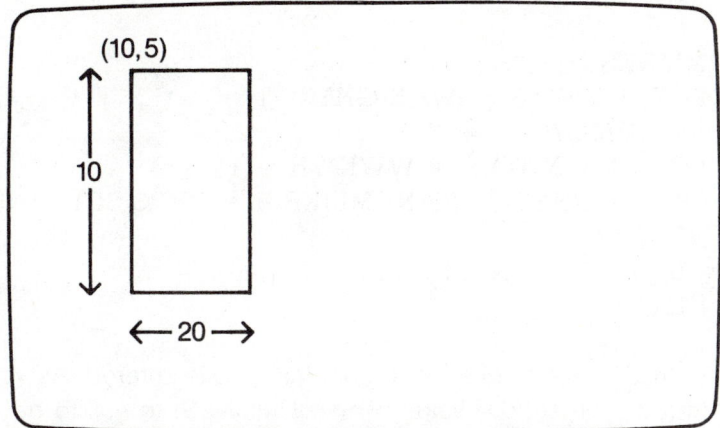

Figure 11-3   *A window at (10,5) on the screen.*

With this information, you can design a subroutine to save the text within the window. The subroutine needs four input parameters:

X, Y	— Location of upper-left corner of window
WWIDTH	—Window width
WHEIGHT	—Window height

To save the characters from this window, you must first determine how to scan across the window and read each character. You can do this with some FOR-NEXT loops.

```
FOR IX = X TO X + WWIDTH − 1
   FOR IY = Y TO Y + WHEIGHT − 1
      CH$ = CHR$(SCREEN(IY, IX))
   NEXT IY
NEXT IX
```

Once the chacters have been read, they are stored using array S$() to save the characters for each row. As you scan across the line, you'll put each character from the screen into S$().

For a window that is four lines high, you need four array elements. S$(1) stores the characters from the first line. S$(2) stores the second line, and so on. To keep track of which array element stores a line, use the variable NUMLINES, which holds the current index into S$(). Here is a routine that copies the characters from a window. The upper-left corner of the window is at (X, Y). The window is WWIDTH characters wide and WHEIGHT lines high.

```
NUMLINES = 1
FOR IY = Y TO Y + WHEIGHT − 1
    S$ (NUMLINES) = ""
    FOR IX = X TO X + WWIDTH − 1
    S$(NUMLINES) = S$(NUMLINES) + CHR$(SCREEN(IY,IX))
    NEXT IX
    NUMLINES = NUMLINES + 1
    NEXT IY
```

NUMLINES is set to one just before the loop is entered. As you begin to scan each row, you set the value of S$(NUMLINES) to null to get rid of any old data that may be in the array. As you scan across the line, you append each character that you find to the end of S$(NUMLINES). After leaving the NEXT IY, S$(NUMLINES) holds the characters that you've extracted from the line within the window. You increment NUMLINES in preparation for scanning the next row. After scanning five lines, NUMLINES is set to 6 (because it stops just after the last line). S$(1) through S$(5) contain the characters from within the boundaries of the window.

That's all there is to saving the lines of text within a single window. The program in Listing 11-1 draws some text on the screen. Next, the program copies the text to S$(). Then the text in S$() is displayed; you can see that it has indeed saved the text within the window. Because IY is incremented only to 30 in line 1040, only the first 30 characters of each line are saved.

Listing 11-1

```
100      CLS                                      ' Clear the screen
110      LOCATE 5, 1
120      PRINT "This is an example of how text is read from the screen"
130      LOCATE 6,1
140      PRINT "and copied into a string variable in a BASIC program."
150      LOCATE 7,1
160      PRINT "The text you see on these lines will be copied into"
170      LOCATE 8,1
180      PRINT "the array S$() in the program"
190      GOSUB 1000
200      LOCATE 15,1
210      FOR I = 1  TO  NUMLINES−1
220        PRINT S$(I)
230      NEXT I
```

```
240       STOP
1000      ' Copy the text off of the screen in lines 5 through 8
1010      NUMLINES = 1
1020      FOR IY = 5  TO  8
1030        S$(NUMLINES) = ""
1040        FOR  IX = 1 TO 30
1050          S$(NUMLINES) = S$(NUMLINES) + CHR$(SCREEN(IY,IX))
1060        NEXT IX
1070        NUMLINES = NUMLINES + 1
1080      NEXT IY
1090      RETURN
```

Drawing a Window

The next step is to actually draw the new window. Here's a routine to do this.

```
1000 REM − DRAW WINDOW at (X,Y) of WWIDTH and
     WHEIGHT
1010 LOCATE Y,X
1020 PRINT CHR$ (218); STRING$(WWIDTH − 2,196);
     CHR$(191);
1030 FOR IY = Y + 1 TO Y + WHEIGHT − 2
1040     LOCATE IY,X
1050     PRINT CHR$(179); SPACE$(WWIDTH − 2); CHR$(179);
1060 NEXT IY
1070 LOCATE Y + WHEIGHT − 1, X
1080 PRINT CHR$(192); STRING$(WWIDTH − 2,196); CHR$(217);
1090 RETURN
```

Line 1010 positions the cursor at the upper-left corner of the window. Then the top window border is drawn. This consists of a string of horizontal graphics characters. The values 218, 196, and 191 are the ASCII codes for the graphics characters you need. All the graphics characters are shown in Appendix G of your IBM PC BASIC manual.

The FOR-NEXT loop draws a vertical line at the left edge of the window, fills the window with blanks, and finishes with another vertical line at the right edge. Finally, the bottom of the window is drawn.

Restoring the Text

Text is easily restored by printing S$() on the screen in the appropriate place. If you define a subroutine RESTORE TEXT with the parameters

X,Y   − Location of upper-left corner of window
WHEIGHT   − Window height

all you need to do is copy the text in S$() back onto the screen. Here is the routine:

```
2000 FOR IY = Y + WHEIGHT - 1 TO Y STEP -1
2010    NUMLINES = NUMLINES - 1
2020    LOCATE IY, X
2030    PRINT S$(NUMLINES);
2040 NEXT IY
2050 RETURN
```

WHEIGHT tells the routine how high the window is, and hence, how many lines it covers on the screen. This corresponds to the number of lines that were saved in the S$() array.

A Package of Window Routines

You now have the basic subroutines needed for producing windows. A few additional features can make the window system really useful, so the next step is to create a full window package.

The package will include a set of subroutines that perform all of the manipulations that you need to draw windows, erase windows, draw text within windows, display menus, and even draw windows on top of other windows. The subroutines are outlined here.

Subroutines

ADD WINDOW	– Draws a window on the screen, including placing a border around the window.
REMOVE WINDOW	– Removes a window from the screen.
WRITE TEXT	– Writes text within a window.
GOTOXY	– Positions the cursor within a window.
HORIZONTAL MENU	– Displays a menu of choices and points to the desired selection.
PULL-DOWN MENU	– Displays a vertical menu of choices.

Multiple and Overlapping Windows

In order to provide multiple windows, you need to expand the SAVE TEXT and RESTORE TEXT subroutines, which have already appeared. The new subroutines should work so that you can say

ADD WINDOW 1

or

ADD WINDOW 2

and then write

WRITE TEXT in window 1

This means that you will need to keep track of some additional information.

For each window, the routines must remember the X and Y coordinates, the width, the height, and the text. You also need a variable to keep track of the number of windows. To store this information, you create five arrays.

DIM WINDOWX(10)   – Stores X coordinates of windows
DIM WINDOWY(10)   – Stores Y coordinates of windows
DIM WINDOWW(10)   – Stores window widths
DIM WINDOWH(10)   – Stores window heights
DIM S$(100)   – Stores up to 100 lines of text

The dimensions are only suggested values; you can change them. With the suggested values, up to 10 windows may appear simultaneously, with up to 100 rows of text appearing within those windows.

You should also add these two variables:

NUMLINES   – Stores number of lines in text storage
                    array S$()
NUMWINDOWS   – Keeps track of number of windows cur-
                    rently defined

Initially, NUMWINDOWS is set to 0. As you add windows, you increment NUM-WINDOWS and use it as an index to the four arrays, WINDOWX, WINDOWY, WINDOWW, and WINDOWH.

The complete set of subroutines is shown in Listing 11-2. In the ADD WINDOW subroutine, NUMWINDOWS is incremented and the input parameters, X, Y, WWIDTH, and WHEIGHT are saved in the corresponding arrays, subscripted by NUMWINDOWS. ADD WINDOW calls SAVE TEXT, which copies the text from the screen into the array S$(). NUMLINES counts the lines copied. ADD WINDOW calls the routine called DRAW WINDOW, which erases the old text from the screen and replaces it with a window boundary.

Listing 11-2

```
31000    REM --------------------------------------------
31010    REM WINDOW DISPLAY ROUTINES
31020    REM
31030    REM
31040    REM --------------------------------------------
31050    REM ADD WINDOW at (X,Y) with WWIDTH and WHEIGHT
31060    WWIDTH = WWIDTH + 2                        ' Add 2 chars. for border
31070    WHEIGHT = WHEIGHT + 2
31080    NUMWINDOWS = NUMWINDOWS + 1
31090    WINDOWX(NUMWINDOWS) = X
31100    WINDOWY(NUMWINDOWS) = Y
31110    WINDOWW(NUMWINDOWS) = WWIDTH
31120    WINDOWH(NUMWINDOWS) = WHEIGHT
31130    GOSUB 31180                               ' Save text within window
31140    GOSUB 31480                               ' Draw the window
31150    RETURN
31160    REM
31170    REM --------------------------------------------
31180    REM SAVE TEXT in window at (X,Y) of WWIDTH and WHEIGHT
31190    FOR IY = Y TO Y + WHEIGHT - 1
31200      S$(NUMLINES) = ""
31210      FOR IX = X TO X + WWIDTH - 1            ' Copy each char. to S$()
31220        S$(NUMLINES) = S$(NUMLINES) + CHR$(SCREEN(IY,IX))
31230      NEXT IX
31240      NUMLINES = NUMLINES + 1
31250    NEXT IY
31260    RETURN
31270    REM
31280    REM --------------------------------------------
31290    REM REMOVE WINDOW
31300    X = WINDOWX(NUMWINDOWS)                    ' Let (X,Y) equal upper left
31310    Y = WINDOWY(NUMWINDOWS)                    ' of window to remove
31320    WWIDTH = WINDOWW(NUMWINDOWS)               ' Window's width
31330    WHEIGHT = WINDOWH(NUMWINDOWS)              ' Window's height
31340    NUMWINDOWS = NUMWINDOWS - 1                ' One less window now
31350    GOSUB 31390                               ' Restore the text
31360    RETURN
31370    REM
31380    REM --------------------------------------------
31390    REM - RESTORE TEXT
31400    FOR IY = Y + WHEIGHT - 1 TO Y STEP - 1
31410      LOCATE IY,X
31420      NUMLINES = NUMLINES - 1
31430      PRINT S$(NUMLINES);                     ' Just print the stuff
31440    NEXT IY
31450    RETURN
31460    REM
31470    REM --------------------------------------------
31480    REM - DRAW WINDOW at (X,Y) of WWIDTH and WHEIGHT
31490    LOCATE Y,X
31500    PRINT CHR$(218);STRING$(WWIDTH-2,196);CHR$(191);
31510    FOR IY = Y+1 TO Y + WHEIGHT-2
31520      LOCATE IY,X
31530      PRINT CHR$(179);SPACE$(WWIDTH-2);CHR$(179);
31540    NEXT IY
31550    LOCATE Y + WHEIGHT - 1, X
31560    PRINT CHR$(192);STRING$(WWIDTH-2,196);CHR$(217);
31570    RETURN
31580    REM
31590    REM --------------------------------------------
31600    REM - WRITE TEXT T$ at relative (X,Y) within window W
31610    IF LEN(T$) > (WINDOWW(W)-2) - X + 1 THEN SIZE = (WINDOWW(W)-
         2) - X + 1 ELSE SIZE = LEN(T$)
31620    LOCATE WINDOWY(W)+Y, WINDOWX(W)+X
```

```
31630    PRINT LEFT$(T$,SIZE);                        ' Truncate the text
31640    RETURN                                       ' if too big to fit
31650    REM
31660    REM ------------------------------------------------
31670    REM GOTOXY (W,X,Y)
31680    LOCATE Y + WINDOWY(W), X + WINDOWX(W)        ' Goto X,Y within
31690    RETURN                                       ' the window
31700    REM
31710    REM ------------------------------------------------
31720    REM INITIALIZE Window Stuff
31730    NUMLINES = 1
31740    DIM WINDOWX(20), WINDOWY(20), WINDOWW(20), WINDOWH(20), S$(100)
31750                                        ' Use   DEF SEG = &HB000
31760                                        '    if using Monochrome display
31770    RETURN
31780    REM
31790    REM ------------------------------------------------
31800    REM HORIZONTAL MENU SELECTION
31810    ' Inputs to this routine:
31820    '   W                Which window to display the menu within
31830    '   HSELECTION$()    The text of each menu selection
31840    '   HNUMSELECTIONS  How many selections are in the menu
31850    '   HSELECTWIDTH    How many columns allocated for each menu item
31860    '   CREATE.WINDOW   Create the window if this is non-zero, otherwise
31870    '                   use the window specified by W
31880    ' Returns the following:
31890    '   SELECTION       The number of the selection chosen (e.g 1, 2, ...)
31900    REM
31910    REM - Set the parameters to create a 1 line window for the menu
31920    X = WINDOWX(W)
31930    Y = WINDOWY(W)
31940    WWIDTH = WINDOWW(W) - 2
31950    WHEIGHT = 1
31960    IF  CREATE.WINDOW  THEN  GOSUB 31050 :
             W = NUMWINDOWS
31970    X = 1:
             Y = 1
31980    T$ = SPACE$(WWIDTH) :
             GOSUB 31600 ' Clear out the current line
31990    FOR IY = 1 TO HNUMSELECTIONS        ' Now, display the selections
32000      T$ = HSELECTION$(IY)
32010      GOSUB 31600
32020      X = X + HSELECTWIDTH
32030    NEXT IY
32040    X = 1 :
             SELECTION = 1
32050    T$ = HSELECTION$(SELECTION)         ' Highlight the current selection
32060    GOSUB 32210
32070    GOSUB 32300                         ' Get an input character
32080    IF K = 13 THEN RETURN               ' Return if ENTER pressed
32090    IF K<>75 AND K<>77 THEN 32070       ' Get another if its not left or right

32100    T$ = HSELECTION$(SELECTION)         ' Change current selection back
32110    GOSUB 31600                         ' to normal display
32120                                        ' If left arrow, then move to previous

32130                                        ' selection on the menu
32140    IF K = 75  AND SELECTION > 1   THEN X = X - HSELECTWIDTH :
             SELECTION = SELECTION - 1
32150                                        ' If right arrow, then move to next
32160                                        ' selection on the menu
32170    IF K = 77  AND SELECTION < HNUMSELECTIONS THEN X = X + HSELECTWIDTH :
             SELECTION = SELECTION + 1
32180    GOTO 32050
32190    REM
```

```
32200   REM --------------------------------------------------
32210   REM - WRITE INVERSE TEXT T$ at relative (X,Y) within window W
32220     IF LEN(T$) > (WINDOWW(W)-2) - X + 1 THEN SIZE = (WINDOWW(W)-
          2) - X + 1 ELSE SIZE = LEN(T$)
32230     LOCATE WINDOWY(W)+Y, WINDOWX(W)+X
32240     COLOR 0, 7, 0
32250     PRINT LEFT$(T$,SIZE);
32260     COLOR 7, 0, 0
32270     RETURN
32280   REM
32290   REM --------------------------------------------------
32300   REM Get a Character from the Keyboard
32310   ' Returns:
32320   '   K = key code
32330   '   E = 1 if an extended code, otherwise E = 0
32340   '   T$ = the input string
32350   T$ = INKEY$
32360   IF T$ = "" THEN 32350
32370   IF LEFT$(T$,1) = CHR$(0) THEN K = ASC(MID$(T$,2)):
          E = 1 ELSE K = ASC(T$):
          E = 0
32380   RETURN
32390   REM
32400   REM --------------------------------------------------
32410   REM Vertical Pull Down Menu
32420   ' Input to this routine:
32430   '   W               The number of the window holding the horizontal menu
32440   '   SELECTION       The item selected on the horizontal menu
32450   '   HSELECTWIDTH    The number of columns for each item in that menu
32460   '   VSELECTION$()   A list of each menu item to appear
32470   '   VNUMSELECTIONS  The number of selections in the pull down menu
32480   '   VSELECTWIDTH    How wide the pull down menu should be
32490   ' Returns:
32500   '   SELECTION       The number of the selection that was chosen
32510   REM
32520   REM Display one line window for menu
32530   Y = WINDOWY(W) + 2
32540   X = WINDOWX(W) + (SELECTION - 1) * HSELECTWIDTH
32550   WWIDTH = VSELECTWIDTH
32560   WHEIGHT = VNUMSELECTIONS
32570   GOSUB 31050 'Draw the tiny window
32580   X = 1:
          Y = 1:
          W = NUMWINDOWS
32590   FOR IY = 1 TO VNUMSELECTIONS
32600     T$ = VSELECTION$(IY)
32610     GOSUB 31600
32620     Y = Y + 1
32630   NEXT IY
32640   X = 1 :
          Y = 1 :
          SELECTION = 1
32650   T$ = VSELECTION$(SELECTION)
32660   GOSUB 32210
32670   GOSUB 32300
32680   IF K = 13 THEN RETURN
32690   IF K<>72 AND K<>80 THEN 32670
32700   T$ = VSELECTION$(SELECTION)
32710   GOSUB 31600
32720   IF K = 72  AND SELECTION > 1  THEN Y = Y - 1 :
          SELECTION = SELECTION - 1
32730   IF K = 80  AND SELECTION < VNUMSELECTIONS THEN Y = Y + 1 :
          SELECTION = SELECTION + 1
32740   GOTO 32650
```

```
Windows are a wonderful addition to the user interface, providing
an easy way of displaying multiple events on one screen.  They can
also be used for menu selections and other prompts, as demonstrated
in the Window Demonstration program.

     To make a selection, just use the arrow keys to 'point' to the
desired selection.  On a horizontal menu, use the left and right
arrow keys to make the selection.  On a vertical, 'pull-down' menu
use the up and down arrow keys.  Once your selection has been made,
press the ENTER key.  That's all there is to making a selection!
```

Figure 11-4(a)

Let's trace through the addition of two windows to the screen. After the windows have been displayed, the second window will be deleted so you can see how the original text is restored. Figure 11-4(a) shows what the screen will look like before any windows are displayed.

Before doing anything, you need to call the initialization routine at line 31720. There are no windows on the screen when you first call ADD WINDOW. There is some text, however, so the routine saves it by calling SAVE TEXT. NUMWINDOWS is incremented by one, and the window definition is stored in the arrays.

```
NUMWINDOWS = 1
WINDOWX (1) = 10
WINDOWY (1) = 5
WINDOWW (1) = 30
WINDOWH (1) = 5
```

After saving the text from the screen, S$(1) through S$(7) each contain 32 characters, representing the saved text from each line. These strings look like this:

```
S$(1) = "re a wonderful addition to the u    "
S$(2) = "ay of displaying multiple events  "
S$(3) = "sed for menu selections and othe "
S$(4) = "ndow Demonstration program.      "
S$(5) = "                                 "
S$(6) = "ake a selection, just use the ar    "
S$(7) = "election. On a horizontal menu     "
```

NUMLINES has the value 8, meaning that the S$() indices up through 7 have been used. Even though only five lines appear within the window, two additional lines of text were saved because of the window border characters. The same is true for the width of the saved line. Even though only 30 characters appear within the window, 2 extra characters are saved to account for the window border.

Next, you draw the window on the screen by creating a border around the window and filling the interior with blanks. This is all taken care of by the DRAW WINDOW routine. Figure 11-4(b) shows the screen with the first window in place.

Figure 11-4(b)

Repeat the operation for the second window. Place the second window at X = 25 and Y = 7; the width is 25 and the height is 10. Note that the second window overlaps the first. Saving the coordinates of the second window gives

```
NUMWINDOWS = 2
WINDOWX (2) = 25
WINDOWY (2) = 7
WINDOWW (2) = 25
WINDOWH (2) = 10
```

Next, the text within the new window is copied from the screen and placed in S$(). This adds 10 lines of data to S$(), so S$() now contains

```
S$(1)  = "re a wonderful addition to the u     "
S$(2)  = "ay of displaying multiple events     "
S$(3)  = "sed for menu selections and othe     "
S$(4)  = "ndow Demonstration program.          "
S$(5)  = "                                     "
S$(6)  = "ake a selection, just use the ar     "
S$(7)  = "election. On a horizontal menu       "
S$(8)  = "                        prompts,     "
S$(9)  = "                                     "
S$(10) = "                                     "
S$(11) = "                        row keys t   "
S$(12) = "                        use the l    "
```

```
S$(13)  =  "election. On a vertical, '        "
S$(14)  =  "w keys. Once your selectio        "
S$(15)  =  "at's all there is to making       "
S$(16)  =  "                                   "
S$(17)  =  "                                   "
S$(18)  =  "                                   "
S$(19)  =  "                                   "
```

NUMLINES is set to 20 (one more than the total of 19). After drawing the second window, the screen looks like the screen in Figure 11-4(c).

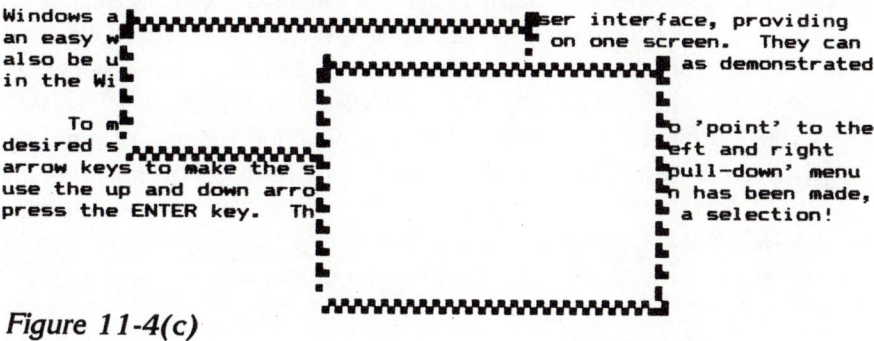

Figure 11-4(c)

Writing text is the easy part. To write the string "Hello There!" in window 2, call the WRITE TEXT subroutine. Pass to it the window number, the string, and the coordinates of the window where the text will appear. For example,

```
T$ = "Hello There!"     ' Set up parameters to WRITE TEXT
X = 1                    ' Print T$ at (1,1)
Y = 1
W = 2                    ' And put it in window 2
GOSUB 31600              ' Call write text
```

A warning is necessary about writing text to windows that are hidden behind other windows. WRITE TEXT is a "dumb" subroutine. It does not know that some windows overlap other windows. If you try to write text in a window overlapped by another, WRITE TEXT will print the text on top of the "higher" window. For this reason, text should only be written to windows that are in the clear, so to speak, or on top of other windows. A rule of thumb is to write text to the most recently drawn window on the display, which will always be on top of any other windows.

The next trick is to remove a window. The window package is set up to remove only the most recently drawn window. This is because the lines of text are saved sequentially in array S$(). If window 1 occupies S$(1) through S$(5) and window 2 occupies S$(6) through S$(12) and you decide to remove window 1, then you would have to restore the text from S$(1) through S$(5). But if you then add a new window, you have no way of reusing the space S$(1) through S$(5). The routines are set up to always add new text at the end of array S$(). Therefore, you can remove only the most recently created window, which is the one that was just added to S$(). This restriction is generally not much of a problem.

REMOVE WINDOW has no parameters because it always removes the most recently drawn window. The actual removal is easy. Just redisplay the original text. This is done by looking at the saved window definition for window 2. WINDOWX(2), WINDOWY(2), WINDOWW(2), and WINDOWH(2) provide the information. You simply begin at the bottom of the window and print S$(NUMLINES) at column WINDOWX(2), row WINDOWH(2) + WINDOWY(2). (These are the coordinates of the last line in the window.) Then you decrement NUMLINES and print the preceding row. The routine continues this way until it reaches the top of the window. At this point, the window is gone and NUM-WINDOWS is decremented. You can now either add or remove a window. The screen returns to the form shown in Figure 11-4(b).

MENUS

One of the features of the new window systems are their support of a mouse input device. The mouse is a small device closely related to the joystick of arcade-game fame. By moving the mouse over a desktop, you can move the cursor about on the screen to perform functions normally relegated to keyboard input. For example, you can create a menu, as shown in Figure 11-5(a), and use the mouse to move from one selection to another. If you don't want to use the mouse to move around the menu, you can use the ARROW keys on the numeric keypad of your IBM PC. By pressing the UP ARROW, you can move up one line. By pressing the DOWN ARROW you can move down one line. Once you've moved to the desired menu selection, you press the ENTER key.

The window package described here has two kinds of menus. In horizontal menus, the selections extend across a line on the display. In vertical, or pull-down menus, the selections are listed vertically on the window. Figure 11-5(a) shows an example of a horizontal menu; Figure 11-5(b) shows a pull-down menu below the horizontal menu.

The programming for these two techniques is quite similar.

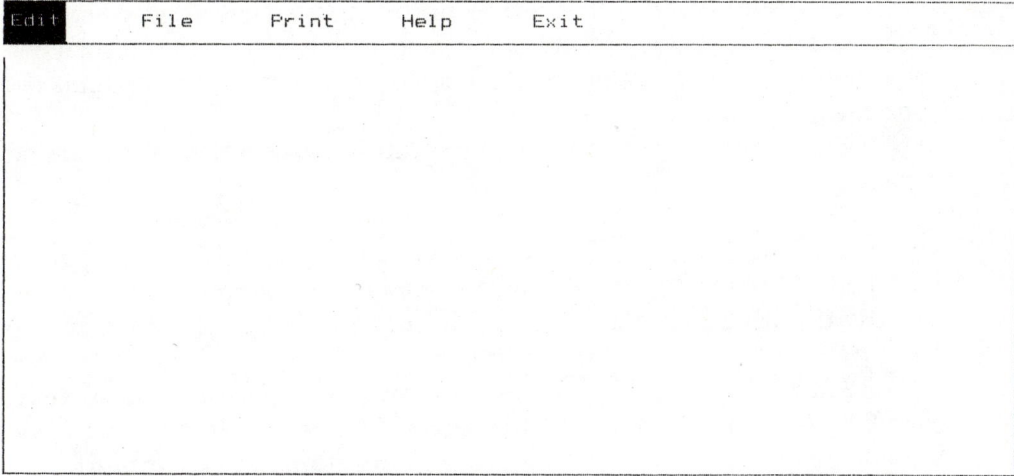

Figure 11-5(a)   *Menu of options on a screen—horizontal menu.*

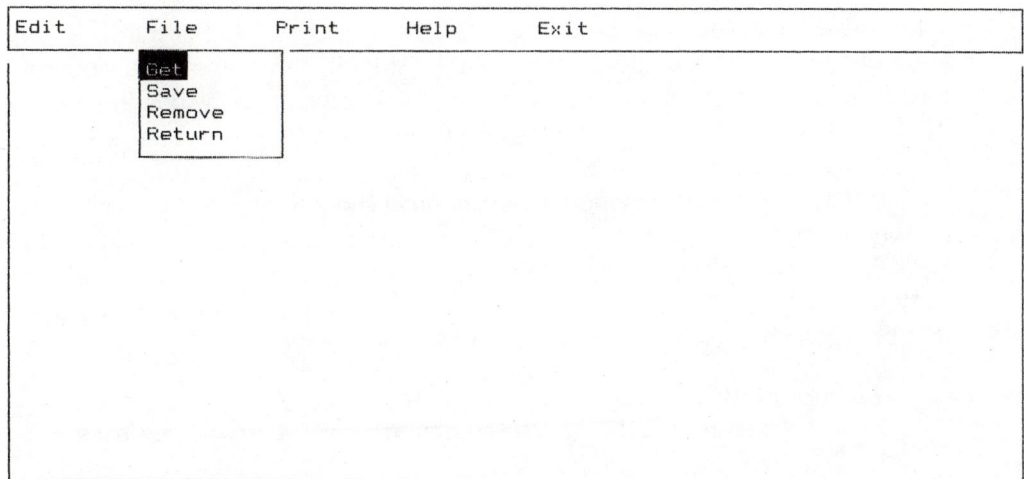

Figure 11-5(b)   *Pull-down menu.*

The Horizontal Menu

A horizontal menu, for the purposes of this window package, is defined as a single line of options that appears at the top of an existing window. The number of selections is limited by the width of the window and the number of columns required for each selection.

You must set several variables before you call the menu selection routine. These values include the number of the window in which you will display the menu, the number of selections, the number of selections to be displayed horizontally, and the text for each item on the menu.

These parameters are passed to the subroutine by setting the following variables:

W	– Which window to use
HSELECTION$()	– The text for each prompt
HNUMSELECTIONS	– The maximum number of items on the menu
HSELECTWIDTH	– The number of columns for each item
CREATE.WINDOW	– This variable is set to 0 if the window that the menu items are to appear in is already on the screen. It is set to 1 if the window needs to be drawn.

After these variables have been assigned, A GOSUB 31800 is made to the subroutine. The subroutine sets the variable SELECTION to the number of the selection that was chosen. Suppose these three items are shown in the menu: EDITING, FILING, GRAPHING. If the third item, GRAPHING, is selected, then SELECTION holds the value 3.

Listing 11-3 uses the horizontal menu. (The corresponding display is shown in Figure 11-5(a).) Be aware that the subroutine does not validate the input parameters. It's quite possible to pass a window number for an undefined window or to try to display more items than can fit on a single line. So be sure that the parameters you select are valid for the operation.

Listing 11-3

```
10       REM - DEMONSTRATION OF WINDOWS ON THE IBM PERSONAL COMPUTER
20       REM
30       REM
40       REM
50       REM
60       REM
70       REM
80       DEFINT A-Z                      ' All variables used here are Integers
90       DIM HSELECTION$(10), VSELECTION$(10)
100                                      ' These hold the menu selections
1000     GOSUB 31710                     ' Initialize Window Stuff
1010     SCREEN.WIDTH = 80
1020     REM - Draw a window around the entire screen
1030     X = 1 :
           Y = 1 :
           WWIDTH =77 :
           WHEIGHT = 21:'
           GOSUB 31050
1040     CREATE.WINDOW = 1
```

```
1050        GOSUB 7000                          ' Display some text on the screen
1060        '
1070        '                                   ' Set up to display main menu
1080        HSELECTION$(1) = "Edit"
1090        HSELECTION$(2) = "Files"
1100        HSELECTION$(3) = "Print"
1110        HSELECTION$(4) = "Help"
1120        HSELECTION$(5) = "Exit"
1130        HNUMSELECTIONS = 5
1140        HSELECTWIDTH = 10
1150        W = 1
1160        GOSUB 31790                         ' Display Horizontal menu
1170        ON SELECTION GOSUB 2000, 3000, 4000, 5000, 6000
1180        CREATE.WINDOW = 0
1190        GOTO 1070
1200        '
1210        '
1220        '
2000        ' Edit Command Selection
2010        T$ = "Edit:  Enter text, Press ESC key when finished"
2020        X = 1:
             Y = 1
2030        W = 2
2040        GOSUB 31600                         ' Display text
2050        WHILE K <> 27
2060          GOSUB 32280                       ' Get input character
2070        WEND
2080        RETURN
2090        '
2100        '
2110        '
3000        ' Files Command
3010        VSELECTION$(1) = "Get"
3020        VSELECTION$(2) = "Save"
3030        VSELECTION$(3) = "Remove"
3040        VSELECTION$(4) = "Return"
3050        VNUMSELECTIONS = 4
3060        VSELECTWIDTH = 10
3070        GOSUB 32390                         ' Display pull-down menu
3080        IF   SELECTION  = 4   THEN   GOSUB 31290 :
             RETURN
3090        X = WINDOWX(NUMWINDOWS) + VSELECTWIDTH
3100        IF X + 2 > SCREEN.WIDTH  THEN X = X - VSELECTWIDTH - 2
3110        Y = WINDOWY(NUMWINDOWS) + VNUMSELECTIONS + 2
3120        WHEIGHT = 1
3130        WWIDTH = 30
3140        GOSUB 31050                         ' Create a new window
3150        T$ = "Enter Filename: "             ' to display this prompt
3160        X = 1
3170        Y = 1
3180        W = NUMWINDOWS
3190        GOSUB 31600                         ' Display the prompt
3200        INPUT FILE.NAME$
3210        GOSUB 31290                         ' Remove filename window
3220        GOSUB 31290                         ' Remove Files window
3230        RETURN
3240        '
3250        '
4000        ' Print Command selection
4010        VSELECTION$(1) = "to Printer"
4020        VSELECTION$(2) = "to File"
4030        VSELECTION$(3) = "Return"
4040        VNUMSELECTIONS = 3
4050        VSELECTWIDTH = 12
4060        GOSUB 32390                         ' Display pull-down menu
```

```
4070       IF  SELECTION = 3   THEN   GOSUB 31290 :
              RETURN
4080       IF  SELECTION = 1   THEN   PRINT.FLAG = 1 :
              GOSUB 31290 :
              RETURN
4090       X = WINDOWX(NUMWINDOWS) + VSELECTWIDTH
4100       IF  X > SCREEN.WIDTH  THEN  X = X - VSELECTWIDTH - 2
4110       Y = WINDOWY(NUMWINDOWS) + VNUMSELECTIONS + 2
4120       WHEIGHT = 1
4130       WWIDTH = 40
4140       GOSUB 31050                        ' Create a window for prompt
4150                                          ' Make sure window will fit
4160       IF X + WWIDTH + 2 > SCREEN.WIDTH  THEN  X = SCREEN.WIDTH - WWIDTH - 2
4170       T$ = "Enter Filename: "
4180       X = 1
4190       Y = 1
4200       W = NUMWINDOWS
4210       GOSUB 31600                        ' Display filename prompt
4220       INPUT FILE.NAME$
4230       GOSUB 31290                        ' Remove the filename window
4240       GOSUB 31290                        ' Remove print window
4250       RETURN
4260       '
4270       '
4280       '
5000       ' Help Selection
5010       VSELECTION$(1) = "for Edit"
5020       VSELECTION$(2) = "for Files"
5030       VSELECTION$(3) = "for Print"
5040       VSELECTION$(4) = "Return"
5050       VNUMSELECTIONS = 4
5060       VSELECTWIDTH = 12
5070       GOSUB 32390                        ' Display help pull-down menu
5080       IF  SELECTION = 4   THEN   GOSUB 31290 :
              RETURN
5090       GOSUB 31290                        ' Remove the menu
5100       RETURN                             ' We could have printed help here
5110       '
5120       '
5130       '
6000       ' Exit program
6010       GOSUB 31290
6020       GOSUB 31290
6030       END
6040       '
6050       '
7000       'Display initial text on screen
7010       X = 1 :
              Y = 3 :
              W = 1
7020       T$ = "Windows are a wonderful addition to the user interface, providing"

7030       GOSUB 31600
7040       Y = Y + 1
7050       T$ = "an easy way of displaying multiple events on one
              screen.  They can"
7060       GOSUB 31600
7070       Y = Y + 1
7080       T$ = "also be used for menu selections and other prompts, as
              demonstrated"
7090       GOSUB 31600
7100       Y = Y + 1
7110       T$ = "in this Window Demonstration program."
7120       GOSUB 31600
7130       Y = Y + 1
```

```
7140      T$ = ""
7150      GOSUB 31600
7160      Y = Y + 1
7170      T$ = "      To make a selection, just use the arrow keys to
          'point' to the"
7180      GOSUB 31600
7190      Y = Y + 1
7200      T$ = "desired selection.  On a horizontal menu, use the left and right"
7210      GOSUB 31600
7220      Y = Y + 1
7230      T$ = "keys to make the selection.  On a vertical, 'pull-down' menu, use"
7240      GOSUB 31600
7250      Y = Y + 1
7260      T$ = "the up and down arrow keys.  Once your selection has been made,"
7270      GOSUB 31600
7280      Y = Y + 1
7290      T$ = "press the ENTER key.  That's all there is to making a selection!"
7300      GOSUB 31600
7310      RETURN
7320      '
7330      '
7340      '
```

The Pull-Down Menu

The pull-down menu is so named because it appears to be pulled down from the top of a window. Sometimes, some of the selections in a horizontal menu need to display another menu. For example, an option labeled FILING may have several suboptions, such as GET, SAVE, and REMOVE. When FILING is selected, the submenu is pulled down from above, like a window shade. This packages the main selection and the suboption menu so that the user is never lost.

Because pull-down menus are almost always used as submenus for a main menu option, the routines provided in this chapter are designed specifically for that use. Listing 11-2 contains the source code for the pull-down menu routine.

Like the horizontal menus, the pull-down menus require their own set of input parameters. These are:

W	– The number of the window containing the horizontal menu
HSELECTION	– The selection chosen on the horizontal menu
HSELECTION	– The width of each horizontal selection
VSELECTION$()	– Each of the pull-down menu choices
VNUMSELECTIONS	– The total number of selections in the menu
VSELECTWIDTH	– The width of the pull-down menu

These parameters are used to create a pull-down menu centered directly below the main menu option on the horizontal menu line.

Figure 11-5(b) shows a pull-down menu. This particular menu was displayed because the FILING option was selected on the main menu. Listing 11-3 is the program that created this menu display.

Running Separate Programs in Windows

The subroutines in this chapter are especially useful within a single program. But you can also use a window to run a different program. When that program ends, its window is erased and the main program takes control. Some window systems display pictures or pictograms illustrating each program on a diskette. When you move the cursor to a picture and press a button on the mouse, the selected program begins execution.

Let's look at an example. Figure 11-6(a) shows a window covering the entire screen. Across the top of the window is a set of options. When the EDITING option is selected, a new window is created on the display, which you can see in Figure 11-6(b). The editing program runs entirely within this window. When it ends, its window is erased and control returns to the horizontal menu. One program acts as a controller, selecting programs one after another.

It's quite possible that one of the called programs could, in turn, call another program. This second program would then begin running in a window of its own, located on top of the windows currently on display. It's not hard to create an application like this. You may wish to modify the programs in this chapter for this type of windowing.

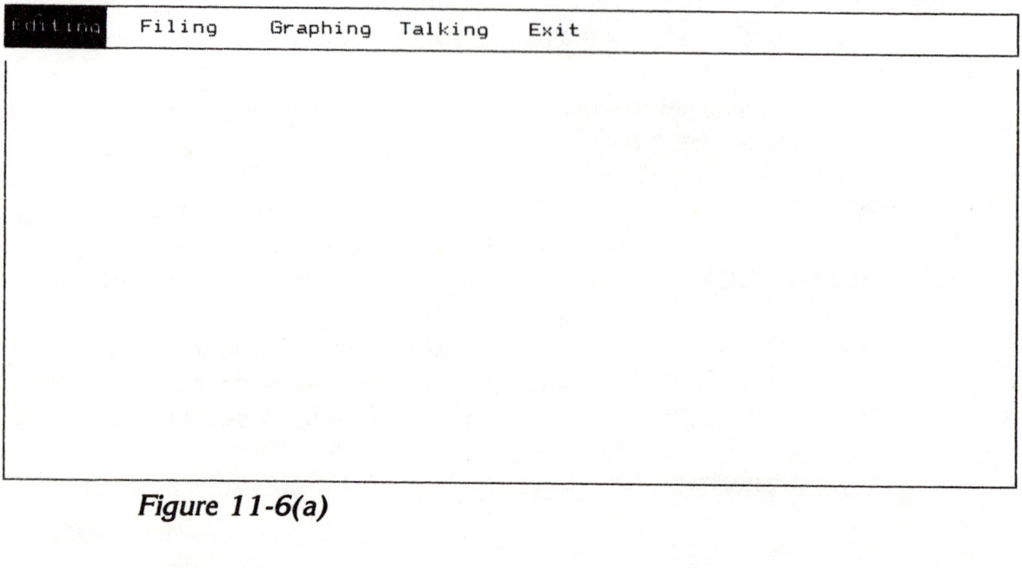

Figure 11-6(a)

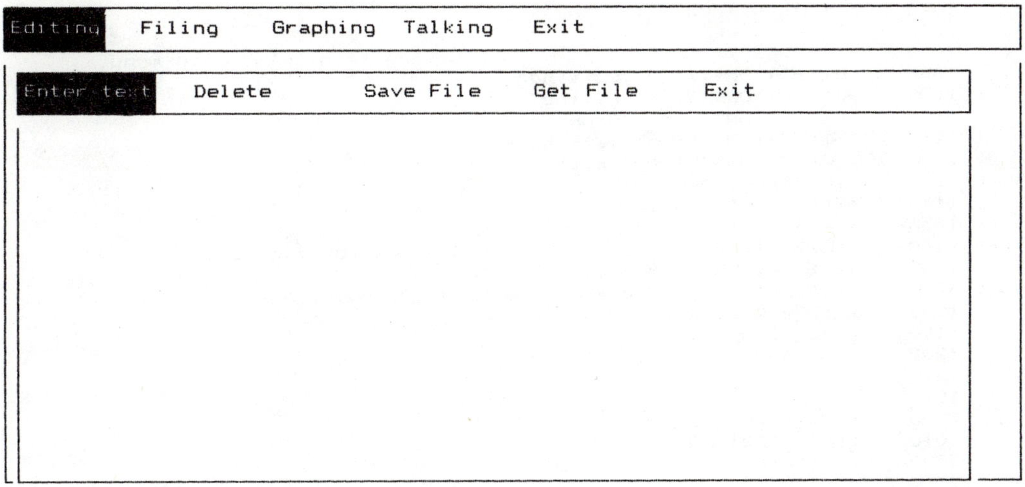

Editing   Filing   Graphing Talking   Exit

Enter text   Delete   Save File   Get File   Exit

Figure 11-6(b)

To experiment with multiple programs, use the program examples in
Listings 11-4(a), 11-4(b), 11-4(c), 11-4(d), and 11-4(e). To each of these listings
you must add the window subroutines, shown in Listing 11-2. An easy way to
copy a large section of one program to another program is to save the portion
of the program you wish to copy into an ASCII text file.

Listing 11-4(a)

```
10        REM - DEMONSTRATION OF WINDOWS ON THE IBM PERSONAL COMPUTER
20        REM
30        REM
40        REM
50        REM - Demonstrates one program calling another
60        REM
70        REM
80        DEFINT A-Z                      ' All variables used here are Integers
84        ' Put all needed variables into COMMON memory
85        COMMON CREATE.WINDOW, SCREEN.WIDTH, HSELECTION$(), VSELECTION$()
86        COMMON HNUMSELECTIONS, VNUMSELECTIONS, SELECTED.PROGRAM,
            NUMLINES, NUMWINDOWS
87        COMMON WINDOWX(), WINDOWY(), WINDOWW(), WINDOWH(), S$()
100                                       ' These hold the menu selections
103       ' If we were RUN, then SELECTED.PROGRAM = 0, so just do next line
104       ' If we were CHAINed, then SELECTED.PROGRAM tells us where to go next
105       ON SELECTED.PROGRAM + 1 GOTO 1000, 2500, 3500, 4500, 5500
1000      DIM HSELECTION$(10), VSELECTION$(10)
1005      GOSUB 31710              ' Initialize Window Stuff
1010      SCREEN.WIDTH = 80
1020      REM - Draw a window around the entire screen
1030      X = 1 :
            Y = 1 :
            WWIDTH =77 :
            WHEIGHT = 21:
            GOSUB 31050
```

```
1040      CREATE.WINDOW = 1
1060      '
1070      '                                  ' Set up to display main menu
1080      HSELECTION$(1) = "Editing"
1090      HSELECTION$(2) = "Filing"
1100      HSELECTION$(3) = "Graphing"
1110      HSELECTION$(4) = "Talking"
1120      HSELECTION$(5) = "Exit"
1130      HNUMSELECTIONS = 5
1140      HSELECTWIDTH = 10
1150      W = 1
1160      GOSUB 31810                        ' Display Horizontal menu
1165      SELECTED.PROGRAM = SELECTION
1170      ON SELECTION GOSUB 2000, 3000, 4000, 5000, 6000
1180      CREATE.WINDOW = 0
1190      GOTO 1070
1200      '
1210      '
1220      '
2000      ' Call the editor
2010      CHAIN "EDITOR"
2500      ' Return from the editor
2510      X = 10 :
            Y = 10
2520      WWIDTH = 30
2530      WHEIGHT = 3
2540      GOSUB 31050
2550      T$ = "Editing completed - Press any key"
2560      X = 1 :
            Y = 1
2570      W = NUMWINDOWS
2580      GOSUB 31600
2590      GOSUB 31290
2600      GOTO 1070
3000      ' Call the filer
3010      CHAIN "FILER"
3500      GOTO 1070
4000      ' Call the grapher
4010      CHAIN "GRAPHER"
4500      GOTO 1070
5000      ' Call the talking utilities
5010      CHAIN "TALKER"
5500      GOTO 1070
6000      ' Exit the program
6010      GOSUB 31290
6020      GOSUB 31290
6030      END
```

Listing 11-4(b)

```
10        REM - Example of a called program using windows
20        REM
30        REM
40        DEFINT A-Z                         ' All variables used here are Integers
50        ' Put all needed variables into COMMON memory
60        COMMON CREATE.WINDOW, SCREEN.WIDTH, HSELECTION$(), VSELECTION$()
70        COMMON HNUMSELECTIONS, VNUMSELECTIONS, SELECTED.PROGRAM,
            NUMLINES, NUMWINDOWS
80        COMMON WINDOWX(), WINDOWY(), WINDOWW(), WINDOWH(), S$()
90        REM - Draw a window for this application
1000      X = 2 :
            Y = 4 :
            WWIDTH =72 :
```

```
                    WHEIGHT = 18:
                    GOSUB 31050
     1010   CREATE.WINDOW = 1
     1020   '
     1030   '                                   ' Set up to display main menu
     1040   HSELECTION$(1) = "Enter text"
     1050   HSELECTION$(2) = "Delete"
     1060   HSELECTION$(3) = "Save File"
     1070   HSELECTION$(4) = "Get File"
     1080   HSELECTION$(5) = "Exit"
     1090   HNUMSELECTIONS = 5
     1100   HSELECTWIDTH = 13
     1110   W = 3
     1120   GOSUB 31810                      ' Display Horizontal menu
     1130   ' Normally, we would use an ON-SELECTION to do some processing
     1140   ' For this example, we'll just erase the menu and return to the caller
     1150   GOSUB 31290
     1160   GOSUB 31290
     1170   CHAIN "MAIN"
     1180   CREATE.WINDOW = 0
     1190   GOTO 1030
     1200   '
     1210   '
     1220   '
```

Listing 11-4(c)

```
     10     REM - Example of a called program using windows
     20     REM
     30     REM
     40     DEFINT A-Z                       ' All variables used here are Integers
     50     ' Put all needed variables into COMMON memory
     60     COMMON CREATE.WINDOW, SCREEN.WIDTH, HSELECTION$(), VSELECTION$()
     70     COMMON HNUMSELECTIONS, VNUMSELECTIONS, SELECTED.PROGRAM,
            NUMLINES, NUMWINDOWS
     80     COMMON WINDOWX(), WINDOWY(), WINDOWW(), WINDOWH(), S$()
     90     REM - Draw a window for this application
     1000   X = 2 :
                    Y = 4 :
                    WWIDTH =72 :
                    WHEIGHT = 18:
                    GOSUB 31050
     1010   CREATE.WINDOW = 1
     1020   '
     1030   '                                   ' Set up to display main menu
     1040   HSELECTION$(1) = "Directory"
     1050   HSELECTION$(2) = "Remove Files"
     1060   HSELECTION$(3) = "Copy File"
     1070   HSELECTION$(4) = "Print File"
     1080   HSELECTION$(5) = "Exit"
     1090   HNUMSELECTIONS = 5
     1100   HSELECTWIDTH = 14
     1110   W = 3
     1120   GOSUB 31810                      ' Display Horizontal menu
     1130   ' Normally, we would use an ON-SELECTION to do some processing
     1140   ' For this example, we'll just erase the menu and return to the caller
     1150   GOSUB 31290
     1160   GOSUB 31290
     1170   CHAIN "MAIN"    /
     1180   CREATE.WINDOW = 0
     1190   GOTO 1030
     1200   '
     1210   '
     1220   '
```

Listing 11-4(d)

```
10      REM - Example of a called program using windows
20      REM
30      REM
40      DEFINT A-Z                      ' All variables used here are Integers
50      ' Put all needed variables into COMMON memory
60      COMMON CREATE.WINDOW, SCREEN.WIDTH, HSELECTION$(), VSELECTION$()
70      COMMON HNUMSELECTIONS, VNUMSELECTIONS, SELECTED.PROGRAM,
          NUMLINES, NUMWINDOWS
80      COMMON WINDOWX(), WINDOWY(), WINDOWW(), WINDOWH(), S$()
90      REM - Draw a window for this application
1000    X = 2 :
          Y = 4 :
          WWIDTH =72 :
          WHEIGHT = 18:
          GOSUB 31050
1010    CREATE.WINDOW = 1
1020    '
1030    '                               ' Set up to display main menu
1040    HSELECTION$(1) = "Enter Data"
1050    HSELECTION$(2) = "Display"
1060    HSELECTION$(3) = "Get/Save"
1070    HSELECTION$(4) = "Rotate"
1080    HSELECTION$(5) = "Exit"
1090    HNUMSELECTIONS = 5
1100    HSELECTWIDTH = 14
1110    W = 3
1120    GOSUB 31810                     ' Display Horizontal menu
1130    ' Normally, we would use an ON-SELECTION to do some processing
1140    ' For this example, we'll just erase the menu and return to the caller
1150    GOSUB 31290
1160    GOSUB 31290
1170    CHAIN "MAIN"
1180    CREATE.WINDOW = 0
1190    GOTO 1030
1200    '
1210    '
1220    '
```

Listing 11-4(e)

```
10      REM - Example of a called program using windows
20      REM
30      REM
40      DEFINT A-Z                      ' All variables used here are Integers
50      ' Put all needed variables into COMMON memory
60      COMMON CREATE.WINDOW, SCREEN.WIDTH, HSELECTION$(), VSELECTION$()
70      COMMON HNUMSELECTIONS, VNUMSELECTIONS, SELECTED.PROGRAM,
          NUMLINES, NUMWINDOWS
80      COMMON WINDOWX(), WINDOWY(), WINDOWW(), WINDOWH(), S$()
90      REM - Draw a window for this application
1000    X = 2 :
          Y = 4 :
          WWIDTH =72 :
          WHEIGHT = 18:
          GOSUB 31050
1010    CREATE.WINDOW = 1
1020    '
1030    '                               ' Set up to display main menu
1040    HSELECTION$(1) = "Terminal"
1050    HSELECTION$(2) = "Elec. Mail"
1060    HSELECTION$(3) = "Auto Dial"
1070    HSELECTION$(4) = "Phone Book"
1080    HSELECTION$(5) = "Exit"
1090    HNUMSELECTIONS = 5
```

```
1100     HSELECTWIDTH = 14
1110     W = 3
1120     GOSUB 31810                      ' Display Horizontal menu
1130     ' Normally, we would use an ON-SELECTION to do some processing
1140     ' For this example, we'll just erase the menu and return to the caller
1150     GOSUB 31290
1160     GOSUB 31290
1170     CHAIN "MAIN"
1180     CREATE.WINDOW = 0
1190     GOTO 1030
1200     '
1210     '
1220     '
```

First, delete any lines that you do not wish to copy. Then, save the lines using the ",A" option of the SAVE command. For example,

SAVE "TEMP", A

creates a copy of the file in text form rather than BASIC's internal form. Next, load the program that you wish to merge the routines into

LOAD "MAIN"

and merge the saved program section by typing

MERGE "TEMP"

That's all that you need to do. If you get the error message BAD FILE MODE, you forgot to use the ",A" option on the SAVE command.

The MAIN program, in 11-4(a), displays the main menu (see Figure 11-6(a). A selected program is called by chaining to it with the CHAIN statement. (Normally, CHAIN wipes out any variables that you are presently using. They may be preserved, however, by placing them in a COMMON statement. Both CHAIN and COMMON are described in Chapter 10.)

The chained program creates a window of its own, displays its own menu (see Figure 11-6(b), and processes all of its commands. When it has finished, it CHAINs back to the MAIN program.

Special processing may be needed on return to the MAIN program. That's why the MAIN program contains an ON-GOTO statement at the beginning. The statement

ON SELECTED.PROGRAM + 1 GOTO 1000, 2000, etc

jumps to the appropriate routine based on the value in SELECTED.PROGRAM. If the MAIN program was RUN instead of CHAINed to, SELECTED.PROGRAM is O. The ON-GOTO then just goes to the next line in the program, so no special return processing is needed. Instead, the initialization subroutine must be called.

The complete set of routines may be easily altered for your own purposes. The CHAIN operations are a bit slow, but there are ways to make them faster. One way is to compile your BASIC programs whenever possible (see Appendix A). Also, if you have a lot of memory on your computer, you may wish to configure a portion of that memory as high-speed "memory disk."

"Memory disk" is a special technique that makes the IBM PC act as though its memory boards were disk drives. The integrated circuit chips on the memory board contain no moving parts and they work at the speed of electricity. And that is much faster than the floppy diskettes. See your computer dealer about this option. The product will make your window programs run faster.

Enhancing the Window Package

The basic window routines can be enhanced by adding *scrolling* within windows, and by saving attributes such as color or underlining. Another enhancement is the ability to copy or transfer text from one window to another.

Scrolling is used to slide entire lines up or down on the screen. Suppose you are typing a program in BASIC. Each time that you press ENTER, the lines on the screen move up one row. A new, blank line appears at the bottom of the screen. This is called scrolling up. When the lines on the screen each move down a row, and the top row becomes blank, the operation is called scrolling down.

In this section you'll see how you can make the text within a single window move up or down. This feature can be used to insert new lines in the middle of an existing window or to delete lines of text.

You also need to save text attributes. So far the window package saves only the text within a window. It ignores the color or flashing attributes of the text. You need to modify the routines to preserve the attributes associated with each character on the screen. These attributes include color, flashing text, and boldfaced or underlined characters.

Saving Attributes

Saving the attributes is easy, because the SCREEN() function, which reads characters from the screen, can also read attributes. Instead of calling SCREEN(), as in

```
SCREEN(Y,X)
```

You can add a third parameter,

    SCREEN(Y,X,A)

If A IS 0, then SCREEN() works as you've been using it, returning the ASCII code of the character at row Y, column X. If A is nonzero, the SCREEN returns the attribute corresponding to the character at row Y, column X. For example, most black and white text is written on the screen with an attribute value of 7. This corresponds to white characters on a black background. If your screen is currently displaying black and white text, and you type

    PRINT SCREEN (10, 10, 1)

you should see the value 7 printed. The attribute value changes according to the character's color, background color, and flashing or nonflashing status. If you let

    ATTR = SCREEN (Y, X, 1)

then we can compute the corresponding colors as follows:

- Foreground Color = ATTR MOD 16
- Background Color = (((ATTR − Foreground Color)/16) MOD 128
- If ATTR > 127 then the character is blinking.

Fortunately, you don't absolutely need to know what the attribute values actually mean. You just need to save them and then restore their values when removing the window.

Saving the text and the attributes is straightforward. Restoring the text is, unfortunately, a bit more complicated. But let's take easy things first. To save the attribute value, modify the line in the SAVE TEXT subroutine where SCREEN is called, so that it reads

    S$(NUMLINES) = S$(NUMLINES) + CHR$(SCREEN(IY,IX)) +
    CHR$(SCREEN(IY,IX,1))

In this form, you'll be saving two bytes for every character on the screen. One will be the actual character, and the other will be the corresponding attribute. You're now done with SAVE TEXT.

The routine called RESTORE TEXT must process the text in the S$() array differently, because it now contains text and attributes. If you simply PRINT S$() to the screen, you'll see some of the text. But you'll see quite a few peculiar characters, too. You need to modify the subroutine so that it actually writes the characters and attributes *into the screen memory* area. Two more BASIC statements are needed for this process. PEEK can be used like SCREEN() to peek at characters on the screen. POKE, as the name implies, pokes a new character onto the screen.

PEEK and POKE

The PEEK() function peeks at a location anywhere in memory and returns the value of the byte at that location. PEEK() reads characters from the screen memory area in the same way that SCREEN() reads characters.

The screen memory contains 4,000 bytes of display information. This corresponds to exactly one screenful of text: remember that the screen is 80 columns wide and 25 rows high. Each character on the screen is represented by two bytes in the screen memory. That's why it takes 4,000 bytes to hold the 2,000 characters on the screen: $80 \times 25 \times 2 = 4,000$.

The screen memory is layed out in rows and columns, as shown in Figure 11-4. The character that appears in row 0, column 0 is the first byte in the screen memory area. The character appearing on the next row down, row 1, appears at byte 161 in the screen memory area. This happens because the first row occupies 160 bytes of memory: two bytes for each of the 80 characters that can appear on a line.

The first byte of each two-byte pair holds the character that appears on the screen. If the character at the upper-left corner of your screen is the letter A, then the first byte in the screen memory has the value 65, which is the ASCII code used internally to represent the letter A. The second byte contains an attribute describing how the letter A should be displayed. On the IBM monochrome display, this attribute indicates if A should be underlined, high or low intensity, or flashing. On the color display, the attribute byte selects both the character color and the background color for the character.

Screen memory, as you can see, is simply arranged as a sequence of 4,000 bytes in memory. Our screen, on the other hand, is generally thought of in terms of 80 rows and 25 columns. Therefore, when you wish to directly manipulate the data in the screen memory, you need to convert the row and column coordinates into memory addresses within the screen memory area.

To convert from rows and columns to screen addresses, you need to multiply the row by 160 (the number of bytes in each row) and then add the number of columns. Then multiply by two, since each character occupies two bytes. This conversion can be expressed as the formula

$$\text{Address} = \text{Row} * 160 + \text{Column} * 2$$

In this form, you are assuming that the row and column are both numbered beginning with zero, as is shown in Figure 11-7. If the row and column are numbered beginning with row 1 and column 1, as is done with BASIC's LOCATE command, you need to subtract one from each coordinate. The address formula then becomes

$$\text{Address} = (\text{Row} - 1) * 160 + (\text{Column} - 1) * 2$$

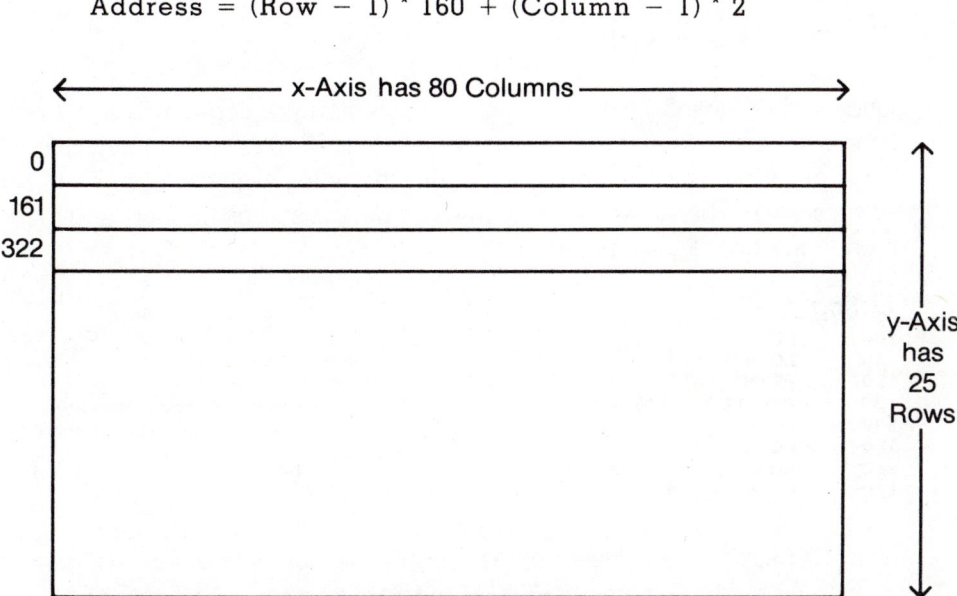

Figure 11-7   *The IBM screen memory.*

You still need one more trick before you can use all this. Memory on the IBM PC is organized into segments. The screen memory is located in a particular segment. Before you can use PEEK(), you need to tell BASIC which segment you wish to PEEK() into. The address that you pass to PEEK() becomes an offset from the start of the segment. For example, if a segment begins at memory address 1000, then PEEK(1) means you want to look at memory address 1001.

Define the segment you wish to PEEK() into with the statement DEF SEG. The location of the screen memory is defined in the IBM PC Technical Reference manual. The manual says that screen memory for the monochrome display is located at segment &HBOOO. The notation &HBOOO may be new to you. The prefix &H means that the following number is written in hexidecimal notation, or base 16. If this seems bewildering, don't worry about it. All you need to do is simply copy the appropriate number into your program. It's not terribly important that you know exactly what it means.

To define the correct segment, type

    DEF SEG = &HBOOO

Note that the above segment is for the monochrome display only. For the color display, use

    DEF SEG = &HB800

Once you've defined the segment, you can start reading characters from the screen memory. Run the program in Listing 11-5 to see how this works. This short program writes a single character, the letter A, in the upper-left corner of the screen. Then it reads the character from the screen memory and displays it on the bottom line of the screen.

Listing 11-5

```
100        CLS
110        LOCATE 1,1
120        PRINT "A"
130        DEF SEG = &HB800          ' Color Screen Memory
140                                  ' Use &HBOOO for monochrome
150        LOCATE 20,1
160        CHARACTER = PEEK (.0 )     ' Look at first char. in screen
170        PRINT  CHARACTER, CHR$(CHARACTER)
```

BASIC's POKE() statement is roughly the opposite of PEEK(). Instead of getting a byte from memory, POKE() puts a byte into memory. POKE() has two parameters. The first parameter is the address at which a byte should be changed, and the second parameter holds the new value. Listing 11-5 can be modified to change the letter A shown in the upper-left corner of the screen to some other character. To do this, add

    180 POKE 0, ASC("*")

The program will change the letter A to an asterisk. The zero value in the address parameter may be changed to any address within the screen memory.

By modifying the RESTORE TEXT routine to use POKE(), you can output both the original character and the original attribute that were stored in the S$() array. The modification is easy to make. It is shown here.

```
REM − RESTORE TEXT
FOR IY = Y + WHEIGHT − 1 to Y STEP − 1
    NUMLINES = NUMLINES − 1
    FOR IX = 1 to WWIDTH − 1
        ADDRESS = (IY − 1)* 160 + (IX − 1)* 2
        ' Restore Character
        POKE ( ADDRESS, MID$(S$(NUMLINES), (IX − 1)*2 ,1))
        ' Restore Atribute
        POKE ( ADDRESS, MID$(S$(NUMLINES), (IX − 1)*2 + 1 ,1))
            NEXT IX
    NEXT IT
```

The FOR-NEXT loop variable IX increases only to the width of the window. But because each character is stored as two bytes—a character and an attribute—you need to double the index IX to reach each byte. That's why the MID$() functions use the index value $(IX − 1)*2$ and $(IX − 1)*2 + 1$. If IX is 1, then these expressions yield 0 and 1, respectively. When IX is 2, the expressions yield 2 and 3. So you can see that even though you increment IX by one only, you are still able to pick each of the character-attribute pairs out of S$().

Scrolling

Scrolling is moving the text of one row onto another and then repeating that operation for the area to be scrolled. To scroll all the text on the screen up one line, you begin at the top of the screen and copy row 2 into row 1, row 3

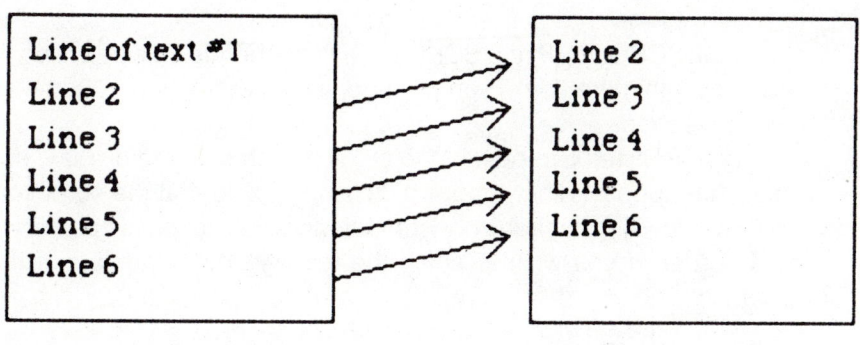

Line of text #1	Line 2
Line 2	Line 3
Line 3	Line 4
Line 4	Line 5
Line 5	Line 6
Line 6	

Before scrolling Up   After scrolling Up

Figure 11-8

into row 2, row 4 into row 3, and so on, all the way down to copying row 24 into row 23. Then you fill row 24 with blanks because there is nothing to scroll into that position. (See Figure 11-8.)

To program scrolling, you use PEEK() and POKE to read characters from one line and then write them to another. The SCROLL UP subroutine is shown in Listing 11-6. On entry to SCROLL UP, X and Y are the coordinates of the upper-left corner of a window that is WWIDTH wide and WHEIGHT high. The subroutine starts at the top of the window and proceeds to scroll by copying the next line on the screen into the current line. (Be sure to change the DEF SEG statement in line 32760 to correspond to your display: &HB000 for the monochrome, &HB800 for color displays.)

Listing 11-6

```
32750    REM - SCROLL UP within the window (X,Y), WWIDTH and WHEIGHT
32760    DEF SEG = &HB800
32770    X = X - 1                                   ' PEEK's and POKE's require
32780    Y = Y - 1                                   ' zero relative X,Y
32790    FOR IY = Y  TO  Y + WHEIGHT - 2
32800      K = IY*160
32810      FOR IX = X TO X + WWIDTH - 1
32820        ADDRESS = K + IX*2
32830        POKE ADDRESS, PEEK(ADDRESS+160)
32840      NEXT IX
32850    NEXT IY
32860    LOCATE Y + WHEIGHT, X+1                     ' Blank out bottom line
32870    PRINT SPACE$(WWIDTH);                       ' of window
32880    RETURN
```

Scrolling down is just the opposite of scrolling up. All of the lines in the window are shifted down by one line. SCROLL DOWN begins at the bottom of the window and copies the preceding row into the current row (see Listing 11-7). Row 9 is copied to row 10, row 8 is copied to row 9, row 7 is copied to row 8. This continues until row 1 is copied into row 2. Since there is nothing to scroll into row 1, it is filled with blanks.

Both SCROLL UP and SCROLL DOWN operate by computing the address of a byte within the row. Then, by adding or subtracting 160, the line needed next is reached.

Both routines can be used to scroll any area on the display, not just those areas that appear within windows. When it is said that the scroll routines work within windows, that means conceptual windows, not physical windows marked by a border. If you wish to scroll the text within a window, set the following variables:

```
X = WINDOWX(W) + 1
Y = WINDOWY(W) + 1
WWIDTH = WINDOWW(W) - 2
WHEIGHT = WWINDOWH(W) - 2
```

Listing 11-7

```
32890    REM - SCROLL DOWN within the window (X,Y), WWIDTH and WHEIGHT
32900    DEF SEG = &HB800
32910    X = X - 1                              ' PEEK's and POKE's require
32920    Y = Y - 1                              ' zero relative X,Y
32930    FOR IY = Y + WHEIGHT - 1  TO  Y + 1 STEP -1
32940      K = IY*160
32950      FOR IX = X TO X + WWIDTH - 1
32960        ADDRESS = K + IX*2
32970        POKE ADDRESS, PEEK(ADDRESS-160)
32980      NEXT IX
32990    NEXT IY
33000    LOCATE Y + 1, X + 1                    ' Blank out top line
33010    PRINT SPACE$(WWIDTH);                  ' in window
33020    RETURN
```

W is the window that will be scrolled. The width and height are both decreased by 2 so that the border characters which are included in the width and height values stored in the arrays, don't scroll.

The scroll routines are not particularly fast, especially when used on large windows. This is because IBM BASIC is interpreted. To speed up the scroll routines, you best bet is to use the IBM BASIC compiler, described in Appendix A. Once the routines have been compiled, they run fast.

The routines shown in Listing 11-6 and 11-7 do not scroll the attribute values. If you have color or boldfaced text on your screen, these routines will have interesting results. The text will move up or down on the screen, but the appropriate colors will stay put. To scroll attributes, simply add the following line to Listing 11-6:

```
32835 POKE ADDRESS + 1, PEEK ( ADDRESS + 161 )
```

Add this line to Listing 11-7:

```
32975 POKE ADDRESS + 1, PEEK ( ADDRESS - 159 )
```

Copying Text between Windows

Transferring text from one window to another is not difficult. You must set X and Y to the upper-left corner of a rectangle that encompasses the text to copy. WWIDTH and WHEIGHT are set to the rectangle's width and height. Save the current value of NUMLINES as

```
TEMP = NUMLINES
```

Then call the SAVE TEXT subroutine. Upon return, the text will have been saved into S$(), beginning at S$(TEMP) and continuing to S$(NUMLINES − 1). This text may be processed as required by your application or simply displayed in another window using the WRITE TEXT subroutine. Once you're finished with the text, you reset NUMLINES = TEMP so that the other window routines will continue to work correctly.

REVIEW

- Windows let you partition the screen into separate viewing areas. Each area can display a program or function.
- To implement windows, save the text that currently occupies the window space. Then draw a window border and fill the interior with blanks. You can display prompts, messages, and menus within the window. Once you've finished using the window, the old text is restored and the window disappears.
- To save text use the BASIC function SCREEN(Y,X), which returns the character code corresponding to the character at row Y, column X on the screen. The characters within a single line are stored in an array variable.
- Text is restored by positioning to the appropriate point on the screen and printing the string.
- CHAIN and COMMON enable programs to run other programs and to pass the values of variables between the programs. By using these statements with the window subroutines, you can create programs that run other programs within a window on the screen.
- Some simple enhancements are scrolling text within windows and saving color attributes.

12

Graphics

IBM BASIC provides easy-to-use graphics statements, such as LINE, CIRCLE, and PAINT. These statements may be used to quickly construct simple drawings and graphics.

To use the graphics statements, you must have the Color/Graphics Monitor Adapter, and you must be using either an RGB, composite, or television display. The graphics operations do not work on the monochrome display.

The graphics statements give you the power to condense large amounts of information into a simple drawing. For example, look at the profits of the fictitious Computers that Glow in the Dark Corporation in Figure 12-1(a). The numbers don't look very inviting, so you might not even take the time to read them. In Fig. 12-1(b), the numbers are displayed in a graph. You can see at a glance that profits increased each month.

This chapter explains techniques for creating and manipulating simple graphics. First, the important IBM BASIC graphics statements are introduced. You'll see how to produce bar and line charts and other simple drawings using these statements. Methods of saving pictures to disk files and some simple animation techniques are also explained.

1983 Profits for Computers That Glow In the Dark Corporation.

Month	Profits
Jan	1,831,617
Feb	1,911,317

Mar	2,123,418
Apr	2,220,113
May	2,311,161
Jun	2,351,298
Jul	2,389,113
Aug	2,418,218
Sep	2,399,561
Oct	2,612,561
Nov	2,599,110
Dec	2,675,126

Figure 12-1(a)

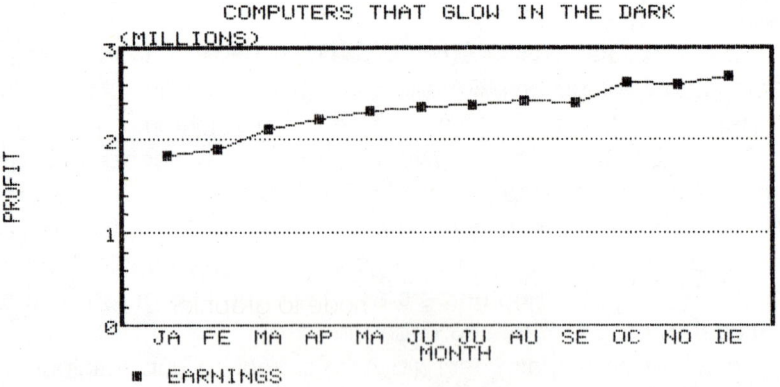

Figure 12-1(b)

OVERVIEW OF PC GRAPHICS

The graphics operations work by treating the screen as a grid of 320 horizontal points and 200 vertical points. Each point can be given one of four different colors. Figure 12-2 illustrates the layout of the graphics screen and the location of the points.

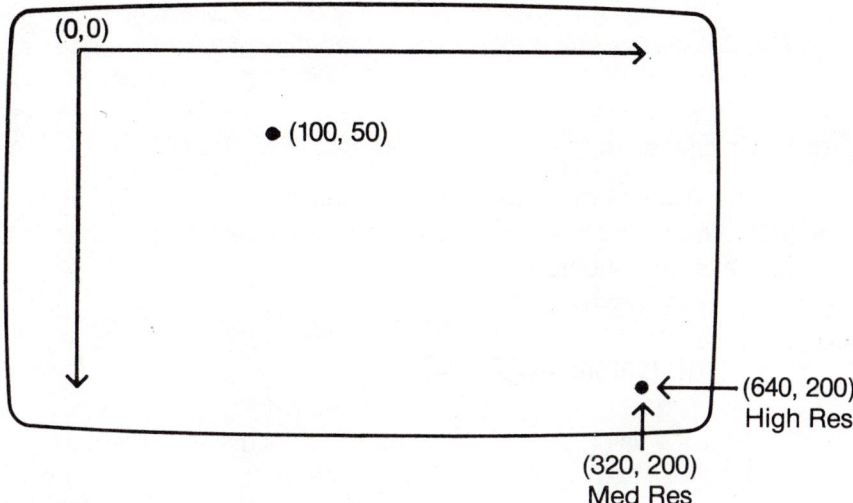

Figure 12-2   *The IBM PC Graphics screen.*

Each of these points is referenced using an X and Y coordinate value To reference a particular point, you refer to its coordinates. The point at coordinate (100,50) is shown in Figure 12-2.

By sacrificing color, the IBM PC can provide an even greater degree of resolution in its graphics. In this form, termed high resolution, the screen is 640 points horizontally and 200 points vertically. In this mode, the graphics appear only in black and white. (See Chapter 13 for a trick that adds color.) This chapter discusses only work with the lower-resolution color graphics (320 × 200).

To switch the screen from text mode to graphics mode, use the SCREEN statement.

SCREEN 1

A value of 2 in the SCREEN statement activates high-resolution graphics.
Try the following statements on your computer.

SCREEN 1
LINE (25,50) – (120,50)

These statements draw a straight, horizontal line near the upper-left corner of the display. The first coordinate (25,50) describes the starting point for the line, while the second coordinate (120,50) describes the ending point. Note that LINE coordinates are in the form (X,Y); LOCATE coordinates are in the form (Y,X).

That's basically all you need to know to make simple drawings. But IBM BASIC provides much more power than this through its repertoire of graphics statements.

The LINE Statement

You have seen how to use the LINE statement to draw a straight line. You can also use the statement to add color to a line. A color is chosen by placing a digit after the ending point.

For example,

LINE (25,50) – (25,120), 2

draws a line using color 2. Up to three colors may be selected using a number from 1 to 3. Color 0 is always the same as the background color and is not normally used. (The terms *palette*, *background*, *foreground*, and *border* are explained in the next section.)

A simple way to draw a square is to use four separate LINE statements, as in

LINE (50,50) – (100,50)
LINE (50,100) – (100,100)
LINE (100,100) – (50,100)
LINE (50,100) – (50,50)

But there's an even easier way to draw a box. The LINE statement has an additional parameter that instructs the PC to draw a box. Suppose you want to draw a box using the points (50,50) and (100,200). The point (50,50) is the upper-left corner of the box and (100,200) is the lower-right corner. The box would look like this:

(50,50)

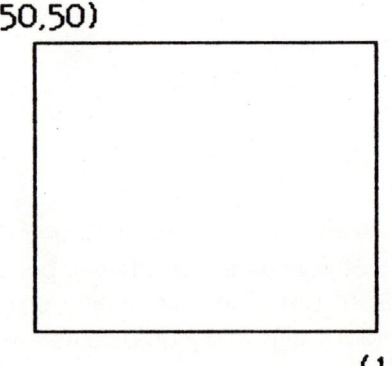

(100,200)

You can draw this box with the statement

LINE (50,50) – (100,200), , B

The B indicates that you want a box drawn. Note that the color parameter was omitted. IBM BASIC uses an assumed color when a color is not specified.

LINE is capable of yet another trick. It can also fill in the box with the same color it uses to draw the border. Indicate box filling by replacing the B with BF, as in

LINE (50,50) – (100,100), , BF

In summary, the LINE statement has the following format:

LINE (point 1) – (point 2), color, B or BF

Both the color and the box parameter may be omitted.

The COLOR Statement

The colors used in graphics are chosen from one of two possible color palettes. You use the COLOR statement to select a palette. The color parameter that is used with the LINE statement, for instance, selects one of the three colors available from the current palette.

In addition, you use the COLOR statement to select the color of the background. If this text was on the IBM PC, the foreground color would be black, and the background color would be white.

The format of the COLOR statement is

COLOR background, palette

The parameters are listed in Tables 1 and 2.

Each palette contains three colors. See Table 1 for a list of numbers and their corresponding colors.

Up to 16 background colors are selected by choosing one of the color numbers in Table 2. Note that colors 8 through 15 are lighter shades of the corresponding colors 0 through 7. Also, the actual color displayed on your monitor or television set depends on the adjustment of the tuning controls. You may need to experiment with the color controls on your television in order to match the colors shown in the chart.

TABLE 1

Color	Palette 0	Palette 1
0	Background	Background
1	Green	Cyan
2	Red	Magenta
3	Brown	White

TABLE 2
THE 16 BACKGROUND COLORS

0 Black	8 Gray
1 Blue	9 Light Blue
2 Green	10 Light Green
3 Cyan	11 Light Cyan
4 Red	12 Light Red
5 Magenta	13 Light Magenta
6 Brown	14 Yellow
7 White	15 High-intensity White

The CIRCLE Statement

CIRCLE is actually more general than the name implies. The CIRCLE statement is used to draw circles, ellipses, and portions of ellipses and circles. The basic statement specifies the center point and the radius. For example,

CIRCLE (100, 100), 50

tells the PC to draw a circle that has radius 50 and a center point at (100,100) on the screen. Figure 12-3 shows the circle that you should see.

The radius value is in points, so 50 means that the radius is 50 points on the screen.

CIRCLE also allows you to specify a color, starting and ending angles, and an aspect ratio. The latter is used to describe ellipses. When the aspect ratio is 1 (the value that the PC uses if you don't specify a value), a circle is drawn. When the aspect ratio is set to .5, for instance, an ellipse is created. See Figure 12-4.

The color value selects a color from the current palette. This color affects the border of the circle only. Unlike the LINE statement, CIRCLE does not have

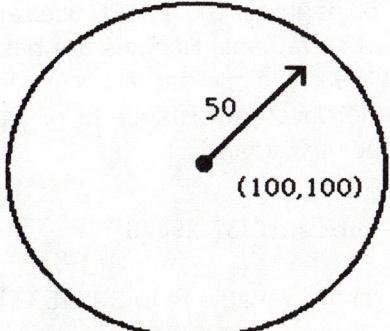

Figure 12-3 *CIRCLE (100,100), 50 draws a circle with a center at (100,100) and a radius of 50 units.*

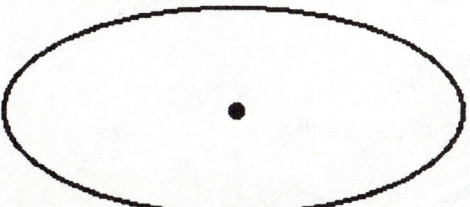

Figure 12-4 *Ellipses are created by setting the aspect ratio parameter to a value other than 1.*

a built-in method of painting its interior. You use PAINT to paint a solid circle; that statement is described in the next section.

The starting and ending angles let you draw a partial circle by telling BASIC where to begin the circle arc and where to end it. The angles are in reference to a horizontal line extending to the right, as shown in the following diagram:

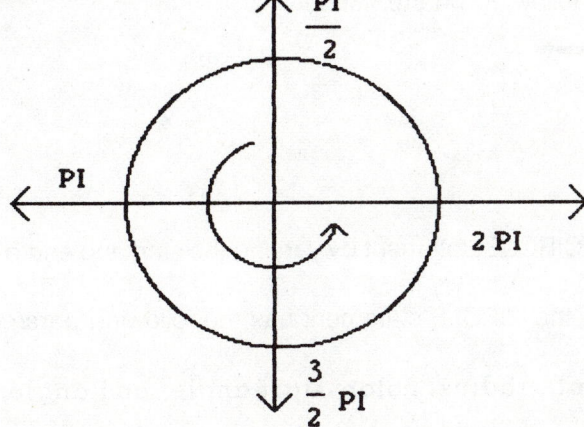

As you know, a circle is divided into 360 degrees. The IBM PC uses an alternate method of circle measurement known as radians. Radians are based on the unit pi, which is approximately 3.141593. A circle has a circumference of 2 times pi. This means that a half circle covers a distance of pi. Perform the following calculation to convert degrees to radians:

radian.measure = degree.measure/57.29578

To simplify the following examples, set the variable PI to 3.141593 by typing

PI = 3.141593

To draw a half circle, enter

CIRCLE (100,100), 50, , 0, PI

You should see a drawing that looks like this:

Now, change the parameters to

CIRCLE (100,100), 50,, PI/2, PI

You should see the following quarter circle:

Experiment with the CIRCLE statement by varying the start and end parameters and the aspect ratio.

To summarize, the CIRCLE statement has the following parameters:

CIRCLE (point), radius, color, start angle, end angle, aspect ratio

The PAINT Statement

PAINT fills an area on the screen with a color. For example, if you drew a box using four individual LINE statements, you might like to later add some color to make the box look solid. To see PAINT in operation, type the following:

        LINE (50,50) – (100,50)
        LINE (50,100) – (100,100)
        LINE (100,100) – (50,100)
        LINE (50,100) – (50,50)

This draws a box on the screen. To use PAINT, specify a point, any point, within the box and a color for painting the box. For example

        PAINT (51,51),2

selects a point just inside the upper-left corner of the box and paints the entire box with color 2.

PAINT operates by painting everything up to a boundary color. In the previous example, the lines marking the box boundary delineate the area to be painted. If the area to be painted is not completely enclosed, the entire screen will be painted, so be careful! To see this, type these statements:

        LINE (50,50) – (100,50)
        LINE (50,100) – (100,100)
        LINE (100,100) – (50,100)
        PAINT (51,51),2

The entire screen should be obliterated! To reset, type

        CLS

which clears the screen.

The format for PAINT is

        PAINT (point), paint color, boundary color

where point is an (X,Y) coordinate somewhere within the object to be painted, paint color is a value from 0 to 3 that designates a color from the current palette, and boundary color is the color of the edges of the figure.

To paint a circle, simply specify the center coordinates that you used in the CIRCLE statement. This will cause the entire circle to be filled with color. If you have drawn only a partial circle, you will need to select a point within the wedge.

The PSET Statement

PSET draws a single point on the screen. For example,

    PSET (100,100)

draws the point at coordinates (100,100). You can color it with a color from the current palette. For example,

    PSET (100,100),2

Type this line on your computer to see how PSET works. Vary the values of the X and Y coordinates and try some different colors.

To erase a point, use the color 0, as in

    PSET (100,100), 0

which sets the point at (100,100) to the background color.

IBM BASIC also provides a PRESET statement, which is virtually identical to PSET. The only difference is that for PRESET, if no color is specified, PRESET automatically uses the current background color. So in effect, PRESET erases points from the screen. It is simpler to use PSET (X,Y),0 than to remember the PRESET command.

The POINT Function

POINT is not a drawing command; it returns the color of a point on the screen. POINT, therefore, is a function, not a statement. Type the following two statements:

    PSET (100,100), 2
    PRINT POINT (100,100)

You should see the value 2, which is the color of the point at (100,100).

The SCREEN Statement

SCREEN selects the screen mode, either text or graphics, medium resolution (320 × 200) or high resolution (640 × 200). SCREEN also sets other parameters that are used in text mode, but this book discusses only those used for graphics.

To change the screen from text to medium-resolution graphics mode, type

SCREEN 1

This clears the screen and sets the foreground to white and the background and border to black. In addition, the number of text columns is set to 40, regardless of the previous column setting.

To restore the screen to text operation, type

SCREEN 0

To return to 80-column operation, type

WIDTH 80

The GET and PUT Statements

GET and PUT are used for both file operations and graphics. In the graphics format, GET reads a section of the image from the display and copies it, in its internal format, into an array. Once the image is in the array, it may be placed elsewhere on the screen with the PUT statement.

GET and PUT are especially useful for producing animated effects, such as balls that bounce around the screen or spaceships that rocket across the display. GET and PUT make it easy to create video game displays. These techniques are described later in this chapter.

Summary of IBM Graphics Statements

- LINE (point 1) – (point 2), color, B or BF. LINE draws a line between points 1 and 2. If B is indicated, LINE draws a box, using the two points as the upper-left and lower-right corners of the box. BF fills the box with color.
- COLOR background, palette. COLOR selects the current color palette and the foreground and background colors.
- CIRCLE (point), radius, color, start angle, end angle, aspect ratio. Circles, ellipses, and arcs are produced with the CIRCLE statement. The basic operation, drawing a circle, is done by telling CIRCLE where the center of the circle is to appear and what size the circle will be (the radius).

Additional parameters select a drawing color, the portion of the circle that should be drawn, and an aspect ratio, which draws an ellipse.

- PAINT (point), paint color, boundary color. PAINT is used to fill any enclosed area with a particular color. Simply specify a point somewhere within the area to be painted and a paint color. PAINT will do the rest.

These are the basic graphics statements available in IBM BASIC. Some of the statements, such as SCREEN and COLOR, have more power than that described here. There are a few other graphics statements, such as DRAW, but they are not necessary for the graphics operations in this book.

SIMPLE GRAPHICS

In this section, you'll use the IBM graphics statements to display bar charts, line charts, and pie charts. These charts are used frequently to display statistical results, such as quarterly earnings or expense reports.

The Bar Graph

The bar graph presents a display of the data after it has been organized into categories. Figure 12-5(a) shows the monthly earnings for the Aerobic Programmer's Institute, a company providing health training for computer programmers. In Figure 12-5(b) these data have been arranged into a bar graph, showing the monthly earnings along the vertical (Y) axis and the corresponding month across the horizontal (X) axis.

To display bar graphs (and also the line and pie graphs), you'll use a subroutine that takes an array of numbers as input and draws the corresponding graph on the screen. The input array will be D(). A variable N will indicate how many elements of D() should be used. Suppose you have the following data in the array:

D(1) = 353
D(2) = 275
D(3) = 250

and N is set to 3.

You could use the values directly to draw lines or boxes on the screen. But it's quite possible that some or all of the values in D() exceed the number of points available in the display. For example, if D(1) = 765, and the screen is only 320 × 200 points, you must scale D(1) down. Note that this routine works only with positive values—negative values require slightly different handling.

Monthly earnings of the
Aerobic Programmer's Institute.

Month	Profits
Jan	1,000
Feb	2,000
Mar	2,713
Apr	3,121
May	4,578
Jun	5,611
Jul	4,618
Aug	7,193
Sep	7,311
Oct	7,819
Nov	8,007
Dec	8,123

Figure 12-5(a)

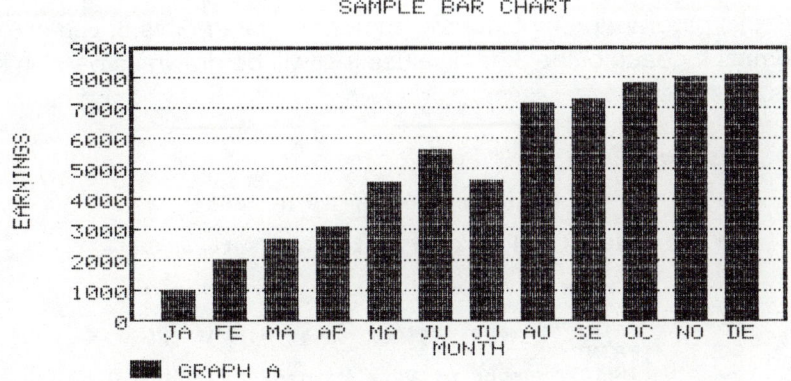

Figure 12-5(b)

To simplify the graphs, assume that each graph must fit into a space that is 101 points high and 201 points wide. Therefore, you need to scale all data to fit within a range of 0 to 100 (vertically) and 0 to 200 (horizontally).

You can see immediately that you'll have to reduce the values listed previously for the D() array before you can graph them. To scale the values in D(), first scan through D looking for the largest value. Call this value MAXIMUM. Next, divide each array value by MAXIMUM. The MAXIMUM value in the D() array is 353. Therefore, you make the following calculations:

$$D(1) = 353 / 353 = 1$$
$$D(2) = 275 / 353 = .779$$
$$D(3) = 250 / 353 = .708$$

These calculations convert the values in D() to the range of 0 to 1. If these values are to appear on the vertical axis, you need to convert them to the range 0 to 100. Do that by multiplying each value by 100. If the values are to appear across the screen, then multiply D() by 200. When you multiply the values by 100, you get

$$D(1) = 1 \quad * 100 = 100$$
$$D(2) = .779 * 100 = 78$$
$$D(3) = .708 * 100 = 71$$

All of these values now fit on the vertical axis. One slight cosmetic problem is that the largest value fills the entire vertical portion of the graph. To avoid this problem, increase the value of MAXIMUM before translating the data values into the proper range.

A program that displays simple bar charts is in Listing 12-1. When it is run, this program prompts for the number of data points. If you enter 3, it then prompts for each of the 3 data values that will be drawn as bars on the vertical axis.

Listing 12-1

```
10        REM - Demonstration of Bar Graphs
20        REM
30        DIM D(100)      ' Array to hold Entered Data
40        CLS
50        SCREEN 1
60        '
70        PRINT "Demonstration of Bar Graphs"
80        PRINT
90        INPUT "Number of Data Points? ",N
100       PRINT
110       PRINT "Enter Y values for each point:"
120       FOR I = 1 TO N
130          PRINT "Point";I;
140          INPUT "? ",D(I)
150       NEXT I
160       GOSUB 200             ' Normalize Data
170       GOSUB 330             ' Draw Graph
```

```
180        CLS
190        GOTO 90
200        REM - Convert all data to range (0..100).
210        MAXIMUM = 0
220        FOR I = 1 TO N        ' Determine maximum value
230           IF  D(I) > MAXIMUM  THEN  MAXIMUM = D(I)
240        NEXT I
250        MAXIMUM = MAXIMUM * 1.1    ' Increase by 10%
260        ' Now scale D() to proper range
270        FOR I = 1 TO N
280           D(I) = D(I) / MAXIMUM * 100
290        NEXT I
300        RETURN
310        '
320        '
330        REM - Draw graph on screen
340        CLS
350        TOPX = 50 :
              TOPY = 50 :
              BOTTOMX = 250 :
              BOTTOMY = 150
360        ' Draw box around the entire graph
370        LINE (TOPX, TOPY) - (BOTTOMX, BOTTOMY),,B
380        ' Determine width of each bar in the bar chart
390        COLUMNS.PER.BAR = INT((BOTTOMX-TOPX)/N) - 4
400        STARTX = TOPX + 3
410        FOR I = 1 TO N
420           LINE ( STARTX, BOTTOMY - D(I)) - (STARTX + COLUMNS.PER.BAR,
              BOTTOMY),,BF
430           LOCATE BOTTOMY/8 + 1, STARTX/8
440           PRINT I;
450           STARTX = STARTX + COLUMNS.PER.BAR + 3
460        NEXT I
470        ' Display legend on left side of graph
480        NUM.ROWS = INT((BOTTOMY - TOPY) / 8)
490        TEMP = 0
500        FOR I = INT(BOTTOMY/8)+1 TO INT(TOPY/8)+1 STEP - 1
510           LOCATE I, 1
520           PRINT INT(TEMP);
530           TEMP = TEMP + MAXIMUM / NUM.ROWS
540        NEXT I
550        '
560        LOCATE 23,1
570        PRINT "Press <SPACE> to continue";
580        T$ = INPUT$(1)
590        RETURN
```

The subroutine at line 200 searches through the data array D() to locate the MAXIMUM value. At line 250, the MAXIMUM is increased by 10% so that there is always a small gap at the top of the chart. Next, the values in D() are normalized to the range 0 to 100 (lines 270 through 290).

The graph is drawn by the routine at line 330. Line 350 initializes the upper-left and lower-right corners of the rectangle that the graph will be displayed within. The LINE statement in line 370 draws a box around the charting area on the screen.

Line 390 determines how wide each bar in the bar chart should be. For example, if the graph is 200 graphics columns wide, and you have five data items to plot, you then have room for 200/5 or 40 columns per item. A small amount is subtracted from the column width; this leaves a gap between each bar.

Lines 410 through 460 draw the actual bar chart columns by displaying a box at each location across the graph. Variable STARTX indicates the current horizontal location across the chart. You use STARTX to indicate the upper-left corner of a box, and you use the value in D(I) to indicate the box's height. Statements 430 and 440 output a label beneath the graph.

Finally, you add a legend along the left side of the graph (lines 480 through 540) by displaying the Y-axis coordinates.

A number of simple improvements can make this a valuable data analysis tool. For example, the values in line 350 may be changed to increase or decrease the size of the chart. Currently, the chart is drawn within a horizontal rectangle centered on the screen. By changing these values, you can change the chart to a vertical rectangle or a square located anywhere on the display.

In addition, the labels written along the bottom of the chart are numbers in the range 1 to N. You might wish to change these to display more meaningful titles. For example, a graph containing sales figures might have labels like MARCH, APRIL, or MAY. A convenient way to add this feature is to prompt for a label name in addition to the data point in line 130. For example, you could use these statements:

```
130 PRINT "Enter name, Point?";
140 INPUT "? "; LABEL$(I), D(I)
```

Then, change statement 520 to read

```
440 PRINT LABEL$(I);
```

The Line Graph

Line graphs display points connected by lines, as shown in Figure 12-6. Because the program statements needed to print a line graph are nearly identical to those for the bar graph, you need only to modify the subroutine at line 330. The changes are in Listing 12-2.

Line 390 determines the width of each point in the display. For example, if there are four points to be displayed within 200 columns, then you can place each item 50 points away from its neighbor.

Lines 410 through 480 draw the graph by displaying a line between item D(I) and D(I + 1). Note that when I is equal to N, the line is already drawn. This is because when I is one less than N (N − 1), I + 1 is equal to N. Hence, there is nothing to do for the last data point.

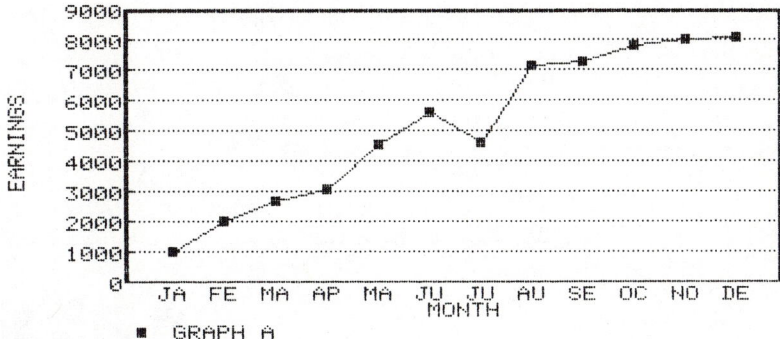

Figure 12-6 *A line chart.*

Listing 12-2

```
330      REM - Draw graph on screen
340      CLS
350      TOPX = 50 :
            TOPY = 50 :
            BOTTOMX = 250 :
            BOTTOMY = 150
360      ' Draw box around the entire graph
370      LINE (TOPX, TOPY) - (BOTTOMX, BOTTOMY),,B
380      ' Determine width of each bar in the bar chart
390      COLUMNS.PER.LINE = INT((BOTTOMX-TOPX)/N) - 4
400      STARTX = TOPX + INT(COLUMNS.PER.LINE/2)
410      FOR I = 1 TO N
420         IF  I<> N  THEN  LINE ( STARTX, BOTTOMY - D(I)) - (STARTX +
            COLUMNS.PER.LINE, BOTTOMY - D(I+1))
430         CIRCLE (STARTX, BOTTOMY - D(I)),3,2
440         PAINT (STARTX, BOTTOMY - D(I)),3,2
450         LOCATE BOTTOMY/8 + 1, STARTX/8
460         PRINT I;
470         STARTX = STARTX + COLUMNS.PER.LINE + 3
480      NEXT I
490      ' Display legend on left side of graph
500      NUM.ROWS = INT((BOTTOMY - TOPY) / 8)
510      TEMP = 0
520      FOR I = INT(BOTTOMY/8)+1 TO INT(TOPY/8)+1 STEP - 1
530         LOCATE I, 1
540         PRINT INT(TEMP);
550         TEMP = TEMP + MAXIMUM / NUM.ROWS
560      NEXT I
570      '
580      LOCATE 23,1
590      PRINT "Press <SPACE> to continue";
600      T$ = INPUT$(1)
610      RETURN
```

The CIRCLE and PAINT statements place a tiny circle at each data item on the screen. These are particularly helpful when a section of the graph is horizontal and the separate data points cannot be distinguished.

The comments concerning column width, data normalization, and the legends of the bar chart also apply to the line graph.

Quite often, line and bar charts are combined. For example, at the beginning of each year, most corporations forecast monthly earnings. At the end of the year, a line graph of the expected earnings is combined with a bar graph of actual earnings. (See Figure 12-7.) In this form, it's easy to see whether the corporation's earnings goals were achieved.

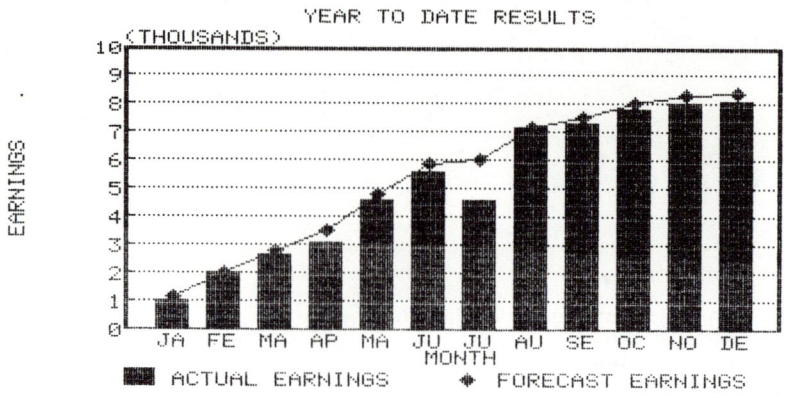

Figure 12-7   *Combined line and bar chart.*

The Pie Graph

Pie charts display data as wedges or pieces of a pie. (See Figure 12-8.) Pie charts are difficult to draw. Fortunately, your DOS diskette (or your DOS 2.0 Supplemental Programs diskette) contains a BASIC program to draw pie charts.

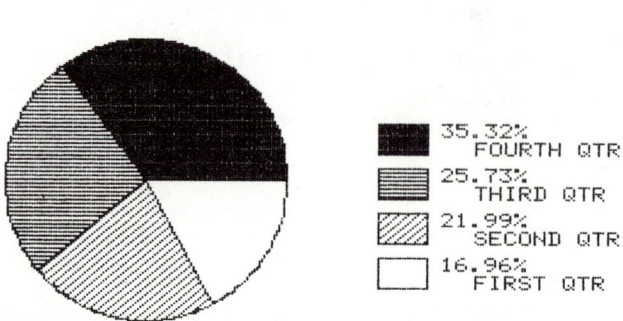

Figure 12-8   *A pie chart.*

To obtain a listing of the IBM Piechart program, load the program into memory and type LLIST:

```
LOAD "PIECHART"
Ok
LLIST
```

The heart of the program appears in lines 1520 through 1670. Line 1520 performs data normalization (similar to the data normalization done for line and bar charts). In IBM Piechart, the array R() contains the data to be graphed. If you wish to add pie chart capability to your program, define array R() as needed and place Piechart lines 1520 through 1670 into a subroutine in your program.

The Piechart program involves trigonometry, a subject best left alone unless you already have some familiarity with it. In essence, the statements at 1580 through 1640 use the CIRCLE command to draw a portion of a circle. PAINT then fills the wedge with a particular color. The trigonometric calculations (lines 1600, 1610, 1630, and 1640) are used to determine the location of the next wedge and the coordinates of the lines that separate each of the wedges. All you need to do to use this routine is to set up R() to contain the data, set up S to contain the sum of the data (see lines 1460 through 1510), and set up N to equal the total number of data points.

ANIMATION

Animation is motion. You have seen how simple objects can be drawn with the LINE and CIRCLE statements. Now, you'll see how those objects can move around on the screen.

IBM BASIC makes animation remarkably easy. All you need to do is draw the object and then use the GET and PUT commands. In graphics mode, the GET statement gets a drawing or portion of a drawing from the screen and places it into an array. PUT copies the drawing from the array back onto the screen. Through proper use of the GET and PUT statements, you can repeatedly put a drawing onto the screen, varying its location by a small amount each time. This produces animation.

The first step is to draw the object. If you wish to draw a circle or a box, just use the CIRCLE or LINE statements. But you can draw much more detailed objects by using combinations of the graphics statements. For example, Figure 12-9 shows a sketch of an airplane on graph paper. This drawing can be mapped to the display screen by graphing each of the points that define the aircraft with PSET or LINE statements. Listing 12-3 on page 294 shows the sequence of LINE statements that creates the airplane sketched in Figure 12-9.

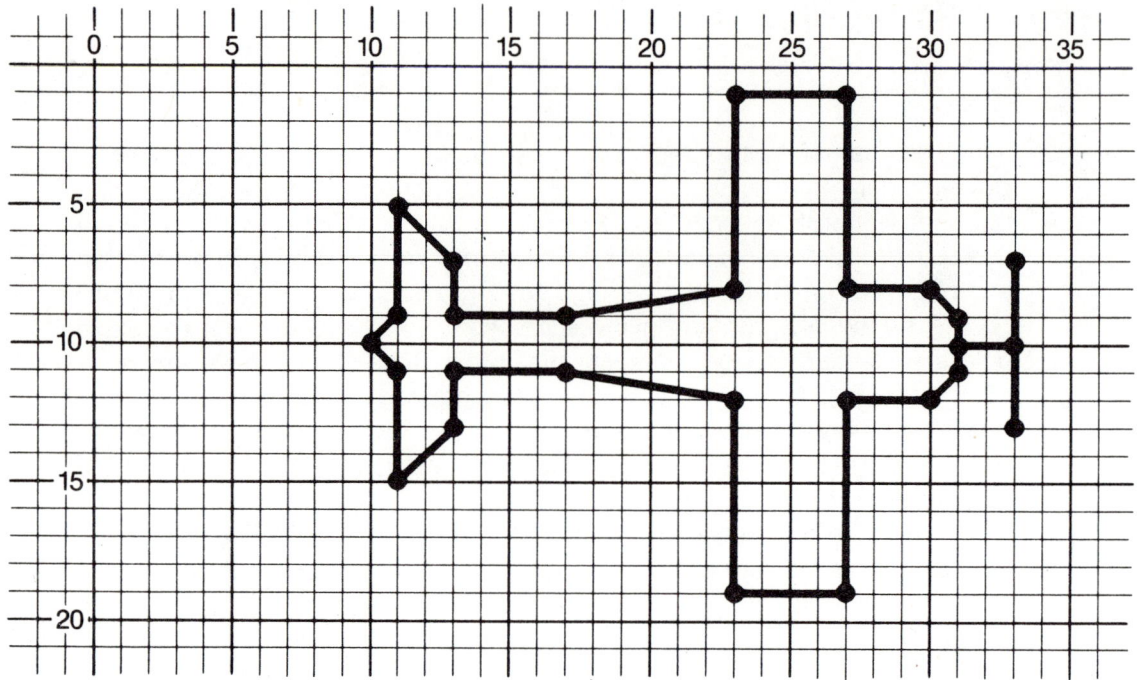

Figure 12-9 *Sketch of an airplane to be graphed on the IBM PC screen.*

At this point, you have a stationary aircraft on the display. Next, you use GET to copy the drawing from the screen into an array. GET has the following format:

GET (x1,y1) – (x2,y2), arrayname

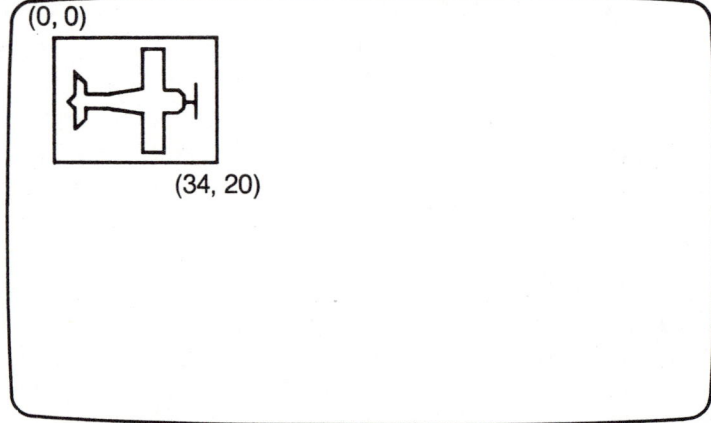

Figure 12-10 *An airplane displayed on the IBM PC screen.*

The first two points describe the upper-left and lower-right corners of a box, just as they do with the LINE statement. Arrayname is the name of the array that will hold the drawing. Figure 12-10 shows the airplane sketched in place at the upper-left corner of the display. To copy this drawing into an array defined as DIM AIRPLANE%(100), you execute

GET (0,0) − (34,20), AIRPLANE%

The coordinates (0,0) and (34,20) mark the upper-left and lower-right corners of a box. The area within this box represents the portion of the graph that is copied to AIRPLANE%.

The actual array can be any nonstring array. These examples use integer variables for the array. To determine the size of the integer array needed to hold a particular graph, compute the following:

DIMENSION = (4 + INT(XWIDTH * GRAPHICS.MODE + 7)/8
    * YHEIGHT) / 2

Here, XWIDTH is the width of the drawing in points. YHEIGHT is the height in points, and GRAPHICS.MODE is 2 for medium-resolution graphs (or 1 for high-resolution graphs). For example, for a medium-resolution drawing containing 35 points horizontally and 21 points vertically, you need an integer array with at least

104 = (4 + INT(35 * 2 + 7)/8 * 21)/2

elements. Here is an example:

DIM OBJECT%(104)

If the drawing were made at the extreme upper-left of the screen, you would execute

GET (0,0) − (34,20), OBJECT%

This would copy the drawing into the array OBJECT%.

To draw the object somewhere else on the display, execute

PUT (X, Y), OBJECT%

This draws whatever was stored in OBJECT% at (X,Y) on the display.

Try these statements to see how GET and PUT work.

```
CLS                          ' Clear the screen
SCREEN 1                     ' Set graphics mode
DIM OBJECT%(104)             ' An array to store the drawing
LINE (3,3) – (31,18),,B      ' Draw a box
GET (0,0) – (34,20),OBJECT%  ' Copy the box to the array
PUT (100,100),OBJECT%        ' And put the box somewhere else
```

You should see two boxes on the computer's display, one at the upper left and another near the middle of the screen.

To animate an object, PUT the object at some initial (X,Y) location on the screen. Then add 1 to X and PUT the object at (X,Y) once again. This has the effect of drawing the box very quickly in successive locations. Listing 12-3 is the code for this operation. The airplane is displayed in the upper-left corner of the screen and is copied into array AIRPLANE%. Statement 410 puts the drawing back onto the screen at (X,Y). Incrementing X (line 420) makes the airplane move across the screen to the right. This particular example moves the airplane down the screen each time it crashes into the right border. (See line 430.) Finally, when the airplane reaches the bottom of the screen, the program stops (line 440).

Listing 12-3

```
10      REM - Demonstration of Animation
20      REM
30      CLS
40      SCREEN 1
50      '
60      REM - Draw airplane at upper left screen
70      LINE (10,10)-(11,9) ' Begin at tail
80      LINE (11,9)-(11,5)
90      LINE (11,5)-(13,7)
100     LINE (13,7)-(13,9)
110     LINE (13,9)-(16,9)
120     LINE (16,9)-(23,8)
130     LINE (23,8)-(23,1) ' Draw left wing
140     LINE (23,1)-(27,1)
150     LINE (27,1)-(27,8)
160     LINE (27,8)-(30,8) ' Draw nose of aircraft
170     LINE (30,8)-(31,9)
180     LINE (31,9)-(31,11)
190     LINE (31,11)-(30,12)
200     LINE (30,12)-(27,12) ' Draw right wing
210     LINE (27,12)-(27,19)
220     LINE (27,19)-(23,19)
230     LINE (23,19)-(23,12)
240     LINE (23,12)-(16,11) ' Draw right side of fuselage
250     LINE (16,11)-(13,11)
260     LINE (13,11)-(13,13) ' Draw right elevator
270     LINE (13,13)-(11,15)
280     LINE (11,15)-(11,11)
```

```
290       LINE (11,11)-(10,10)
300       LINE (31,10)-(33,10) ' Draw propeller
310       LINE (33,7)-(33,13)
320       '
330       ' Allocate enough space to hold the drawing
340       DIM AIRPLANE% (100)
350       GET (0,0)-(34,20), AIRPLANE%
360       '
370       '
380       ' Now move the airplane across the screen
390       X = 0 :
            DX = 1
400       Y = 0 :
            DY = 21
410       PUT (X,Y),AIRPLANE%,PSET
420       X = X + DX
430       IF X >= 320-35 THEN   CLS :
            Y = Y + DY :
            X = 0
440       IF Y >= 200 - 21  THEN STOP
450       GOTO 410
```

In Listing 12-3, the variables DX and DY determine the speed of the plane. Increasing the values of DX and DY makes the aircraft move farther at each display; it therefore appears to move faster. By adding a call to INKEY$ within the display loop, you could check for input of the arrow keys. These keys could be used to change the direction of the airplane.

PUT has an optional parameter that tells how the drawing should be placed on the screen. This extra parameter appears just after the array name and may be one of the following:

PUT (X,Y), AIRPLANE%, PSET
PUT (X,Y), AIRPLANE%, PRESET
PUT (X,Y), AIRPLANE%, XOR
PUT (X,Y), AIRPLANE%, OR
PUT (X,Y), AIRPLANE%, AND

PSET is the value that is assumed by BASIC if no parameter is placed after the array name. In this form, PUT copies the saved drawing directly onto the screen. Note that if you are moving an object across the display, you must erase the drawing at the old location. An easy way to do this is make the boxed area read by GET somewhat larger than the actual drawing. In Figure 12-9, there is a large, unused area at the rear of the airplane. When you move the aircraft forward, this blank area erases the previous drawing of the aircraft.

PRESET is like PSET, except that a negative image is drawn. For example, if PSET draws white lines on a black background, then PRESET draws the inverse image—black lines on a white background.

The AND option makes the AIRPLANE% appear only if there is already a drawing at that location on the screen. OR, on the other hand, merges two pictures. With the OR option, the object that is PUT onto the screen is super-imposed on any existing drawings.

XOR is similar to the OR operation, but it has one important difference. Like OR, an object drawn with XOR is merged with any existing object. But if you PUT XOR the same drawing to the same place twice, the drawing will disappear. For example,

```
PUT (X,Y), AIRPLANE%, XOR
```

draws the airplane on the screen. If you follow that with a second PUT statement,

```
PUT (X,Y) AIRPLANE%, XOR
```

where X and Y have not been changed, the object will be erased.

XOR is particularly useful for moving objects around on a screen that is full of other objects. Use XOR the first time that the object is drawn on the screen. When it's time to move it, use PUT and XOR to erase the existing object, change the (X,Y) coordinates, and PUT the object at the next location.

By all means, experiment! PUT and GET are not difficult to use and they let you create dazzling, animated displays for games or serious simulations.

Saving Picture Files

BASIC's BSAVE and BLOAD statements can be used to copy the screen to a disk file, and vice versa. To save the graph in a disk file, type

```
DEF SEG = &HB800
BSAVE "DRAWING1",0, 16384
```

This creates a file containing 16,384 bytes.

To copy a drawing from disk back to the screen, execute

```
DEF SEG = &HB800
BLOAD "DRAWING1",0
```

REVIEW

- IBM BASIC provides a powerful set of easy-to-use graphics statements: LINE, CIRCLE, PSET, COLOR, and SCREEN.

- You can create bar, line, and pie charts and many other artistic displays using just five graphics statements.
- You create animation by drawing an object on the screen and moving the object across the screen with GET and PUT. By varying the distance that the object moves between each successive display, you create the appearance of speed.

13

IBM BASIC Hints and Tricks

IBM BASIC is rich with features and capabilities. But occasionally, your programs need to do things that BASIC cannot do directly. For example, how does a BASIC program determine how much memory is on the computer? Or how can a program tell if a color monitor is attached to the system?

This chapter discusses hints and tricks that will help you solve problems like those just mentioned and that will help you make IBM BASIC even more powerful. After reading this chapter, you will know how to:

- determine memory size
- use more than 64K of memory in BASIC
- determine what type of display monitor is in use
- determine how many disk drives are attached
- protect programs from unauthorized LISTing and unprotect protected programs
- obtain a disk directory from within a program
- activate the PRINT SCREEN function from within BASIC
- BASIC's internal SCROLL WINDOW
- clear part of a screen
- evaluate an arithmetic expression entered by a user
- determine if CAPS LOCK or NUM LOCK have been pressed
- disable keyboard input
- convert lower case to upper case
- add color to the high-resolution graphics

- save the screen image to disk
- use simple statistics routines

Many of these methods require the use of PEEK, POKE and DEF SEG, which are described in Chapter 11.

DETERMINING MEMORY SIZE

Many programs need to know how much memory is available on the computer on which they are running. If not enough memory is available, a program may need to store extra data in a temporary—and very slow—disk file. But if the progam knows that memory is available, it may be able to avoid the slow disk processing.

When the IBM PC is first turned on, PC DOS automatically determines how much memory is available and stores this value in a special location. You can look at the stored value with DEF SEG and PEEK. The following statements show how:

```
100 DEF SEG = &H40
110 MEMORY.SIZE = PEEK(19) + PEEK(20)*256
```

MEMORY.SIZE is set to the size of memory, in 1K increments. If your PC has 64K of memory, this will set MEMORY.SIZE to 64.

USING EXTRA MEMORY FOR BASIC DATA

Because of the way it was programmed BASIC ignores most extra memory on your computer system. The largest BASIC program (including data and variables) is limited to about 61K; it makes no difference that your computer has more memory. This is because BASIC is rather dumb.

That extra memory can be accessed if you make clever use of PEEK and POKE. To take advantage of this technique, your system must have more than 96K of memory if it uses DOS 1.0 or 1.1 or more than 128K if it uses DOS 2.0 or 2.1'

To determine how much memory is available outside of BASIC's memory area, you need to sum the memory required by your DOS, the memory required by the BASICA program, and the memory required for your BASIC program. DOS 1.0 and 1.1 take about 12K of memory. DOS 2.0 and 2.1 take about 25K.

BASICA uses about 10K. The maximum size of your program is 64K. Therefore, once everything is loaded, you have:

> 12K (DOS 1.1) + 10K (BASICA) + 64K (space for your
> program)

This adds up to 86K. To be on the safe side, say that everything up through 96K is in use. (On DOS 2.0/2.1, it would be everything up to 128K.)

Any other memory is free. To get at the free memory areas, you set DEF SEG to the base of the free area. Then you use POKE to place data into that area and PEEK to copy data back into your program's data area.

On DOS 1.0/1.1 you'd type

> DEF SEG = 96*64

On DOS 2.0/2.1, you'd type

> DEF SEG = 128*64

The entire 64K of memory immediately following the address in the DEF SEG statement can be referenced with PEEK and POKE. For example, the letter A may be written to the first byte of the new storage area with the statement.

> POKE 0, ASC("A")

and retrieved with

> PRINT CHR$(PEEK (0))

The power of this feature lies in the ability it gives you to store large amounts of data outside the 64K limit of BASIC. For example, a word-processing program needs to keep the text that is being edited in memory. But because BASIC limits the total size of programs plus data to 64K, and because a word-processing program is likely to be quite large, there will be little room to store the lines of text within BASIC's 64K work area.

But by using the trick just described, you could (assuming that there is enough memory on the machine) easily store text just outside of BASIC, and read the characters one by one with the PEEK statement.

By using the same technique, you can place data in some other rather unsuspecting places. The IBM Color/Graphics Monitor Adaptor (IBM PC only) contains an extra 16K of memory on the adaptor board. When a color display is used to display 80-column text, only the first 4K of the graphics memory is actually used. (A mere 2K is used in 40-column mode.) The remaining 12K is not used. So you have an additional 12K of storage.

The graphics memory is located at segment &HB800. To use the extra 12K, set DEF SEG to the segment just beyond the first 4K, as in

$$DEF\ SEG\ =\ \&HB800\ +\ 4096/16$$

Then use PEEK and POKE to access the 12K, beginning with location 0 and continuing up through $12 * 1024 - 1$.

DETERMINING DISPLAY TYPE
AND NUMBER OF DISK DRIVES

The type and number of each type of equipment, such as monitors, disk drives, printers, and so on, is stored in a location in memory. To fetch this information, set the default segment to 0, and peek at locations 16 and 17.

```
100 DEF SEG = &H40
110 EQUIPMENT1% = PEEK(17)
120 EQUIPMENT2% = PEEK(16)
```

Each value contains 8 bits. The particular pattern of bits determines what type of equipment is attached to the computer. The method of extracting the bits uses BASIC's AND and division operators. It is not necessary to understand how this works. Listing 13-1 shows how to evaluate the equipment bytes.

Listing 13-1

```
130 NUMBER.PRINTERS = (EQUIPMENT1 AND 192)/64
140 NUMBER.RS232.CARDS = (EQUIPMENT1 AND 14)/2
150 NUMBER.DISKS = (EQUIPMENT2 AND 192)/64 + 1
160 IF  NUMBER.DISKS = 4  THEN
       IF  (EQUIPMENT2% AND 1)=0  THEN  NUMBER.DISKS = 3
170 DISPLAY.MODE = (EQUIPMENT2 AND 48)/16
180 ' DISPLAY.MODE = 1, MEANS 40 X 25 COLOR DISPLAY
190 ' DISPLAY.MODE = 2, MEANS 80 X 25 COLOR DISPLAY
200 ' DISPLAY.MODE = 3, MEANS 80 X 25 MONOCHROME DISPLAY
210 ' NOTE:  DISPLAY.MODE = 3,  EVEN IF BOTH COLOR AND
220 ' MONOCHROME CARDS ARE INSTALLED.
```

Protecting and Unprotecting BASIC Programs

BASIC programs may be protected from unauthorized listing by saving them with the ",P" option:

```
SAVE "SAMPLE", P
```

This creates a program called SAMPLE.BAS that may only be RUN, or LOADed and then RUN. Any attempt to LIST or edit the file creates an error message.

But the protection is hardly foolproof. In fact, there is a very simple way to undo the protection. Type:

```
NEW
DEF SEG
BSAVE "SCRATCH.FIL", 1124, 1
LOAD "SAMPLE"
BLOAD "SCRATCH.FIL", 1124
```

Now, type LIST and you will be able to see the program.

When a program file is protected, BASIC sets byte 1124 to 255. To unprotect the program, you need to set byte 1124 back to 0. It would seem that all you need to do is execute

```
POKE 1124, 0
```

but BASIC is smart enough to not let you POKE around in a protected program. So POKE won't work.

But BSAVE lets you save an unprotected program's protection setting. After loading the protected SAMPLE.BAS file, you can reset the protection byte by BLOADing the unprotected value back to byte 1124. In the steps outlined above, you create a new empty program. Then you use BSAVE to save the unprotected protection setting. Then you load SAMPLE.BAS. Finally, you BLOAD the saved unprotected byte and clobber SAMPLE's protection.

Obtaining Disk Directories from BASIC

The FILES command is normally used as a command, but it may also be used as a statement within a BASIC program. For example,

```
100 CLS
110 LOCATE 1,1
120 FILES "A:*.*"
```

is a short routine that clears the screen and displays a file directory of disk A beginning at the top line of the screen.

An example use of this feature might be as a prompt asking for a filename. You could code this as:

```
1000 CLS
1010 LOCATE 1,1
1020 PRINT "Current List of Files on ";DIRECTORY$
1030 LOCATE 3,1
1040 DIRECTORY$ = DIRECTORY$ + "*.*"
1050 FILES DIRECTORY$
1060 FOR I = 20 TO 24        ' Clear out bottom lines
1070     LOCATE I,1          ' in case directory was
1080     PRINT SPACE$(79);   ' too big
1090 NEXT I
1100 LOCATE 21, 10
1110 INPUT "Enter Filename? ", FILE.NAME$
```

After displaying the filenames, you could use the cursor keys to point to the desired filename. You would do this by highlighting the first filename in the directory and accepting cursor keys to move from one filename to another until the desired filename is selected. Then the actual filename could be read directly from the screen memory area using PEEK and POKE. (See Chapter 11 for details on accessing the screen memory.)

Note that in statement 1050, you can't say

```
FILES DIRECTORY$ + "*.*"
```

It simply will not work. Instead, you must append the "*.*" before executing the FILES statement.

ACTIVATING THE PRINT SCREEN FUNCTION*

Whatever is presently on the IBM display screen may be copied to the printer by pressing the SHIFT and PRTSC keys simultaneously. Assuming that the

*This feature does not work on the PCjr.

printer is connected and online, each line of the screen will be copied to the printer, one by one.

Alternately, a BASIC program can activate the PRINT SCREEN function by using the following statements:

```
1000 ' Subroutine to print the screen
1010 TEMP$ = "" : TEMP% = 0 : PRINT.SCREEN = 0
1020 TEMP$ = CHR$(&HCA) + CHR$(5) + CHR$(&HCB)
1030 TEMP% = VARPTR(TEMP$)
1040 PRINT.SCREEN = PEEK(TEMP% + 2) * 256 +
      PEEK(TEMP% + 1)
1050 DEF SEG
1060 CALL PRINT.SCREEN
1070 RETURN
```

No user input is required to dump the screen contents to the printer. Simply call the above subroutine whenever you wish to have the screen image printed. Remember, though, that this is for text only and will not work for graphics.

The routine works by placing a 3-byte 8088 machine language program into string TEMP$. Next, PRINT.SCREEN% is assigned the memory location where the bytes of TEMP$ are stored. Executing the CALL statement causes a jump to the first machine byte in TEMP$. These three bytes represent this sequence of 8088 instructions:

```
INT 5
RET
```

which translates roughly to

```
Call the DOS print screen subroutine
And then return to who called us
```

SETTING THE SCROLL WINDOW

In BASIC, the screen is 24 lines high and 80 columns wide. If you move the cursor to the bottom of the screen and type LIST to see a large program, the lines scroll upward on the screen. Before long, the entire screen is covered with your program listing. The same thing happens if your program outputs to the screen with PRINT statements. Old information scrolls off the top of the screen, never to be seen again.

The height and size of the scroll window does not have to be 24 × 80. For example, you might like to display a graph on the top portion of the screen, and then scroll text on the bottom without causing the graph to scroll off the screen. You can do this by changing both the dimension and the location of the scroll area. Type this routine; set TOP.EDGE to 5 and BOTTOM.EDGE to 10.

```
2000 ' Set the Scroll area.
2010 ' On entry:
2020 '    TOP.EDGE = top most line of the scroll area
2030 '    BOTTOM.EDGE = bottom most line of the scroll area
2040 '    RIGHT.EDGE = right most column of the scroll area
2050 DEF SEG
2060 POKE &H5B TOP.EDGE
2070 POKE &H5C, BOTTOM.EDGE
2080 POKE &H29, RIGHT.EDGE
2090 RETURN
```

Type LIST and see what happens.

The statement in line 2080, which sets the RIGHT.EDGE, is equivalent to typing

```
WIDTH RIGHT.EDGE
```

Be sure that the values you enter are valid for the current display mode. If the screen is only 40 columns wide, then set RIGHT.EDGE to values less than or equal to 40.

CLEARING PART OF A SCREEN

The CLS statement clears the entire screen all at once. Sometimes you need to clear only a portion of the screen. The standard way to do this is as follows:

```
1000 FOR Y = TOP TO BOTTOM
1010    LOCATE Y,1
1020    PRINT SPACE$(80);
1030 NEXT Y
```

This is the only way to do it on a monochrome display. But on a graphics display, you can use a sneaky way of clearing out a section of the display.

Just use the LINE statement to draw a box.

The LINE statement has the format,

LINE (X1,Y1) — (X2,Y2), color, BF

In spite of its name, LINE can also be used to draw boxes on the display by appending the BF parameter (See Chapter 12.) The points (X1,Y1) and (X2,Y2) are set to the upper-left and lower-right corners, respectively, of a rectangular area. If you set the color to 0, the box is filled with the current background color. Presto! The specified section of the screen is erased.

Since the points (X1,Y1) and (X2,Y2) are intended as graphics points, you need to convert text rows and columns to graphics rows and columns. Each character on the screen is eight dots high by eight dots wide. Therefore, to convert character positions to graphics positions, you need to multiply the text row number by eight and the column number by eight. A subroutine to clear a rectangular area of text on the screen becomes

```
1000 ' Clear the area bounded by (X1,Y1) to (X2,Y2)
1010 LINE ((X1 − 1)*8,(Y1 − 1)*8) − ((X2 − 1)*8,(Y2 − 1)*8), 0, BF
1020 RETURN
```

Note that you subtract 1 from each text coordinate because text coordinates always begin at 1. (LOCATE 1,1 is the extreme upper-left corner of the screen), while graphics coordinates always begin at 0.

EVALUATING ARITHMETIC EXPRESSIONS

There are two ways to evaluate an arithmetic expression, such as (78 + 89)/ (41 − 37). One way is to write a lengthy program that parses the expression. The other way is to cheat and let BASIC do all the work!

If your program needs to accept arithmetic expressions for input, as in

Enter Expression: 45 + SQR(2)/SIN(30)

you can take advantage of a feature of the CHAIN statement. CHAIN has a special MERGE option that allows you to merge the CHAINed program into the lines of the currently running program. Using this format of CHAIN means you do not lose the currently executing program.

The CHAIN statement with the MERGE option has the format

CHAIN MERGE "Filename", line number

You can use this statement to your advantage. When the expression

45 + SQR(2)/SIN(30)

is entered, you can create a new statement and use CHAIN MERGE to merge the new statement right into the body of the program.

Listing 13-2 illustrates the basic method. Line 10 prompts for the expression and stores the result in L$. Lines 20 through 40 create a new statement consisting of

1020 RESULT =

followed by the entered expression. This statement is written to a temporary file. Next, at line 50, CHAIN MERGE merges the created file into the program, causing line 1020 to be overwritten by whatever is in XYZ.BAS. The program jumps to line 1000. The expression has now become part of the program and is executed like any other statement. After obtaining RESULT, control returns to line 70.

The ON ERROR GOTO statement is needed to catch expressions that were entered incorrectly. For example, 3*/5 makes no sense. BASIC will issue an error if you attempt to evaluate 3*/5. ON ERROR GOTO causes a jump to line 1040 if any error occurs. At line 1040 you print an error message and return to the caller.

Listing 13-2

```
10 INPUT "Enter Expression? ",L$
20 OPEN "XYZ.BAS" FOR OUTPUT AS 1
30 PRINT #1, "1020 RESULT="+L$
40 CLOSE 1
50 CHAIN MERGE "XYZ.BAS",1000
60 PRINT "Result = ";RESULT
70 GOTO 10
1000 ' Evaluate expression
1010 ON ERROR GOTO 1040
1020 RESULT=10+5
1030 GOTO 60
1040 ON ERROR GOTO 0
1050 PRINT "Invalid Expression"
1050 RESUME 1060
1070 ON ERROR GOTO 0
1080 GOTO 70
```

CHECKING THE CAPS LOCK AND NUM LOCK KEYS*

IBM really blundered when they built the keyboard for the IBM PC. You cannot tell whether the CAPS LOCK or NUM LOCK keys have been pressed. When CAPS LOCK is depressed, pressing the SHIFT key causes lower case characters to appear. The result of this is that touch typists may find an entire paragraph written in upper case or all of their upper case written in lower case.

Your software can overcome this error in the IBM PC keyboard design by either displaying the current setting of the CAPS LOCK and NUM LOCK keys on the screen or by automatically setting the locks to appropriate assumed values.

Whenever you press CAPS LOCK, the PC updates a location in memory. Each time that CAPS LOCK is pressed, the value is toggled from CAPS LOCK ON to CAPS LOCK OFF, or vice versa. Press CAPS LOCK once, and the memory location is changed to CAPS LOCKED PRESSED. Press it again, and the memory location is changed back to CAPS LOCK NOT PRESSED. You can access the current setting by PEEKing at the keyboard status memory location, and you can change the value by POKEing. The following examples show how the LOCK keys may be checked and set.

```
DEF  SET = &H40
IF   PEEK(&H17) AND 64 THEN
        PRINT "CAPS LOCK ON"
IF   PEEK(&H17) AND 32 THEN
        PRINT "NUM LOCK ON"
```

To set CAPS LOCK to the ON state, execute this statement:

```
POKE &H17, PEEK(&H17) OR 64
```

To set NUM LOCK to ON, execute this statement:

```
POKE &H17, PEEK(&H17) OR 32
```

To set CAPS LOCK OFF, use this statement:

```
POKE &H17, PEEK(&H17) AND (255-64)
```

*The PCjr does not have a NUMLOCK key, so this function does not apply to the PCjr.

To set NUM LOCK OFF, use this statement:

POKE &H17, PEEK(&H17) AND (255-32)

Disabling Keyboard Input*

Sometimes a program must run with absolutely no interruptions. To make this possible, disable the keyboard with the statement

OUT 97, 204

To turn the keyboard back on, use the statement

OUT 97, 76

If you forget to re-enable the keyboard, you'll have to turn off the PC, wait a bit, and then turn it back on. There's no way to regain control except by executing the second OUT command.

Adding Color to High-Resolution Graphics*

High-resolution graphics provides 640 horizontal points and 200 vertical points on the screen. High-resolution mode is selected with the SCREEN statement:

SCREEN 2

(See Chapter 12 for additional details.)

According to the IBM PC BASIC manual, only two colors are possible in high resolution mode: black and white. But actually, the display circuitry is capable of showing any one of eight possible colors on a black background when the display is either a color television or a composite monitor. (RGB monitors will still be just black and white in high-resolution mode.) Use this statement to access color:

OUT &H3D9, color

The color parameter may be varied from 1 to 15. Experiment!

*This feature does not work on the PCjr.

CENTERING A STRING

To center a string S$ on the display, execute the following code:

```
LOCATE Y, 40 - LEN(S$) / 2
PRINT S$
```

Y is the row S$ should be centered on. Change 40 to 20 if you are using a 40-column screen.

CONVERTING LOWER CASE TO UPPER CASE

Listing 13-3 is a routine that takes a string L$ and converts any lower case characters within L$ to upper case.

Listing 13-3

```
10        INPUT L$
15        GOSUB 1000
20        PRINT L$
30        GOTO 10
1000      ' Convert lower case characters in L$ into upper case
1010      TEMP$ = L$
1020      L$ = ""
1030      FOR I = 1 TO LEN(TEMP$)
1040        CH$ = MID$(TEMP$,I,1)
1050        IF  CH$ >= "a"  AND  CH$ <= "z"  THEN L$ =
            L$ + CHR$(ASC(CH$)-32) ELSE L$ = L$ + CH$
1060      NEXT I
1070      RETURN
```

PRINTING A BACK SPACE

To move the cursor backwards one character position, you can't just print the ASCII code for a backspace. Instead, you must use LOCATE to move the cursor backward, as shown here:

```
LOCATE CSRLIN, POS(0) - 1
```

The variable CRSLIN is automatically set by BASIC to the current row on the screen. POS(0) is always equal to the horizontal column on the screen where the cursor is currently located. So this statement moves the cursor left one space. To erase the character and move the cursor back one space, execute the following commands:

```
LOCATE CSRLIN, POS(0) − 1
PRINT " ";
LOCATE CSRLIN, POS(0) − 1
```

SAVING SCREEN IMAGES

An easy way to create fast help messages is to display them on the screen and then save the entire image on disk by using BASIC's BSAVE command. When the message must be displayed, you simply BLOAD the file back into screen memory.

BSAVE copies an area of memory to a disk file. If you specify the screen memory area, then you copy the contents of the screen to the disk. For example, to save the current display, type

```
1000 DEF SEG = &HB000      ' For monochrome display
1010                       ' Use &HB800 for color display
1020 BSAVE "SCREEN", 0, 4096
```

This copies the 4K screen buffer to the disk file. To copy graphics images, use

```
1020 BSAVE "SCREEN", 0, 16384
```

because you'll need to save the entire 16K graphics memory. Be sure to specify

```
DEF SEG = &HB800
```

so that the BSAVE will reference the graphics memory area.

To load the screen image back from disk, type

```
BLOAD "SCREEN", 0
```

Be sure that DEF SEG is still set to the correct memory area before making the call.

SWITCHING DISPLAY SCREENS

If your program depends on the use of a color graphics card, you can use the entire 16K of memory in some interesting ways. Earlier in this chapter, you saw how data can be temporarily stored in this extra memory. You can also use the extra memory space to store additional screen images.

In 40-column text mode, only 2K is used for the current screen image. This leaves 14K, or the equivalent of seven screens of memory. Using the SCREEN statement, you can select which of the eight possible screens (numbered 0 through 7) will appear on the display. Meanwhile, your program can be writing data to one of the other screens. Then, quick as a flash, the current display can be switched to one of the other screens.

In 80-column text mode, you can do the same, except that you have enough memory for only four screens, numbered 0 through 3.

SCREEN has the format

SCREEN mode, color select, apage, vpage

To set the screen to text mode, set the mode parameter to 0. If the current width is 40, the screen enters 40-column mode; otherwise, 80-column mode is selected. The color select parameter determines if true color should be allowed. If color select is 0, then only black and white images are displayed. If color select is 1, then a color display will be created.

The last two parameters, apage and vpage, select which screen appears on the display and to which screen subsequent PRINTs output data. VPage selects the visual page, which is the screen, or page, that appears on the display. Normally, both apage and vpage are the same value. Execute a PRINT and the output immediately appears on the screen.

By changing the values of the apage and vpage parameters, you can prepare a new screen image while the current screen is displayed. Then, once the new image is ready, you select it for presentation by setting the vpage parameter to the new screen number. For example, initially, both the vpage parameter and the apage parameter are set to 0. To prepare a new screen, you execute

SCREEN 0, 0, 1, 0

This leaves screen 0 on the display, but it sets the active page to screen 1. Subsequent PRINT will send their output to screen 1, but the current display will remain unchanged. Once screen 1 is ready, you execute

SCREEN 0, 0, 0, 1

which sets the visual page to 1 and the active page to 0. Your program can now modify the contents of screen 0.

Here is an example of how screen switching works:

```
 5 CLS
10 PRINT "Hi There!"
20 SCREEN 0,0,1,0
30 PRINT "Peek a Boo!"
40 INPUT "", A$
50 SCREEN 0,0,0,1
60 INPUT "", A$
70 SCREEN 0,0,1,0
```

When the program runs, all you will see is,

Hi There!

When you press the ENTER key, the screen instantly switches to show

Peek a Boo!

Pressing ENTER again restores the message,

Hi There!

A handy way to use this technique is to display help messages without destroying the current display. For example, the screen might show part of a word-processing document. If the HELP key is pressed, you write the help message to an unused screen and then switch to that screen display. You can switch back to the original screen when you are done.

A note of caution is necessary. Since there is only one cursor, your program must keep track of where the cursor was on the original screen. Before switching from one active page to another, save the current cursor location using POS(0) and CSRLIN. Here is an example:

```
SAVED.X = POS(0)
SAVED.Y = CSRLIN
```

On return to the active page, restore the cursor location by executing

```
LOCATE SAVED.Y, SAVED.X
```

Using the Cursor Keys During Input

When entering data in response to an INPUT statement, you can use BASIC's editing keys to edit the input.

An interesting variation is to not only edit the current input line but to move the cursor somewhere else on the screen and to use the other text as input. For example, try the following:

```
10 INPUT "Name? ", N1$
20 INPUT "Name? ", N1$
30 PRINT N1$,N2$
```

When you run this program, you'll see

```
Name? ED
Name?
```

At the second prompt, use the UP ARROW key to move to the previous input. Move the cursor to the right past ED and press ENTER. You'll see ED printed twice.

Simple Statistics Routines

The remainder of this chapter provides a number of commonly used statistical routines. Some, like the *mean*, are easy to program. Others, like *standard deviation, median*, and *mode* are less obvious.

The Mean

The most common statistic is the mean, or average. It is frequently used to describe an entire set of data with a single number. For example, suppose three lawyers earn $50,000, $100,000 and $150,000 respectively. You know that the average salary is $100,000.

The mean is easily computed by adding together all of the values and then dividing by the number of values. This is the computation of the average of the three lawyers' salaries:

$$\frac{50000 + 100000 + 150000}{3} = 100000$$

Computing the Mean of an Array of Data

Often, the data for which you must compute a mean has been stored in an array. To compute the mean of the array, you let N equal the number of values in the array, and you let each of the values be represented by X(1), X(2), X(3), and so on, up to X(n). The three salaries just shown might be stored in arrays as

    X(1) = 50000
    X(2) = 100000
    X(3) = 150000

and

    N = 3

Once the values have been entered into the array, the mean is easily computed as shown in Listing 13-4.

Listing 13-4

```
10 SUM = 0
20 FOR I = 1 TO N
30    SUM = SUM + X(I)
40 NEXT I
50 MEAN = SUM / N
```

Computing the Mean During Input

In some instances, the set of data may not have been stored in an array. Instead, each value may be entered from the keyboard. In this case, the sum and the count N are produced as the data are entered. Listing 13-5 shows how to do this.

Listing 13-5

```
10 N=0
20 SUM = 0
30 PRINT "Enter Observation # ";N+1;"(999 when finished)";
40 INPUT X
50 IF X=999 THEN GOTO 90
60 SUM = SUM + X
70 N = N + 1
80 GOTO 30
90 REM - COMPUTE MEAN
100 IF N = 0   THEN MEAN = 0
    ELSE  MEAN = SUM / N
```

THE MEDIAN

The median is that value that falls in the middle of a range of data. Consider this list of numbers:

5   13   17   23   53   67   513

The median is 23 because half of the numbers are less and half are greater than 23.

Note that the median is not the same as the mean.

$$\frac{5 + 13 + 17 + 23 + 53 + 67 + 513}{7} = 73.3$$

An interesting property of the median is that a median value is rarely affected by extremely large or very small values. The value of 513 could have been 93 or 1,100 or 10,137—but the median would still be 23. On the other hand, a large value like 513 makes the mean greater, which can lead to erroneous conclusions about the data. In fact, the mean of the above list, 73.3, is hardly representative. Of the seven numbers, six are less than 73.3 .

Computing the Median

To compute a median, you first sort the data into numerical order. Then you select the number in the middle of the list. Simple, right?

Actually, the method used to select the middle of the list depends on whether the total number of values is odd or even. For example, it's obvious that 7 is the middle number in the list.

3   7   11

But what is the middle number in the list

5   8   9   12?

When N, the number of values in the list, is odd, you select the $(N+1)/2$ element. When N is 3, as shown in the first list, you select the $(3+1)/2$, or 2d element, which gives the number 7. When N is even, as in the second list, there is no single middle element because $(4+1)/2$ is 2.5. The correct solution is to average the numbers at positions 2 and 3, which gives the correct value for the median.

An Algorithm that Computes the Median

Assume that an array X() holds the numbers whose median is to be determined. Let N equal the size of the list. The steps to compute the median are:

1. Sort array X() into ascending order.
2. If N is odd the
     Median = X((N+1)/2)
   Otherwise, if N is even then
     Median = (X (N/2) + X((N+2)/2))/2

The sorting step may use any sorting algorithm. Listing 13-6 implements the above algorithm using a Shellsort.

Listing 13-6

```
10        DIM X(100)
20        INPUT "Enter # (999 when done) ? ",X
30        IF X = 999 THEN 100
40        N = N + 1
50        X(N) = X
60        GOTO 20
70        '
80        '
100       GOSUB 1000
110       PRINT "Median = ";MEDIAN
120       STOP
130       '
140       '
150       '
1000      ' Shellsort array X() into ascending order
1010      D = 4
1020      IF D < N THEN D = D + D :
            GOTO 1020
1030      D = D - 1                          ' Let D =
          largest power of 2 < N
1040      D = INT (D/2)
1050      IF D < 1 THEN 1170
1060      FOR J = 1 TO N - D
1070        FOR I = J TO 1 STEP -D
1080          IF X(I + D) > X(I) THEN GOTO 1130
1090          T = X(I)
1100          X(I) = X(I + D)
1110          X(I + D) = T
1120        NEXT I
1130      NEXT J
1140      GOTO 1040
1150      '
1160      '
1170      ' Compute Median
1180      IF (N MOD 2) <> 0  THEN  MEDIAN = X( (N+1)/2 )
            ELSE  MEDIAN = ( X(N/2) + X((N + 2)/2))/2
1190      RETURN
```

THE MODE

Both the mean and the median are used to describe the middle of a group of data. Another measure, called the mode, is the value that occurs most frequently. Consider this list:

10   12   17   17   17   18   19   23   23   25

The mode is 17 because it occurs most often. Some data do not have a mode, as in

5   7   9   11

Other data have more than one mode, as in

7   7   8   9   23   33   37   41   53   57   57

This list has two modes, 7 and 57.

Computing the Mode

If you know the possible range of values in the array X() for which you are to compute a mode, then the computation is fairly easy. Define an array COUNT(MAX.VALUE) where MAX.VALUE is the largest value that can be stored in X(I). Use each value X(i) as an index to another array. For each X(i), increment a counter to keep track of how many times that value has occurred. Suppose you have the following list of numbers:

4   5   4   7   4   3   5   4   8

You define

DIM COUNT(8)

since 8 is the largest number in the X() values. For each X(I), you increment the corresponding COUNT:

COUNT(4) = COUNT(4) + 1
COUNT(5) = COUNT(5) + 1

```
COUNT(4) = COUNT(4) + 1
COUNT(7) = COUNT(7) + 1
COUNT(4) = COUNT(4) + 1
```

After going through the entire list, you are left with COUNT() having the values

```
COUNT(1) = 0
COUNT(2) = 0
COUNT(3) = 1
COUNT(4) = 4
COUNT(5) = 2
COUNT(6) = 0
COUNT(7) = 0
COUNT(8) = 1
```

Obviously, the value 4 occurs the most often, and is, therefore, the mode. Listing 13-7 shows how this simple version is programmed. Note that Listing 13-7 only finds one mode, even though there may be more than one mode for the array of data, X().

Listing 13-7

```
1000 ' Compute the Mode
1010 DIM COUNT(MAX.VALUE)
1020 FOR I = 1 TO MAX.VALUE
1030     COUNT(I) = 0
1040 NEXT I
1050 FOR I = 1 TO N
1060     COUNT(X(I)) = COUNT(X(I)) + 1
1070 NEXT I
1080 MODE = 0
1090 FOR I = 1 TO MAX.VALUE
1100     IF COUNT(I) > MODE  THEN  MODE = COUNT(I)
1110 NEXT I
```

If the range of permissible values includes negative numbers, you can add a constant to each value, so that each index into COUNT is always positive. For example, if the range of numbers is from -4 to $+5$, then you define COUNT as DIM COUNT(10), and add 5 to each X(I) value. This gives a range from 1 to 10.

If the range of numbers is too large to be used as indices into an array, you can place the numbers into a symbol table. (See Chapter 4.) Then you search the table for each value in array S(). If the value is in the table, then you increment a counter associated with that data value. After checking all the numbers in the array X(), you can quickly scan through the symbol table looking for the largest counts. The corresponding numbers are the modes for the array X().

THE STANDARD DEVIATION AND VARIANCE

Knowing only the average value for a group of numbers can be misleading. Suppose that a city has an average high temperature of 70 degrees during the month of April.

A 70 degree average seems quite nice—but if the high temperature ranges from 20 degrees on April 1 to 120 degrees on April 30, you might not want to live there. What you need is a measure of variation. The standard deviation of a set of data provides this measurement.

Other measurements may seem to gauge variation. You could try to measure the average difference from the mean by subtracting each value from the mean. Unfortunately, since some of the numbers are less than the mean and some greater, the average of the differences will always be zero.

Given the list of numbers

$$17 \quad 31 \quad 37 \quad 41 \quad 59$$

with mean equal to 37, the average difference would be computed as

$$(17-37) \; + \; (31-37) \; + \; (37-37) \; + \; (41-37) \; + \; (59-37)$$
$$-20 \quad + \quad -6 \quad + \quad 0 \quad + \quad 4 \quad + \quad 22 \quad = 0$$

An alternate approach is to square the differences; this will always yield a positive value. This is the technique used in calculating the standard deviation.

Calculating the Standard Deviation

the *sample standard deviation* is defined mathematically as

$$S = \sqrt{\frac{\Sigma (x - \bar{x})^2}{n - 1}}$$

The notation $\Sigma (x - \bar{x})^2$ means to sum or add together *each value x minus the mean and square the result.*

The mean (x) of this list of numbers

$$7 \quad 13 \quad 23 \quad 11$$

is 13.5. The standard deviation is then calculated as

$$S^2 = \frac{(7 - 13.5)^2 + (13 - 13.5)^2 + (23 - 13.5)^2 +)(11 - 13.5)^2}{3}$$

$S^2 = 139/3$

$S^2 = 46.3$

$S = 6.8$

A major problem with the formula just given is that you must first compute the mean and then go back through the entire list and recompute the differences from the mean.

When you deal with large data sets or when you use a computer, a better formula is:

$$S = \sqrt{\frac{n\,(\Sigma x^2) - (\Sigma x)^2}{n\,(n - 1)}}$$

Using this formula, the computer can compute the standard deviation in a single pass through the list of numbers.

Three totals are computed as each number in the list is examined:

1. the size of the list, n
2. the sum of each of the numbers squared (Σx^2)
3. the sum of each of the numbers (Σx)

To represent these values in a BASIC program, let N equal the size of the list. SUMSQRD holds the sum of each of the numbers squared. SUM holds the sum of all the numbers. Listing 13-8 is a sample program that computes the standard deviation of a set of entered numbers.

Listing 13-8

```
10        N = 0
20        SUM = 0
30        SUMSQRD = 0
40        INPUT "Enter # (999 when done) ? ",X
50        IF X = 999 THEN 120
60        N = N + 1
70        SUM = SUM + X
80        SUMSQRD = SUMSQRD + X * X
90        GOTO 40
100       '
110       '
120       ' Compute Standard Deviation
130       STANDARD.DEVIATION = SQR ( ( N * SUMSQRD - SUM
            * SUM ) / ( N * (N - 1)))
140       PRINT "Standard Deviation = "; STANDARD.DEVIATION
```

APPENDIX
A

The IBM BASIC Compiler

The IBM BASIC compiler translates BASIC programs into a form that makes them run up to 40 times faster than normal programs.

All that you need to do is to run the BASIC compiler and let it automatically convert your program. The compiler is a separate software product; it is available from your IBM software dealer.

UNDERSTANDING THE COMPILER

Deep inside your PC is a *microchip* or *integrated circuit* called the *8088 microprocessor.* This chip contains the brainpower of your PC.

But the 8088 does not speak BASIC. It speaks a peculiar dialect of bits, bytes and hex digits known as *machine language.* Another program, called the *BASIC interpreter,* acts as an intermediary between your program and the 8088. The interpreter is similar to a translator translating one language into another. In this case, the interpreter translates the language of BASIC into the specialized machine language of the 8088. Each and every time a statement is executed, it must be translated. This results in a great deal of inefficiency, and hence, a much slower program than is possible with the 8088 machine language. The use of the compiler eliminates the intermediate interpretation step, thereby making your programs run fast. Figure A–1 illustrates this.

You may be wondering why you don't just dispense with the interpreter. It's mainly kept around for convenience. You see, the compiler translates only *entire programs,* all in one big gulp.

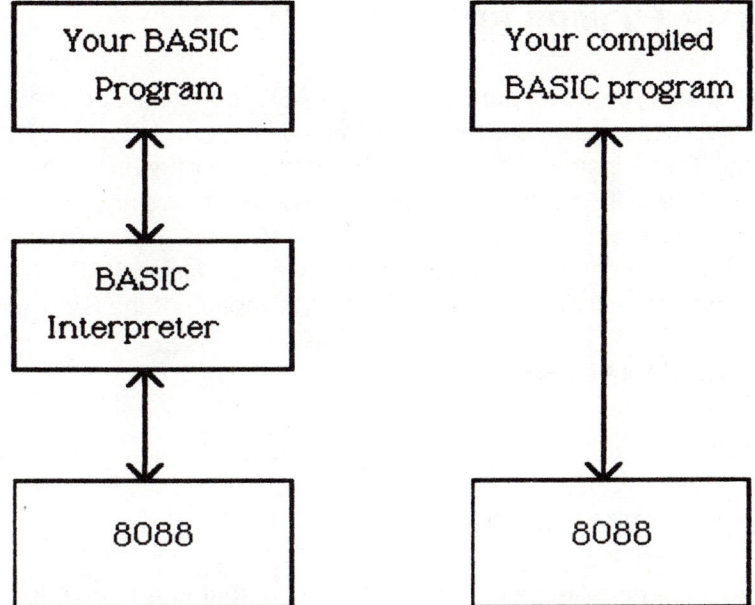

Figure A-1   *Normal BASIC must be translated into the 8088's language by way of the BASIC interpreter, as shown on the left. The compiler eliminates the need for the interpreter, allowing programs to directly execute on the 8088.*

The interpreter, on the other hand, is interactive, working line by line on the program. If a mistake occurs, you can just re-enter the line or lines that are incorrect, and then run the program again. If there is a mistake in a compiled program, you must recompile *the entire program,* even if only a minor change is needed to fix the problem. This requirement makes the compiler rather awkward to use during program development and debugging.

Ideally, what programmers need is a compiler that works line by line. Unfortunately, a line-by-line compiler is a difficult and large program to construct, requiring a great deal more memory than is appropriate for a personal computer. Interactive BASIC is a nice compromise. The interpreter translates each statement into a sequence of intermediate steps that taken individually are relatively easy to translate into a sequence of 8088 instructions. This translation, while much slower than the actual 8088 machine language, produces a BASIC program that takes a fairly small amount of memory.

Compilation makes sense once you have completed the program and are satisfied that it works correctly. Together, the two forms of BASIC give the best of both worlds: *interactive* for program development and testing; *compiled* for fast execution of a finished masterpiece.

USING THE COMPILER

Assuming that you have purchased the BASIC compiler and made at least one backup copy, these are the steps that you need to follow to compile your program. (These instructions assume the presence of two disk drives and at least 64K of memory, but the compiler may also be run on single drive systems.)

If you have already written your BASIC program, you need to save it as an ASCII text file before handing it to the compiler. Using BASICA, load your program into memory and save it with the ",A" option of the SAVE command:

LOAD "ANALYSIS"

Ok

SAVE "ANALYSIS. TXT",A

This creates a new file called "ANALYSIS.TXT" that is a normal text file. Text files can be read by word-processing programs, and text editors. The text files can be printed and have all manner of other things done to them that are unacceptable for a normal .BAS program file.

Next, you place the diskette containing the compiler in drive A. Place the diskette containing your program text file in drive B and make this your default drive, if it is not already:

A>B:
B>

Type this statement next:

B>A:BASCOM ANALYSIS.TXT;

Note the semicolon at the end. This begins execution of the BASIC compiler. On the screen you should see a message similar to

IBM Personal Computer BASIC Compiler
(C) Copyright IBM Corp 1982 Version 1.00
(C) Copyright Microsoft, Inc. 1982

and after a long pause during which it compiles your program,

nnnnn Bytes Available
nnnnn Bytes Free

nn Warning Error(s)
nn Severe Error(s)

Any other messages that you see are warning or error messages indicating that there is a problem in the compilation.

Next, type

B>A:LINK ANALYSIS;

Again, note the semicolon. When the linker finishes, you will again see the DOS B> prompt. To run the program, type

B>ANALYSIS

Review of Compilation Steps

- SAVE your program using the ",A" option of the SAVE command.
- Run the compiler by typing

B>A:BASCOM programname;

- Link the compiled program by typing

B>A:LINK programname;

- And finally, run your program by entering its name

B>programname

and pressing ENTER.

That is about all there is to compiling and executing your BASIC programs. The sections that follow discuss some additional features of the BASIC compiler and some of the changes that you may have to make to your program so that it will be acceptable for the compiler.

OTHER FEATURES OF THE COMPILER

If you omit the semicolon at the end of each command line, the compiler, or linker, will display a series of prompts. Depending on how you answer these questions, you can create an executable program file named differently than your source file or you can have the compiler produce a listing of the program on the attached printer. These particular options are described in detail in the IBM BASIC Compiler manual. Normally, you will find it most convenient to place a semicolon at the end of the command line, bypassing these prompt messages.

You can use several features when you compile programs that you cannot use in interactive BASIC. You can compile programs whose statements do not include line numbers. You can also use the INCLUDE FILES option, which allows one program to include portions of another program file. In addition, a better assembly language interface is available when you compile programs.

The Run-Time Library

Normally, compiled BASIC programs require the use of an auxiliary program called the run-time module. The run-time module is kept in a file called BAS-RUN.EXE and is automatically invoked whenever you run a compiled program. In many instances, you do not need to use the BASRUN run-time module.

BASRUN is required in order to support the CHAIN statement and the COMMON statement, and is especially helpful if your application consists of several programs. If you do not use the CHAIN or COMMON statements, you will probably wish to avoid invocation of the run-time module. Further, if you wish to distribute your programs to others, and your programs use the BASRUN module, then you must sign a license agreement and pay a royalty to IBM Corporation for each copy of your program that you give or sell to others. Therefore, it may be in your best interests to avoid the run-time module.

The BASIC compiler automatically produces programs that require the run-time module. You may instruct the compiler to not use the run-time module, by appending "/O" to the end of the compiler command line:

    B>A:BASCOM ANALYSIS/O;

"O" is mnemonic for "old" or "original." Older versions of the BASIC compiler did not have a run-time module. When the run-time module was added, the compiler authors decided to add an option to allow compatibility with the older compiler.

Programs created with the /O option do not use the run-time module and do not require a royalty payment to IBM if the program is distributed. If you must do chaining between programs, consider using the RUN statement in place of CHAIN. RUN can begin execution of another program when used as a statement:

```
1000 RUN "PROGR3"
```

In addition, variables that are normally placed in COMMON may be copied to a disk file for temporary storage and then restored by the called program. Or they may be placed in an unused area of memory by using POKE, and then read back by the called program using PEEK.

As an example, consider the steps needed to copy a single precision real number into a memory area. Using the VARPTR function, you can obtain the location of the variable's four data bytes. Using PEEK, you can copy the bytes to a temporary location. Then, with POKE, the four bytes can be safely stored elsewhere in memory. For example, to save the value of variable X, use the following statements:

```
I% = VARPTR(X)
B1 = PEEK(I%)
B2 = PEEK(I% + 1)
B3 = PEEK(I% + 2)
B4 = PEEK(I% + 3)
DEF SEG = &H1800       'Choose some unused area of memory
POKE 0, B1
POKE 1, B2
POKE 2, B3
POKE 3, B4
```

In the called program, execute the following statements to restore the value of X:

```
X = 0
I% = VARPTR(X)
DEF SEG = &H1800       'Use same segment as in calling
                        program
B1 = PEEK(0)
B2 = PEEK(1)
B3 = PEEK(2)
B4 = PEEK(3)
```

```
DEF SEG              'Set to BASIC's Data Segment
POKE I%, B1
POKE I% + 1, B2
POKE I% + 2, B3
POKE I% + 3, B4
```

Appendix I, "Technical Tips and Information," in the IBM BASIC Reference manual describes how variables are stored in BASIC's memory area. Other types of variables have different representations inside BASIC. With the technique just described, combined with the information in Appendix I, all types of variables may be saved and restored without resorting to the use of the COMMON statement.

Differences between Interpreted BASIC and Compiled BASIC

For the most part, compiled BASIC is identical to interpreted BASIC. There are a few quirks that require special attention. They may require you to make changes to your program. The following paragraphs summarize the most important differences and what steps should be taken to alleviate the conflicts.

CHAIN

The compiled version of CHAIN does not support the options ALL, MERGE, LINE, and DELETE. The use of CHAIN will normally require the use of the run-time module. It is still possible to use CHAIN without the run-time module, however, by using the following format:

```
RUN "programname"
```

COMMON

In compiled program, COMMON should appear at *the beginning of the program,* just *after* any DIM statements. Interpretive BASIC allows the COMMON statement to appear almost anywhere in the program.

DEF FN and DEF type

All definition statements should appear at the beginning of a compiled program before the main body of executable statements.

DIM

In compiled programs, arrays defined with DIM must have integer subscripts, rather than variable subscripts. For example, the following statements

```
MAX = 100
DIM N(MAX)
```

must be changed to

```
DIM N(100)
```

Variables may not be used to define the size of arrays.

In compiled BASIC, all variables must be DIMensioned *before* they are first referenced. This means that DIM statements should almost always be placed at the beginning of your program. In addition, the compiler allows DIMensioned variables to have up to 60 subscripts. Interpreted BASIC allows only two.

PEEK and POKE

Some PEEKs and POKEs will not work in the compiler. For example, PEEKs and POKEs preceded by

```
DEF SEG
```

without an address, parameter may not work the same as in interpretive BASIC.

REVIEW

- The compiler provides an easy method of making BASIC programs run much, much faster.
- A program is compiled by saving the source as an ASCII file, running the BASCOM compiler, the linker, and the newly compiled program.
- If you use the run-time compiler, remember that you must pay IBM a royalty if you distribute your compiled program to others. To avoid using the run-time module, use the /0 compiler option.
- A few differences exist between interactive BASIC and compiled BASIC. The chief differences involve the location of the DIM and COMMON statements, the use of variables to define array subscripts, and specialized code, like PEEK and POKE. Additional differences are described in the IBM BASIC Compiler manual.

APPENDIX
B

The "Pretty Printer" Program

Most of the BASIC program listings in this book were not made by typing LIST in BASIC. Instead, a special program called a "pretty printer" was used to display the listings in a more readable format.

A pretty printer program takes an ordinary BASIC listing and arranges the lines and statements into a format that makes the listing easier to read and understand. IBM BASIC allows you to place multiple statements on a single line, separating each statement with a colon. The following line

10 A = 1: B = 3: C = 5: GOSUB 700: PRINT "Finished"

is equivalent to these five separate lines:

10 A = 1
20 B = 3
30 C = 5
40 GOSUB 700
50 PRINT "Finished"

When all the statements appear on a single line, the listing can be difficult to read and understand. A pretty printer program takes a single line of multiple statements and arranges them like this:

10 A = 1:
    B = 3:
    C = 5:

```
GOSUB 700:
PRINT "Finished"
```

This is easier to read, especially when there are many long lines in the listing.

The pretty printer program is itself written in IBM BASIC. (See Listing B-1.) All you need to do to create pretty printed listing is to type in the program and follow a few easy steps.

Listing B-1

```
10        PRINT "BASIC Program Source Pretty Printer   V1.1"
20        REM
30        REM
40        PRINT
50        DEFINT A-Z                            ' Use only integers
60        QUOTE$ = CHR$(34)                     ' The double quote "
70        INPUT "Enter name of ASCII Source file to Print? ",FILE.NAME$
80        INPUT "List to Printer (Y/CR)? ",C$:
            IF C$="y" OR C$="Y" THEN LIST.TO.PRINTER=-1 ELSE LIST.TO.PRINTER=0
90        INPUT "Line Width (CR=80)? ",LINE.WIDTH:
            IF LINE.WIDTH = 0 THEN LINE.WIDTH = 80
100       OPEN FILE.NAME$ FOR INPUT AS #1:
            PAGE.LENGTH = 66 :
            LINES.PER.PAGE = 60:
            LINE.NUMBER = (PAGE.LENGTH-LINES.PER.PAGE)/2:
            IF LIST.TO.PRINTER THEN FOR I = 1 TO LINE.NUMBER:
            LPRINT:
            NEXT I:
            WIDTH "LPT1:",LINE.WIDTH:
            LPRINT CHR$(27);CHR$(69);
110       COL = 8 ' Column at which to begin line's text
120       GOSUB 160
130       PRINT:
            PRINT:
            PRINT
140       PRINT "****** FINISHED *********"
150       STOP
160       IF EOF(1) THEN RETURN ELSE LINE INPUT #1, L$
170       T = INSTR(L$," "):
            L$ = LEFT$(L$,T) + SPACE$(COL-T) + MID$(L$,T+1)
180                                             ' Find first blank after line #
190                                             ' and add spaces for indentation
200       STARTING.POINT = 1 :
            INDENTATION = 0
210       FIRST.QUOTE = INSTR(1,L$,QUOTE$)      ' Find first quote on line
220       IF  FIRST.QUOTE = 0   THEN  FIRST.QUOTE = LEN(L$)+1
230       IF  STARTING.POINT > LEN(L$)  GOTO 160
240       ENDING.POINT = INSTR(STARTING.POINT,L$,":")
250                                             ' Find next colon in line
260       IF  ENDING.POINT = 0  THEN  ENDING.POINT = LEN(L$)+1
270                                             ' If the colon is not within a
280                                             ' a string, then it must be a
290                                             ' statement separator, so
300                                             ' print the statement
310       IF  ENDING.POINT <= FIRST.QUOTE  THEN  T$ = MID$(L$,
            STARTING.POINT,ENDING.POINT-STARTING.POINT+1):
            GOSUB 380:
            GOSUB 360:
            STARTING.POINT = ENDING.POINT + 1:
            INDENTATION = COL + 3:
            GOTO 230
```

```
320      SECOND.QUOTE = INSTR(FIRST.QUOTE+1,L$,QUOTE$)
330      IF   SECOND.QUOTE = 0   THEN   T$ = MID$(L$,STARTING.POINT):
         GOSUB 380:
         GOSUB 360:
         GOTO 160
340      IF   ENDING.POINT > SECOND.QUOTE   THEN   FIRST.QUOTE =
         INSTR(SECOND.QUOTE+1,L$,QUOTE$):
         IF   FIRST.QUOTE = 0   THEN   FIRST.QUOTE = LEN(L$)+1:
         GOTO 310 ELSE GOTO 310
350      ENDING.POINT = INSTR(SECOND.QUOTE+1,L$,":"):
         GOTO 260
360      IF   LIST.TO.PRINTER   THEN   IF PAGE.LENGTH-LINE.NUMBER =
         (PAGE.LENGTH-LINES.PER.PAGE)/2   THEN   LPRINT CHR$(12);:
         LINE.NUMBER = (PAGE.LENGTH-LINES.PER.PAGE)/2:
         FOR I1 = 1 TO LINE.NUMBER:
         LPRINT:
         NEXT I1
370      RETURN
380      IF   (LEN(T$) + INDENTATION) <= LINE.WIDTH   THEN   PRINT
         TAB(INDENTATION);T$:
         GOSUB 480:
         RETURN
390                                              ' If the line fits, print it
400                                              ' Otherwise, find a spot to
410                                              ' break it into two pieces
420      I = LEN(T$) :
         IF I > (LINE.WIDTH - 10)   THEN I = LINE.WIDTH - 10
430      WHILE I > 0
440      IF   INSTR("=+-/*, ",MID$(T$,I,1)) THEN PRINT
         TAB(INDENTATION);LEFT$(T$,I):
         GOSUB 490:
         T$ = MID$(T$,I+1):
         IF   LEN(T$) = 0   THEN   RETURN   ELSE INDENTATION = COL + 3:
         GOTO 380
450      I = I-1
460      WEND
470      PRINT T$:
         RETURN
480      IF   LIST.TO.PRINTER   THEN   LPRINT TAB(INDENTATION);T$:
         LINE.NUMBER = LINE.NUMBER  + 1:
         GOSUB 360:
         RETURN
490      IF   LIST.TO.PRINTER   THEN   LPRINT TAB(INDENTATION);LEFT$(T$,I):
         LINE.NUMBER = LINE.NUMBER + 1:
         GOSUB 360:
         RETURN
500      RETURN
```

First, save the program that you wish to have pretty printed by using the ",A" option of the SAVE command. This option saves your program as an ASCII text file:

SAVE "TEMP.BAS", A

Next, run the pretty printer program:

RUN "PRETTY"

When you see this prompt:

Enter name of ASCII Source file to Print?

type the name of the text file listing produced by step 1, above. When you see this prompt:

List to Printer (Y/CR) ?

enter a single letter Y if you want the listing sent to the printer. Otherwise, the listing will be displayed only on the screen. The next prompt you see is:

Line Width (CR = 80)?

The pretty printer can break long lines into shorter sections when you indicate a line length of less than 80 columns. This feature is useful when making listings for publication or when you need a wide right margin so that you will have room to pencil in corrections or changes.

HOW THE PROGRAM WORKS

Several variables and statements within the program may be changed so that the listings can be customized to your needs. Variable PAGE.LENGTH sets the length of each piece of paper. For most printers, an 8½-by-11-inch paper is 66 lines long. If you are making listings on paper that is longer or shorter, change the value of PAGE.LENGTH in line 100. In addition, you may also need to change the variable LINES.PER.PAGE. Even though there are 66 lines on each sheet of paper, only 60 of those lines will contain the listing. This leaves top and bottom margins of three blank lines, each.

At the end of the line 100, the statement

LPRINT CHR$(27);CHR$(69);

initializes the printer. This particular statement causes the Epson or IBM dot matrix printers to print in *emphasized* mode, resulting in listings that have somewhat higher clarity than normal mode.

Another common selection for the IBM and Epson printers is *condensed* mode. In condensed mode, the printer outputs slightly narrower characters so that it can display 128 characters on each line. Condensed mode is selected by LPRINTing:

LPRINT CHR$(15);

Other print options are available. See your printer reference manual for details.

At line 160, a line of the program to be pretty printed is read into variable L$. Line 170 locates the blank after the leading line number, and inserts additional spaces so that the program statement will appear indented. For example,

10 PRINT

becomes

10   PRINT

To change the indentation size, change the value assigned to variable COL (mnemonic for "column") in line 110.

The block of lines at 200 through 350 perform the bulk of the processing. The pretty printer looks for the statement separator and splits long lines into individual statements whenever colons are found. A few extra steps are needed to avoid detecting colons within character strings.

Line 210 locates the first quote within the source line. For example, in the statement

10 PRINT "Here is a colon: see it?" : INPUT C$

you need to skip over the first colon because it appears within the character string and is not a statement separator. FIRST.QUOTE is assigned the location of the first quote within the line. ENDING.POINT locates the first colon. If ENDING.POINT is less than FIRST.QUOTE, then you know that the colon is not within a character string:

```
10 A = 1: INPUT "Name?" : PRINT
       /\         /\
       |        FIRST. QUOTE
     ENDING.POINT
```

But, if ENDING.POINT is greater than FIRST.QUOTE, you need to see if it comes within or after the string:

```
10 PRINT "Here is a colon: see it?" : INPUT C$
        /\                   /\
     FIRST.QUOTE    |
                    ENDING.POINT
```

In line 320, SECOND. QUOTE locates the end of the string:

```
10 PRINT "Here is a colon: see it?" : INPUT C$
        ∧                    ∧     ∧
     FIRST.QUOTE  |       SECOND.QUOTE
                     ENDING.POINT
```

SINCE ENDING.POINT is between the two quotes, you know that the colon that you have found is not a statement separator. So you resume searching after the second quote. If ENDING.POINT is past the second quote, then you have a geniune statement-separating colon. Here is an example:

```
10 PRINT "Here is a colon: see it?" : INPUT C$
        ∧                          ∧∧
     FIRST.QUOTE                 | ENDING.POINT
                  SECOND.QUOTE
```

T$, a temporary variable, is assigned the midsection of L$, either from the start of the line or between existing colons and is then output by the print subroutine at line 380.

Transcribing the Listings

When transcribing a listing made by the pretty printer program, be sure to place all of the statements of a multiple statement line onto a single line. In other words, when you see a statement like

```
10 A = 1:
     B = 3:
     C = 5:
     GOSUB 700:
     PRINT "Finished"
```

type it at your computer as

```
10 A = 1: B = 3: C = 5: GOSUB 700: PRINT "Finished"
```

References

Aho, Alfred V. and Jeffrey D. Ullman. *Principles of Compiler Design.* Reading, Mass.: Addison-Wesley Publishing Co., 1977.

Algorithms 63, 64, 75, and 201. From *Collected Algorithms from CACM.*

Boies, S. J. "User behaviour on an interactive computer system." *IBM Systems Journal* 13, no. 1 (1974).

Bourne, Lyle E., Jr., and Bruce R. Ekstrand. *Psychology.* New York: Holt, Rinehart and Winston, 1979.

Bowyer, Kevin W. "The Role of Computer Systems in the Nuclear Power Debate." *Computers and Society* (Spring/Summer 1980): 6.

Cheriton, David R. "Man-Machine Interface Design for Timesharing Systems." *Proc. of the ACM Natl. Conf., 1976:* 362–380.

Cuff, Rodney N. "On casual users." *Int. J. of Man-Machine Studies,* 12, no. 2 (Feb 1, 1980): 163–187.

Dwyer, Barry. "A User-Friendly Algorithm," *Comm. of the ACM* 24, no. 9 (September 1981): 556–561.

Freund, John E. *Modern Elementary Statistics.* Englewood Cliffs, N.J.: Prentice-Hall, 1979.

Gaines, Brian R., and Peter V. Facey. "Some Experience in Interactive System Development and Application." *Proc. of the IEEE* 63, no. 6 (June 1975): 894.

Gorney, Leu. "Queuing Theory, the Science of Wait Control, Part 1: Queue Representation." *BYTE* 4, no. 4 (April 1979): 132.

———. "Queuing Theory, the Science of Wait Control, Part 2: System Types." *BYTE* 4, no. 5 (May 1979): 176.

Gotlieb, C. C., and L. R. Gotlieb. *Data Types and Structures.* Englewood Cliffs, N.J.: Prentice-Hall, 1978.

Grappel, Robert. "The My Dear Aunt Sally Algorithm." *BYTE* 2, no. 2: 19.

Hayes, Phil, Eugene Ball, and Raj Reddy. "Breaking the Man-Machine Communication Barrier." *Computer* 14, no. 3 (March 1981): 19.

Helmers, Carl. "The Era of Off-the-Shelf Personal Computers Has Arrived." *BYTE* 6, no. 5: 46.

Hines, Theodore C., and Lois Winked. "Sorting and Filing Complex Alphanumeric Entries." *Creative Computing.* 7, no. 7 (July 1981): 128–129.

Howard, Jim. "What is Good Documentation?" *BYTE* 6, no. 3 (March 1981): 132.

International Business Machines Corporation. *IBM BASIC.* 2nd Ed. Version 1.1. 1981.

International Business Machines Corporation. *IBM Technical Reference.* 1981.

Joyce, James. "Human Factors in Software Engineering." *Proc. of the First West Cost Computer Faire* (April 1977): 56.

Kennedy, T.C.S. "The Design of Interactive Procedures for Man Machine Communication." *Int. J. of Man-Machine Studies* 6 no. 3 (May 1974): 309–334.

Kennedy, T. C. S. "Some Behavioural Factors Affecting the Training of Naive Users of an Interactive Computer System." *Int. J. of Man-Machine Studies* 7, no. 6 (November 1975): 817–834.

Knuth, Donald E. "Algorithms." *Scientific American* 236, no. 4 (April 1977): 63.

Knuth, Donale E. *The Art of Computer Programming: Fundamental Algorithms.* Vol. 3, Reading, Mass: Addison-Wesley Publishing Co., 1973.

Knuth, Donald E. *The Art of Computer Programming: Sorting and Searching.* Reading, Mass.: Addison-Wesley Publishing Co., 1973.

Ledgard, Henry, John A. Whiteside, Andrew Singer, and William Seymour. "The Natural Language of Interactive Systems." *Comm. of the ACM* 23, no. 10 (October 1980): 556.

Lorin, Harold. *Sorting and Sort Systems.* Reading, Mass.: Addison-Wesley Publishing Co., 1975.

Martin, James. *Design of Man-Computer Dialogues.* Englewood Cliffs, N.J.: Prentice-Hall, 1973.

Maurer, W. Douglas. "Processing Algebraic Expressions." *BYTE* 2, no. 2: 25.

Miller, L. A. and John C. Thomas, Jr. "Behavioral issues in the use of interactive systems." *Int. J. of Man-Machine Studies* 9 (1977): 509–536.

Miller, L. A. "Natural language programming: Styles, strategies, and contrasts." *IBM Systems Journal* 20, no. 2 (1981).

Mills, H. D. "Principles of software engineering." *IBM Systems Journal* 19, no. 4 (1980): 414.

Mitchell, Edward. "Searching Techniques." *Creative Computing* 8, no. 9 (1982): 160.

———. "Introduction to Data Structures." *Creative Computing* 8, no. 10 (October 1982): 210.

———. "Programming Data Structures." *Creative Computing* 8, no. 11 (November 1982): 207.

———. "Searching Techniques: A Survey of Sorts." *Creative Computing* 8, no. 12 (December 1982): 284.

Montgomery, Christine A. "Is Natural Language an Unnatural Query Language?" *Proc. of the ACM* (August 1975): 1075.

Nijenhuis, Albert N. "How Not To Be Out of Sorts, Part 1: Insertion Sort." *Creative Computing* 6, no. 8 (August 1980).

———. "Part II: Heapsort." *Creative Computing* 6, no. 9 (September 1980): 136–137.

———. "Part III: Linked Merge Sort." *Creative Computing* 6, no. 10 (October 1980).

Shneiderman, Ben. "Human Factors Experiments in Designing Interactive Systems." *Computer* 12, no. 12 (December 1979): 9–19.

Shneiderman, Ben. *Software Psychology.* Cambridge: Winthrop Publishers, Inc., 1980.

Simon, David E. *IBM BASIC From the Ground Up.* Hasbrouck Heights, N.J.: Hayden Book Company, 1983.

Standish, Thomas A. *Data Structure Techniques.* Reading, Mass.: Addison-Wesley Publishing Co., 1980.

Swanson, Paul. "PDQ: A Data Manager for Beginners, Don't Reinvent the Wheel." *BYTE* 6, no. 11 (November 1981): 236.

Tannenbaum, Andrew S. *Structured Computer Organization.* Englewood Cliffs, N.J.: Prentice-Hall, 1976.

Teich, Albert H., ed. "Daedulus of New Scientist." In *Technology and Man's Future.* New York: St. Martin's Press, 1977. 35.

Walker, Bill. "Sorting with Binary Trees." *BYTE* 5, no. 10 (October 1980): 96.

Weizenbaum, Joseph. *Computer Power and Human Reason.* San Francisco: W. H. Freeman and Co., 1976.

Williams, Gregg. "The Commodore VIC 20 Microcomputer." *BYTE* 6, no. 5 (May 1981): 46.